Mark G. Costello   MAy, 1989

O9-AIC-346

Internetworking With TCP/IP
Principles, Protocols, and Architecture

DOUGLAS E. COMER

Department of Computer Sciences
Purdue University
West Lafayette, IN 47907

PRENTICE HALL
Englewood Cliffs, New Jersey 07632

Library of Congress Cataloging-in-Publication Data

COMER, DOUGLAS.
    Internetworking with TCP/IP : principles, protocols, and
architecture / Douglas Comer.
        p.   cm.
    Bibliography: p.
    Includes index.
    ISBN 0-13-470154-2
    1. Computer networks.   2. Computer network protocols.   3. Data
transmission systems.   I. Title.
TK5105.5.C59 1988   87-35201
004.6—dc19   CIP

Editorial/production supervision: Ellen B. Greenberg
Cover illustration: Jim Kinstrey
Cover design: Bruce Kenselaar
Manufacturing buyer: Cindy Grant

UNIX is a registered trademark of AT&T Bell Laboratories.
proNET-10 is a trademark of Proteon Corporation.
VAX, Microvax, and LSI 11 are trademarks of Digital Equipment Corporation

© 1988 by Prentice-Hall, Inc.
A Division of Simon & Schuster
Englewood Cliffs, New Jersey 07632

All rights reserved. No part of this book may be reproduced, in any form
or by any means, without permission in writing from the publisher.

Printed in the United States of America

10   9   8   7   6   5   4

ISBN   0-13-470154-2   025

Prentice-Hall International (UK) Limited, *London*
Prentice-Hall of Australia Pty. Limited, *Sydney*
Prentice-Hall Canada Inc., *Toronto*
Prentice-Hall Hispanoamericana, S.A., *Mexico*
Prentice-Hall of India Private Limited, *New Delhi*
Prentice-Hall of Japan, Inc., *Tokyo*
Simon & Schuster Asia Pte. Ltd., *Singapore*
Editora Prentice-Hall do Brasil, Ltda., *Rio de Janeiro*

To Chris

Contents

Chapter 6   Determining an Internet Address at Startup (RARP)   59

Chapter 7   Internet Protocol: Connectionless Datagram Delivery (IP)   65

Chapter 8   Routing IP Datagrams   79

Chapter 9   Internet Protocol: Error and Control Messages (ICMP)   89

Chapter 10   Protocol Layering   101

Chapter 11   User Datagram Protocol   119

Chapter 12   Reliable Stream Transport Service (TCP)   129

Chapter 13   The Core Gateway System (GGP)   153

Chapter 14   Autonomous Systems and Confederations (EGP)   163

Chapter 18   The Domain Name System   215

Chapter 19   Application Level Services   233

Foreword

In this book Professor Douglas Comer has provided a long sought overview and introduction to TCP/IP. There have been many requests for *the* article, report, or book to read to get started on understanding the TCP/IP protocols. At last, this book satisfies those requests. Writing an introduction to TCP/IP for the uninitiated is a very difficult task. While combining the explanation of the general principles of computer communication with the specific examples from the TCP/IP protocol suite, Doug Comer has provided a very readable book.

While this book is specifically about the TCP/IP protocol suite, it is a good book for learning about computer communications protocols in general. The principles of architecture, layering, multiplexing, encapsulation, addressing and address mapping, routing, and naming are quite similar in any protocol suite, though, of course, different in detail (See Chapters 3, 10, 17, and 18).

Computer communication protocols do not do anything themselves. Like operating systems, they are in the service of application processes. Processes are the active elements that request communication and are the ultimate senders and receivers of the data transmitted. The various layers of protocols are like the various layers in a computer operating system, especially the file system. Understanding protocol architecture is like understanding operating system architecture. In this book Doug Comer has taken the "bottom up" approach – starting with the physical networks and moving up in levels of abstraction to the applications.

Since application processes are the active elements using the communication supported by the protocols, TCP/IP is an "interprocess communication" (IPC) mechanism. While there are several experiments in progress with operating system style message passing and procedure call types of IPC based on IP, the focus in this book is on more traditional applications that use the UDP datagram or TCP logical connection forms of IPC (See Chapters 11, 12, 17, 18, and 19).

One of the key ideas inherent in TCP/IP and in the title of this book is "internetworking." The power of a communication system is directly related to the number of entities in that system. The telephone network is very useful because (nearly) all the telephones are in (as it appears to the users) one network. Computer communication systems and networks are currently separated and fragmented. The goal of interconnection and internetworking, to have a single powerful computer communication network, is fundamental to the design of TCP/IP. Essential to internetworking is addressing (See Chapters 4, 5, and 6), and a universal protocol – the Internet Protocol (See Chapters 7, 8, and 9).

To have an internetwork the individual networks must be connected. The connecting devices are called gateways. Further, these gateways must have some procedures for forwarding data from one network to the next. The data is in the form of IP datagrams and the destination is specified by an IP address, but the gateway must make a routing decision based on the IP address and what it knows about the connectivity of the networks making up the Internet. The procedures for distributing the current connectivity information to the gateways are called routing algorithms, and these are currently the subject of much study and development (See Chapters 13, 14, 15, and 16).

Like all communication systems, the TCP/IP protocol suite is an unfinished system. It is evolving to meet changing requirements and new opportunities. Thus, this book is, in a sense, a snapshot of TCP/IP circa 1987. And, as Doug Comer points out, there are many loose ends (See Chapter 20).

Most chapters end with a few pointers to material ''for further study''. Many of these refer to memos of the RFC series of notes. This series of notes is the result of a policy of making the working ideas and the protocol specifications developed by the TCP/IP research and development community widely available. This availability of the basic and detailed information about these protocols, and the availability of the early implementations of them, has had much to do with their current widespread use. This commitment to public documentation at this level of detail is unusual for a research effort, and has had significant benefits for the development of computer communication (See Appendix 3).

This book brings together information about the various parts of the TCP/IP architecture and protocols and makes it accessible. Its publication is a very significant milestone in the evolution of computer communications.

                                        Jon Postel,
                                        Internet Protocol Designer and
                                        Deputy Internet Architect

                                        December, 1987

Preface

In the last century, railroads revolutionized the world by providing a transportation network that moved raw materials and manufactured products. They made an industrialized society possible. Digital communication networks have started a new revolution by providing the technology that transports the data needed by a society in which information plays a key role. Networking already permeates industry, education, and government. It has already begun to change the way we view the world by shrinking geographic distances and forming new communities of people who interact frequently. More important, network growth is explosive. The revolution is well underway.

To understand networking and the selection of topics discussed in this book, it is important to realize that network research and development occurred in three stages. Before the 1960s, the main question was, "How can we transmit bits across a communication medium efficiently and reliably?" The results include the development of information theory, the sampling theorem, and other ideas commonly referred to as signal processing. Beginning around the mid 1960s, emphasis shifted to packet switching and the question became, "How can we transmit packets across a communication medium efficiently and reliably?" The results include the development of packet switching technologies, local area networks, and statistical analysis of network response to load. From approximately the mid 1970s to the present, emphasis has centered on network architecture and the question, "How can we provide communication services across a series of interconnected networks?" The results include the development of internetwork technologies, protocol layering models, datagram and stream transport services, and the client-server interaction paradigm.

Most textbooks and network courses concentrate on the first two stages of network research, presenting the well-known theories of data communications and queueing analysis. Although such information is important to engineers who design network technologies and hardware products, most network architects purchase commercially available network hardware. Instead of detailed knowledge about how bits or packets flow across communication media, they need to know how to interconnect such hardware and how to use the resulting system.

This text concentrates on the third stage of networking. It examines the architecture of interconnected networks and explains the principles and protocols that make such interconnected architectures function as a single unified communication system. More important, it shows how an interconnected architecture can be used for distributed computation.

The entire text focuses on the concept of internetworking in general and the TCP/IP internet technology in particular. Internetworking is a powerful abstraction that allows us to deal with the complexity of multiple underlying communication technologies. It hides the details of network hardware and provides a high level communication environment. As the book shows, the ultimate goal of internetworking is maximal interoperability, that is, maximizing the ability of programs on diverse computer and network systems to communicate reliably and efficiently.

The text reviews both the architecture of network interconnections as well as internet communication services and the protocols needed to provide those services. By the end of the book, the reader will understand how it is possible to interconnect multiple physical networks into a coordinated system, how internet protocols operate in that environment, and how application programs use the resulting system. As a specific example, the reader learns the details of the DARPA (TCP/IP) Internet, including the architecture of the gateway system and the application protocols it supports. In addition, the book discusses some of the limitations of the internet approach.

Writing about internetworking is both exciting and challenging. It is challenging because, as in any rapidly changing research area, nothing is stable. It is exciting because the TCP/IP Internet is an active, rapidly expanding entity. Researchers working on it generate new ideas constantly and the possibilities seem endless. Looking back over TCP/IP and the DARPA Internet makes it clear that much has been accomplished. Knowing that the research has taken a little over a decade makes one realize how intense the effort has been.

Designed as both a college text and as a professional reference, the book is written at an advanced undergraduate or graduate level. For professionals, the book provides a comprehensive introduction to the TCP/IP technology and the architecture of the Internet. Although it is not intended to replace protocol standards, the book is a good starting point for learning about internetworking because it provides a uniform overview that emphasizes principles. Moreover, it gives the reader perspective that can be extremely difficult to obtain from individual protocol documents.

When used in the classroom, the text provides more than sufficient material for a single semester network course at either the undergraduate or graduate level. Such a course can be extended to a 2-semester sequence if accompanied by programming projects and readings from the literature. For undergraduate courses, it can be taken at face value. Students should be expected to grasp the basic concepts described in the text, and they should be able to describe or use them. At the graduate level, students should be expected to use the material here as a basis for further exploration of current research. They should understand it well enough to answer exercises or solve problems that require them to explore subtleties and consequences. Many of the exercises suggest such subtleties; solving them often requires students to read protocol standards and apply creative energy to comprehend consequences.

At all levels, hands-on experience sharpens the concepts and helps students gain intuition. Thus, I encourage instructors to invent projects that force students to use internetwork services and protocols. Although such experimentation is safest when the instructional laboratory network is isolated from production computing facilities, we have found that students exhibit the most enthusiasm, and benefit the most, when they have access to the ''real'' TCP/IP Internet.

The book is organized into four main parts. Chapters 1 and 2 form an introduction that provides an overview and discusses existing technologies. In particular, Chapter 2 reviews physical network hardware. The intention is to provide basic intuition about what is possible, not to spend inordinate time on hardware details. Chapters 3-12 describe the TCP/IP Internet from the viewpoint of a single host, showing the basic services available and the protocols a host uses to access them. They cover the basics of Internet addressing and routing as well as the notion of protocol layering. Chapters 13-16 describe the architecture of the Internet when viewed globally. They explore the core gateway system and the protocols gateways use to exchange routing information. Finally, Chapters 17-19 discuss application level services available in the Internet. They present the client-server model of interaction and give several examples of how one can organize client and server software. The last section discusses electronic mail and the domain name system, two topics that are extremely popular.

The chapters have been organized "bottom up." They begin with an overview of hardware and continue to build new functionality on top of it. This view will appeal to anyone who has developed Internet software because it follows the same pattern one uses in implementation. The concept of layering does not appear until Chapter 10. The discussion of layering emphasizes the distinction between conceptual layers of functionality and the reality of layered protocol software in which multiple objects appear at each layer.

Although it is difficult to omit any chapter completely, the instructor will find that students are often satisfied to know that something is possible without knowing the details. For example, one can skim through Chapters 5, 6, and 9 by covering only the functionality and not the details of the protocols. In addition, several chapters (especially 16) contain engineering techniques. While such techniques are crucial to efficient implementations, they can be skipped to save time.

A modest background is required to understand the material. The reader is expected to have programmed in a high level language and to be familiar with basic data structures like stacks, queues, and trees. Readers need basic intuition about the organization of computer software into an operating system that supports concurrent programming and application programs that users invoke to perform computation. Readers do not need sophisticated mathematics, nor do they need to know information theory or theorems from data communications; the book describes the physical network as a black box around which an internetwork can be built. It states design principles in English and discusses motivations and consequences.

Many people have contributed to this book. I thank Steve Chapin, Jim Griffioen, Chris Kent, Tim Korb, Dan Lynch, Thomas Narten, Shawn Ostermann, John Steele, and Raj Yavatkar, who all read drafts and made valuable comments. Craig Partridge supplied numerous suggestions, including a few exercises, and corrected several technical errors. He and Van Jacobson supplied the graph of Internet round trip delays in Chapter 12. Barry Shein graciously allowed me to use his example UNIX client and server code in Appendix 1. Charlotte Tubis provided valuable editing. Special thanks go to my wife, Chris, who has read the text more times than I can count and made extensive suggestions.

1

Introduction and Overview

1.1 The Need For An Internet

Data communication has become a fundamental part of computing. World-wide networks gather data about such diverse subjects as atmospheric conditions, crop production, and airline traffic. Groups establish electronic mailing lists so they can share information of common interest. Hobbyists exchange programs for their home computers. In the scientific world, data networks are essential because they allow scientists to send programs and data to remote supercomputers for processing, to retrieve the results, and to exchange scientific information with colleagues.

Unfortunately, most networks are independent entities, established to serve the needs of a single group. The users choose a hardware technology appropriate to their communication problems. More important, it is impossible to build a universal network from a single hardware technology, because no single network suffices for all uses. Some users need a high-speed network to connect machines, but such networks cannot be expanded to span large distances. Others settle for a slower speed network that connects machines thousands of miles apart.

Recently, however, a new technology has emerged that makes it possible to interconnect many disparate physical networks and make them function as a coordinated unit. The new technology, called an *internetwork*, or *internet*, accommodates multiple, diverse underlying hardware technologies by adding both physical connections and a new set of conventions. The internet technology hides the details of network hardware and permits computers to communicate independent of their physical network connections.

To appreciate internet technology, think of how it affects research. Imagine for a minute the effects of interconnecting all the computers used by scientists. Any scientist would be able to exchange data resulting from an experiment with any other scientist. It would be possible to establish national data centers to collect data from natural phenomena and make the data available to all scientists. Computer services and programs available at one location could be used by scientists at other locations. As a result, the speed with which scientific investigations proceed would increase. In short, the changes would be dramatic.

1.2 The TCP/IP Internet

Government agencies have realized the importance and potential of internet technology for many years and have been funding research that will make possible a national research internet. This book discusses principles and ideas underlying the leading internet technology, one that has resulted from research funded by the *Defense Advanced Projects Research Agency (DARPA)*. The DARPA technology includes a set of network standards that specify the details of how computers communicate, as well as a set of conventions for interconnecting networks and routing traffic. Commonly referred to as *TCP/IP* (after the names of its two main standards), it can be used to communicate across any set of interconnected networks. For example, some colleges use TCP/IP to interconnect all networks on the college campus, even though the college has no connection to outside networks. Other groups use TCP/IP for long haul communication among geographically distant sites.

Although the TCP/IP technology is noteworthy by itself, it is especially interesting because its viability has been demonstrated on a large scale. It forms the base technology for a large internet that connects most major research institutions, including several government labs. The *National Science Foundation (NSF)*, the *Department of Energy*, and the *National Aeronautics and Space Administration (NASA)* all participate, using TCP/IP to connect many of their research sites with those of DARPA. The resulting entity, known as the *DARPA Internet*, the *TCP/IP Internet*, or just the *Internet*†, allows researchers at connected institutions to share information with colleagues across the country as easily as they share with researchers in the next room. An outstanding success, the Internet demonstrates the viability of the TCP/IP technology and shows how it can accommodate a wide variety of underlying network technologies.

Most of the material in this book applies to any internet built to use TCP/IP, but some chapters refer specifically to the Internet built by DARPA. Readers interested only in the technology should be careful to watch for the distinction between the Internet architecture as it exists and general TCP/IP internets as they might exist.

1.3 Internet Services

One cannot appreciate the technical details underlying the Internet without understanding the services it provides. This chapter reviews Internet services briefly, highlighting the services most users understand, and leaving to later chapters the discussion of how computers connect to the Internet and how the functionality is implemented.

---

†We will capitalize *internet* when referring specifically to the DARPA Internet, and use lower case otherwise.

Much of our discussion of services will focus on standards called *protocols*. Protocols, like TCP/IP, give the formulas for passing messages, specify the details of message formats, and describe how to handle error conditions. Most important, they allow us to discuss communication standards independent of any particular vendor's network hardware. In a sense, protocols are to communication what programming languages are to computation. A programming language allows one to specify or understand computation without knowing the details of any particular CPU instruction set. Similarly, a communication protocol allows one to specify or understand data communication without depending on detailed knowledge of a particular vendor's network hardware.

We will see that all network services are described by protocols. The next sections refer to protocols used to specify application-level services as well as those used to define network-level services. Later chapters explain each of these Internet protocols in more detail.

1.3.1 Application Level Internet Services

From the point of view of a user, the Internet appears to be a set of application programs that use the network to carry out useful communication tasks. We use the term *interoperability* to refer to the ability of diverse computing systems to cooperate in solving computational problems. We say that Internet application programs exhibit a high degree of interoperability. Most users that access the Internet do so merely by invoking application programs without understanding the Internet technology or even the path their data travels to its destination; they rely on the application programs to handle such details. Only programmers who write such application programs view the Internet as a network and need to understand the details of the technology.

The most popular and widespread Internet application programs include:

- *Electronic mail.* Electronic mail allows a user to compose memos and send them to individuals or groups of individuals. Another part of the mail application allows users to read memos that they have received. Electronic mail has been so successful that many Internet users depend on it for normal business correspondence. Although many electronic mail systems exist, it is important to understand that the Internet makes mail delivery more reliable. Instead of relying on intermediate machines to relay mail messages, Internet mail delivery operates by having the sender's machine contact the receiver's machine directly. Thus, the sender knows that once the message leaves the local machine, it has been successfully received at the destination machine.
- *File transfer.* Although users sometimes transfer files using electronic mail, mail is designed primarily for short, text files. The Internet has a file transfer application program that allows users to send or receive arbitrarily large files of programs or data. For example, using the file transfer program, one can copy large data banks containing satellite images, programs written in FORTRAN or Pascal, or an English dictionary. The system provides a way to check for authorized users, or even to prevent all access. Like mail, file transfer across the Internet is reliable because

the two machines involved communicate directly, without relying on intermediate machines to make copies of the file along the way.

- *Remote login.* Perhaps the most interesting Internet application, remote login allows a user sitting at one computer to connect to a remote machine and establish an interactive login session. The remote login makes it appear that the user's terminal connects directly to the remote machine by sending every keystroke from the user's keyboard to the remote machine and displaying every character the remote computer prints on the user's terminal screen. When the remote login session terminates, the application returns the user to the local system.

We will return to each of these applications in later chapters, to examine them in more detail. We will see exactly how they use the underlying Internet protocols, and why having Internet standards for the applications has helped ensure that they are widespread.

1.3.2 Network-Level Internet Services

A programmer who writes application programs that use the Internet has an entirely different view of it than a user who merely executes the applications. At the network level, the Internet provides two broad types of service that all application programs use. While it is unimportant at this time to understand the details of these services, they cannot be omitted from any overview of the Internet:

- *Connectionless Packet Delivery Service.* This service, explained in detail throughout the text, forms the basis for all other Internet services. Connectionless delivery is an abstraction of the service that most packet-switching networks offer. It means simply that the Internet routes small messages from one machine to another based on address information carried in the message. Because the connectionless service routes each packet separately, it does not guarantee reliable delivery. Because it usually maps directly onto the underlying hardware, the connectionless service is extremely efficient. More important, having connectionless packet delivery as the basis for all Internet services makes the Internet protocols adaptable to a wide range of network hardware.

- *Reliable Stream Transport Service.* Most applications need much more than packet delivery because they require the Internet to recover from transmission errors, lost packets, or failures of intermediate computers along the path. The reliable transport service handles such problems. It allows an application on one computer to establish a ''connection'' with an application on another, and then send a large volume of data across as if it were a permanent, direct hardware connection. Underneath, of course, the Internet protocols divide the stream of data into small messages and send them, one at a time, waiting for the receiver to acknowledge reception.

Many networks provide basic services similar to those outlined above, so one might wonder what distinguishes Internet services from others. The primary distinguishing features are:

- *Network Technology Independence.* While the Internet is based on conventional packet switching technology, it is independent of any particular vendor's hardware. More important, the Internet includes a variety of network technologies ranging from networks designed to operate within a single building to those designed to span large distances. Internet protocols define the unit of transmission, called a *datagram*, and specify how to transmit datagrams on a particular network.
- *Universal interconnection.* The Internet allows any pair of computers to which it attaches to communicate. Each computer is assigned an *address* that is universally recognized throughout the Internet. Every datagram carries the addresses of its source and destination. The destination address is used to make routing decisions.
- *End-to-End Acknowledgements.* The Internet protocols provide acknowledgements between the source and ultimate destination instead of between successive machines along the path, even when the two machines do not connect to a common physical network.
- *Application Protocol Standards.* In addition to the basic transport-level services (like reliable stream connections), the Internet includes standards for many common applications including electronic mail, file transfer, and remote login. Thus, when designing application programs that use the Internet, programmers often find that existing software provides the communication services they need.

Later chapters will discuss the details of the services provided to the programmer as well as many of the application protocol standards.

1.4 History And Scope Of The Internet

Part of what makes the Internet so exciting is its size and growth rate. DARPA began working toward an internet in the mid 1970s, with the architecture and protocols taking their current form around 1978-79. At that time, DARPA was known as the primary funding agency for packet-switched network research and had pioneered many ideas in packet-switching with its well-known *ARPANET*. The ARPANET used conventional point-to-point leased line interconnection but DARPA had also funded exploration of packet-switching over radio networks and satellite communication channels. Indeed, the growing diversity of network hardware technologies helped force DARPA to study network interconnection, and pushed internetworking forward.

The first pieces of the Internet began around 1980 when DARPA first started converting machines attached to its research networks to use the new TCP/IP protocols. The transition to Internet technology became complete in January of 1983 when DARPA demanded that all computers connected to the ARPANET use TCP/IP.

To encourage university researchers to adopt and use the new protocols, DARPA decided to make an implementation available at low cost. At that time, most university computer science departments were running a version of the UNIX operating system available as part of the University of California's "Berkeley Software Distribution." By funding Bolt Beranek and Newman, Inc. (BBN) to implement its Internet protocols under UNIX, and Berkeley to integrate them with its distribution, DARPA was able to reach over 90% of the university computer science departments. The new protocol software came at a particularly significant time because many departments were just acquiring second or third machines and connecting them together with local area networks.

The Berkeley software distribution became popular because it offered more than basic Internet protocols. In addition to standard Internet application programs, Berkeley offered a set of utilities for network services that resembled those in UNIX. The chief advantage of the Berkeley utilities lay in their similarity to standard UNIX. For example, an experienced UNIX user can learn how to use Berkeley's remote file copy utility (*rcp*) quickly because it behaves exactly like the UNIX file copy utility except that it allows users to copy files to or from remote machines.

Besides a set of utility programs, Berkeley provided a new operating system abstraction, the *socket*, that allows application-level programs to access the Internet. A generalization of the UNIX mechanism for I/O, the socket has options for several types of network and Internet access. Its design has been debated since its introduction, and many operating systems researchers have proposed alternatives. Independent of its overall merits, however, the introduction of the socket abstraction had an important impact on use of the Internet because it allowed application programs to use the facility. Thus, it encouraged researchers to experiment with TCP/IP.

The success of the TCP/IP technology and the Internet among computer science researchers led other groups to adopt it. The National Science Foundation understands that network communication will soon be a crucial part of scientific research and has taken an active role in expanding the Internet to reach as many scientists as possible. Starting in 1985, it began a program to establish access networks centered around its six supercomputer centers, and in 1986 it expanded networking efforts by funding a new long haul backbone network, called *NSFnet*†, that reaches all its supercomputer centers and ties them to the ARPANET. Finally, in 1986 it provided seed money for a dozen regional networks, each of which connects major scientific research institutions in a given area. All the NSF-funded networks use TCP/IP protocols, and all are part of the Internet.

Within seven years the Internet had grown to span several thousand individual networks located throughout the United States and Europe and had connected over 20,000 computers at universities and government research laboratories. More important, both the size and the use of the Internet continued to grow much faster than anticipated. By late 1987 it was estimated that the growth had reached 15% per month.

Rapid expansion introduced problems of scale unanticipated in the original design and motivated research into ways to manage distributed resources. In the original arrangement, for example, the names and addresses of all computers attached to the Internet were kept in a single file that was edited by hand and then distributed to every site on the Internet. By the mid 1980s, it became apparent that a central file would not suffice

---

†The term *NSFnet* is sometimes used loosely to mean all the NSF-funded networking activities, but we will use it to refer to the NSF-funded backbone that links supercomputer centers.

for long. First, requests to update the file would soon exceed the capacity of people to process them. Second, even if a correct central file existed, network capacity was insufficient to allow either frequent distribution to every site or on-line access by every site.

1.5 The Internet Activities Board

The *Internet Activities Board*, or *IAB*, provides the focus for much of the research and development underlying the Internet. Originally organized by DARPA to encourage exchange among the principals involved in Internet research, the IAB has evolved into an autonomous organization. Each member of the IAB chairs an *Internet task force* charged with investigating a problem or set of issues deemed to be important. The IAB consists of approximately ten task forces, with charters ranging from one that investigates how the traffic load from various applications affects the Internet to one that handles short term Internet engineering problems. The IAB meets several times each year to hear status reports from each task force, review and revise technical directions, discuss policies, and exchange information with representatives from agencies like DARPA and NSF who are supporting Internet operations and research.

The chairman of the IAB is the *Internet architect* and is responsible for suggesting technical directions, and coordinating the activities of the various task forces. The IAB chairman establishes new task forces on the advice of the IAB. The chairman also represents the IAB to others.

Members of the IAB are responsible for recruiting volunteers to serve on their task forces, for calling and running task force meetings, and for reporting progress to the IAB. Usually, active researchers participate in Internet task force activities for two reasons. On one hand, serving on a task force provides opportunities to learn about new research problems. On the other hand, because new ideas and problem solutions designed and tested by task forces often become part of the Internet technology, members sense that their work can have a direct, positive influence on the field.

Some IAB task forces are joint with a parallel organization, the *Distributed Systems Architecture Board*, or *DSAB*. While the DSAB concentrates on distributed computing and distributed operating systems in particular, there is much overlap in the technical research. Finally, the IAB and DSAB are interlocked because the IAB chairman is a member of the DSAB, and the DSAB chairman is a member of the IAB.

1.6 Internet Research And Request For Comments

The Internet is not yet a commercial product. It is instead a large, active research project. Reports of work, proposals for protocols, and protocol standards all appear in a series of technical reports called Internet *Request For Comments*, or *RFCs*. RFCs may be short or long; they may cover broad concepts or details. The Network Information Center distributes RFCs to the community electronically, using the Internet or by postal mail. While RFCs are edited, they are not refereed in the same way as academic research papers. Also, some reports pertinent to the Internet are published in a parallel series of *Internet Engineering Notes*, or *IENs*. There are references to RFCs and IENs throughout the text. Ask a local network expert how to obtain RFCs at your site, or refer to Appendix *3* for instructions on how to retrieve them through electronic mail or order them by phone.

1.7 Internet Protocols and Standardization

Readers familiar with data communication networks realize that many communication protocol standards exist. Many of them precede the Internet, so the question arises, ''Why did the Internet designers invent new protocols when so many international standards already existed?'' The answer is complex, but follows a simple maxim:

> *Use existing protocol standards whenever such standards apply; invent new protocols only when existing standards are insufficient, but be prepared to migrate to international standards when they become available.*

So, despite appearances to the contrary, the Internet protocol suite was not intended to ignore or avoid international standards. It came about merely because none of the existing protocols satisfied the need. The philosophy of adopting standards when they become available also means that when international standards arise, the Internet will migrate from TCP/IP to the new standards.

1.8 Future Growth

Both the TCP/IP technology and the Internet continue to evolve. New protocols are being proposed; old ones are being revised. NSF has added considerable complexity to the system by introducing its backbone network, several regional networks, and hundreds of campus networks. Other groups continue to connect to the Internet as well. The most significant change comes not from added network connections, however, but from additional traffic. Physicists, chemists, and space scientists manipulate and exchange much larger volumes of data than computer science researchers who accounted for much of the early Internet traffic. These other scientists introduced substantial load when they began using the Internet; as they expand their use, a new generation of computer and communication technology will be needed.

1.9 Organization Of This Text

So far we have talked about the TCP/IP technology and the Internet in general terms, summarizing the services provided and the history of their development. The remainder of this book looks at the architecture of the Internet, the TCP/IP technology, and the applications that use it in more detail. It discusses the fundamentals of protocols like TCP/IP as well as showing how they fit into the Internet. In addition to giving details, it highlights the general principles underlying network protocols and explains why the TCP/IP protocols adapt easily to so many underlying network technologies.

The next chapter provides a brief summary of the network hardware used throughout the Internet. Its purpose is not to illuminate nuances of particular vendor's hardware, but to focus on the features of each technology that are of primary importance to an Internet architect. Later chapters delve into the Internet itself, filling three purposes: they explore general concepts and review the Internet architectural model, they examine the details of Internet protocols, and they look at Internet standards for high-level services like electronic mail and file transfer.

Several appendices follow the main text. The first appendix presents an example of the interface between application programs that use the Internet and the Internet protocol software located in the operating system. Strictly speaking, such an interface is not part of the Internet protocols. However, seeing such an example may help make some of the concepts clear. The second appendix presents an assorted list of hints for programmers who must implement Internet protocols, and the third contains a guide to RFCs. The fourth appendix contains an alphabetical list of terms and abbreviations used throughout the literature and the text. Because beginners often find the new terminology overwhelming and difficult to remember, they are encouraged to use the alphabetical list instead of scanning back through the text. Finally, the fifth appendix, intended as a reference, contains a list of the official Internet protocols.

1.10 Summary

An internet consists of a set of connected networks that act as a coordinated whole. The chief advantage of an internet is that it provides universal interconnection while allowing individual groups to use whatever network hardware is best suited to their needs. We will examine principles behind internet communication and a specific internet technology as well as an example operational Internet. Our example technology, called TCP/IP after its two basic protocols, was developed by the Defense Advanced Research Projects Agency. It provides the basis for an Internet that connects most major scientific research institutions including many universities and government laboratories. The Internet is expanding rapidly and has support from the National Science Foundation, the Department of Energy, the National Aeronautics and Space Administration, and other government agencies.

2

Review of Underlying Network Technologies

2.1 Introduction

It is important to understand that the Internet is not a new kind of physical network. It is, instead, a method of interconnecting physical networks and a set of conventions for using networks that allow the computers they reach to interact. While hardware technology plays only a minor role in the overall design, it is important to be able to distinguish between the low-level mechanisms provided by the hardware itself and the higher-level facilities that the Internet protocol software provides. It is also important to understand how packet-switched technology affects our choice of high-level abstractions.

This chapter introduces basic packet-switching concepts and terminology and then reviews some of the underlying network hardware technologies that have been used in the Internet. Later chapters describe how these networks are interconnected and how the Internet accommodates the vast differences. While the list presented here is certainly not comprehensive, it clearly demonstrates the variety among physical networks that comprise the Internet. The reader can safely skip many of the technical details, but should try to imagine building a homogeneous system using such heterogeneous hardware.

2.2 Two Approaches To Network Communication

Whether they provide connections between one computer and another or between terminals and computers, communication networks can be divided into two basic types: *circuit-switched* and *packet-switched*. Circuit-switched networks operate by forming a dedicated connection (circuit) between two points. The U.S. telephone system uses circuit switching technology – a telephone call establishes a circuit from the originating phone through the local switching office, across trunk lines, to a remote switching office, and finally to the destination telephone. While a circuit is in place, no other traffic can travel over the wires that form the circuit. The advantage of circuit switching lies in its guaranteed capacity: once a circuit is established, no other network activity will decrease the capacity of the circuit. One disadvantage of circuit switching is cost: circuit costs are fixed, independent of traffic. For example, one pays a fixed rate when making a phone call, independent of how rapidly the two parties talk.

Packet-switched networks, the type usually used to connect computers, take an entirely different approach. In a packet-switched network, traffic on the network is divided into small segments called *packets* that are multiplexed onto high capacity intermachine connections. A packet, which contains only a few hundred bytes of data, carries identification that enables computers on the network to know whether it is destined for them or how to send it on to its correct destination. For example, a file to be transmitted between two machines may be broken into many packets that are sent across the network one at a time. The network delivers the packets to the specified destination where network software reassembles them into a single file again. The chief advantage of packet-switching is that multiple communications among computers can proceed concurrently, with intermachine connections shared by all pairs of machines that are communicating. The disadvantage, of course, is that as activity increases, a given pair of communicating computers can use less of the network capacity.

Despite the potential drawback of not being able to guarantee network capacity, packet-switched networks have become extremely popular. The motivations for adopting packet switching are cost and performance. Because multiple machines can share a network, fewer interconnections are required, and cost is kept low. Because engineers have been able to build high speed network hardware, capacity is not a problem. So many computer interconnections use packet-switching that, throughout the remainder of this text, the term *network* will refer only to packet-switched networks.

2.3 Long Haul And Local Area Networks

Packet-switched networks that span large geographical distances (e.g., the continental U.S.) are fundamentally different from those that span short distances (e.g., a single room). First, *long haul networks* operate at slower speeds than *local area networks*. Typical speeds for a long haul network range from 9.6 Kbps (thousand bits per second) to 1.54 Mbps (million bits per second), while local area networks usually operate between 3 Mbps and 100 Mbps. Second, computers attach directly to local area network media. Typically, each computer on a local area network has a network device interface that connects directly to a passive interconnection media like coaxial cable or copper wire cable. Long haul networks, on the other hand, usually consist of special purpose packet switching computers that are interconnected by leased lines. Connecting to the network means connecting to a packet switching computer. Third, long haul networks introduce high delay between transmission and receipt of a packet, whereas local area networks introduce little delay.

The goal of network protocol design is to hide the technological differences between networks, making interconnection independent of the underlying hardware technology. The next sections present six examples of such network technologies used throughout the Internet, showing some of the differences among them. Later chapters show how the Internet isolates such differences and makes the communication system independent of hardware technology.

2.4 Ethernet Technology

Ethernet is the name given to a popular local area packet-switched network technology invented at Xerox PARC in the early 1970s. The version described here was standardized by Xerox Corporation, Intel Corporation, and Digital Equipment Corporation in 1978. As Figure 2.1 shows, an Ethernet consists of a coaxial cable about 1/2 inch in diameter and up to 500 meters in length. Resistance is added between the center wire and shield at each end to prevent reflection of electrical signals. Called the *ether*, the cable itself is completely passive; all the active electronic components that make the network function are associated with computers that are attached to the network.

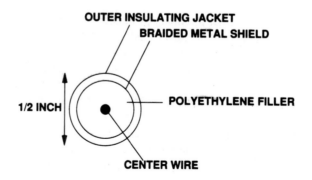

Figure 2.1 Coaxial cable used in an Ethernet

Ethernets may be extended with hardware devices called *repeaters* that relay electrical signals from one cable to another. Figure 2.2 shows a typical use of repeaters in an office building. A single backbone cable runs vertically up the building, and a repeater attaches the backbone to an additional cable on each floor. Computers attach to the cables on each floor. Only two repeaters may be placed between any two machines, so the total length of a single Ethernet is still rather short (1500 meters).

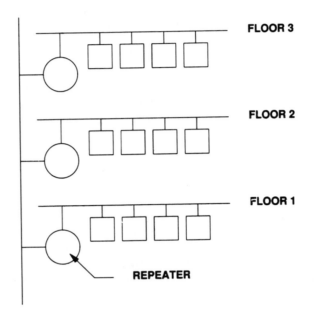

Figure 2.2 Repeaters used to join Ethernet cables in a building.

Connections to the ether are made by *taps* as Figure 2.3 shows. At each tap, a small hole in the outer layers of cable allows small pins to touch the center wire and the braided shield (some manufacturers' connectors require that the cable be cut and a "T" inserted). Each connection to an Ethernet has two major electronic components. A *transceiver* connects to the center wire and braided shield on the ether, sensing and sending signals on the ether. A *host interface* connects to the transceiver and communicates with the computer (usually through the computer's bus).

The transceiver is a small piece of hardware usually found physically adjacent to the ether. In addition to the analog hardware that senses and controls the ether, a transceiver contains digital circuitry that allows it to communicate with a digital computer. The transceiver can sense when the ether is in use and can translate analog electrical signals on the ether to (and from) digital form. The transceiver cable that runs between the transceiver and host interface carries both power to operate the transceiver as well as signals to control its operation.

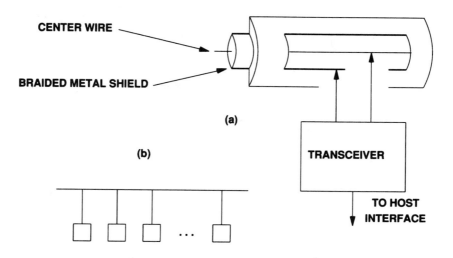

Figure 2.3 (a) A cutaway view of the cable showing the details of 2 electrical connections between a transceiver and the cable at a tap, and (b) the schematic diagram of an Ethernet with many taps.

Figure 2.4 shows the interconnection between a host and a transceiver. Each host interface controls the operation of one transceiver according to instructions it receives from the computer. To the operating system, the interface appears to be an input/output device that accepts basic data transfer instructions from the computer, controls the transceiver to carry them out, interrupts when the task has been completed, and reports status information. While the transceiver is a simple hardware device, the host interface can be complex (e.g., it may use a microprocessor to control transfers).

2.4.1 Properties of an Ethernet

The Ethernet is a 10 Mbps broadcast bus technology with distributed access control. It is a *bus* because all stations share a single communication channel; it is *broadcast* because all transceivers receive every transmission. The method used to direct packets from one station to just one other station or a subset of all stations will be discussed later. For now, it is enough to understand that transceivers do not filter transmissions – they pass all packets onto the host interface that chooses packets the host should receive and filters out all others. Ethernet access control is distributed because, unlike some networks, there is no central authority granting access. The Ethernet access scheme is called *Carrier Sense Multiple Access* with *Collision Detect* (*CSMA/CD*). It is *CSMA* because each multiple access point senses a carrier wave to determine when the network is idle. Each host interface that wants to transmit a message listens to the ether to see if a message is being transmitted (i.e., performs carrier sensing). When no transmission is sensed, the host interface starts transmitting. Each transmission is limited in duration (because there is a maximum packet size), and there is a required minimum idle time between transmissions, which means that no single pair of communicating machines can use the network without giving other machines an opportunity for access.

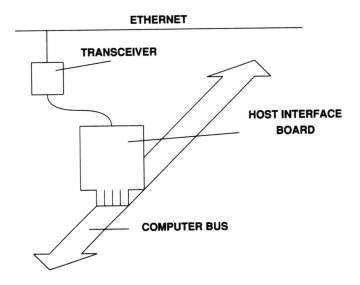

Figure 2.4 The connection between an Ethernet cable and a computer.

2.4.2 Collision Detection and Recovery

When a transceiver begins transmission, the signal does not reach all parts of the network simultaneously. Instead it travels along the cable at approximately 80% of the speed of light. Thus, it is possible for two transceivers to both sense that the network is idle and begin transmission simultaneously. When the two electrical signals cross they become scrambled, such that neither is meaningful. Such incidents are called *collisions*.

The Ethernet handles collisions in an ingenious fashion. Each transceiver monitors the cable while it is transmitting to see if a foreign signal interferes with its transmission. Technically, the monitoring is called *collision detect* (*CD*), making the Ethernet a CSMA/CD network. When a collision is detected, the host interface aborts transmission, waits for activity to subside, and tries again. Care must be taken or the network could wind up with all transceivers busily attempting to transmit and every transmission producing a collision. To help avoid such situations, Ethernet uses a binary exponential backoff policy where a sender delays 1 time unit after the first collision, 2 time units if a second attempt to transmit also produces a collision, 4 time units if a third attempt results in a collision, and so on. In addition, a sender adds a small random variation to its delay to prevent two transceivers from using exactly the same delay steps.

2.4.3 Ethernet Capacity

The standard Ethernet is rated at 10 Mbps, which means that data can be transmitted onto the cable at 10 million bits per second. This speed should not be thought of as the rate at which two computers can exchange data. Indeed, few computers are fast enough to supply or consume data continuously at Ethernet speed, which is close to the speed of a memory system. Network hardware speed is important, however, because it gives a measure of network total traffic capacity. Think of the network as a highway connecting multiple cities. High speeds make it possible to carry high traffic loads, while low speed means the highway cannot carry as much traffic. A 10 Mbps Ethernet, for example, can handle a few computers that generate heavy loads, or many computers that generate light loads.

2.4.4 Ethernet Variations

When high capacity is not needed, the network can still use Ethernet-like technology, but operate at slow speed. The advantages are primarily economic. Lower speed means less complicated hardware and lower cost. One reason cost is lower for slow-speed networks is that engineers can build entirely digital network interface hardware, completely avoiding analog transceivers. Single chip drivers for slow speed networks are already available, making the cost extremely low.

Costs can also be reduced if high-speed digital circuits can connect directly to the cable without using a transceiver. In such cases, an Ethernet can be implemented with standard coaxial cable like that used for cable television. Called *thin-wire Ethernet*, the thin cable is inexpensive, but supports fewer connections and covers shorter distances than standard Ethernet cable.

Another method of reducing costs uses a single physical cable to carry multiple, independent Ethernets. Known as *broadband*, the technology works much like broadcast radio. The transmitter multiplexes multiple Ethernets onto a single cable by assigning each Ethernet a unique frequency. Receivers must be "tuned" to the correct frequency so they can receive only the desired signal and ignore others. Although the equipment needed to connect to a broadband cable is somewhat more expensive than equipment needed to connect to a conventional *baseband* cable, broadband eliminates the cost of laying multiple cables.

2.4.5 Ethernet Addressing

An Ethernet host interface also provides an *addressing mechanism* that keeps unwanted frames from being passed to the host computer. Recall that each interface receives a copy of every packet, even those addressed to other machines. The hardware filters packets, ignoring those that are addressed to other machines and passing the host only those packets addressed to it. The address mechanism and filter are needed to prevent a computer from being overwhelmed with incoming data.

Each computer attached to an Ethernet is assigned a 48-bit integer known as its *Ethernet address*. These addresses are assigned by vendors of Ethernet hardware and are usually fixed in machine readable form on the host interface hardware. Because Ethernet addresses belong to hardware devices, they are sometimes called *hardware addresses* or *physical addresses*. Note the following important property of physical addresses:

Physical addresses are associated with the interface hardware; moving the hardware interface to a new machine or replacing a hardware interface that has failed changes physical addresses.

Knowing that Ethernet physical addresses can change will make it clear why higher levels of the network software are designed to accommodate such changes.

The 48-bit Ethernet address does more than specify a single hardware interface. It can be one of three types:

- The physical address of one network interface,
- The network *broadcast* address, or
- A *multicast* address.

Vendors purchase blocks of physical addresses and assign them in sequence as they manufacture Ethernet interface hardware. Thus, no two hardware interfaces have the same physical address. By convention, the broadcast address (all 1s) is reserved for sending to all stations simultaneously. Multicast addresses provide a limited form of broadcast in which a subset of the computers on a network agree to respond to a multicast address. Every computer in a multicast group can be reached simultaneously without affecting computers outside the multicast group.

To accommodate broadcast and multicast addressing, Ethernet interface hardware must recognize more than its physical address. A host interface usually accepts at least two kinds of transmissions: those addressed to the interface physical address and those addressed to the broadcast address. Some interfaces can be programmed to recognize multicast addresses or even alternate physical addresses. When the operating system starts, it initializes the Ethernet interface, giving it a set of addresses to recognize. The interface then scans each transmission, passing on to the host only those transmissions designated for one of the specified addresses.

2.4.6 Ethernet Frame Format

The Ethernet should be thought of as a link-level connection among machines. Thus, it makes sense to view the data transmitted as a *frame*†. Ethernet frames are of variable length, with no frame larger than 1526 octets‡. As in all packet-switched networks, a frame must identify its destination. Figure 2.5 shows the Ethernet frame format that contains both the sender's physical address as well as the destination physical address.

---

†The term *frame* derives from communication over serial lines in which the sender "frames" the data by adding special characters before and after the transmitted data.

‡The term *octet* refers to an 8-bit quantity, often called a *byte*.

In addition to identifying the source and destination, each frame transmitted across the Ethernet contains a *preamble, type field, data field*, and *Cyclic Redundancy Check (CRC)*. The preamble consists of 64 bits of alternating *0*s and *1*s to help receiving nodes synchronize. The 32-bit CRC helps the interface detect transmission errors: the sender computes the CRC as a function of the data in the frame, and the receiver recomputes the CRC to verify that the packet has been received intact. The packet type field contains a 16-bit frame type.

From the Internet point of view, the important idea is that Ethernet frames are *self-identifying*. They contain the addresses of both the sender and the destination, as well as a frame type identification. When a frame arrives at a given machine, the operating system uses the frame type to determine which protocol software module to use to process the frame. The chief advantages of self-identifying frames are that they allow multiple protocols to be used together on a single machine and they allow multiple protocols to be intermixed on the same physical network without interference. For example, one could have an application program using Internet protocols while another used a local experimental protocol. The operating system would decide where to send incoming packets based on their frame type. We will see that the Internet uses self-identifying Ethernet frames to distinguish among several of its protocols.

Preamble	Destination Address	Source Address	Packet Type	Data	CRC
64 bits	48 bits	48 bits	16 bits	368-12000 bits	32 bits

Figure 2.5 The format of a frame (packet) as it travels across an Ethernet.

2.5 ProNET Ring Technology

ProNET-10 is the name of a commercial local area network product that offers an interesting alternative to the Ethernet. Based on networking research at universities, and manufactured by Proteon Incorporated, a proNET-10 consists of a passive wiring system that interconnects computers. Like the Ethernet, it operates at 10 Mbps†, is limited to short geographic distances, and requires attached computers to have an active host interface.

Unlike the Ethernet or related bus technologies, proNET-10 requires hosts to be wired in a one-way ring and uses an access technology known as *token passing*. The primary distinguishing feature of token-passing systems is that they achieve fair access by having all machines take turns using the network. At any time, exactly one machine holds a *token* which grants that machine the right to send a packet. After sending its packet, the machine passes the token to the next machine in sequence, and so on. Thus, when none of the machines has anything to send, they continually pass the token around; when they all have packets to send, they take turns sending them.

---

†A related Proteon product operates at 80 Mbps.

Although token passing can be used with Ethernet-like bus topologies, the proNET-10 ring arrangement makes token passing especially simple because the physical connections determine the sequence through which the token passes. The key is that a given machine does not know the identity of the machine to which it passes the token. We will soon see why token circulation based on physical order is important, and how it can be used to make the ring more reliable.

To understand how a ring operates, we need to look at the hardware. Physically, the ring network is not a continuous wire – it consists of point-to-point connections among the host interfaces of computers on the net. At each host, one wire carries incoming signals, and another carries outgoing signals.

Conceptually, each host interface operates in one of three modes: *copy mode*, *transmit mode*, or *recovery mode*. As Figure 2.6 shows, the first two modes represent normal operation, with the choice depending on whether the machine currently holds the token.

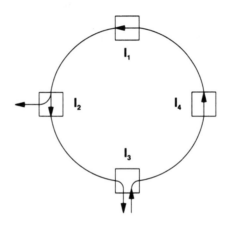

Figure 2.6 A token ring network with interface I_3 in transmit mode, holding the token and sending a packet to interface I_2. Other interfaces are in copy mode. The sender always receives back the bits being sent; other interfaces extract a copy of the packet for their host only if the address matches.

When not holding the token, an interface runs in copy mode, reading bits from the incoming wire and copying them to the outgoing wire. In copy mode, the interface also watches the data stream to find packets addressed to the local machine, placing a copy of such packets in the machine's memory. When holding the token, the interface operates in transmit mode, sending a packet on the outgoing wire and verifying correctness by reading it back from the incoming wire.

Quite unlike the Ethernet, proNET-10 interface hardware does not have fixed addresses assigned by the manufacturer. Instead, each interface comes with a set of 8 switches that allows a system administrator to choose any of 255 possible addresses (thus, a given proNET-10 network is limited to 255 machines). The address must be selected and configured using physical switches on the board. It cannot be changed quickly or easily once the interface is installed. Unlike Ethernet addresses, the configurable address scheme used by proNET-10 allows address conflicts. An installer is required to ensure that each interface on a given ring is assigned a unique address. An address of all *1*s is reserved for broadcast traffic.

2.5.1 proNET-10 Frame Format

Figure 2.7 shows the proNET-10 frame format. Most fields are specified in numbers of bits because the network is bit-oriented and does not always align data on octet boundaries. The network hardware requires the data field to be an exact multiple of octets, making it easy to transfer data to the host computer's memory. Like the Ethernet, the hardware only understands some parts of the frame format; software supplies and uses other parts. From the Internet designer's point of view, however, the distinction is unimportant.

Start of Msg	Dest. Addr.	Src. Addr.	Packet Type	Data	End of Msg.	Par.	Ref.
10 bits	8 bits	8 bits	24 bits	0-16352 bits	9 bits	1 bit	1 bit

Figure 2.7 The proNET-10 frame format.

Each frame begins with a *start of message* field, followed by two octets of *destination* and *source* address. The packet type field consists of three octets, but only the first is currently used; the last two must contain 0. Following the *data* portion of the packet comes an *End of Message* field, a single *parity* bit, and a *refused* bit. Either another packet or the token follows immediately after the end of a packet. Note that, like the Ethernet, proNET-10 frames are self-identifying.

The hardware uses a *flag* consisting of 7 contiguous 1 bits to distinguish fields like end-of-message from user data. The token and beginning of message also start with a flag. Whenever 7 contiguous 1 bits occur in the user's data, the hardware modifies the sequence to ensure that the receiver can distinguish it from a flag. The receiver reverses the modification to deliver exactly the same data that was sent.

2.5.2 proNET-10 Token Recovery

Because a token passing ring relies on all hosts to forward the token when they finish transmitting, failures at one node can stop the ring. Suppose, for example, that a malfunction or electrical interference damaged the token. Unless the ring included a mechanism to recover, all transmission would cease. To recover from token loss, the proNET-10 has each station run two timers. One timer is reset whenever the station detects an activity (e.g., a packet) and the other is reset when a token arrives. If either timer has expired when the station has a packet to send, the station changes to recovery mode and eventually generates a new token for the ring.

Usually, the first station to enter recovery mode assumes it holds the token and transmits its packet. Then it transmits the token as if nothing had gone wrong. As it transmits, the station monitors the ring to check that the packet circulates completely. If so, the ring has recovered and everything proceeds as usual. In the improbable case that two stations simultaneously try to transmit after a token loss, they detect the problem because they do not receive back their own transmission. The two stations back off, wait a random time, and try again. To ensure that they do not both wait exactly the same amount of time, each station computes a delay proportional to its hardware address. Thus, if two boards begin circulating packets simultaneously, only one survives. The recovery algorithm is both efficient and reliable. It guarantees that in only a few trips around the ring, one station will decide it holds the token and all other stations will agree.

2.5.3 proNET-10 Star-Shaped Ring

In practice, most installations configure proNET-10 networks into star-shaped rings to improve reliability. The idea is to use a passive wire center as a physical hub even though the network operates logically as a ring. The wire center has no active components, but uses sensitive relays powered by current flowing over the network wires. As long as a machine has power, its relay at the wire center keeps it connected into the ring. When the machine is powered down, however, current stops flowing to the wire center, and the machine's relay opens in such a way that it reconnects the ring for the other machines. Thus, the network will continue to operate even if some of the attached machines lose power (of course, a machine failure may stop the network for a few milliseconds while the remaining nodes recover the token). Adding to the reliability, the vendor has designed the proNET-10 interface in two pieces, one that can participate in copy mode and token recovery without any help from the CPU, and another that depends on the CPU to read or write packets. Thus, the network is also isolated from operating system failures.

2.6 ARPANET Technology

One of the oldest long haul packet-switched networks, the ARPANET, was built by the Defense Advanced Research Projects Agency (DARPA†) starting in the late 1960s

†The name of the network arises because the agency was known as *ARPA*, not *DARPA*, when the network was built.

and has served as a testbed for research in packet-switching. In addition to its use for network research, researchers in several universities, a few military bases, and government labs regularly use the ARPANET to exchange files and electronic mail and to provide remote login among their sites. In 1984 the Department of Defense partitioned the ARPANET into two connected networks, leaving the ARPANET for experimental research and forming the MILNET for production use by the military. Although under normal circumstances, both ARPANET and MILNET agree to pass traffic to the other freely, controls can be applied to disconnect them if needed. Because the ARPANET and MILNET use the same hardware technology, our description of the technical details will apply to both even though we will refer mainly to the ARPANET.

The ARPANET has influenced the Internet from its inception. Because the ARPANET was already in place and used daily by the researchers who developed the Internet architecture, it had a profound effect on their work. They came to think of the ARPANET as a dependable long haul backbone around which the Internet could be hung. The influence of a central, long haul backbone is still painfully obvious in some of the Internet protocols that we will discuss later, and has prevented the Internet from accommodating additional long haul backbones gracefully.

Physically, the ARPANET consists of approximately 50 BBN Corporation C30 and C300 minicomputers called *Packet Switched Nodes*‡ or *PSNs* scattered across the continental U.S. and in western Europe (the MILNET has approximately 160 PSNs, including 24 in Europe and 11 in the Pacific and Far East). One PSN resides at each site participating in the network and is dedicated to the task of switching packets; it cannot be used for general-purpose computation. Indeed, the PSN is considered to be part of the ARPANET and is controlled by the *Network Operation Center* (*NOC*†) located at BBN in Cambridge, Massachusetts.

Point-to-point data circuits leased from long haul carriers connect the PSNs together to form a network. For example, leased data circuits connect the ARPANET PSN at Purdue University to the ARPANET PSNs at Carnegie Mellon and at the University of Wisconsin. Currently, all leased data circuits in the ARPANET operate at 56 Kbps, but we think of the speed more as a measure of capacity than a measure of delivery speed. Line speeds will be increased only when traffic on the ARPANET saturates line capacity (which many observers believe to be imminent). When building the ARPANET, DARPA decided that reliability was important, so they mandated that each PSN must have at least two leased line connections to other PSNs. Thus, the ARPANET can continue switching packets even if one of its data circuits fails.

In addition to connections for leased data circuits, each PSN has up to 8 *ports* that connect it to user's computers, which are called *hosts*. Originally, all computers that needed to access the ARPANET connected directly to one of the ports on a PSN. Normally, direct connections are formed with a special-purpose interface board that plugs into the computer's I/O bus and attaches to a PSN port. When programmed properly, the

---

‡PSNs were formerly called *Interface Message Processor*s or *IMP*s, and the terminology persists.
†called "the knock" after its acronym.

interface allows the computer to contact the PSN to send and receive packets.

The original PSN port hardware used a complex protocol for transferring data across the ARPANET. Fondly known as 1822, after the number of a technical report that described it, this bizarre protocol survives and is still used on most PSN ports. In general, 1822 permits a host to send a packet across the ARPANET to a specified destination PSN and a specified port on that PSN. Performing the transfer is complicated, however, because 1822 offers reliable, flow-controlled delivery. To prevent a given host from saturating the net, 1822 limits the number of packets that can be in transit. To guarantee that each packet arrives at its destination, 1822 forces the sender to await a *Ready For Next Message (RFNM)* signal from the PSN before transmitting each packet. The RFNM acts as an acknowledgement. It includes a buffer reservation scheme that requires the sender to reserve a buffer at the destination PSN before sending a packet.

Although there are many parts of 1822 not discussed here, the key idea to understand is that underneath all the detail, the ARPANET is merely a transfer mechanism. When a computer connected to one port sends a packet to another port, the data delivered is exactly the data sent. Because the ARPANET does not deliver a network-specific header, packets sent across it do not have a fixed field to specify packet type. Thus, unlike other network technologies, the ARPANET does not deliver self-identifying packets. In summary:

> *The ARPANET does not understand contents of packets that travel across it; it is only by convention that machines attached to the AR-PANET agree on the format and contents of packets sent or received at a specific PSN port.*

Unfortunately, 1822 is not an industry standard. So few vendors manufacture 1822 interface boards that it is difficult to connect new machines to the ARPANET. To solve the problem, DARPA has developed a new PSN interface that uses an international data communications standard known as *CCITT X.25* (the designator was assigned by the standards committee that developed it). The first version of an X.25 PSN port used only the data transfer part of the X.25 standard (known as HDLC/LAPB), but later versions made it possible to use all of X.25 when connecting to a PSN (i.e., ARPANET appears to be an X.25 network). It is likely that, in the future, more ports will use X.25 than 1822.

Internally, of course, the ARPANET uses its own set of protocols that are invisible to users. For example, there is a special protocol that allows one PSN to request status from another, another protocol that PSNs use to send packets among themselves, and still another that allows PSNs to exchange information about link status and optimal routes.

Because the ARPANET was originally built as a single, independent network to be used for research, its protocols and addressing structure were designed without much thought given to expansion. By the mid 1970's, it became apparent no single network would solve all communication problems, and DARPA began to investigate satellite and packet radio network technologies. This experience with a variety of network technologies led to the concept of an internetwork.

Today, the ARPANET and MILNET form the backbones of the research and production side of the Internet. The Network Operation Center, located at BBN, monitors traffic 24 hours a day, detects malfunctions in the hardware and communications lines, and coordinates the installation of new software in the PSNs. DARPA and NSF pay for ARPANET operation and maintenance, including the leased lines charges, using the *Defense Communication Agency (DCA)* to carry out contracts and fill work orders.

2.7 National Science Foundation Networking

Realizing that data communication would soon be crucial to scientific research, in 1987, the National Science Foundation established a *Division of Network and Communications Research and Infrastructure* to help ensure that requisite network communications will be available for U.S. scientists and engineers. Although the division funds basic research in networking, its emphasis so far has been concentrated on providing seed funds to build extensions to the Internet.

NSF's Internet extensions form a hierarchy consisting of a new cross-country backbone connecting the 6 NSF supercomputer centers, a set of mid-level (or regional) networks that each span a geographic area and connect it to the backbone, and a set of access networks (e.g., a campus network) that attach researchers to the regional or backbone networks. We will look at each of these briefly.

2.7.1 NSFnet Backbone

Originally built to provide scientists with access to NSF supercomputers, the backbone consists of six Digital Equipment Corporation LSI-11 microcomputers located at the NSF supercomputer centers. Geographically, the backbone spans the continental United States from Princeton, NJ to San Diego, CA, using 56 Kbps leased lines as Figure 2.8 shows.

At each site, the microcomputer runs software affectionately known as *fuzzball* code. The fuzzballs reach local computers by an Ethernet and attach to the leased line through serial line controllers that use the vendor's link-level protocols. The primary connection between the NSFnet backbone and the rest of the Internet occurs at Carnegie Mellon, which has both an NSFnet backbone node and an ARPANET PSN.

2.7.2 NSFnet Mid-level Networks

NSF has funded almost a dozen mid-level networks that span almost every state. A typical mid-level network includes 6 to 12 universities clustered in a geographic area. The original NSF goal was to cover initial costs and then allow each mid-level network to operate in fiscal and administrative autonomy. While the goal of fiscal independence is still firm, the mid-levels have recently realized the need to form a federation to help coordinate technical work and interactions.

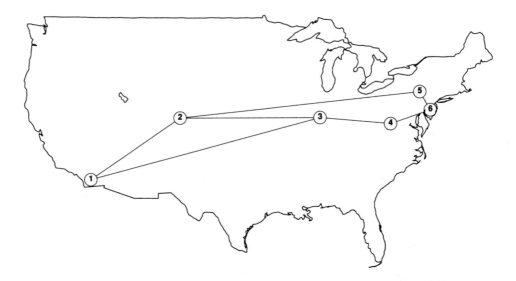

Figure 2.8 The NSF backbone network sites in (1) San Diego CA, (2) Boulder CO, (3) Champaign IL, (4) Pittsburgh PA, (5) Ithaca NY, and (6) Princeton NJ, shown in approximate geographical locations.

Each mid-level network is free to choose whatever technology will serve it best; NSF will provide access from a mid-level to the rest of the Internet. Most mid-levels have proposed using point-to-point leased line interconnections similar to that of the NSFnet backbone; almost all plan to upgrade to higher speed lines in the near future. Many of the mid-levels are just getting organized, so it is difficult to predict how or when they will evolve.

2.7.3 NSFnet Access Networks

The final component of NSFnet consists of a random collection of access networks. Some were funded as experiments using new technology (e.g., a satellite bridge), while others were funded to provide supercomputer access for a specific research individual or group. In the latter category, each supercomputer center includes a consortium of research groups that connect to it over leased lines. A consortium sometimes includes geographically distant sites, making these so-called *consortium networks* quite extensive.

2.8 X25NET

CSNET, an organization formed in 1980 to help provide Internet services to industry and small schools, uses X25NET technology to connect some of its subscribers to the Internet. Originally developed at Purdue University, X25NET runs Internet protocols over public packet-switched networks. The motivation is to allow organizations that cannot afford direct ARPANET connections to lease a network connection from a common carrier (e.g., AT&T) and use it to send Internet traffic.

Readers who know about public packet-switched networks may find X25NET strange because such networks use the CCITT X.25 protocols exclusively while the Internet uses Internet protocols. When used in X25NET, however, the underlying X.25 network merely provides a path over which Internet traffic can be transferred. We have already stated that many underlying technologies can be used to carry Internet traffic. The technique, sometimes called *tunneling*, simply means that a complex network with its own protocols is treated like any other hardware delivery system. What makes the use of X.25 so peculiar is the interface X.25 provides. Unlike most network hardware, X.25 protocols provide a reliable transmission stream, sometimes called a *virtual circuit*, from the sender to the receiver, while the Internet protocols have been designed for a packet delivery system, making the two (apparently) incompatible.

Viewing X.25 connections merely as delivery paths produces a strange twist. It turns out that X.25 networks exhibit substantially better throughput with multiple simultaneous connections. Thus, instead of opening a single connection to a given destination, an X25NET sender often opens multiple connections and distributes packets among them to improve performance. The receiver accepts packets over all the X.25 connections and combines them together again.

The addressing scheme used by X.25 networks is given in a related standard known as X.121. X.121 physical addresses each consist of a 14-digit number, with the last 10 digits assigned by the vendor that supplies the X.25 network service. Resembling telephone numbers, one popular vendor's assignments includes an area code based on geographic location. The addressing scheme is not surprising because it arises from an organization that determines international telephone standards. It is unfortunate, however, because it makes assignment of Internet addresses difficult. Subscribers using X25NET must each maintain a table of mappings between Internet addresses and X.25 addresses. Chapter 6 discusses the address mapping problem in detail and gives an alternative to using fixed tables.

Because X.25 networks operate independently of the Internet, a point of contact must be provided between the two. Both DARPA and CSNET operate dedicated machines that provide the interconnection between X.25 and the ARPANET. The primary interconnection is known as the *VAN gateway*. The VAN agrees to accept X.25 connections and route incoming Internet traffic to its destination.

X25NET is significant, not because it is an optimal interconnection strategy, but because it illustrates the flexibility and adaptability of the Internet protocols. In particular, it shows how tunneling makes it possible to use an extremely wide range of complex network technologies in the Internet.

2.9 Cypress Network

Most of the network technologies we have discussed so far are expensive. But Internet access need not be limited to large institutions that connect directly to the ARPANET or major NSFnet sites; many small schools and individuals need access as well. Small institutions cannot afford high speed leased lines, or the equipment that connects to it. Cypress is designed to fill that need by providing a low cost and low volume Internet access technology.

Cypress consists of a set of minicomputers interconnected by low or medium speed (9.6 Kbps to 56 Kbps) leased lines. As Figure 2.9 shows, each minicomputer resides at a subscriber's site, where it connects to the local computing environment over an Ethernet local area network. It connects to the rest of Cypress over leased serial lines. At least one site on a Cypress network connects to the Internet and passes traffic between the Cypress net and the rest of the Internet.

Originally, Cypress was designed to have a ''growing vine'' topology in which each new site leased a serial line to the closest existing site. The advantage of using a vine topology is low cost; the disadvantage is delay, which becomes noticeable for traffic that passes through several intermediate machines. The Cypress topology has changed for two reasons: first, NSFnet has increased the number of potential Internet connection points dramatically, and second, most subscribers seem to be willing to pay more to avoid delays. Thus, the current Cypress network has a single hub located at Purdue University, where it connects to the ARPANET. In the future, many ARPANET and NSFnet sites will serve as hubs using Cypress, or a Cypress-like technology to provide low cost access to small sites nearby.

Cypress is based on a few key ideas. First, to achieve low cost, Cypress consolidates functionality, using a single computer to serve several purposes. Second, the Cypress protocols are based on *best-effort delivery*, with no attempt made to correct errors or recover lost packets at the link level. Later chapters will explain why best-effort delivery works well in the Internet environment. Third, Cypress operates as a network, not merely as a set of point-to-point links. Fourth, Cypress connects to a network at subscriber sites, not merely to a single machine. Thus, many hosts at the subscriber's site can use the Cypress connection by treating it as their path to the rest of the Internet. Fifth, Cypress allows its packet switches to be monitored from any site in the Internet because it uses IP to transport monitoring information.

The minicomputers that comprise a Cypress network are called *implets*, and each implet provides three conceptual functions in a single machine. At the lowest level, an implet operates like a packet switch, accepting packets over serial lines and routing them on to their destination. At the next level, an implet connects two networks, the local Ethernet at the subscriber's site and the Cypress network. At the highest level, an implet is a general purpose computer that executes network control and monitoring programs as user processes.

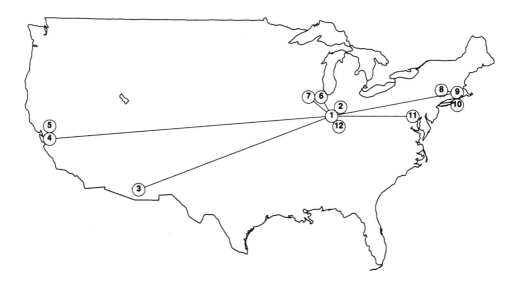

Figure 2.9 The Cypress network centered at (1,2) Purdue with sites in (3) Tucson AZ, (4,5) Palo Alto CA, (6,7) Chicago IL, (8) Williamstown MA, (9) Cambridge MA, (10) Boston MA, (11) Lewisburg PA, and (12) Indianapolis IN. At each site the implet connects to an Ethernet.

In addition to its technical contributions Cypress demonstrates three important ideas. First, it illustrates why network speed should be thought of as a measure of capacity. Sites with low traffic volumes perceive Cypress as an adequate, viable interconnection technology. Low speed does not mean limited functionality. Second, Cypress shows that the Internet protocols work well over a best-effort delivery system with minimum link level protocols. Third, Cypress shows that designing control and monitoring software to use the Internet protocols makes monitoring flexible and debugging easier.

2.10 Summary And Conclusion

We have reviewed several network hardware technologies used throughout the Internet, ranging from high-speed, local area networks like Ethernet and proNET-10 to slower-speed, long haul networks like the ARPANET and Cypress. We have also seen that it is possible to run the Internet protocols over other general-purpose network protocols. While the details of specific network technologies are not important, a general idea has emerged:

The Internet protocols are extremely flexible in that almost any under-lying technology can be used to transfer Internet traffic.

FOR FURTHER STUDY

Early computer communication systems employed point-to-point interconnection, often using general-purpose serial line hardware that McNamara [1982] describes. Metcalf and Boggs [1976] introduced the Ethernet, with a 3 Mbps prototype version. Digital [1980] specifies the 10 Mbps standard adopted by most vendors, with IEEE standard 802 reported in Nelson [1983]. Shoch, Dalal, and Redell [1982] provides a historical perspective of the Ethernet evolution. Related work on the ALOHA network is reported in Abramson [1970], with a survey of technologies given by Cotton [1979].

Token passing ring technology was proposed in Farmer and Newhall [1969]. Miller and Thompson [1982], as well as Andrews and Shultz [1982], give recent summaries. Another alternative, the slotted ring network was proposed by Pierce [1972]. For a comparison of technologies, see Rosenthal [1982].

For more information on the ARPANET see BBN [1981]. The ideas behind X25NET are summarized in Comer and Korb [1983], while Cypress is described in Comer et al [1987].

3

Internetworking Concept and Architectural Model

3.1 Introduction

So far we have looked at the low-level details of transmission across individual networks, the foundation on which all computer communication is built. This chapter makes a giant conceptual leap by describing a scheme that allows us to collect the diverse network technologies into a coordinated whole. The primary goal is a scheme that hides the details of underlying network hardware while providing universal communication services. The primary result is a high level abstraction that provides the framework for all design decisions. Succeeding chapters show how we use this abstraction to build the necessary layers of internet communication software and how the software hides the underlying physical transport mechanisms. Later chapters also show how applications use the resulting communication system.

3.2 Application-Level Interconnection

Designers have taken two different approaches to hiding network details, using application programs to handle heterogeneity or hiding details in the operating system. Early heterogeneous network interconnections provided uniformity through application-level programs. In such systems, an application-level program, executing on each machine in the network, understands the details of the network connections for that machine and interoperates with the application programs across those connections. For example, some electronic mail systems consist of mailer programs that forward a memo one machine at a time. The path from source to destination may involve many different networks, but that does not matter as long as the mail systems on all the machines cooperate by forwarding each message.

Using application programs to hide network details may seem natural at first, but results in limited, cumbersome communication. Adding new functionality to the system means building a new application program for each machine. On a given machine each application program understands the network connections for that machine, resulting in duplication of code. Users who are experienced with networking understand that once the interconnections grow to hundreds or thousands of networks, no one can possibly build all the necessary application programs. Furthermore, success of the step-at-a-time communication scheme requires correctness of all application programs executing along the way. If a single application program fails, communication fails even though the user has no knowledge or control of the failure.

3.3 Network-Level Interconnection

The alternative to providing interconnection with application-level programs is a system based on network-level interconnection. A network-level interconnect provides a mechanism that delivers packets from the source to their destination in real time. Switching small units of data instead of files or large messages has several advantages. First, it maps directly onto the underlying network hardware. Second, it separates data communication activities from application programs, permitting machines to handle network traffic without understanding the applications that use it. Third, it keeps the system flexible, making it possible to build general purpose networking protocols.

The key to designing universal network-level interconnection can be found in an abstract communication system concept known as *internetworking*. The internetwork, or *internet*, concept is an extremely powerful one. It detaches the notions of communication from the details of network technologies and hides low-level details from the user. More important, it drives all our design decisions and explains how to handle physical addressing. After reviewing basic motivation for internetworking, we will consider the properties of an internet in more detail.

Recall that we began with two fundamental observations about the design of communication systems:

- No single network can serve all users.
- Users desire universal interconnection.

The first observation is a technical one. Local area networks that provide the highest speed communication are limited in geographic span; long-haul networks span large distances but cannot supply high speed connections. Thus, no single network technology satisfies all needs, so we are forced to consider multiple underlying technologies.

The second observation is self evident. Ultimately, we would like to be able to communicate between any two points. In particular, we desire a communication system that is not constrained by the boundaries of physical networks.

The goal is to build a unified, cooperative, interconnection of networks that supports a universal communication service. Within each network, computers will use underlying technology-dependent communication primitives like the ones described in Chapter 2. New software, inserted between the technology-dependent communication mechanisms and application programs, will hide the low-level details and make the collection of networks appear to be a single large network. Such an interconnection scheme is called an *internetwork* or *internet*.

The idea of building an internet follows a standard pattern of system design: researchers imagined a high level computing facility and worked from the available computing technology, adding layers of software until they had a system that efficiently implemented the imagined high-level facility. The next section shows the first steps of that design process by defining the goal more precisely.

3.4 Properties Of The Internet

The notion of universal service is important, but it alone does not capture all the ideas we have in mind for a unified internet because there can be many implementations of universal services. In our design, we want to hide the underlying internet architecture from the user. That is, we do not want to require users to understand the details of hardware interconnections to use the internet. We also do not want to mandate a network interconnection topology. In particular, adding a new network to the internet should not mean connecting to a centralized switching point, nor should it mean adding direct physical connections between the new network and all existing networks. We want to be able to send data across intermediate networks even though they are not connected to the source or destination machines. We want all machines in the internet to share a universal set of machine identifiers (which can be thought of as *names* or *addresses*).

Our notion of a unified internet also includes the idea of a network independence in the interface. That is, we want the set of operations used to establish communication or to transfer data to remain independent of the underlying network technologies or the destination machine. Certainly, a user should not have to understand the network interconnection topology when writing programs that communicate.

3.5 Internet Architecture

We have seen how machines connect to individual networks. The question arises, "How are networks interconnected to form an internetwork?" The answer has two parts. Physically, two networks can only be connected by a computer that attaches to both of them. A physical attachment does not provide the interconnection we have in mind, however, because such a connection does not guarantee that the computer will cooperate with other machines that wish to communicate. To have a viable internet, we need computers that are willing to shuffle packets from one network to another. Computers that interconnect two networks and pass packets from one to the other are called *internet gateways*.

Consider an example consisting of two networks shown in Figure 3.1. In the figure, machine *G* connects to both network *1* and network *2*. For *G* to act as a gateway, it must capture packets on network *1* that are bound for machines on network *2* and transfer them. Similarly, *G* must capture packets on network *2* that are destined for machines on network *1* and transfer them.

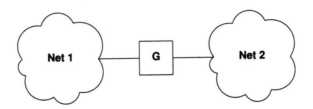

Figure 3.1 Two networks interconnected by a gateway G.

3.6 Interconnection Through Gateways

When internet connections become more complex, gateways need to understand about the internet topology beyond the networks to which they connect. For example, Figure 3.2 shows three networks interconnected by two gateways.

Figure 3.2 Three networks interconnected by two gateways.

In this example, gateway *G1* must shuffle from network *1* to network *2* all packets destined for machines on either network *2* or network *3*. As the size of the Internet expands, the gateway's task of making decisions about where to send packets becomes more complex.

The idea of a gateway seems simple, but it is important because it provides a way to interconnect networks, not just machines. In fact, we have already discovered the principle of interconnection used throughout the Internet:

> *In the Internet, computers called gateways provide all interconnections among physical networks.*

You might suspect that gateways, which must know how to route packets to their destination, are large machines with enough primary or secondary memory to hold information about every machine in the internet. However, internet gateways are usually minicomputers; they often have little or no disk storage and limited main memories. The trick to building a small internet gateway lies in the following concept:

> *Gateways route packets based on destination network, not on destination host.*

If routing is based on networks, the amount of information that a gateway needs to keep is proportional to the number of networks in the Internet, not the number of machines.

Because gateways play a key role in Internet communication, we will return to them in later chapters and discuss the details of how they operate and how they learn about routes. For now, we will assume that it is possible, and practical to have correct routes for all networks in each gateway in the Internet. We will also assume that only gateways provide connections between physical networks in the Internet.

3.7 The User's View

Remember that the Internet is designed to provide a universal interconnection among machines independent of the particular network to which they attach. Thus, we want the user to view the Internet as a single, virtual network to which all machines connect despite its physical connection. Figure 3.3 shows how thinking of the Internet instead of constituent networks simplifies the details and makes it easy for the user to conceptualize communication. In addition to gateways that interconnect physical networks, Internet access software is needed on each host to allow application programs to use the Internet as if it were a single, real hardware network.

The advantage of providing interconnection at the network level now becomes clear. Because application programs that communicate over the Internet do not know the details of underlying connections, they can be run without change on any machine. Because the details of each machine's physical network connections are hidden in the Internet software, only that software needs to change when new physical connections appear or old ones disappear. In fact, it is possible to optimize routing by altering physical connections without even recompiling application programs.

A second advantage of having communication at the network level is more subtle: users do not have to understand or remember how networks connect or what traffic they carry. As Figure 3.3 shows, gateways do not provide direct connections among all pairs of networks. It may be necessary for traffic traveling from one machine to another to pass across several intermediate networks. Thus, networks participating in the Internet are analogous to highways in the U.S. interstate system: each net agrees to handle transit traffic in exchange for the right to send traffic throughout the Internet. Typical users are unaffected and unaware of extra traffic on their local network.

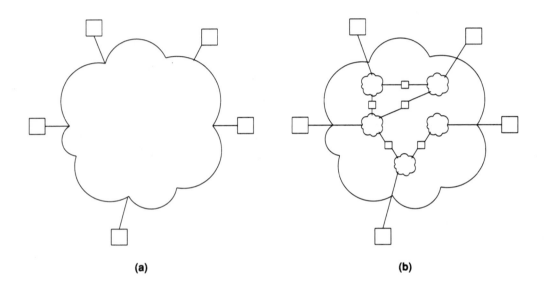

(a)   **(b)**

Figure 3.3 (a) The user's view of an Internet in which each computer appears
to attach to a single large network, and (b) the structure of physical
networks and gateways that provide interconnection.

3.8 The Unanswered Questions

Our sketch of internets leaves many unanswered questions. For example, you might wonder about the exact form of Internet machine addresses or how such addresses relate to the Ethernet, proNET-10, or ARPANET physical hardware addresses described in Chapter 2. The next three chapters confront these questions, showing the format of Internet addresses and how hosts map between physical addresses and Internet addresses. You might also want to know exactly what a packet looks like when it travels through the Internet, or what happens when packets arrive too fast for some host or gateway to handle. Chapter 7 answers these questions. Finally, you might wonder how multiple processes on a single machine can send and receive packets to multiple destinations without becoming entangled in each other's transmissions, or how Internet gateways learn about routes. All of these questions will be answered as well.

Although it may seem vague now, the direction we are following will let us learn about both the structure and use of Internet protocol software. We will examine each part, looking at the concepts and principles as well as technical details. We began by establishing a physical transport layer on which the Internet is built. Each of the next chapters will explore one part of the Internet, until we understand how the pieces fit together.

3.9 Summary

An internet is more than a collection of networks interconnected by computers; it also implies that the interconnected systems agree to conventions that allow each computer to communicate with every other computer. In particular, the internet will allow two machines to communicate even if the communication path between them passes across a network to which neither connects directly. Such cooperation is only possible when computers agree on a set of universal identifiers and a set of procedures for moving data to its final destination.

In the Internet, interconnections among networks are formed by computers called gateways that attach to two or more networks. Gateways route packets between networks by reading them from one network and sending them on another.

FOR FURTHER STUDY

Our model of an internetwork comes from Cerf and Cain [1983]. More information on the DARPA Internet architecture can be found in Postel [1980]; Postel, Sunshine, and Chen [1981], and in Hinden, Haverty, and Sheltzer [1983]. Shoch [1978] presents issues in internetwork naming and addressing. Boggs *et. al.* [1980] describe the internet developed at Xerox PARC, an alternative to the Internet we will examine. Cheriton [1983] describes internetworking as it relates to the V-system.

EXERCISES

3.1 Changing a gateway routing table can be tricky because it is impossible to change all gateways simultaneously. Investigate algorithms that guarantee to either install a change on all machines or install it on none.

3.2 In the Internet, gateways periodically exchange information from their routing tables, making it possible for a new gateway to appear and begin routing packets. Investigate the algorithms used to exchange routing information.

3.3   Compare the organization of the DARPA Internet to the one designed by Xerox Corporation.

3.4   What processors have been used as gateways in the Internet? Does the size and speed of the gateways surprise you? Why?

4

Internet Addresses

4.1 Introduction

We have said that the Internet is a virtual network built by interconnecting physical networks with gateways. This chapter discusses addressing, an essential ingredient that helps TCP/IP software hide physical network details and makes the Internet appear to be a single, uniform entity.

4.2 Universal Identifiers

A communication system is said to supply *universal communication service* if it allows any host to communicate with any other host. To make our communication system universal, we need to establish a globally accepted method of identifying computers.

Often, host identifiers are classified as *names*, *addresses*, or *routes*. Shoch [1978] suggests that a name identifies *what* an object is, an address identifies *where* it is, and a route tells *how* to get there. Although these definitions are intuitive, they can be misleading. Names, addresses, or routes really refer to successively lower-level ways to identify hosts. In general, people usually prefer pronounceable names to identify machines, while software works better with a more compact representation of identifiers that we think of as addresses. Either could be chosen as the Internet universal host identifiers, with mappings defined between them. The decision was made to standardize on compact, binary addresses that make computations like routing decisions efficient. For now, we will discuss only the binary form, postponing the questions of how to map between binary addresses and pronounceable names and how addresses are used in routing until later.

4.3 Three Primary Classes Of Internet Addresses

The way to think of the Internet is as a large network like any other physical network. The difference, of course, is that the Internet is a virtual structure, imagined by its designers, and implemented entirely in software. Thus, the designers were free to choose packet formats and sizes, addresses, delivery techniques, and so on; nothing was dictated by hardware. For addresses, they chose a scheme analogous to physical network addressing in which each host on the Internet is assigned an integer address called its *Internet address*. The clever part of Internet addressing is that the integers are carefully chosen to make operations like routing efficient. Specifically, an Internet address encodes network identification as well as the identification of a unique host on that network. We can summarize:

> *Each host on the Internet is assigned a unique 32-bit Internet address*
> *that is used in all communication with that host.*

The details of Internet addresses help clarify the abstract ideas. For now, we give a simplified view and expand it later. In the simplest case, each host attached to the Internet is assigned a 32-bit universal identifier as its Internet address. The bits of Internet addresses for all hosts on a given network share a common prefix.

Conceptually, each address is a pair (*netid*, *hostid*), where *netid* identifies a network, and *hostid* identifies a host on that network. In practice, Internet addresses have three† primary forms, as Figure 4.1 shows. Given an Internet address, its class can be determined from the three high-order bits, with two bits being sufficient to distinguish among the primary classes. Class *A* addresses, which are used for the handful of networks that have more than 2^{16} (i.e., 65,536) hosts, devote 7 bits to netid and 24 bits to hostid. Class *B* addresses, which are used for intermediate size networks that have between 2^8 (i.e., 256) and 2^{16} hosts, allocate 14 bits to the netid and 16 bits to the hostid. Finally, class *C* networks, which have less than 2^8 hosts, allocate 22 bits to the netid and only 8 bits to the hostid. Note that the Internet address has been defined in such a way that it is possible to extract the hostid or netid portions in constant time. Gateways, which base routing on the netid, depend on such efficient extraction.

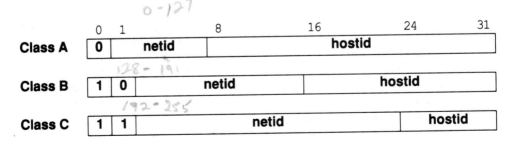

Figure 4.1 The three primary forms of Internet addresses.

---

†A fourth form is reserved for Internet multicasting, an idea still being researched. We will restrict our comments to the forms that specify addresses of individual objects.

4.4 Addresses Specify Network Connections

To simplify discussion, we said that an Internet address identifies a host, but that is not strictly accurate. Consider a gateway that attaches to two physical networks. How can we assign a single Internet address if the address encodes a network identifier as well as a host identifier? In fact, we cannot. Machines that have two or more physical connections are called *multi-homed hosts* and require multiple Internet addresses. Each address corresponds to one of the host's network connections. Looking at multi-homed hosts leads to the following important idea:

> *Because Internet addresses encode both a network and a host on that network, they do not specify a host, but a connection to a network.*

Thus, a gateway connecting *n* networks has *n* distinct Internet addresses, one for each network connection.

4.5 Network And Broadcast Addresses

We have already cited the major advantage of encoding network information in Internet addresses: it makes possible efficient routing. Another advantage is that Internet addresses can refer to networks as well as hosts. By convention, hostid *0* is never assigned to an individual host. Instead, an internet address with hostid zero is used to refer to the network itself. In summary:

> *Internet addresses can be used to refer to networks as well as individual hosts. By convention, the network address has host id with all bits 0.*

Another significant advantage of the Internet addressing scheme is that it includes a *broadcast address* that refers to all hosts on the network. According to the standard, any hostid consisting of all *1s* is reserved for broadcast. On many network technologies (e.g., Ethernet) broadcasting can be as efficient as normal transmission; on others (e.g., Cypress) broadcasting is supported by the network software but requires substantially more delay than single transmission. Other networks do not support broadcast at all. Thus, having an Internet broadcast address does not guarantee the availability or efficiency of broadcast delivery. In summary,

> *Internet addresses can be used to specify broadcast and map to hardware broadcast if available. By convention, a broadcast address has host id with all bits 1.*

As a general rule, the Internet protocols restrict broadcasting to the smallest possible set of machines. We will see how this rule affects multiple networks that share addresses in Chapter 16 when we discuss subnet addressing.

4.6 Interpreting Zero To Mean "This"

We have seen that a field consisting of *1*s can be interpreted to mean "all," as in "all hosts" on a network. In general, Internet software interprets fields consisting of *0*s to mean "this." The interpretation appears throughout the literature. Thus, an Internet address with host id *0* refers to "this" host, and an Internet address with network id *0* refers to "this" network. It is only meaningful, of course, to use such an address in a context where it can be interpreted unambiguously. For example, if a machine receives a packet with network id *0* and host field equal to the host's id, the host interprets the network field to mean "this" network (i.e., the network over which the packet arrived).

Using network id *0* is especially important in those cases where a host wants to communicate over a network but does not yet know its Internet network address. The host uses network id *0* temporarily, and other hosts on the network interpret the address as meaning "this" network. In most cases, replies will have the network address fully specified, allowing the original sender to record it for future use. Chapters 6 and 9 will discuss in detail how a host determines its network address and how it uses network id *0*.

4.7 Weaknesses In Internet Addressing

Encoding network information in the Internet address does have some disadvantages. The most obvious disadvantage is that addresses refer to connections, not to hosts:

If a host moves from one network to another, its Internet address must change.

To understand the problem, consider travelers who wish to disconnect their personal computers, carry them along on a trip, and connect them to the Internet after reaching the destination.

Another weakness of the Internet addressing scheme is that when any class *C* network grows to more than 255 hosts, it must have its address changed to a class *B* address. While this may seem like a minor problem, changing network addresses can be incredibly time-consuming and difficult to debug. Because most software is not designed to handle multiple addresses for the same physical network, administrators cannot usually cause a smooth transition by introducing new addresses slowly. Instead, they must abruptly stop using one network address and start using the other.

The most important flaw in the Internet addressing scheme has not emerged from our discussion and will not become fully apparent until we examine routing. However, its importance warrants a brief introduction here. We have suggested that routing will be based on Internet addresses, with the network id used to make routing decisions. Consider a host with two connections to the Internet. We know that such a host must have more than one Internet address. The following will be true:

Because routing uses the network portion of the Internet address, the path taken by packets traveling to a host with multiple Internet addresses depends on the address used.

The implications are surprising. Humans think of each host as a single entity and want to use a single name. They are often surprised to find that they must learn more than one name and even more surprised to find that multiple names behave differently.

Another surprising consequence of the Internet addressing scheme is that merely knowing one Internet address for a destination may not be sufficient because it may be impossible to reach the destination using that address. Consider the example network shown in Figure 4.2. In the figure, two hosts, *A* and *B*, both attach to network *1*, and usually communicate directly using that network. Thus, users on host *A* address host *B* using Internet address I_4. An alternate path from *A* to *B* exists through gateway *G* and is used whenever *A* sends packets to Internet address I_5. Now suppose *B*'s connection to network *1* fails, but the machine itself remains running (e.g., a wire breaks between *B* and network *1*). Users on *A* who specify internet address I_4 cannot reach *B*, although users who specify address I_5 can. These problems with naming and addressing will arise again in later chapters when we consider routing and name binding.

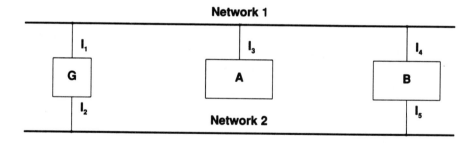

Figure 4.2 An example Internet with a multi-homed host, *B*, that demonstrates a weakness in the Internet addressing scheme. If interface I_4 becomes disconnected, *A* must use address I_5 to reach *B*, routing packets through gateway *G*.

4.8 Dotted Decimal Notation

When communicated to humans, either in technical documents or through application programs, Internet addresses are written as four decimal integers separated by decimal points, where each integer gives the value of one octet of the Internet address. Thus, the 32-bit Internet address

$$10000000 \quad 00001010 \quad 00000010 \quad 00011110$$

is written

$$128.10.2.30$$

We will use dotted decimal notation when expressing Internet addresses throughout the remainder of this text.

4.9 Internet Addressing Authority

All Internet addresses are assigned by a central authority, the *Network Information Center†* (*NIC*) located at *SRI International*. The central authority only assigns the network portion of the address and delegates responsibility for assigning host addresses to the requesting organization. Local area networks like Ethernets are usually assigned Class C numbers because many local area networks are expected, but none has more than 255 hosts. Large networks, like the ARPANET, are assigned class A numbers because only a few such networks are expected.

It should be clear that the NIC only handles Internet address assignment for networks that are (or will be) attached to the DARPA Internet. Many groups that use TCP/IP protocols assign network addresses on their own because they never need to interconnect with the Internet. For example, the NIC has assigned address 10.0.0.0 to the ARPANET. If a college campus decides to use TCP/IP technology on one ethernet with only three hosts (and no other gateway connections), that college could choose to use address 10.0.0.0 for its local network. Authorization is required, however, when assigning addresses to parts of the Internet, to guarantee uniqueness.

4.10 An Example

To make the Internet addressing scheme concrete, consider the example in Figure 4.3 that shows just a few of the connections and hosts on the Internet at the Purdue University Department of Computer Science. The example shows three networks: the ARPANET (10.0.0.0), an Ethernet (128.10.0.0), and a proNET-10 token ring network (192.5.48.0). Writing out the addresses in binary shows them to be class *A*, *B*, and *C*, respectively. Thus, the current address assignment limits the proNET-10 to less than 255 hosts.

---

†called ''The Nick'' after its acronym.

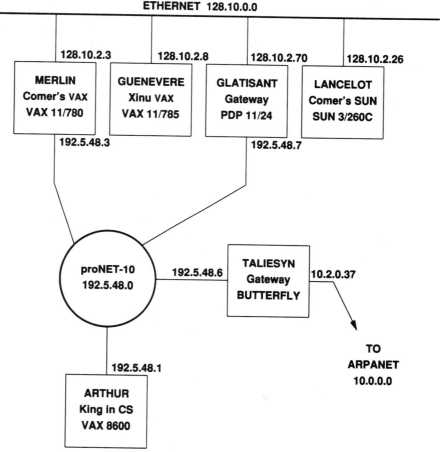

Figure 4.3 Example connections for an Ethernet, ring network and ARPANET.

In the figure, four hosts attach to these networks, labeled *Arthur*, *Merlin*, *Guenevere*, and *Lancelot*. Machine *Taliesyn* serves as a gateway between the ARPANET and the proNET-10, and host *Glatisant* serves as a gateway between the proNET-10 and Ethernet. Host *Merlin* has connections to both the Ethernet and proNET-10, so it can reach hosts on either network without using a gateway. Although *Merlin* could also operate as a gateway, it is primarily a timesharing system in which any additional work reduces the amount of processing available to users (traffic is much higher than this configuration suggests because it shows only a handful of the departmental hosts). Thus, the dedicated gateway, *Glatisant*, was installed to keep the gateway traffic load off the timesharing systems.

Figure 4.3 shows the Internet addresses of each host's network connections. *Lancelot*, which connects only to the Ethernet, has been assigned 128.10.2.26 as its only Internet address. Host *Merlin* has address 128.10.2.3 for its connection to the Ethernet and 192.5.48.3 for its connection to the proNET-10. Choosing the same value for the low-order byte of its two addresses makes it easier for systems programmers to remember all of *Merlin's* Internet addresses.

4.11 Network Byte Order

To create an Internet that is independent of any particular vendor's machine architecture or network hardware, we must define a standard representation for data. Consider what happens, for example, when one machine sends a 32-bit binary integer to another. The physical transport hardware moves the sequence of bits from the first machine to the second without changing the order. However, not all machines store 32-bit integers in the same way. On some (called *Little Endian*), the lowest memory address contains the low-order byte of the integer. On others (called *Big Endian*), the lowest memory address holds the high-order byte of the integer. Still others store integers in groups of 16-bit words, with the lowest addresses holding the low-order word, but with bytes swapped. Floating point is much worse because a vendor sometimes offers multiple floating point representations for a single machine. Thus, direct copying of bytes from one machine to another may change the value of the number.

Standardizing byte-order for integers is especially important because Internet packets carry binary numbers that specify information like destination Internet addresses and packet length. Such quantities must be understood by both the sender and receiver. The Internet solves the byte-order problem by defining a *network standard byte order* that all machines must use for binary fields in Internet packets. Each host converts binary items from the local representation to network standard byte order before sending a packet; it converts from network byte order to the host-specific order when a packet is received. Naturally, the user data field in a packet is exempt from this standard – users are free to format their own data however they choose. Of course, most users rely on standard application programs, and do not have to deal with the problem directly.

The Internet standard for byte order specifies that integers are sent most significant byte first (i.e., *Big Endian* style). That is, if one considers the successive bytes in a packet as it travels from one machine to another, binary integers in that packet have their most significant byte nearest the beginning of the packet and their least significant byte nearest the end of the packet. Many arguments have been offered about which data representation should be used, and the Internet standard still comes under attack from time to time. However, everyone agrees that having a standard is crucial, and the exact form of the standard is far less important.

4.12 Summary

The Internet uses 32-bit binary addresses as universal machine identifiers. They are divided into three classes, allowing a few hundred networks with over a million hosts each, thousands of networks with thousands of hosts each, and over a million networks with up to two hundred fifty four hosts each. To make such addresses easier for humans to understand, they are written in dotted-decimal notation, with the values of the four octets written in decimal, separated by decimal points.

Because the Internet address encodes network identification as well as the identification of a specific host on that network, it makes routing efficient. An important property of Internet addresses is that they refer to network connections, so hosts with multiple connections have multiple addresses. One advantage of the Internet addressing scheme is that the same form of address can be used to refer to hosts, networks, and all hosts on a network (broadcast). The biggest disadvantage of the Internet addressing scheme is that if a machine has multiple addresses, knowing one address may not be sufficient to reach it when some network(s) are unavailable.

To permit the exchange of binary data among machines, the Internet enforces a standard for byte-ordering within binary fields. In general, a host must convert all binary data from its internal form to network standard byte order before sending a packet and it must convert from network byte order to internal order upon receipt.

FOR FURTHER STUDY

The Internet addressing scheme presented here can be found in Reynolds and Postel [RFCs 990 and 997], which also discuss class *D* multicasting addresses. Chapter 16 covers an important extension of addressing that allows a single network address to be used with multiple physical networks.

EXERCISES

4.1   Read the standard and find out exactly how many class *A*, *B*, and *C* networks can exist. Be careful to allow for class *D* networks.

4.2   A machine readable list of assigned addresses is sometimes called an Internet *host table*. If your site has a host table, find out how many class *A*, *B*, and *C* network numbers have been assigned.

4.3   How many hosts are attached to each of the local area networks at your site?

4.4   What is the chief difference between the Internet addressing scheme and the U.S. telephone numbering scheme?

4.5   A single central authority cannot manage to assign Internet addresses fast enough to accommodate the demand. Can you invent a scheme that allows the central authority to divide its task among several groups but still ensure that each assigned address is unique?

5

Mapping Internet Addresses to Physical Addresses (ARP)

5.1 Introduction

We have described the Internet address scheme in which each host is assigned a 32-bit address and have said that the Internet behaves like a virtual network, using only these assigned addresses when sending and receiving packets. We also reviewed several physical network technologies and noted that two machines on a given physical network can communicate *only if they know each other's physical network addresses*. What we have not mentioned is how a host or a gateway maps an Internet address into the correct physical hardware address when it needs to send a packet across a physical net. This chapter considers that mapping, showing how it is implemented for the two most common physical network address schemes.

5.2 The Address Resolution Problem

Consider two machines *A* and *B* that share a physical network. Each has an assigned Internet address I_A and I_B and a physical hardware address P_A and P_B. The goal is to devise low-level software that hides physical addresses and allows higher-level programs to work only with Internet addresses. The ultimate communication, however, must be carried out by physical networks using whatever physical addressing schemes the hardware supplies. So the question arises, suppose machine *A* wants to send a packet to machine *B* across a physical network to which they both attach, but has only *B*'s Internet address I_B, how does it map that address to *B's* physical address, P_B?

The problem of mapping Internet addresses to physical addresses is known as the *address resolution problem* and has been solved in several ways. Some internet protocols keep tables in each machine that contain pairs of internet and physical addresses. Others solve the problem by encoding hardware addresses in the internet addresses. Using either approach exclusively makes internet addressing awkward at best.

5.3 Two Types Of Physical Addresses

There are two basic types of physical addresses, exemplified by the Ethernet, which has large, fixed physical addresses, and proNET-10, which has small, easily configured physical addresses. Address resolution is difficult for Ethernet-like networks, but easy for networks like proNET-10. We will consider the easy case first.

5.4 Resolution Through Direct Mapping

Consider a proNET-10 ring network. Recall from Chapter 2 that it uses small integers for physical addresses and allows the user to choose a hardware address when installing the interface board in a computer. The key to making address resolution easy for a proNET ring lies in observing that as long as one has the freedom to choose both Internet and physical addresses, they can be selected such that parts of them are the same. Typically, one assigns Internet addresses with the host id portion equal to 1, 2, 3, and so on, and then, when installing network interface hardware, selects a physical address that corresponds to the Internet address. For example, one would select physical address 3 for a machine with the Internet address 192.5.48.3 because 192.5.48.3 is a class *C* address with the host portion equal to 3.

For networks like proNET-10, computing a physical address from an Internet address is trivial. The computation consists of extracting the host id portion of the Internet address. It is computationally efficient because it requires only a few machine instructions. It is easy to maintain because the mapping can be performed without reference to external data. Finally, new machines can be added to the network without changing data or recompiling code.

Conceptually, choosing a numbering scheme that makes address resolution efficient means selecting a function, *f*, that maps Internet addresses to physical addresses. The designer may be able to select a physical address numbering scheme as well, depending on the hardware. Resolving Internet address I_A means computing

$$P_A = \mathrm{f}(I_A)$$

We want the computation of *f* to be efficient. If the set of physical addresses is constrained, it may be possible to arrange efficient mappings other than the one given in the example above. For instance, when using X.25 physical addresses, one cannot choose physical addresses. Usually, gateways on X.25 networks store pairs of Internet and X.25 physical addresses in a table and search it when resolving an Internet address. To make address resolution efficient in such cases, software can use a hash function to store and search the table. The exercises suggest another alternative.

5.5 Resolution Through Dynamic Binding

To understand why address resolution is difficult for some networks, consider the Ethernet. Recall from Chapter 2 that the Ethernet has 48-bit physical addresses assigned by vendors when they manufacture interface boards. As a consequence, replacing a board that fails changes the machine's physical address. Furthermore, because the Ethernet address is 48 bits long, there is no hope it could be encoded in a 32-bit Internet address.

Designers of the Internet found a creative solution to the address resolution problem for networks like the Chaosnet or Ethernet. The solution allows new machines to be added to the network without recompiling code, but does not require maintenance of a centralized database. To avoid maintaining a table of mappings, they chose to use a low-level protocol to bind addresses dynamically. Termed the *Address Resolution Protocol* (*ARP*), it provides a mechanism that is both efficient and easy to maintain.

As Figure 5.1 shows, the idea behind dynamic resolution with ARP is simple: when host A wants to resolve Internet address I_B, it broadcasts a special packet that asks the host with Internet address I_B to respond with its physical address, P_B. All hosts, including B, receive the request, but only host B recognizes its Internet address and sends a reply that contains its physical address. When A receives the reply, it learns B's physical hardware address and uses that address to send the Internet packet directly to B. We can summarize:

> *The Address Resolution Protocol, ARP, allows a host to find the physical address of a target host on the same physical network, given only the target's Internet address.*

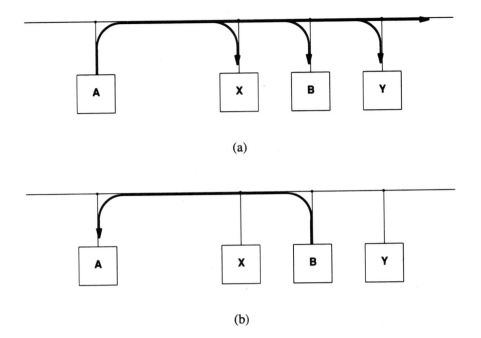

(a)

(b)

Figure 5.1 The ARP protocol. To determine P_B, B's physical address, from I_B, its Internet address, (a) host A broadcasts an ARP request containing I_B to all machines, and (b) host B responds with an ARP reply that contains the pair (I_B, P_B).

5.6 The Address Resolution Cache

It may seem silly that for A to send a packet to B it first sends a broadcast that reaches B. Or it may seem even sillier that A broadcasts the question, "how can I reach you?" instead of just broadcasting the packet it wants to deliver. But there is an important reason for the exchange. Broadcasting is far too expensive to be used every time one machine needs to transmit a packet to another because it requires every machine to process the broadcast packet. To reduce communication costs, hosts that use ARP maintain a cache of recently acquired Internet-to-physical address bindings so they do not have to use ARP repeatedly. When the host receives an ARP reply, it saves the result in its cache for successive lookups. When transmitting a packet, the host always looks in its cache for a binding before sending an ARP request. If the host finds the desired binding in its cache, it need not use the network. Experience shows that because most network communication involves more than one packet transfer, even a small cache is worthwhile.

5.7 ARP Refinements

Several refinements of ARP are possible. First, observe that if host *A* is about to use ARP because it needs to send to *B*, there is a high probability that host *B* will need to send to *A* in the near future. If we anticipate *B*'s need, we can avoid extra network traffic by arranging for *A* to include its Internet-to-physical address binding when sending a request to *B*. Second, notice that because *A* broadcasts its initial request, all machines on the network receive it and can extract and store in their cache *A*'s Internet-to-physical address binding. Third, when a new machine appears on the net (e.g., when an operating system reboots), we can avoid having every other machine run ARP by broadcasting the new pair of Internet address and physical address.

The following rule summarizes refinements:

> *The sender's Internet-to-physical address binding is included in every ARP broadcast; receivers update the Internet-to-physical address binding information in their cache before processing an ARP packet.*

5.8 Relationship Of ARP To Other Protocols

ARP provides one possible mechanism to map from Internet addresses to physical addresses; we have already seen that some network technologies do not need it. The point is that ARP would be completely unnecessary if we could make all network interfaces understand their Internet address. Thus, ARP merely imposes a new addressing scheme on top of whatever low-level addressing mechanism the hardware uses. The idea can be summarized:

> *ARP is a low-level protocol that hides the underlying network physical addressing, permitting us to assign Internet addresses of our choosing to every machine. We think of it as part of the physical network system, and not as part of the Internet protocols.*

5.9 ARP Implementation

Functionally, ARP is divided into two parts. One part determines physical addresses when sending a packet, and the other answers requests from other machines. Address resolution for outgoing packets seems straightforward, but small details complicate an implementation. Given a destination Internet address the host consults its ARP cache to see if it knows the mapping to physical address. If it does, it extracts the physical address, places the data in a frame using that address, and sends the frame. If it does not know the mapping, it must broadcast an ARP request and wait for a reply.

Broadcasting an ARP request to find an address mapping can become complex. The target machine could be down or just too busy to accept the request, in which case, the sender may not receive a reply or the reply may be delayed. Or the initial ARP broadcast request could be lost (in which case the sender should retransmit, at least once). Meanwhile, the host must store the original outgoing packet so it can be sent once the address has been resolved. In fact, the host must decide whether to allow multiple outstanding ARP requests (most do not), and if allowing multiple requests, it must take care not to broadcast multiple ARP requests for a given target Internet address. Finally, the cached value could be out of date, making successful transmission impossible.

The second part of the ARP code handles ARP packets that arrive from the network. The handler examines its cache to see if it already has an entry for the sender and, if an entry exists, the handler updates that entry by copying the sender's physical address from the packet. It then processes the packet.

The host must handle two types of incoming ARP packets. It must examine incoming ARP request packets to see if it is the target of a request from another machine. If so, the ARP handler forms and sends a reply, supplying its physical address. If not, the packet is requesting a mapping for another machine and can be ignored.

The second interesting case occurs when an ARP reply arrives. Depending on the implementation, the handler may need to create a cache entry and fill in the sender's Internet-to-physical binding before processing. If the reply answers a previously issued query, the handler must also arrange to have the waiting outgoing packet(s) sent. If the host is not interested in the reply, it simply stops processing the packet.

5.10 ARP Encapsulation And Identification

When ARP messages travel from one machine to another, they must be carried in physical frames as Figure 5.2 shows

| Frame Header | Complete ARP message treated as data |

Figure 5.2 An ARP message encapsulated in an Ethernet frame

To identify the frame as carrying an ARP request or ARP reply, the sender assigns a special value to the type field in the frame header and places the ARP message itself in the frame's data field. When a frame arrives at a host, the system examines the frame type to determine what it contains. For example, on an Ethernet, ARP requests have a type field of 0806_{16} and replies have a type of 8035_{16}. These are standard values, assigned by the authority that sets Ethernet standards, and are universally accepted.

5.11 ARP Protocol Format

Unlike most protocols, the data in ARP packets does not have a fixed-format header. Instead, the message is designed to be useful with a variety of network technologies, so early header fields contain counts that specify lengths of succeeding fields. In fact, ARP can be used with arbitrary physical addresses and arbitrary protocol addresses. The example in Figure 5.3 below shows the 28-octet ARP message format used on Ethernet hardware (where physical addresses are 48-bits or 6 octets long), when resolving DARPA Internet protocol addresses (4 octets long). Unlike most of the Internet protocols, the variable-length fields in ARP packets do not align on 32-bit boundaries, making the diagram difficult to read. For example, the sender's hardware address, labeled *SENDER HA*, occupies 6 contiguous octets, so it spans two lines in the diagram. Nevertheless, we have chosen this format because it is standard throughout the Internet literature.

0	8	16	31
HARDWARE		PROTOCOL	
HLEN	PLEN	OPERATION	
SENDER HA (octets 0-3)			
SENDER HA(octets 4-5)		SENDER IA (octets 0-1)	
SENDER IA (octets 2-3)		TARGET HA (octets 0-1)	
TARGET HA (octets 2-5)			
TARGET IA (octets 0-4)			

Figure 5.3 The format of ARP/RARP messages used for Internet-to-Ethernet address resolution.

Field *HARDWARE* specifies a hardware interface type for which the sender seeks an answer; it is *1* for Ethernet. Field *OPERATION* specifies an ARP request (*1*), ARP response (*2*), RARP† request (*3*), or RARP response (*4*). Fields *HLEN* and *PLEN* allow ARP to be used with arbitrary networks because they specify the length of the physical hardware address and the length of the protocol address. The sender supplies its hardware address and Internet address, if known, in fields *SENDER HA* and *SENDER IA*.

When making a request, the sender also supplies the target Internet address (ARP), or target hardware address (RARP), using fields *TARGET HA* and *TARGET IA*. A response carries both the target machine's hardware and Internet addresses.

---

†RARP, which uses the same message format, will be described in the next chapter.

5.12 Summary

Internet addresses are assigned independent of the physical hardware address. However, high-level network software that uses Internet addresses must ultimately map them into physical hardware addresses when delivering packets to their final destination. If hardware addresses consist of small integers that can be changed easily, a direct mapping can be established by having the physical address be encoded in the Internet address; otherwise, the mapping must be performed dynamically. The ARP protocol performs dynamic address resolution, using only the low-level network communication system. It permits machines to resolve addresses without keeping a permanent record of bindings.

A machine uses ARP to find the hardware address of another machine by broadcasting an ARP request that contains the Internet address for which it searches. Each machine responds to requests for its physical hardware address and sends replies that contain the needed binding.

To make ARP efficient, each machine caches Internet-to-physical address bindings. Because Internet traffic tends to consist of a sequence of interactions between pairs of machines, the cache eliminates most ARP broadcast requests.

FOR FURTHER STUDY

The address resolution protocol used here is given by Plummer [RFC 826] and has become an Internet standard. Dalal and Printis [1981] describe the relationship between Ethernet and Internet addresses, and Clark [RFC 814] discusses addresses and bindings in general. Comer [1987] examines an example implementation for the Xinu operating system.

EXERCISES

5.1   Given a small set of physical addresses (positive integers), can you find a function, f, and an assignment of Internet addresses such that f maps the Internet addresses 1-to-1 onto the physical addresses, and computing f is efficient?

5.2   In what special case does a host connected to an Ethernet not need to use ARP or an ARP cache before transmitting an IP datagram?

5.3   One common algorithm for managing the ARP cache replaces the least recently used entry when adding a new one. Under what circumstances can this algorithm produce unnecessary network traffic?

5.4   Should ARP update the cache if an old entry already exists for a given Internet address? Why or why not?

5.5   Why should ARP modify the cache even when it receives information without specifically requesting it? Why or why not?

5.6   Any implementation of ARP that uses a fixed-size cache can fail when used on a network that has many hosts and much ARP traffic. Explain how.

5.7   ARP is often cited as a security weakness. Explain why.

5.8   Explains what can happen if the hardware address field in an ARP response becomes corrupted during transmission. Hint: ARP implementations do not usually remove cache entries if they are frequently used.

5.9   Suppose machine C receives an ARP request sent from A looking for target B, and suppose C has the binding from I_B to P_B in its cache. Should C answer the request? Why or Why not?

6

Determining an Internet Address at Startup (RARP)

6.1 Introduction

We now know that physical network addresses are both low-level and hardware dependent, and we understand that machines on the Internet each have an assigned 32-bit Internet address that is independent of the machine's underlying physical network address. Although application programs always use the Internet address when specifying a destination, hosts and gateways must use physical addresses to transmit datagrams across underlying networks. Usually, a machine's Internet address is kept on its secondary storage, where the operating system finds it at startup. The question arises, "How does a diskless machine, one without access to secondary storage, determine its Internet address?" The problem is critical for diskless workstations that use Internet addresses to communicate with a file server. This chapter explores that question and describes a protocol that diskless machines use to obtain an address.

To allow a single operating system image to be used on a set of machines, it must be built without fixed notions of Internet addresses. When such an operating system starts execution on a diskless machines, it must use the network to contact a server and obtain its Internet address. The procedure sounds paradoxical: a machine communicates with a remote server to obtain an address used for communication.

The paradox is only imagined because the machine *does* know how to communicate. It can use its physical address to communicate over a single network. Thus, the machine must resort to physical network addressing temporarily in the same way that the operating systems use physical memory addressing to set up page tables that allow virtual addressing. Once the machine knows its Internet address, it can communicate across the Internet.

The idea behind finding an Internet address is simple: the diskless machine sends a request to a server and waits until the server sends a response. We assume the server has a disk where it keeps a database of Internet addresses. In the request, the machine needing to know its an Internet must uniquely identify itself so the server can look up the correct Internet address and send a reply. Both the machine that issues the request and the server that responds use physical network addresses during their brief communication. How does the diskless machine know the physical address of the server? Usually, it does not – it simply broadcasts the request to all machines on the local network. One or more servers respond.

When the diskless machine broadcasts its request, it must uniquely identify itself. What information can the operating system broadcast that will uniquely identify the machine on which it is executing? Any hardware identification suffices (e.g., the CPU serial number), but such information may be difficult to obtain, and the length or format may vary among CPUs.

6.2 Reverse Address Resolution Protocol (RARP)

The Internet designers realized that there is another piece of uniquely identifying information readily available, namely, the machine's physical network address. Using the physical address as a unique identification has two advantages. Because a host obtains its physical addresses from the network interface hardware, such addresses are always available and do not have to be bound into the operating system image. Because the identifying information depends on the network and not on the CPU vendor or model, all machines on a given network will supply uniform, unique identifiers. Thus, the problem becomes the reverse of address resolution: given a physical network address, a server map it into an Internet address.

The protocol diskless machines use to communicate with a server that can supply their Internet addresses is called the *Reverse Address Resolution Protocol (RARP)*. It is adapted from the ARP protocol of the previous chapter and uses the same message format†. In practice, the RARP message sent to request an Internet address is a little more general than what we have just outlined: it allows a machine to request the Internet address of a third party as easily as its own. It also allows for multiple types of physical networks.

Like an ARP message, a RARP message is sent from one machine to another encapsulated in the data portion of an Ethernet frame. An Ethernet frame carrying the RARP request has the usual preamble, Ethernet source and destination addresses, and packet type fields in front of the frame. The frame type contains a value that identifies the contents of the frame as a RARP request. The data portion of the frame contains the 28-octet RARP message.

Figure 6.1 illustrates how a host uses RARP. The sender broadcasts a RARP request that specifies itself as the target machine and supplies its physical network address in the target hardware field. All machines on the network receive the request, but only those authorized to supply the RARP service process the request and send a reply; such

---

†See Figure 5.3 for ARP/RARP message format details.

machines are known as *RARP servers*. For RARP to succeed, the network must contain at least one RARP server.

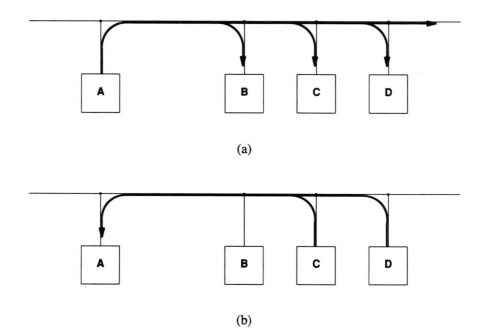

(a)

(b)

Figure 6.1 Example exchange using the RARP protocol. (a) host *A* broadcasts a RARP request specifying itself as a target, and (b) those machines authorized to supply the RARP service reply directly to *A*.

Servers answer requests by filling in the target protocol address field, changing the message type from *request* to *reply*, and sending the reply back directly to the machine making the request. The original machine receives replies from all RARP servers, even though only the first is needed.

Keep in mind that all communication between the host seeking its Internet address and the server supplying it must be carried out using only the physical network. Furthermore, the protocol allows a host to ask about an arbitrary target. Thus, the sender supplies its hardware address separate from the target hardware address, and the server is careful to send the reply using the sender's hardware address. On an Ethernet, having a field for the sender's hardware address may seem redundant because the information is also contained in the Ethernet frame header. However, not all Ethernet hardware provides the operating system with access to the physical frame header.

6.3 Timing RARP Transactions

Like any network communication, RARP requests are susceptible to loss or corruption. Because RARP uses only the physical network, RARP software must handle time out and retransmission. In general, RARP is used only on local area networks like the Ethernet, where the probability of failure is low. If a network has only one RARP server, however, that machine may not be able to handle the load, so packets may be dropped.

Many diskless machines rely on RARP to boot and may choose to retry indefinitely until they receive a response. Other implementations announce failure after only a few tries to avoid flooding the network with unnecessary broadcast traffic (e.g., in case the server is unavailable). On an Ethernet, network failure is less likely than overload at the server. Making the RARP retransmit quickly may have the unwanted effect of flooding a congested server with more traffic. Thus, a large delay ensures that servers have ample time to satisfy the request and return an answer.

6.4 Primary And Backup RARP Servers

The chief advantage of having several machines function as RARP servers is that it makes the system more reliable. If one server is down, or too heavily loaded to respond, another answers the request. Thus, it is highly likely that the service will be available. The chief disadvantage of using many servers is that when a machine broadcasts a RARP request, the network becomes overloaded when they all attempt to respond. On an Ethernet, for example, using multiple RARP servers makes the probability of collision high.

How can the RARP service be arranged to keep it available and reliable without incurring the cost of multiple, simultaneous replies? There are at least two possibilities, and they both involve delaying responses. In the first solution, each machine that makes RARP requests is assigned a *primary server*. Under normal circumstances, only the machine's primary server responds to its RARP request. All nonprimary servers receive the request but merely record its arrival time. If the primary server is unavailable, the original machine will timeout waiting for a response and then rebroadcast the request. Whenever a nonprimary server receives a second copy of a RARP request within a short time of the first, it responds.

The second solution uses a similar scheme but attempts to avoid having all nonprimary servers transmit responses simultaneously. Each nonprimary machine that receives a request computes a random delay and then sends a response. Under normal circumstances, the primary server responds immediately, and successive responses are delayed so there is low probability that they arrive at the same time. When the primary server is unavailable, the requesting machine experiences a small delay before receiving a reply. By choosing delays carefully, the designer can guarantee that requesting machines do not timeout and rebroadcast before they receive an answer.

6.5 Summary

At system startup, a diskless machine must contact a server to find its Internet address before it can communicate on the Internet. We examined the RARP protocol that uses physical network addressing to obtain the machine's Internet address. The RARP mechanism supplies the target machine's physical hardware address to uniquely identify the processor and broadcasts the RARP request. Servers on the network receive the message, look up the mapping in a table (presumably from secondary storage), and reply to the sender.

FOR FURTHER STUDY

The details of RARP are given in Finlayson, *et. al.* [RFC 903]. Comer [1987] discusses an example implementation of RARP for the Xinu operating system. Often, a diskless machine needs to boot a new image at startup. To handle such cases, Croft and Gilmore [RFC 951] propose an alternative to RARP called BOOTP. Finlayson [RFC 906] describes workstation bootstrapping using the TFTP protocol.

EXERCISES

6.1   A RARP server can broadcast RARP replies to all machines or transmit each reply directly to the machine that makes the request. Can you characterize a system in which broadcasting is beneficial?

6.2   RARP is a narrowly focused protocol in the sense that replies only contain one piece of information (i.e., the requested Internet address). When diskless machines boot, they usually want to know at least the time, their Internet address, and their machine name. Extend RARP to supply the additional information.

6.3   How much larger will the Ethernet frames become when information is added to RARP as described in the previous exercise?

6.4   Adding a second RARP server to a network increases reliability. Does it ever make sense to add a third? How about a fourth? Why or Why not?

7

Internet Protocol: Connectionless Datagram Delivery (IP)

7.1 Introduction

We have been reviewing pieces of network hardware and software that make Internet communication possible, explaining the underlying network technologies and address resolution. This chapter considers the fundamental principle of connectionless delivery and discusses how it is provided by *IP*, one of the two major protocols used in the Internet. We will study the format of Internet datagrams and see how they form the basis for all Internet communication.

7.2 A Virtual Network

Chapter 3 discussed the architecture of an internet in which gateway machines connect multiple physical networks. Looking at the architecture may be misleading, because the focus should not be on the interconnection technology, but on the interface that an internet provides to a user.

> *A user thinks of an internet as a single virtual network that intercon-*
> *nects all hosts, and through which communication is possible; its*
> *underlying architecture is both hidden and irrelevant.*

In a sense, the Internet is an abstraction of physical networks because, at the lowest level, it provides the same functionality: accepting packets and delivering them. Higher levels of Internet software add most of the rich functionality users perceive.

7.3 Internet Architecture And Philosophy

Conceptually, the Internet provides three sets of services as shown in Figure 7.1; their arrangement in the figure suggests dependencies among them. At the lowest level, a connectionless delivery system provides a foundation on which everything rests. At the next level, a reliable transport service provides a higher level platform on which applications depend. We will soon explore each of these services, understand what they provide, and see the Internet protocols associated with them.

Figure 7.1 The three conceptual sets of Internet services.

7.4 The Concept Of Unreliable Delivery

Although we can associate protocol software with each of the services in Figure 7.1, the reason for identifying them as conceptual parts of the Internet is that they clearly point out the philosophical underpinnings of the design. The point is:

> *Internet software is designed around three conceptual networking ser-*
> *vices arranged in a hierarchy; much of its success has resulted because*
> *this architecture is surprisingly robust and adaptable.*

One of the most significant advantages of this conceptual separation is that it becomes possible to replace one service without disturbing others. Thus, research and development can proceed concurrently on all three.

7.5 Connectionless Delivery System

The most fundamental Internet service consists of an unreliable, best-effort, connectionless, packet delivery system, analogous to the service provided by network hardware. The service is called *unreliable* because delivery is not guaranteed. The packet may be lost, duplicated, or delivered out of order, but the Internet will not detect such conditions, nor will it inform the sender or receiver. The service is called *connectionless* because each packet is treated independently from all others. A sequence of packets sent from one machine to another may travel over different paths, or some may be lost while others are delivered. Finally, the service is called *best-effort* because the Internet makes an earnest attempt to deliver packets. That is, the Internet does not discard packets capriciously; unreliability arises only when resources are exhausted or underlying networks fail.

7.6 Purpose Of The Internet Protocol

The protocol that defines the unreliable, connectionless delivery mechanism is called the *Internet Protocol* and is usually referred to by its initials, *IP*. IP defines the basic unit of data transfer and the exact format of all data as it passes across the Internet. In addition to the formal specification of data formats, IP includes a set of rules that specify how packets should be processed and how errors should be handled. In particular, IP embodies the idea of unreliable delivery and the associated ideas of packet routing. It is such a fundamental part of the design that the Internet is sometimes called an *IP-based technology*.

We begin our consideration of IP in this chapter by looking at the packet format it specifies. We leave until later chapters the topics of IP routing and error handling.

7.7 The Internet Datagram

The analog between a physical network and the Internet is strong. On a physical network, the unit of transfer is a frame that contains a header and data, where the header gives information like the (physical) source and destination addresses. The Internet calls its basic transfer unit an *Internet datagram*, sometimes referred to as an *IP datagram* or merely a *datagram*. Like the frame from a typical physical network, a datagram is divided into header and data areas. Also like a frame, the datagram header contains the source and destination addresses. The difference, of course, is that the datagram contains Internet addresses. Figure 7.2 shows the general form of a datagram:

| DATAGRAM HEADER | DATA AREA |

Figure 7.2 General form of an IP datagram, the basic unit of Internet transfer.

7.7.1 Datagram Encapsulation

How large can a datagram be? Unlike physical network frames that must be recognized by hardware, datagrams are handled by software. They can be of any length the Internet designers choose. However, as datagrams move from one machine to another, they must always be transported in physical frames.

The idea of carrying datagrams in a network frame is called *encapsulation*. To the underlying network, a datagram is like any other message sent from one machine to another. Thus, as Figure 7.3 shows, the datagram travels in the data portion of the network frame:

| FRAME HEADER | COMPLETE DATAGRAM TREATED AS DATA |

Figure 7.3 The obvious encapsulation of an Internet datagram in a frame.

In the ideal case, the entire datagram fits into one frame, making transmission efficient.

7.7.2 Datagram Size and Network MTU

Knowing that datagrams travel in network frames might lead us to choose a maximum datagram size such that the datagram always fits into one frame. But which frame size should we use? After all, a datagram might travel across many networks as it moves from gateway to gateway or from a gateway to its destination host.

Each packet-switching network places a fixed upper bound on the size of data that can be transferred in one physical frame. For example, the Ethernet limits transfers to 1500 octets, while the proNET-10 allows 2000 octets per frame. We refer to these limits as the network's *maximum transfer unit* or *MTU*. MTU sizes can be quite small: some networks limit transfers to 128 octets or less. Limiting datagrams to such small values makes transfers inefficient when those datagrams pass across a network that can carry larger size frames. However, allowing datagrams to be larger than the minimum network MTU means that a datagram may not always fit into a single network frame.

The choice should be obvious: the point of the Internet is to hide underlying network technologies and make communication convenient for the user. Thus, instead of designing datagrams that adhere to the constraints of physical networks, we will choose a convenient datagram size and arrange a way to divide large datagrams into small pieces called *fragments*, so they can be shipped across a physical network with small MTU and then *reassembled* into a complete datagram. The Internet does not limit datagrams to a specific size, but suggests that networks and gateways should be prepared to handle datagrams of up to 576 octets without fragmenting them. (Hosts are required to accept, and reassemble if necessary, datagrams of 576 octets.)

Fragmenting a datagram means dividing it into several pieces. It may surprise you to learn that each piece has the same format as the original datagram. Each one contains a header that duplicates most of the original datagram header (except for a few bits that show it is a fragment), followed by as much data as will fit in that fragment and still be smaller than the network MTU being used.

Should a datagram be reassembled after passing across one network, or should the fragments be carried to the final host before reassembly? In the Internet, once a datagram has been fragmented, the fragments usually travel as separate datagrams all the way to the ultimate destination, where they must be reassembled. If any fragments are lost, the datagram cannot be reassembled and the surviving pieces will eventually be discarded without processing.

7.7.3 Datagram Format

Now that the basic datagram content has been described, we will look at the fields in more detail. Figure 7.4 shows the arrangement of fields in a datagram:

0	4	8	16	19	24	31

VERS	LEN	TYPE OF SERVICE	TOTAL LENGTH			
IDENT			FLAGS	FRAGMENT OFFSET		
TIME		PROTO	HEADER CHECKSUM			
SOURCE IP ADDRESS						
DESTINATION IP ADDRESS						
OPTIONS					PADDING	
DATA						
. . .						

Figure 7.4 Format of an Internet datagram, the basic unit of transfer on the Internet.

The 4-bit version field (*VERS*) specifies the IP protocol version and is used to verify that the sender, receiver, and gateways in between them agree on the format of the datagram. If standards change, machines will reject datagrams with protocol versions different from theirs, preventing them from misinterpreting datagram contents according to an outdated format. The current protocol version is *4*.

The length field (*LEN*), also 4 bits, gives the datagram header length measured in 32-bit words. The most common header, without options, contains 20 octets, and has a length field equal to 5.

The *TOTAL LENGTH* field gives the length of the IP datagram measured in octets, including the length of the header and data. The size of the data area is computed from the *TOTAL LENGTH* and *LEN* fields.

7.7.4 Datagram Type of Service and Precedence

The 8-bit *TYPE OF SERVICE* field specifies how the datagram should be handled and is broken down into five subfields as shown in Figure 7.5:

Figure 7.5 The five subfields that comprise the type-of-service field.

Three *PRECEDENCE* bits specify datagram precedence, with values ranging from 0 (normal precedence) through 7 (network control), allowing sender's to indicate the importance of each datagram. Although most hosts and gateways in the Internet ignore type of service, it is an important concept because it provides a mechanism that will eventually allow control information to have precedence over data. For example, if all hosts and gateways honor precedence, it is possible to implement congestion control algorithms that are not affected by the congestion they are trying to control.

Bits *D*, *T*, and *R* specify the type of service the datagram desires. When set, the *D* bit requests low delay, the *T* bit requests high throughput, and the *R* bit requests high reliability. Of course, it may not be possible for the Internet to guarantee the type of service requested (i.e., if no path to the destination has that property). Thus, we think of the type of service request as a hint to the routing algorithms, not as a demand. If a gateway does know more than one possible route to a given destination, it can use the type of service field to select one with characteristics closest to those desired. For example, suppose the gateway can select between a low capacity leased line or a high bandwidth (but high delay) satellite connection. Datagrams carrying keystrokes from a user to a remote computer could have the *D* bit set requesting that they be delivered as quickly as possible, while datagrams carrying a bulk file transfer could have the *T* bit set requesting that they travel across the high capacity satellite path.

It is also important to realize that routing algorithms must choose from among underlying physical network technologies that each have characteristics of delay, throughput, and reliability. Often, a given technology trades off one characteristic for another (e.g., it achieves higher data rates at the expense of longer delay). Thus, the idea is to give the algorithm a hint about what is most important; it seldom makes sense to specify all three types of service. To summarize:

> *We regard the type of service specification as a hint to the routing al-
> gorithm that helps it choose among various paths to a destination
> based on its knowledge of the hardware technologies available on
> those paths. The Internet cannot guarantee the type of service request-
> ed.*

7.7.5 Fragmentation Control

Three fields in the datagram header, *IDENT*, *FLAGS*, and *FRAGMENT OFFSET*,
control fragmentation and reassembly of datagrams. Field *IDENT* contains a unique integer that identifies the datagram. Its primary purpose is to allow the destination to collect all fragments from a datagram. As a fragment arrives, the destination uses the
IDENT field along with the source address to identify the datagram to which the fragment belongs. Hosts usually generate a unique value for identification by incrementing a
global counter each time they create a datagram. The host assigns the new counter value
to the datagram's *IDENT* field. Any gateway that fragments the datagram copies the
IDENT field into every fragment.

The low-order 2 bits of the 3-bit *FLAGS* field control fragmentation. The first
specifies whether the datagram may be fragmented (it is called the *do not fragment* bit
because setting it to *1* specifies that the datagram should not be fragmented). The low
order *FLAGS* bit specifies whether this is the last fragment (i.e., the fragment with the
highest offset). It is called the *more fragments* field. Because the length field in a fragment header refers to the size of the fragment and not the size of the original datagram,
the destination cannot use the length to tell whether it has collected all fragments. Thus,
it needs the *more fragments* bit to mark the end of the original datagram.

Recall that each fragment has exactly the same format as a complete datagram. For
a fragment, field *FRAGMENT OFFSET* specifies the offset of this fragment in the original datagram, measured in units of 8 octets, starting at offset zero. To reassemble the datagram, the destination must obtain all fragments starting with offset *0* through the fragment with highest offset. Fragments do not necessarily arrive in order, and there is no
communication between the destination that receives fragments and the gateway that
fragmented the datagram. If one or more fragments are lost, the entire datagram must be
discarded.

7.7.6 Time to Live (TTL)

The time to live field (*TIME*) specifies how long, in seconds, the datagram is allowed to remain in the Internet system. In principle, the idea is both simple and important: whenever a host injects a datagram into the system, it sets a maximum time that the
datagram should survive. Each gateway along the path from source to destination checks
the time remaining when they process a datagram and discards it when the time to live
reaches zero. Thus, datagrams do not travel around the Internet forever, even if routing
tables become corrupt and point in circles.

Estimating exact times is difficult because gateways do not usually know the transit time for a physical network. To simplify processing, hosts and gateways assume that each network transfer takes unit time. Thus, they must decrement the time to live field by one each time they process a header.

7.7.7 Other Datagram Header Fields

Field *PROTO* is analogous to the type field in an Ethernet frame. Higher level protocols use *PROTO* to specify the format and contents of the data by identifying the high-level protocol type. The mapping between a high level protocol and the integer value used in *PROTO* to identify it must be administered by a central authority to guarantee standardization across the entire Internet.

Field *HEADER CHECKSUM* ensures integrity of header values. The IP checksum is formed by treating the header as a sequence of 16-bit integers (in network byte order), adding them together using one's complement arithmetic, and then taking the one's complement of the result. For purposes of computing the checksum, field *HEADER CHECK-SUM* is assumed to contain zero.

Separating the checksum for headers and data has advantages and disadvantages. Because the header usually occupies fewer octets than the data, having a separate checksum reduces processing time at gateways which only need to compute header checksums. The separation also allows higher level protocols to choose their own checksum scheme for the data. The chief disadvantage is that higher level protocols are forced to add their own checksum or risk having corrupted data go undetected.

Fields *SOURCE IP ADDRESS* and *DESTINATION IP ADDRESS* contain the 32-bit Internet addresses of the datagram's sender and intended recipient.

The field labeled *DATA* in Figure 7.4 shows the beginning of the data area of the datagram. Its length depends, of course, on what is being sent in the datagram.

The last field of an IP header, labeled *PADDING*, represents octets containing zero that may be needed to ensure that the Internet header extends to an exact multiple of 32 bits (recall that the header length field is specified in units of 32-bit words).

7.8 Internet Datagram Options

The *OPTIONS* field following the destination address is not required in every datagram; options are included mostly for network testing or debugging. Options processing is an integral part of IP, however, so all standard implementations must include it.

The length of the *OPTIONS* field varies depending on which options are selected. Some options are one octet long; they consist of a single octet option code. Other options are variable length. When options are present in a datagram, they appear contiguously, with no special separators between them. Each option consists of a single octet option code, a single octet length, and a set of data octets for the option. The option code octet is divided into three fields as Figure 7.6 shows.

COPY	OPTION CLASS	OPTION NUMBER

Figure 7.6 The division of the option code octet into three fields.

The fields consist of a 1-bit *COPY* flag, a 2-bit *OPTION CLASS*, and the 5-bit *OPTION NUMBER*. The *COPY* flag controls how gateways treat options during fragmentation. When the copy bit is set to *1*, it specifies that the option should be copied into all fragments. When set to *0*, the copy bit means that the option will only be copied into the first fragment and not into all fragments.

The *OPTION CLASS* and *OPTION NUMBER* bits specify the general class of the option and give a specific option in that class. The table in Figure 7.7 shows how classes are assigned.

Option Class	Meaning
0	Datagram or network control
1	Reserved for future use
2	Debugging and measurement
3	Reserved for future use

Figure 7.7 Classes of IP options as encoded in the *OPTION CLASS* bit of an option code octet.

The table in Figure 7.8 lists the possible options that can accompany an IP datagram and gives their *OPTION CLASS* and *OPTION NUMBER* values. As the list shows, most options are used for control purposes.

Option Class	Option Number	Length	Description
0	0	1	End of option list. Used if options do not end at end of datagram (also see header padding).
0	1	1	No operation.
0	2	11	Security and handling restrictions.
0	3	var	Loose source routing. Used to route datagram along a specified path.
0	7	var	Record route. Used to trace a route.
0	8	4	Stream identifier. Used to carry a SATNET stream identifier.
0	9	var	Strict source routing. Used to route datagram along a specified path.
2	4	var	Internet timestamp. Used to record timestamps along the route.

Figure 7.8 The eight possible IP options with their numeric class and number codes. The value *var* in the length column stands for *variable*.

7.8.1 Record Route Option

The routing and timestamp options are the most interesting because they provide a way to monitor or control how Internet gateways route datagrams. The *record route* option allows the source to create an empty list of IP addresses and arrange for each gateway that handles the datagram to add its name to the list. Figure 7.9 shows the format of the record route option.

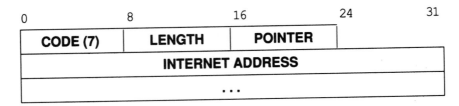

Figure 7.9 The format of the record route option in an IP datagram.

As described above, the *CODE* field contains the option number and class (7 for record route). The length field specifies the total length of the option as it appears in the IP datagram, including the first three octets. The field labeled *INTERNET ADDRESS* denotes the area reserved for Internet addresses, with the *POINTER* field giving the offset within the option of the next available slot. Each machine that handles the datagram adds its address to the record route list (enough space must be allocated in the option by the original source to hold all entries that will be added). To add itself to the list, a machine first compares the pointer and length fields. If the pointer is greater than the length, the list is full, so the machine forwards the datagram without inserting its entry. If the list is not full, the machine inserts its (4-octet) address and increments the pointer by four.

7.8.2 Source Route Options

Another option that network builders find interesting is the *source route* option. The idea behind source routing is that it provides a way for the sender to dictate a path through the Internet. For example, to test the throughput over a particular physical network, system administrators can arrange to force IP datagrams over that network using source routing. Of course, such routing is only useful to people who understand the network topology; the average user has no need to know or use it.

In practice, IP supports two forms of source routing. One form, called *strict source routing*, includes a sequence of Internet addresses. It means that the addresses specify the path the datagram must follow to reach its destination. The path between two successive addresses in the list must consist of a single physical network; an error results if a gateway cannot follow a strict source route. The other form, called *loose source routing*, also includes a sequence of Internet addresses. It specifies that the datagram must follow the sequence of Internet addresses, but allows multiple network hops between successive addresses on the list.

Both source route options require gateways along the path to overwrite items in the address list with their local network addresses. Thus, when the datagram arrives at its destination, it contains a list of all addresses visited, exactly like the list produced by the record route option.

The format of a source route option is like that of the record route option shown in Figure 7.9. Each gateway examines the *POINTER* and *LENGTH* fields to see if the list has been exhausted. If it has, the pointer is greater than the length; the gateway routes the datagram to its destination as usual. If the list is not exhausted, the gateway follows the pointer, picks up the Internet address, replaces it with the gateway's address, and routes the datagram using the address it obtained from the list.

7.8.3 Timestamp Option

The *timestamp option* works like the record route option in that the timestamp option contains an initially empty list and each gateway along the path from source to destination fills in one item in the list. Unlike the record route option, however, entries in the timestamp option list contain the time and date at which a gateway handles the datagram, expressed as milliseconds since midnight, Universal Time (see Chapter 17 for more information on Internet time representation). Of course, timestamps issued by independent computers are not always consistent, so they must be treated as estimates.

The timestamp also has an option that allows the source to request each gateway to insert both a timestamp and its Internet address into the list. Usually, the timestamp option is used for monitoring network performance. Having the route recorded along with timestamps is useful because it allows the receiver to know exactly which path the datagram followed.

7.9 Summary

The fundamental service provided by Internet software is a connectionless, unreliable, best-effort, packet delivery system. The Internet Protocol (IP) formally specifies the format of Internet packets, called *datagrams*, and informally embodies the ideas of connectionless delivery. This chapter concentrated on datagram formats; later chapters will discuss IP routing and error handling. Among other information, the datagram header contains the source and destination Internet addresses, fragmentation control, precedence, and a checksum used to catch transmission errors. We learned that in addition to fixed fields, each datagram header can contain a variable length options field. Intended to help monitor and control the Internet, the options allow one to specify or record routing information, or to gather timestamps as the datagram traverses the Internet.

FOR FURTHER STUDY

Postel [1980] discusses possible ways to approach internet protocols, addressing, and routing. In later publications, Postel [RFC 791] gives the standard for the Internet Protocol, and Hornig [RFC 894] specifies the standard for the transmission of Internet datagrams across an Ethernet. In addition to the packet format, Internet administrators also specify many constants needed in the network protocols. These values can be found in Reynolds and Postel [RFC 1010]. An alternative internet protocol suite known as *xns*, is given in Xerox [1981]. Boggs *et. al.* [1980] describe the PARC Universal Packet (PUP) protocol. Kent and Mogul [1987] discuss the disadvantages of fragmentation.

EXERCISES

7.1 What is the single greatest advantage of having the IP checksum cover only the datagram header and not the data? What is the disadvantage?

7.2 Is it ever necessary to use an IP checksum when sending packets over an Ethernet?

7.3 What is the MTU size for the ARPANET? NSFnet? X25NET?

7.4 Do you expect high-speed local area networks to have larger or smaller MTU size than slower, long-haul networks?

7.5   Argue that fragments should have small, nonstandard headers.

7.6   Find out when the IP protocol version last changed. Is having a protocol version number really useful?

7.7   Can you imagine why a one's complement checksum was chosen for IP instead of a cyclic redundancy check?

7.8   What are the advantages of doing reassembly at the ultimate destination instead of doing it after the datagram travels across one network?

8

Routing IP Datagrams

8.1 Introduction

We have seen that all Internet services build on an unreliable, connectionless packet delivery system, and that the basic unit of transfer in this system is an IP datagram. This chapter adds to the description of connectionless service by describing how gateways route IP datagrams and deliver them to their final destination. Later chapters show how other services use IP. In a sense, the routing algorithm characterizes the operational aspects of IP while the datagram format characterizes static aspects.

Routing can be difficult, especially in machines with multiple physical network connections where the routing code must select a network over which to send the datagram. Ideally, the routing software would examine such things as network load, datagram length, or the type of service specified in the datagram header, when selecting the best path. Most Internet routing software is much less sophisticated, however, and selects routes based on fixed assumptions about shortest paths.

8.2 Routing In The Internet

The term *routing* refers to the process of choosing a path over which to send packets, and *router* refers to any computer making such a choice. Routing occurs at several levels. For example, within a network like the ARPANET that has multiple physical connections between packet switches, the network itself is responsible for routing packets from the time they enter until they leave. Such internal routing is completely self-contained, so machines on the outside cannot participate in decisions; they merely view the network as an entity that delivers packets.

Remember that our goal is to provide a virtual network that provides a connection-less IP datagram delivery service. Thus, we will focus on *IP routing*. Analogous to routing within a physical network, IP routing occurs at a higher level than physical network routing.

To understand IP routing completely, we must go back and look at the Internet architecture. Recall that the Internet is composed of multiple physical networks interconnected by computers called *gateways*. Hosts connect directly to one or more physical nets. Both hosts and gateways participate in IP routing, and hosts with multiple network connections can act as gateways. For now, we will distinguish hosts from gateways and assume that hosts do not perform the gateway function of transferring packets from one network to the other.

Loosely speaking, we can divide routing into two forms: *direct routing* and *indirect routing*. Direct routing, the transmission of a datagram from one machine directly to another, is the basis on which all Internet communication rests. It is performed using an underlying physical transmission system. *Indirect routing* occurs when the destination is not on a directly attached network, forcing the sender to pass the datagram to a gateway for delivery.

8.3 Datagram Delivery Over A Single Network

We know that one machine on a given physical network can send a physical frame directly to another machine on the same network. To transfer an IP datagram, the sender encapsulates the datagram in a physical frame, maps the destination IP address into a physical address, and uses the network hardware to deliver it. Chapter 5 discussed datagram encapsulation and presented several possible mechanisms for address resolution, including dynamic binding with the ARP protocol used on Ethernet-like networks. Thus, we have reviewed all the pieces needed for direct delivery. To summarize:

> *Transmission of an IP datagram between two machines on a single physical network does not involve gateways; the sender encapsulates the datagram in a physical frame and sends it directly to the destination.*

How does the sender know whether the destination lies on a directly connected network? The test is straightforward. We assume that each machine knows the Internet addresses of all its network connections. To see if a destination lies on one of the directly connected networks, the sender extracts the network portion of the destination Internet address and compares it to the network portion of its own Internet address(es). A match means the datagram can be sent directly. Here we see one of the advantages of the Internet address scheme, namely, that because the Internet addresses of all machines on a single network include a common network id, and because extracting that id can be done in a few instructions, testing whether a machine can be reached directly is extremely efficient.

8.4 Indirect Routing

Indirect routing is more difficult than direct routing because the sender must identify a gateway to which the datagram can be sent. The gateway must then forward the datagram on toward its destination network.

To visualize how indirect routing works, imagine a large internet with many networks interconnected by gateways, but with only two hosts at the far ends. When one host wants to send to the other, it encapsulates the datagram and sends it to the nearest gateway. We know that it can reach a gateway because all networks are interconnected, so there must be a gateway attached to each one. Thus, the originating host can reach a gateway using a single physical network. Once the frame reaches the gateway, software extracts the datagram and the routing routines select the next gateway along the path toward the destination. The datagram is again placed in a frame and sent over the next physical network to a second gateway, and so on, until it can be delivered directly. These ideas can be summarized:

> *Gateways in the Internet form a cooperative, interconnected structure.*
> *Datagrams pass from gateway to gateway until they reach a gateway*
> *that can deliver the datagram directly.*

How can a gateway know where to send each datagram? How can a host know which gateway to use for a given destination? The two questions are related because they both involve IP routing. We will answer them in two stages, considering the basic table-driven routing algorithm in this chapter, and postponing a discussion of how gateways learn new routes until later.

8.5 Table-Driven IP Routing

The usual Internet routing algorithm employs an *Internet routing table* on each machine that contains information about possible destinations. If every routing table contained information about every possible destination address, it would be impossible to keep the tables current. Furthermore, because the number of possible destinations is large, machines would have insufficient space to store the information.

Conceptually, we would like to isolate information about specific hosts to the local environment in which they exist, allowing gateways that are far away to route packets without knowing such details. Fortunately, the IP address scheme makes such routing possible. Gateways do not need to know all details as long as they know the interconnection structure of the networks and the destination network to which a datagram has been sent. When a datagram arrives at a gateway, IP software locates the destination Internet address and extracts the network portion from it. The gateway then uses the network id to make routing decisions.

Using destination network addresses instead of destination host addresses makes routing efficient and keeps routing tables small. Typically, a routing table contains pairs (*N*, *G*), where *N* is a destination Internet *network* address, and *G* is the Internet address of a gateway to which to send datagrams destined for network *N*. All gateways listed in a routing table used by machine *M* must lie on networks to which *M* connects directly, making it possible to reach them directly.

Figure 8.1 shows an example Internet that consists of 4 networks and 3 gateways. In the figure, the routing table gives the routes that gateway *G* uses. Because *G* connects directly to networks 20.0.0.0 and 30.0.0.0, it can reach any host on those networks directly (possibly using ARP to find physical addresses). Given a datagram destined for a host on network 40.0.0.0, *G* routes it to address 30.0.0.7, the address of gateway *H*. *H* will then deliver the datagram directly. *G* can reach address 30.0.0.7 because it attaches directly to network 30.0.0.0.

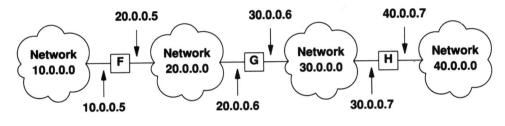

(a)

TO REACH HOSTS ON NETWORK	ROUTE TO THIS ADDRESS
20.0.0.0	DELIVER DIRECT
30.0.0.0	DELIVER DIRECT
10.0.0.0	20.0.0.5
40.0.0.0	30.0.0.7

(b)

Figure 8.1 (a) An example Internet with 4 networks and 3 gateways, and (b) the routing table for gateway *G*.

As Figure 8.1 demonstrates, the size of the routing table remains fixed, independent of the number of hosts in the Internet. It only grows when new networks are added. We can summarize the underlying principle:

To keep table size small, IP routing software bases decisions on destination network addresses, not on individual host addresses.

Choosing routes based on destination network id alone has several consequences. First, in most implementations, it means that all traffic headed for a given network takes the same path. As a result, even when multiple paths exist, they may not be used concurrently. Also, all types of traffic follow the same path without regard to the delay or throughput of physical networks. Second, because only the final gateway along the path attempts to communicate with the destination host, only it learns if the host exists or is operational. Thus, we need to arrange a way for that gateway to send reports of problems back to the original source. Third, because each gateway routes traffic independently, traffic traveling from host *A* to host *B* may follow an entirely different path than traffic traveling from host *B* back to A. We need to ensure that gateways cooperate to guarantee that two-way communication is always possible.

8.6 Default Routes

Another technique used to keep routing table sizes small consolidates multiple entries into a default case. The idea is to have the IP routing software first look in the routing table for the destination network. If no route appears in the table, the routing routines send the datagram to the default.

Default routing is especially useful when a site has a small set of local addresses and only one connection to the rest of the Internet. For example, default routes work well in host machines that attach to a single physical network and reach only one gateway leading to the remainder of the Internet. The entire routing decision consists of two tests: one for the local net, and a default that points to the only possible gateway. Even if the site contains a few local networks, the routing is simple because it consists of a few tests for the local networks plus a default for all other destinations.

8.7 Host-Specific Routes

Although we said that all routing is based on networks and not on individual hosts, most IP routing software allows per-host routes to be specified as a special case. Having per-host routes gives the local network administrator more control over network use and can also be used to control access. When debugging network connections or routing tables, the ability to specify a special route for one individual machine turns out to be especially useful.

8.8 The Final Algorithm

Taking into account everything we have said, the IP routing algorithm becomes:

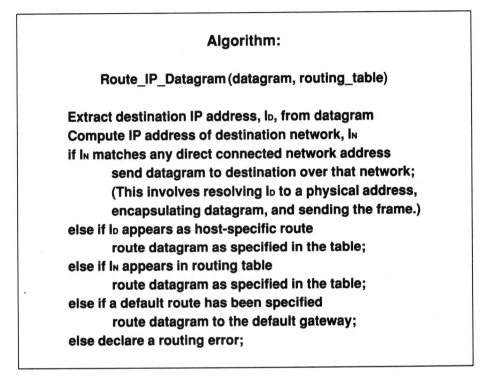

Algorithm:

Route_IP_Datagram(datagram, routing_table)

Extract destination IP address, I_D, from datagram
Compute IP address of destination network, I_N
if I_N matches any direct connected network address
      send datagram to destination over that network;
      (This involves resolving I_D to a physical address,
      encapsulating datagram, and sending the frame.)
else if I_D appears as host-specific route
      route datagram as specified in the table;
else if I_N appears in routing table
      route datagram as specified in the table;
else if a default route has been specified
      route datagram to the default gateway;
else declare a routing error;

Figure 8.2 The IP routing algorithm. Given an IP datagram and a routing table, this algorithm selects a next machine to which the datagram should be sent. Routing tables always specify a next machine that lies on a directly connected network.

8.9 Handling Incoming Datagrams

So far, we have discussed IP routing by describing how decisions are made about outgoing packets. It should be clear, however, that incoming packets are involved in routing as well. When an IP datagram arrives at a host, the device drivers deliver it to the IP software for processing. Two cases arise: the datagram could have reached its final destination, or it may need to travel further. In the first case, IP should pass the datagram to the local operating system for processing. In the second case, IP retains the datagram and routes it using the standard algorithm.

Determining whether an IP datagram has reached its final destination is not quite as trivial as it seems. Remember that a machine may have multiple physical connections, each with its own Internet address. When an IP datagram arrives, the host must compare the destination Internet address to each of its network addresses. If any match, it passes the datagram to the local operating system. If none match, IP decrements the time-to-live field in the datagram header, discarding it if the count reaches zero, or routing it if the count remains positive.

Should every machine route the IP datagrams it receives? Gateways must route incoming datagrams because that is their main function. Some multiply-homed hosts act as gateways even though they are really general purpose computing systems. While using a host as a gateway is not usually a good idea, if one chooses to use that arrangement, the host must be configured to route datagrams just like a gateway. But what about other hosts, those that are not intended to be gateways? The answer is that hosts not designated to be gateways should probably *not* route datagrams that they receive; they should discard them.

There are four reasons why a host not designated to serve as a gateway should refrain from performing any gateway functions. First, when such a host receives a datagram intended for some other machine, something has gone wrong with Internet addressing or routing. The problem may not be revealed if the host takes corrective action by rerouting the datagram. Second, rerouting will cause unnecessary network traffic (and may steal CPU time from legitimate uses of the host). Third, simple errors can cause chaos. Suppose, that every host reroutes traffic. What happens if an error causes the broadcast of a datagram that is destined for some host, *H*? Every host on the network receives the datagram and reroutes it to *H*, which will be bombarded with multiple copies. Fourth, as later chapters show, gateways use a special protocol to report errors; hosts that are not designated to serve as gateways do not report errors.

8.10 Establishing Routing Tables

We have discussed how IP routes datagrams based on the contents of routing tables, without saying how systems initialize their routing tables or update them as the network changes. Later chapters deal with these questions and discuss protocols that allow gateways to keep routes consistent. For now, it is only important to understand that IP bases all routing decisions on tables, so changing those tables will change the routes datagrams follow.

8.11 Summary

IP routing consists of deciding where to send a datagram based on its destination address. The route is direct if the destination machine lies on a network to which the sending machine attaches; the route is indirect if the datagram must be sent to a gateway for delivery. Direct delivery involves encapsulating the datagram in a physical frame, mapping the destination Internet address to a physical address, and sending the frame using the underlying hardware. A host sends indirectly routed packets to an Internet gateway for delivery. The gateways transfer packets among themselves until the datagram can be delivered directly across a physical network.

The Internet routing algorithm is table driven. It bases routing decisions on the destination network address instead of the destination host address, keeping routing tables small while retaining efficiency. Default routes help keep tables small, especially for hosts that can access only one gateway.

FOR FURTHER STUDY

Routing is an important topic. Frank and Chou [1971] and Schwartz and Stern [1980] discuss routing in general; Postel [1980] discusses Internet routing. Braden and Postel [RFC 1009] provide a summary of how Internet gateways handle IP datagrams. Fultz and Kleinrock [1971] analyze adaptive routing schemes; and McQuillan, Richer, and Rosen [1980] describe the ARPANET adaptive routing algorithm.

EXERCISES

8.1 Complete routing tables for all gateways in Figure 8.1. Which benefit most from default routes?

8.2 Examine the routing algorithms used in 4.3 BSD UNIX. Are all the cases mentioned here covered? Does the algorithm allow anything not mentioned?

8.3 What does a gateway do with the *time to live* value in the IP header?

8.4 Consider a machine with two physical network connections and two Internet addresses I_1 and I_2. Is it possible for that machine to receive a datagram destined for I_2 over the network with address I_1? Explain.

8.5 Consider two hosts, A and B, that both attach to a common physical network, N. Is it ever possible, when using our routing algorithm, for A to receive a datagram destined for B? Explain.

8.6 Modify the routing algorithm to accommodate the IP source route options discussed in Chapter 7.

8.7 An IP gateway must perform a computation that takes time proportional to the length of the datagram header each time a packet passes through it. Explain.

8.8 A network administrator argues that to make monitoring and debugging his local network easier, he wants to rewrite the routing algorithm so it tests host-specific routes *before* it tests for direct delivery. Can you imagine how he could use the revised algorithm to build a network monitor?

8.9 Is it possible to address a datagram to a gateway's Internet address? Does it make sense to do so?

8.10 Consider a modified routing algorithm that examines host-specific routes testing for delivery on directly connected networks. Under what circumstances might such an algorithm be desirable?

8.11 Play detective: after monitoring IP traffic on a local area network for 10 minutes one evening, someone notices that all frames destined for machine *A* carry IP datagrams that have destination equal to *A*'s Internet address, while all frames destined for machine *B* carry IP datagrams with destination *not* equal to *B*'s Internet address. Explain.

8.12 How could you change the IP protocol to support high-speed packet switching at gateways? Hint: a gateway must recompute a header checksum after decrementing the time-to-live field.

8.13 Compare the ISO connectionless delivery protocol (ISO standard 8473) with IP. How well will the ISO protocol support high-speed switching? Hint: variable length fields are expensive.

9

Internet Protocol: Error and Control Messages (ICMP)

9.1 Introduction

We have seen that the Internet Protocol provides an unreliable, connectionless packet delivery service, and that packets travel from gateway to gateway until they reach a gateway that can deliver them directly to the destination host. If a gateway cannot route or deliver a datagram, or if the gateway detects an unusual condition like network congestion that affects the host, it needs to instruct the host to take action to avoid or correct the problem. This chapter discusses a mechanism that gateways and hosts use to communicate such control or error information. We will see how gateways use the mechanism to report delivery problems and how hosts use the mechanism to test whether destinations are reachable.

9.2 The Internet Control Message System

In the connectionless system we have described so far, each gateway or host operates autonomously, routing and delivering datagrams that arrive without coordinating with the original sender. The system works well if all machines operate correctly and agree on routing, but no system works correctly all the time. Besides failures of communication lines and processors, the Internet fails to deliver packets when the destination machine is temporarily or permanently disconnected from the network, when the time-to-live counter expires, or when intermediate gateways become so congested that they cannot process more traffic. The important difference between having a real, hardware network and a software-based Internet is that in the former, the designer can often rely on network hardware to inform machines when such problems arise. In the Internet, which has no such hardware mechanism, a sender cannot tell whether delivery failure results from a local malfunction or a remote one. Debugging becomes extremely difficult. The IP protocol itself contains nothing to help the sender test connectivity or learn about such failures.

To allow machines on the Internet to report errors or provide information about unexpected circumstances, the designers added a special-purpose message mechanism to the Internet protocols. The mechanism, known as the *Internet Control Message Protocol* (or *ICMP*), is considered a required part of IP, and must be included in every IP implementation.

ICMP messages travel across the Internet in the data portion of IP datagrams like all other traffic. The ultimate destination of an ICMP message is not a user process on the destination machine, but the Internet software on that machine. That is, when an ICMP error message arrives, the IP software module handles the problem itself; it does not pass the ICMP message to the application program whose datagram caused the problem. We can summarize:

> *The Internet Control Message Protocol allows gateways and hosts to send error or control messages to other gateways or hosts; ICMP provides communication between the Internet software on one machine and the Internet software on another.*

Initially designed to allow gateways to report the cause of delivery errors to hosts, ICMP is not restricted to gateways. An arbitrary machine can send an ICMP message to any other machine. Thus, a host can correspond with a gateway or another host. The chief advantage of allowing hosts to use ICMP is that it provides a single mechanism used for all control and information messages.

9.3 ICMP Message Format And Delivery

Each ICMP message travels across the Internet in the data portion of an IP datagram, as Figure 9.1 shows.

IP Datagram Header	Complete ICMP Message Treated as Data

Figure 9.1 The encapsulation of an ICMP message in an IP datagram.

Datagrams carrying ICMP messages are routed exactly like datagrams carrying information for users; there is no additional reliability. Thus, error messages themselves may be lost or discarded. An exception is made if an IP datagram carrying an ICMP message causes an error. The exception, established to avoid the problem of having error messages about error messages, specifies that ICMP messages are not generated for errors that result from datagrams carrying ICMP messages.

It is important to keep in mind that even though ICMP messages are encapsulated and sent using IP, ICMP is not considered a higher level protocol – it is a required part of IP. The reason for using IP to deliver ICMP messages is that they may need to travel across several physical networks to reach their final destination. Thus, they cannot be delivered by the physical transport alone.

Although each ICMP message has its own format, they all begin with three fields: an 8-bit integer message *TYPE* field, an 8-bit *CODE* field that provides further information about the message type, and a 16-bit *CHECKSUM* field (ICMP uses the same checksum algorithm as IP, but the ICMP checksum only includes the ICMP message). In addition, ICMP messages that report errors always include the Internet header and first 64 data bits of the datagram causing the problem. The reason for returning more than the datagram header alone is to allow the receiver to determine more precisely which protocol(s) were used and which application program was responsible for the datagram. As we will see later, most higher-level protocol formats are designed so that crucial information is encoded in the first 64 bits.

The ICMP *TYPE* field defines the meaning of the message and the format of the rest of the packet. The types include:

Type Field	ICMP Message Type
0	Echo Reply
3	Destination Unreachable
4	Source Quench
5	Redirect (change a route)
8	Echo Request
11	Time Exceeded for a Datagram
12	Parameter Problem on a Datagram
13	Timestamp Request
14	Timestamp Reply
15	Information Request
16	Information Reply
17	Address Mask Request
18	Address Mask Reply

The next sections describe each of these messages, giving details of the message format and its meaning.

9.4 Testing Destination Reachability And Status

A host or gateway sends an ICMP *echo request* message to test whether a destination is alive and reachable. Any machine that receives an echo request addressed to it must formulate an echo reply and return it to whichever machine sent the request. Figure 9.2 shows the format of the echo message.

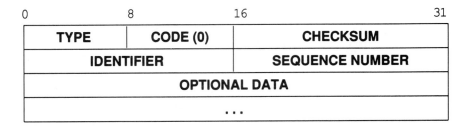

Figure 9.2 ICMP echo request or reply message format.

The field listed as *OPTIONAL DATA* is a variable length field that contains data to be returned to the client. An echo reply must return exactly the same data as was received in the request. Fields *IDENTIFIER* and *SEQUENCE NUMBER* are used by the client to match replies to requests. The value of the *TYPE* field specifies whether the message is a request (*8*) or a reply (*0*).

The ICMP echo request/reply mechanism has proven to be among the most useful tools in the Internet. Many systems provide an application program that users can invoke to send ICMP echo requests and time replies. Because the destination machine's Internet software handles ICMP, it is usually possible to obtain an echo even if the machine is so overloaded that user level processes are not responsive.

9.5 Reports Of Unreachable Destinations

When a gateway cannot deliver an IP datagram, it sends a *destination unreachable message* back to the original source, using the format shown in Figure 9.3.

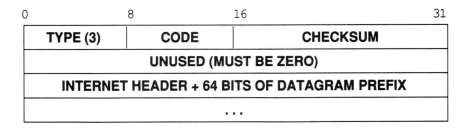

Figure 9.3 ICMP destination unreachable message format.

The *CODE* field in a destination unreachable message contains an integer that further describes the problem. Possible values are:

Code Value	Meaning
0	Network Unreachable
1	Host Unreachable
2	Protocol Unreachable
3	Port Unreachable
4	Fragmentation Needed and DF set
5	Source Route Failed

A gateway sends network or host unreachable messages when it cannot route or deliver datagrams. Destinations may be unreachable because hardware is temporarily out of service, because the sender specified a nonexistent destination address, or (in rare circumstances) because the gateway does not have a route to the destination network. ICMP includes a short prefix of the datagram that caused the problem so protocol software at the original source can know exactly which datagram caused the problem. The meaning of protocol and port unreachable messages will become clear when we study how higher level protocols use abstract destination points called ''ports''.

Most of the remaining messages are self explanatory. If the datagram contains the source route option with an incorrect route, it may trigger a source route failure message. If a gateway needs to fragment a datagram but the ''don't fragment'' bit is set, the gateway sends a fragmentation needed message back to the source.

9.6 Datagram Flow Control

When datagrams arrive too quickly for a gateway or host to process, it must discard them. The machine discarding datagrams sends an ICMP *source quench* message to request that the original source slow down its rate of sending datagrams. Usually, machines send one source quench for every datagram that must be discarded. However, there are many algorithms gateways use to select which sources to quench. Some attempt to avoid discarding datagrams by arranging for gateways to send quench requests just as their queues start to become long.

There is no ICMP message to reverse the effect of a source quench. Instead, a host that receives source quench messages from some destination, *D*, lowers the rate at which it sends datagrams to *D* until it stops receiving requests; it then gradually increases the rate as long as no further source quench requests are received.

Source quench messages contain, in addition to the *TYPE*, *CODE*, and *CHECKSUM* fields, an unused 32-bit field, and a *DATAGRAM PREFIX* field as Figure 9.4 shows.

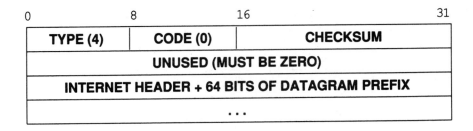

Figure 9.4 ICMP source quench message format.

As with most ICMP messages that report an error, the datagram prefix field contains a prefix of the datagram that triggered the source quench request.

9.7 Route Change Requests From Gateways

Internet routing tables usually remain static over long periods of time. Hosts initialize them from a disk file at system startup, and system administrators seldom make routing changes during normal operations. If network interconnections change, routing tables in a particular host may become incorrect. The changes can be temporary (e.g., when hardware needs to be repaired) or permanent (e.g., when a new network is added to the Internet). As we will see in later chapters, gateways exchange routing information periodically to accommodate network changes and keep their routes up-to-date. Thus, a gateway usually knows better routes than hosts. When a gateway detects that some host is using a non-optimum route, the gateway sends an ICMP *redirect* message to that host. It also forwards the original datagram on to its destination. Redirect messages do not solve the problem of propagating routes in a general way, however, because they are limited to interactions between a gateway and a host on a directly connected network. Later chapters explore the problem of how to propagate routes across multiple networks.

Each redirect message contains, in addition to the requisite *TYPE*, *CODE*, and *CHECKSUM* fields, a 32-bit *GATEWAY INTERNET ADDRESS* field and a *DATAGRAM PREFIX* field, as Figure 9.5 shows.

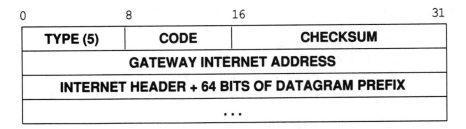

Figure 9.5 ICMP redirect message format.

The *GATEWAY INTERNET ADDRESS* field contains the address of a gateway that the host is to use to reach the destination mentioned in the datagram header. The *INTERNET HEADER* field contains the IP header plus the next 64 bits of the datagram that triggered the message. Thus, a host receiving an ICMP redirect examines the datagram prefix to determine the datagram's destination address. The *CODE* field of an ICMP redirect message further specifies how to interpret the destination address, based on values assigned as follows:

Code Value	Meaning
0	Redirect datagrams for the Net
1	Redirect datagrams for the Host
2	Redirect datagrams for the Type of Service and Net
3	Redirect datagrams for the Type of Service and Host

Gateways only send ICMP redirect requests to hosts on directly connected networks and not to other gateways.

9.8 Detecting Circular Or Excessively Long Routes

Each IP datagram contains a time-to-live counter, sometimes called a *hop count*. To prevent datagrams from circling in the Internet forever, each gateway decrements the count and discards the datagram when it reaches zero. Whenever a gateway discards a datagram because its hop count reaches zero, it sends an ICMP *time exceeded* message back to the datagram's source; using the format shown in Figure 9.6.

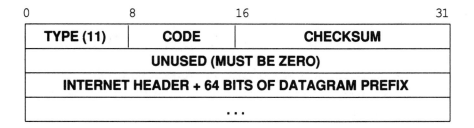

Figure 9.6 ICMP time exceeded message format.

The *CODE* field explains the nature of the timeout:

Code Value	Meaning
0	Time to live count exceeded
1	Fragment reassembly time exceeded

Fragment reassembly refers to the task of collecting all the fragments from a datagram. Whenever the first fragment of a datagram arrives, the receiving host starts a timer and considers it an error if the timer expires before all the pieces of the datagram arrive. Code value *1* is used to report such errors to the sender; one message is sent for each such error.

9.9 Reporting Incorrect Datagram Headers

When a gateway or host finds problems with a datagram header, it sends a *parameter problem* message to the original source. One possible cause of such problems occurs when arguments to an option are incorrect. The message, formatted as shown in Figure 9.7, is only sent when the problem is so severe that the datagram must be discarded.

```
0                 8                16                           31
┌─────────────────┬─────────────────┬───────────────────────────┐
│    TYPE (12)    │    CODE (0)    │         CHECKSUM          │
├─────────────────┼─────────────────┴───────────────────────────┤
│     POINTER     │        UNUSED (MUST BE ZERO)               │
├─────────────────┴───────────────────────────────────────────┤
│      INTERNET HEADER + 64 BITS OF DATAGRAM PREFIX           │
├─────────────────────────────────────────────────────────────┤
│                          . . .                              │
└─────────────────────────────────────────────────────────────┘
```

Figure 9.7 ICMP parameter problem message format.

The *POINTER* field identifies the octet in the datagram's header that caused the problem.

9.10 Clock Synchronization And Transit Time Estimation

A client sends a *timestamp request* message to another to request that the destination machine return its current value for the time of day. The receiving machine sends a *timestamp reply* back to the machine making the request. Figure 9.8 shows the format of timestamp request and reply messages.

The *SEQUENCE* and *IDENTIFIER* fields are used by the source to associate replies with requests. The *TYPE* field identifies the message as a request (*13*) or a reply (*14*). Remaining fields specify times, given in milliseconds since midnight, universal time. The *ORIGINATE* field is filled in by the original sender just before the packet is transmitted, the *RECEIVE* field is filled immediately upon receipt of a request, and the *TRANSMIT* field is filled immediately before the reply is transmitted.

Hosts use the three timestamp fields to compute estimates of the delay time between them and to synchronize their clocks. Because the reply includes the *ORIGINATE TIMESTAMP* field, a host can compute the total time required for a request to travel to a destination, be transformed into a reply, and return. Because the reply carries both the time at which the request entered the remote machine, as well as the time at which the reply left, the host can compute the network transit time, and from that, estimate the differences in remote and local clocks. To obtain an accurate estimate of round trip delay, of course, many measurements must be taken and averaged.

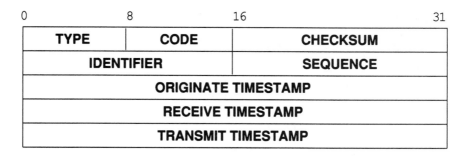

Figure 9.8 ICMP timestamp request and reply message format.

9.11 Obtaining A Network Address

Machines use the ICMP *information request* message to obtain an Internet address for a network to which they attach; it is an alternative to RARP. The sender fills in a request, sends it with the network portion of the IP destination address set to *0*, and awaits a reply. The reply arrives with the network portion of the sender's IP filled in. Gateways respond to requests for network address and send their reply with both the source and destination fields of the IP datagram fully specified. Figure 9.9 shows the format of request and reply messages.

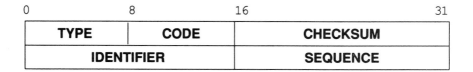

Figure 9.9 ICMP information request and reply message format.

The *IDENTIFIER* and *SEQUENCE* fields contain values that the sender uses to associate replies with requests. The *TYPE* field specifies whether the packet contains a request (*15*) or a reply (*16*).

9.12 Obtaining A Subnet Mask

Subnet addressing allows multiple physical networks to share a single IP network address. For example, at Purdue University, two physical Ethernets share the class B address 128.10.0.0. All hosts on one physical network have Internet addresses of the form 128.10.2.XX, while hosts on the other physical network have addresses of the form 128.10.1.XX (where XX denotes the hostid portion of the address).

Chapter 16 discusses the motivation for subnet addressing as well as the details of how subnets operate. For now, it is only important to understand that to use subnet addressing, machines need to know which bits of the Internet address correspond to their physical network, and which correspond to other physical networks. Information about the interpretation of address bits is kept in a 32-bit quantity called the *subnet mask*.

To learn its subnet mask, a machine can send an *address mask request* message to a gateway and receive an *address mask reply*. The machine making the request can either send the message directly if it knows the gateway's address or broadcast the message if it does not. Figure 9.10 shows the format of address mask messages.

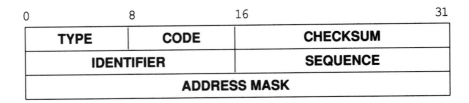

Figure 9.10 ICMP address mask request and reply message format.

The *TYPE* field in an address mask message specifies whether the message is a request (*17*) or a reply (*18*). A reply contains the network's subnet address mask in the *ADDRESS MASK* field. As usual, the *IDENTIFIER* and *SEQUENCE* fields allow a machine to associate replies with requests.

9.13 Summary

Normal communication across the Internet involves sending messages from a user process on one host to a user process on another host. Gateways may need to communicate directly with the network software on a particular host to report abnormal conditions or to send the host new routing information.

The Internet Control Message Protocol that provides for extranormal communication among gateways and hosts on the Internet is an integral, required part of IP. ICMP includes *source quench* messages that retard the rate of transmission, *redirect* messages that request a host to change its routing tables, and *echo request/reply* messages that hosts can use to determine whether a destination can be reached. An ICMP message travels in the data area of an Internet datagram and has three fixed-length fields at the beginning of the message: an ICMP message *type* field, a *code* field, and an ICMP *checksum* field. The message type determines the format of the message as well as its meaning.

FOR FURTHER STUDY

Both Tanenbaum [1981] and Stallings [1985] discuss control messages in general and relate them to various network protocols. The central issue is not how to send control messages but when. Grange and Gien [1979], as well as Driver, Hopewell, and Iaquinto [1979], concentrate on a problem for which control messages are essential, namely, flow control. Gerla and Kleinrock [1980] compare flow control strategies analytically.

The Internet Control Message Protocol described here is a DARPA standard defined by Postel [RFC 792]. Nagle [RFC 896] discusses ICMP source quench messages and shows how gateways should use them to handle congestion control. Prue and Postel [RFC 1016] discusses a more recent idea. Nagle [1987] argues that congestion is always a concern in packet switched networks. Mogul and Postel [RFC 950] discuss subnet mask request and reply messages. Finally, Jain, Ramakrishnan and Chiu [1987] discuss how gateways and transport protocols could cooperate to avoid congestion.

EXERCISES

9.1 Devise an experiment to record how many of each ICMP message type appear on your local network during a day.

9.2 Experiment to see if you can send packets through a gateway fast enough to trigger an ICMP source quench message.

9.3 Devise an algorithm that synchronizes clocks using ICMP timestamp messages.

9.4 In network jargon, the verb *to ping* means "send an ICMP echo request and wait for an ICMP echo reply to see if a host is alive." Ping is derived from the name of a program, the Packet INternet Groper. See if your local operating system lets you build a program to ping a specified host.

9.5 If you connect to the Internet, try to ping host *xinu.cs.purdue.edu*.

9.6 Should a gateway give ICMP messages priority over normal traffic? Why or why not?

9.7 Consider an Ethernet that has one conventional host, *H*, and 12 gateways connected to it. Find a single (slightly illegal) frame carrying an IP packet that, when sent by host *H*, causes *H* to receive exactly 24 packets.

9.8 Compare ICMP source quench packets with Jain's 1-bit scheme. Which is a more effective strategy for dealing with congestion? Why?

9.9 There is no ICMP message that allows a machine to inform the source that transmission errors are causing datagrams to arrive corrupted. Under what circumstances might such a message be useful?

9.10 Should ICMP error messages contain a timestamp that specifies when they are sent?

10

Protocol Layering

10.1 Introduction

Previous chapters have reviewed the architectural foundations of internetworking, described how gateways route Internet datagrams among themselves or to hosts, and presented mechanisms used to map Internet addresses to physical network addresses. This chapter considers the general structure of software found in gateways and hosts that carries out network communication. It presents the general principle of layering, shows how layering makes Internet protocol software easier to understand and build, and traces the path of datagrams through the protocol software they encounter when traversing the Internet.

10.2 The Need For Multiple Protocols

We have said that protocols allow one to specify or understand communication without knowing the details of a particular vendor's network hardware. They are to communication what programming languages are to computation. It should be apparent by now how closely the analogy fits. Like assembler language, some protocols describe communication across a physical network. For example, the details of the Ethernet frame format, network access policy, and frame error handling comprise a protocol that describes physical communication on an Ethernet. Similarly, the details of Internet addresses, the Internet datagram format, and the concept of unreliable, connectionless delivery comprise the Internet Protocol.

Complex data communication systems do not use a single protocol to handle all transmission tasks. Instead, they require a set of cooperative protocols, sometimes called a *protocol family*. To understand why, think of the problems that arise when machines communicate over a data network:

● *Hardware failure.* A host or gateway may fail either because the hardware fails or because the operating system crashes. A network transmission link may fail or accidentally be disconnected. The protocol software needs to detect such failures and recover from them if possible.

● *Network congestion.* Even when all hardware and software operates correctly, networks have finite capacity which may be exceeded. The protocol software needs to arrange ways that a congested machine can suppress further traffic.

● *Packet delay or loss.* Sometimes, packets are lost or experience extremely long delays. The protocol software needs to learn about failures or adapt to long delays.

● *Data corruption.* Electrical or magnetic interference can cause transmission errors that corrupt the contents of transmitted data. Protocol software needs to detect and recover from such errors.

● *Data duplication or sequence errors.* Networks that offer multiple routes may deliver data out of sequence. The protocol software needs to reorder packets and remove any duplicates.

Taken together, all these problems seem overwhelming. It becomes difficult to understand how to write a single protocol that will handle them all. From the analogy with programming languages, we can see how to conquer the complexity. Program translation has been partitioned into four conceptual subproblems identified with the software that handles the subproblem: compiler, assembler, link editor, and loader. The division makes it possible for the designer to concentrate on one subproblem at a time, and for the implementor to build and test each piece of software independently.

Two final observations about our programming language analogy will help clarify the organization of protocols. First, it should be clear that pieces of translation software must agree on the exact format of data passed between them. For example, the data passed from the compiler to the assembler consists of a program defined by the assembler programming language. Thus, we see how the translation process involves multiple programming languages. The analogy will hold for protocols software, where we will see that multiple protocols describe the interfaces between protocol processing software modules. Second, the four parts of the translator form a linear sequence in which output from the compiler becomes input to the assembler, and so on. Protocol software also uses a linear sequence.

10.3 The Conceptual Layers Of Protocol Software

Think of the modules of protocol software on each machine as being stacked vertically into *layers*, as in Figure 10.1. Each layer takes responsibility for handling one part of the problem.

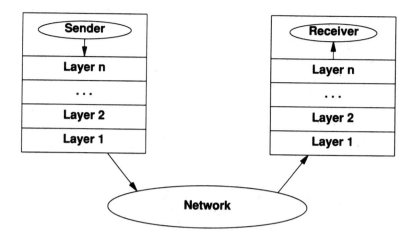

Figure 10.1 The conceptual organization of protocol software in layers.

Conceptually, sending a message from an application program on one machine to an application program on another means transferring the message down through successive layers of protocol software on the sender's machine, transferring the message across the network, and transferring the message up through successive layers of protocol software on the receiver's machine.

In practice, the protocol software is much more complex than the simple model of Figure 10.1 indicates. Each layer makes decisions about the correctness of the message and chooses an appropriate action based on the message type or destination address. For example, one layer on the receiving machine must decide whether to keep the message or forward it to another machine. Another layer must decide which application program should receive the message.

To understand the difference between the conceptual organization of protocol software and the implementation details, consider the comparison shown in Figure 10.2. The conceptual diagram shows an Internet layer between a high level protocol layer and a network interface layer. The realistic diagram shows that the IP software may communicate with multiple high-level protocol modules and with multiple network interfaces.

Although a diagram of conceptual protocol layering does not show all details, it does help explain the general ideas. For example, Figure 10.3 shows the layers of protocol software used by a message that traverses three networks. We understand that any machine attached to two networks must have two network interface modules, even though the conceptual layering diagram shows only a single network interface layer in each machine.

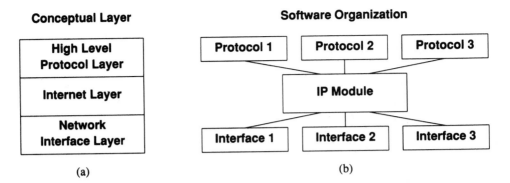

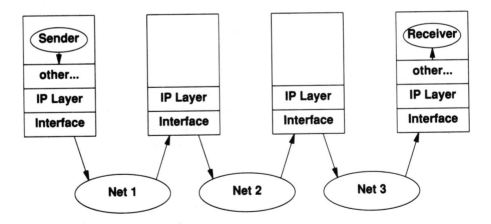

Figure 10.2 A comparison of (a) conceptual protocol layering and (b) a realistic view of software organization showing multiple network interfaces below IP and multiple protocols above it.

As the figure shows, a sender on the original machine transmits a message which the IP
layer places in a datagram and sends across network *1*. On intermediate machines the datagram passes up to the IP layer which routes it back out again (on a different network).
Only when it reaches the final destination machine does IP extract the message and pass
it up to higher layers of protocol software. The diagram does not show that each intermediate machine has at least two distinct network interfaces below the IP layer.

Figure 10.3 The path of a message traversing the Internet from the sender
through two intermediate machines to the receiver. Intermediate
machines only send the datagram to the IP software layer.

10.4 Functionality Of The Layers

Once the decision has been made to partition the communication problem into sub-problems and organize the protocol software into modules that each handle one subproblem, the question arises, "what functionality should reside in each module?" The question is not easy to answer for several reasons. First, given a set of goals and constraints governing a particular communication problem, it is possible to choose an organization that will optimize protocol software for that problem. Second, even when considering general network-level services such as reliable transport, there are multiple fundamental approaches to solving the problem. Third, the design of network (or internet) architecture and the organization of the protocol software are interrelated; one cannot be designed without the other.

10.4.1 ISO 7-Layer Reference Model

Two ideas about protocol layering dominate the field. The first, based on work done by the *International Standards Organization (ISO)*, is known as the ISO *Reference Model of Open System Interconnection*. The ISO model contains 7 conceptual layers organized as shown in Figure 10.4.

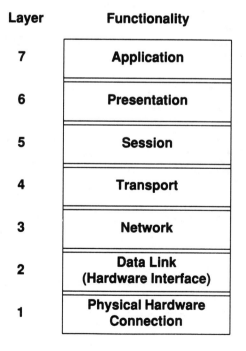

Figure 10.4 The ISO 7-layer reference model for protocol software.

The ISO model, built to describe protocols for a single network, does not contain a specific level for internetwork routing in the same way the Internet protocols do.

10.5 X.25 And Its Relation To The ISO Model

Although it was designed to provide a conceptual model and not an implementation guide, the ISO layering scheme has been the basis for several protocol implementations. Among the protocols commonly associated with the ISO model, the set of protocols known as X.25 is probably the best known and most widely used. X.25 has been adopted by public data networks in the United States and Europe.

In the X.25 view, a network operates much like a telephone system. Like the ARPANET described in Chapter 2, an X.25 network is assumed to consist of complex packet switches that contain the intelligence needed to route packets. Hosts do not attach directly to communication wires of the network. Instead each host attaches to one of the packet switches using a serial communication line. In one sense the connection between a host and an X.25 packet switch is a miniature network consisting of one serial link. The host must follow a complicated procedure to transfer packets onto the network.

●*Physical Layer*. X.25 specifies a standard for the physical interconnection between host computers and network packet switches, as well as the procedures used to transfer packets from one machine to another. In the reference model, level *1* specifies the physical interconnection including electrical characteristics of voltage and current. The corresponding protocol, X.21, gives the details used by public data networks.

●*Data Link Layer*. The level *2* portion of the X.25 protocol specifies how data travels between a host and the packet switch to which it connects. X.25 uses the term *frame* to refer to a unit of data as it passes between a host and a packet switch (it is important to understand that the X.25 definition of *frame* differs from the way we have used it). Because the hardware delivers only a stream of bits, the level *2* protocol must define the format of frames and specify how the two machines recognize frame boundaries. Because transmission errors can destroy data, the level *2* protocol includes error detection (e.g., a frame checksum). Finally, because transmission is unreliable, the level *2* protocol specifies an exchange of acknowledgements that allows the two machines to know when a frame has been transferred successfully.

One commonly used level *2* protocol, named the *High Level Data Link Communication*, is best known by its acronym, *HDLC*. Several versions of HDLC exist, with the most recent known as *HDLC/LAPB*. It is important to remember that successful transfer at level *2* means a frame has been passed to the network packet switch for delivery; it does not guarantee that the packet switch accepted the packet or was able to route it.

●*Network Layer*. The ISO reference model specifies that the third level contains functionality that completes the definition of the interaction between host and network. Called the *network* or *communication subnet* layer, this level defines the basic unit of transfer across the network and includes the concepts of destination addressing and routing. Remember that in the X.25 world, communication between host and packet switch is conceptually isolated from the traffic that is being passed. Thus, the network might allow packets defined by level 3 protocols to be larger than the size of frames that can be transferred at level 2. The level 3 software assembles a packet in the form the network expects and uses level 2 to transfer it (possibly in pieces) to the packet switch. Level 3 must also respond to network congestion problems.

 • *Transport Layer.* Level 4 provides end-to-end reliability by having the destination host communicate with the source host. The idea here is that even though lower layers of protocols provide reliable checks at each transfer, the end-to-end layer double checks to make sure that no machine in the middle failed.

 • *Session Layer.* Higher levels of the ISO model describe how protocol software can be organized to handle all the functionality needed by application programs. The ISO committee considered the problem of remote terminal access so fundamental that they assigned layer 5 to handle it. In fact, the central service offered by many public data networks consists of terminal to host interconnection. The carrier provides a special purpose host computer called a *Packet Assembler And Disassembler (PAD)* on the network with dialup access. Subscribers, usually travelers who carry their own terminal and modem, dial up the local PAD, make a network connection to the host with which they wish to communicate, and log in. Using the network for long distance communication is less expensive than direct dialup.

 • *Presentation Layer.* ISO layer 6 is intended to include functions that many application programs need when using the network. Typical examples include standard routines that compress text or convert graphics images into bit streams for transmission across a network. Although it is not completely understood, much work has been expended on this layer in recent years. A standard, called *Abstract Syntax Notation 1*(ASN.1), has been drafted that provides an interface for application programs.

 • *Application Layer.* Finally, ISO layer 7 includes application programs that use the network. Examples include electronic mail or file transfer programs. In particular, ISO has devised a protocol for electronic mail called the X.400 standard.

10.5.1 The TCP/IP Internet Layering Model

The second major layering model did not arise from a standards committee, but came instead from research that led to the TCP/IP protocol family used throughout the Internet. With a little work, the ISO model can be stretched to describe the TCP/IP layering scheme, but the underlying assumptions are different enough to warrant distinguishing the two.

Broadly speaking, TCP/IP protocol software is organized into four conceptual layers that build on a fifth layer of hardware. Figure 10.5 shows the conceptual layers as well as the form of data as it passes between them.

 • *Application Layer.* At the highest level, users invoke application programs that access the Internet. An application interacts with the transport level protocol(s) to send or receive data. Each application program chooses its own form of data, which can be thought of as a sequence of messages or a stream of bytes. Whatever the form, it passes the data to the transport level for delivery.

 • *Transport Layer.* The primary duty of the *transport layer* is to provide communication from one application program to another. Such communication is often called *end to end*. The transport layer may regulate flow of information. It may also provide reliable transport, ensuring that data arrives without error and in sequence. To do so, it arranges to have the receiving side send back acknowledgements and retransmit lost packets. The transport software divides the stream of data being transmitted into small pieces sometimes called *packets* (from the ISO terminology) and passes each packet along with a destination address to the next level for transmission.

Although Figure 10.5 uses a single block to represent the application level, a general purpose computer can have multiple application programs accessing the network at one time. The transport layer must accept data from several user programs and send it to the next lower level. To do so, it adds additional information to each packet, including codes that identify which application program sent it and which application program should receive it, as well as a checksum. The receiving machine uses the checksum to verify that the packet arrived intact, and uses the destination code to identify the application program to which it should be delivered.

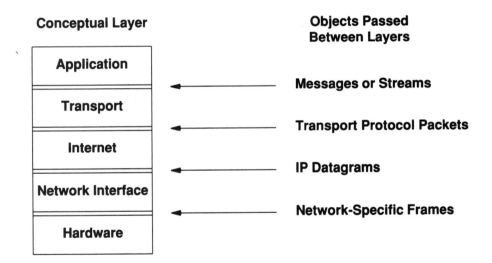

Figure 10.5 The 5 conceptual layers of hardware and protocol software used in the Internet, and the form of objects passed between layers. The layer labeled *network interface* is sometimes called the *data link* layer.

 • *Internet layer*. As we have already seen, the Internet layer handles machine to machine communication. It accepts a request to send a packet from the transport layer along with an identification of the machine to which the packet should be sent. It encapsulates the packet in an IP datagram, fills in the datagram header, uses the routing algorithm to determine whether to deliver the datagram directly or send it to a gateway, and passes the datagram to the appropriate network interface for transmission. The Internet layer also handles incoming datagrams, checking their validity, deleting the header, and using the routing algorithm to decide whether the datagram should be processed locally or forwarded. For datagrams addressed to the local machine, the Internet layer software chooses from among several transport protocols the one that will handle the packet. Finally, the Internet layer sends ICMP messages as needed and handles all incoming ICMP messages.

• *Network Interface Layer*. The lowest level Internet protocol software comprises a network interface layer, responsible for accepting IP datagrams and transmitting them over a specific network. A network interface may consist of a device driver (e.g., when the network is a local area network to which the machine attaches directly) or a complex subsystem that uses its own data link protocol (e.g., when network consists of packet switches that communicate with hosts using HDLC).

10.6 Differences Between ISO And Internet Layering

There are two subtle and important differences between the Internet protocol layering scheme and the X.25 scheme. The first difference revolves around the focus of attention on reliability, while the second involves the location of intelligence in the overall system.

10.6.1 End-To-End vs. Link-Level Reliability

One major difference between the TCP/IP protocols and the X.25 protocols lies in their approach to providing reliable data transfer services. In the X.25 model, protocol software detects and handles errors at all levels. At the link level, complex protocols guarantee that the transfer between a host and the packet switch to which it connects will be correct. Checksums accompany each piece of data transferred, and the receiver acknowledges each piece of data received. The link level protocol includes timeout and retransmission algorithms that prevent data loss and provide automatic recovery after hardware fails and restarts.

Successive levels of X.25 provide reliability of their own. At level *3*, X.25 also provides error detection and recovery for packets transferred onto the network, using checksums as well as timeout and retransmission techniques. Finally, level *4* must provide end to end reliability, having the source correspond with the ultimate destination to verify delivery.

In contrast to the ISO scheme, the Internet bases its protocol layering on the idea that reliability is an end to end problem. The architectural philosophy is simple: construct the Internet so it can handle the expected load, but allow individual links or machines to lose data or corrupt it without trying to repeatedly recover. In fact, there is little or no link level reliability in most Internet link level software. Instead, the transport layer handles the error detection and recovery problem.

The resulting freedom from link level verification makes Internet software much easier to understand and implement correctly. Intermediate gateways can discard datagrams that become corrupted because of transmission errors. They can discard any datagrams that cannot be delivered. They can discard datagrams when the arrival rate exceeds machine capacity. They can reroute datagrams through paths with shorter or longer delay without informing the source or destination.

Having unreliable links means that some datagrams do not arrive. Detection and recovery of datagram loss is carried out between the source host and the ultimate destination and is, therefore, called *end to end* checking. The end to end software located in the transport layer uses checksums, acknowledgements, and timeouts to control transmission. Thus, unlike the ISO layering, Internet protocol software focuses most of its reliability control in one layer.

10.6.2 Locus of Intelligence and Decision Making

Another difference between the X.25 model and the Internet model emerges when one considers the locus of authority and control. As a general rule, networks using X.25 adhere to the idea that a network is a utility that provides a transport service. The vendor that offers the service controls network access and monitors traffic to keep records for accounting and billing. The network vendor handles problems like routing, flow control, and acknowledgements internally, making transfers reliable. This view leaves little that the hosts can (or need to) do. In short, the network is a complex, independent system to which one can attach relatively simple host computers; the hosts themselves participate in the network operation very little.

By contrast, the Internet requires hosts to participate in almost all of the network protocols. We have already mentioned that hosts actively implement end to end error detection and recovery. They also participate in routing because they must choose a gateway when sending datagrams, and they participate in network control because they must handle ICMP control messages. Thus, when compared to an X.25 network, the Internet can be viewed as a relatively simple packet delivery system to which intelligent hosts attach.

10.7 The Protocol Layering Principle

Independent of the particular layering scheme used, or the functions of the layers, the operation of layered protocols is based on a fundamental idea. The idea, called the *layering principle*, can be summarized succinctly:

> *Layered protocols are designed so that layer* n *at the destination receives exactly the same object sent by layer* n *at the source.*

The layering principle explains why layering is such a powerful idea. It allows the protocol designer to focus attention on one layer at a time, without worrying about how lower layers perform. For example, when building a file transfer application, the designer thinks only of two copies of the application program executing on two machines and concentrates on the messages they need to exchange for file transfer. The designer assumes that the application on one host receives exactly what the application on the other host sends.

Figure 10.6 illustrates how the layering principle works:

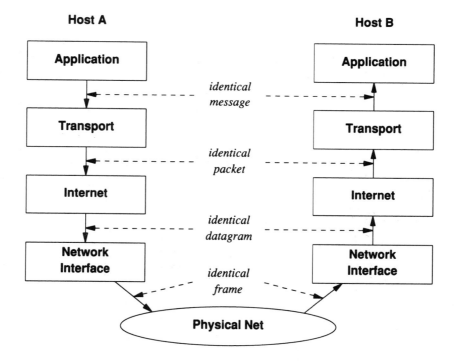

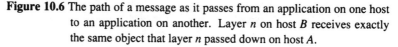

Figure 10.6 The path of a message as it passes from an application on one host to an application on another. Layer *n* on host *B* receives exactly the same object that layer *n* passed down on host *A*.

10.7.1 Layering in an Internet Environment

Our statement of the layering principle is somewhat vague, and the illustration in Figure 10.6 skims over an important issue because it fails to distinguish between transfers from source to ultimate destination and transfers across multiple machines. Figure 10.7 illustrates the distinction, showing the path of a message sent from an application program on one host to an application on another through a gateway.

As the figure shows, message delivery uses two separate network frames, one for the transmission from host *A* to gateway *G*, and another from gateway *G* to host *B*. The network layering principle states that the frame delivered to *G* is identical to the frame sent by host *A*. By contrast, the application and transport layers deal with end to end issues and are designed so the software at the source communicates with its peer at the ultimate destination. Thus, the layering principle states that the packet received by the transport layer at the ultimate destination is identical to the packet sent by the transport layer at the original source.

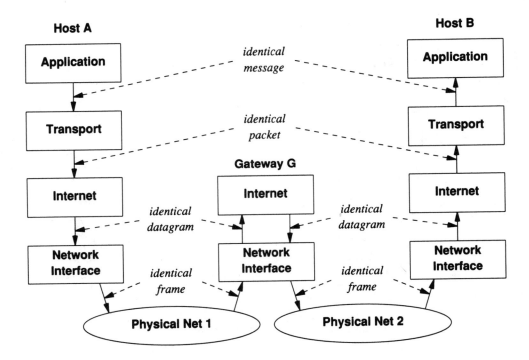

Figure 10.7 The layering principle when a gateway is used. The frame delivered to gateway *G* is exactly the frame sent from host *A*, but differs from the frame sent between *G* and *B*.

It is easy to understand that at higher layers, the layering principle refers to end to end transfers, and that at the lowest layer it applies to a single machine transfer. It is not as easy to see how the layering principle applies to the Internet layer. On one hand, we have said that hosts attached to the Internet should view it as a large, virtual network, with the IP datagram taking the place of a network frame. In this view, datagrams travel from source to ultimate destination, and the layering principle guarantees that the ultimate destination receives exactly the datagram that the source sent. On the other hand, we know that the datagram header contains fields like a *time to live* counter that change every time the datagram passes through a gateway. Thus, the ultimate destination will not receive exactly the same datagram as the source sent. We conclude that although most of the datagram stays intact as it passes across the Internet, the layering principle only applies to datagrams across single machine transfers. To be accurate, we should not view the Internet layer as providing end to end service.

10.8 Layering In The Presence Of Network Substructure

Recall from Chapter 2 that the Cypress network consists of gateways that connect to an Ethernet local area network as well as to other Cypress gateways over leased serial lines. Cypress transfers IP datagrams but uses its own protocol when transferring them across serial lines. The Cypress serial line protocol software must be merged with other protocols, and the question arises, "How do the Cypress protocols fit into the Internet layering scheme?" The answer depends on how the designer views the serial line interconnections.

From the perspective of IP, the set of point to point connections among gateways can either function like a set of independent physical networks, or they can function collectively like a single physical network. In the first case, each physical link is treated exactly like any other network in the Internet. It is assigned a unique (class C) network number, and the two hosts that share that link each have a unique IP address assigned for their connection. Routes are added to the IP routing table as they would be for any other network. A new software module is added at the network interface layer to control the new link hardware, but no substantial changes are made to the layering scheme. The main disadvantage of the independent network approach is that it proliferates network numbers causing routing tables to be larger than necessary.

The second approach to accommodating point to point connections avoids assigning multiple IP addresses to the physical wires. Instead, it treats all the connections collectively as a single, independent network with its own frame format, hardware addressing scheme, and data link protocols. Cypress uses the single network approach and has only one network number for all connections.

Using the single network approach means extending the protocol layering scheme to add a new intranetwork routing layer between the network interface layer and the physical hardware devices. For machines with only one point to point connection, an additional layer seems unnecessary. To see why it is needed, consider a machine with several physical point to point connections, and recall from Figure 10.2 how the network interface layer is divided into multiple software modules that each control one network. We need to add one new network interface for the new point to point network, but the new interface must control multiple physical hardware devices. Furthermore, given a datagram to send, the new interface must choose the correct link over which the datagram should be sent. Figure 10.8 shows the organization.

The Internet layer passes to the network interface all datagrams that should be sent out on any of the point to point connections. The interface passes them to the intranet routing layer that must further distinguish among multiple physical connections and route the datagram across the correct one.

The programmer who designs the intranet routing software determines exactly how the software chooses a physical link. Usually, the algorithm relies on an intranet routing table. The intranet routing table is analogous to the internet routing table in that it specifies a mapping of destination address to route. It contains pairs of entries, (D, L), where D is a destination host address and L specifies one of the physical lines used to reach that destination.

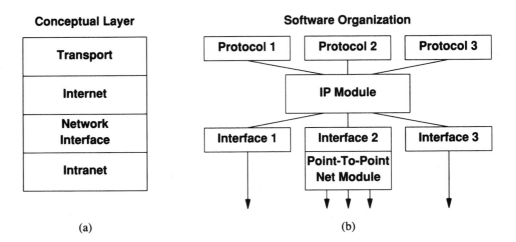

Figure 10.8 (a) conceptual protocol layers when multiple point to point connections are treated as a single IP network, and (b) detailed diagram of software modules showing intranet routing. Each arrow corresponds to one physical device.

The difference between the internet routing table and the intranet routing table is that intranet routing tables are quite small. They only contain routing information for hosts directly attached to the point to point network. The reason is simple: the Internet layer maps an arbitrary destination address to a specific gateway address before passing the datagram to a network interface. Thus, the intranet layer is only asked to distinguish among machines on a single point to point network.

10.9 The Disadvantage Of Layering

We have said that layering is a fundamental idea that provides the basis for protocol design. It allows the designer to divide a complicated problem into subproblems and solve each one independently. Unfortunately, the software that results from strict layering can be extremely inefficient. As an example, consider the job of the transport layer. It must accept a stream of bytes from an application program, divide the stream into packets, and send each packet across the Internet. To optimize transfer, the transport layer should choose the largest possible packet size that will allow one packet to travel in one network frame. In particular, if the destination machine attaches directly to one of the same networks as the source, only one physical net will be involved in the transfer, so the sender can optimize packet size for that network. If the software preserves strict layering, however, the transport layer cannot know how the Internet module will route traffic, or which networks attach directly. Furthermore, the transport layer will not understand the datagram or frame formats or be able to determine how many octets of header will be added to a packet. Thus, strict layering will prevent the transport layer from optimizing transfers.

Usually, implementors relax the strict layering scheme when building protocol software. They allow information like route selection and network MTU to propagate upward. When allocating buffers, they often leave space for headers that will be added by lower layer protocols and may retain headers on incoming frames when passing them to higher layers protocols. Such optimizations can make dramatic improvements in efficiency while retaining the basic layered structure.

10.10 The Basic Idea Behind Multiplexing And Demultiplexing

Communication protocols use a technique called *multiplexing* and *demultiplexing* throughout the layered hierarchy. When sending a message, the source computer includes extra bits that encode the message type, originating process, and protocols used. Eventually, all messages are placed into network frames for transfer and combined into a stream of packets. At the receiving end, the destination machine uses the extra information to guide processing.

Consider an example of demultiplexing shown in Figure 10.9.

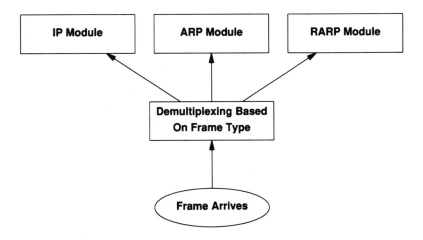

Figure 10.9 Demultiplexing of incoming packets based on the protocol type found in the packet header.

The figure illustrates how software in the network interface layer uses the frame type to choose a procedure that handles the incoming frame. We say that the network interface *demultiplexes* the frame based on its type. To make such a choice possible, software in the source machine must set the frame type field before transmission. Thus, each software module that sends frames uses the type field to specify frame contents.

Multiplexing and demultiplexing occur at almost every protocol layer. For example, after the network interface demultiplexes frames and passes those frames that contain IP datagrams to the IP module, the IP software extracts the datagram and demultiplexes further based on the protocol. Figure 10.10 demonstrates demultiplexing at the Internet layer.

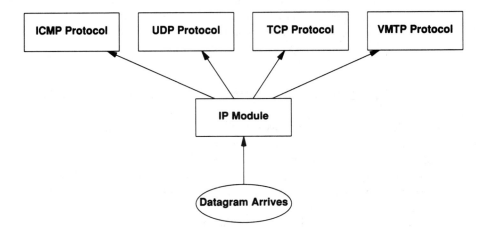

Figure 10.10 Demultiplexing at the Internet layer. IP software chooses an appropriate procedure to handle a datagram based on the type field in the datagram header.

To decide how to handle a datagram, Internet software examines the header of a datagram, and selects a protocol handler based on the datagram type. In the example, the possible datagram types are: *ICMP*, which we have already examined, and *UDP*, *TCP*, and *VMTP*, which we will examine in later chapters.

10.11 ISO Connectionless Delivery Protocols

The International Standards Organization has an effort underway to develop a set of protocols that follow the 7-layer reference model. There are currently 5 proposed transport standards, known as *TP-0*, *TP-1*, *TP-2*, *TP-3*, and *TP-4*. They range in sophistication from simple to complex and are intended for use in a variety of environments. The simplest of the protocols, *TP-0*, provides little in the way of flow control or reliability. It is meant for use in an environment like the one provided by X.25 where the underlying network offers a reliable, stream oriented delivery service.

The most complex of the ISO transport protocols, *TP-4*, resembles TCP. It assumes that the underlying environment only provides connectionless, unreliable packet delivery. Thus, it handles the problems of lost data, flow control, window management, and data that arrives out of sequence. Most Internet researchers and developers believe that ISO's TP-4 will eventually replace TCP because the general policy among Internet leaders is to adopt International standard protocols when feasible. Therefore, despite its current popularity, they view TCP as a protocol that must ultimately migrate the TP-4 standard.

10.12 Summary

Protocols are the standards that specify how data is represented when being transferred from one machine to another. Protocols specify how the transfer occurs, how errors are detected, and how acknowledgements are passed. To simplify protocol design and implementation, communication problems are segregated into subproblems that can be solved independently. Each subproblem is assigned a separate protocol.

The idea of layering is fundamental in protocol design because it provides a conceptual framework for protocol design. In a layered model, each layer handles one part of the communication problem and usually corresponds to one protocol. Layered protocols follow the layering principle, which states that layer *n* on the destination machine receives exactly what layer *n* on the source machine sent.

We examined the International Standards Organization's 7-layer reference model as well as the layering used by the Internet protocols. In both cases, the layering model provides only a conceptual framework for protocol software. The CCITT X.25 protocols follow the ISO reference model and provide an example of reliable communication service offered by a commercial utility, while the TCP/IP protocols provide an example of a slightly different layering scheme used by the Internet.

In practice, protocol software uses multiplexing and demultiplexing to distinguish among multiple protocols within a given layer, making protocol software more complex than the layering model suggests.

FOR FURTHER STUDY

Postel [RFC 791] provides a sketch of the Internet protocol layering scheme and Clark [RFC 817] discusses the effect of layering on implementations. Chesson [1987] makes the controversial argument that layering produces intolerably bad network throughput. Comer [1987] shows an example implementation that achieves efficiency by making compromising strict layering and passing pointers between layers.

A description of the ISO protocols TP-0 through TP-4 can be found in the International Standards Organization documents [1986a] and [1986b]. The ISO protocol documents [1987a] and [1987b] describe ASN.1 in detail. An example presentation protocol used in the Internet, XDR, is described in Sun [RFC 1014].

EXERCISES

10.1   Study the ISO layering model in more detail. How well does a local area network like the Ethernet fit it?

10.2   Build a case that the Internet is moving toward a five-level protocol architecture that includes a presentation layer. (hint: various Internet programs use the XDR protocol, Courier, and ASN.1.)

10.3   Do you think any single presentation protocol will eventually emerge that replaces all others? Why or why not?

10.4   Compare and contrast the tagged data format used by the ASN.1 presentation scheme with the untagged format used by XDR. Characterize situations in which one is better than the other.

10.5   Find out how 4.3 BSD UNIX uses the *mbuf* structure to make layered protocol software efficient.

11

User Datagram Protocol

11.1 Introduction

Previous chapters described an Internet capable of transferring IP datagrams among host computers, where each datagram is routed through the Internet based on the destination's Internet address. At the Internet protocol layer, a destination address identifies a host computer; no further distinction is made regarding which user or which application program on that computer will receive the IP datagram. This chapter extends the Internet protocol suite by adding a mechanism that distinguishes among multiple destinations within a given host, allowing multiple application programs executing on a given host to send and receive datagrams independently.

11.2 Identifying The Ultimate Destination

Most modern computers support multiprocessing, which means they permit multiple application programs to execute simultaneously. Using operating system jargon, we refer to each executing program as a *process*, or a *user level process*. It may seem natural to say that a process is the ultimate destination for a message. However, specifying that a particular process on a particular machine is the ultimate destination for a datagram is somewhat misleading. First, because processes are created and destroyed dynamically, senders seldom know enough to identify a process on another machine. Second, we would like to be able to replace processes that receive datagrams without informing all senders (e.g., rebooting a machine may change all the processes, but rebooting should not require senders to learn about such changes). Third, we need to identify destinations based on the functions they implement without knowing the process that implements the function (e.g., to allow a sender to contact a file server without knowing which process

119

on the destination machine implements the file server function). More important, in systems that allow a single process to handle two or more functions, it is essential that we arrange a way for a process to decide exactly which function the sender desires.

Instead of thinking of processes as the ultimate destination, we will imagine that each machine contains a set of abstract destination points called *protocol ports*. Typically, each protocol port is identified by a positive integer. The local operating system chooses a mechanism that processes use to specify a port or access it.

Most operating systems provide synchronous access to ports. The protocol software located inside the operating system queues packets that arrive for a particular protocol port until a process extracts them. Similarly, the operating system blocks processes that attempt to extract data from a port until a message arrives.

To communicate with a foreign port, a sender needs to know both the Internet address of the destination machine and the protocol port number of the destination within that machine. With each message, the sender supplies both a port number on the foreign machine to which the message is sent, as well as a port number on the source machine to which replies should be addressed. Thus, it is possible for any process receiving a message to reply to the sender.

11.3 The User Datagram Protocol

In the TCP/IP protocol suite, the *User Datagram Protocol* or *UDP* provides one mechanism that senders use to distinguish among multiple recipients on a single machine. In addition to the data sent by a user process, each UDP message contains both a destination port number and source port number, making it possible for the UDP software to deliver the message to the correct recipient and for the recipient to send a reply.

Because UDP depends on the underlying Internet Protocol to transport a UDP message from one machine to another, it provides the same unreliable, connectionless delivery service as IP. It does not use acknowledgements to make sure messages arrive, it does not order incoming messages, and it does not provide feedback to control the rate at which information flows between the machines. Thus, UDP messages can be lost, duplicated, or arrive out of order. Furthermore, packets can arrive faster than the recipient can process them. We can summarize:

> *The User Datagram Protocol (UDP) provides unreliable connectionless delivery service using IP to transport messages among machines. It adds the ability to distinguish among multiple destinations within a given host computer.*

11.4 Format Of UDP Messages

Each UDP message is called a *user datagram* and consists of two parts as Figure 11.1 shows: a UDP header and UDP data area.

Figure 11.1 The two components of a UDP message. Such messages are called *user datagrams*.

The user datagram header is divided into four 16-bit fields that specify the port from which the message was sent, the port to which the message is destined, the message length, and a UDP checksum. Figure 11.2 gives the details, showing a UDP datagram in 32-bit segments:

0	16	31

SOURCE PORT	DESTINATION PORT
LENGTH	UDP CHECKSUM

Figure 11.2   The format of fields in the UDP datagram header.

The *SOURCE PORT* and *DESTINATION PORT* fields contain the 16-bit UDP protocol port numbers used to demultiplex datagrams among the processes waiting to receive them. The *SOURCE PORT* is optional. When used, it specifies the port to which replies should be sent; if not used, it should be zero.

The *LENGTH* field contains a count of octets in the UDP datagram, including the UDP header as well as the user data. Thus, the minimum value for *LENGTH* is eight, the length of the header alone.

The UDP checksum is optional; a value of zero in the *CHECKSUM* field means that the checksum has not been computed. Recall that IP does not compute a checksum on the data portion of a datagram. Thus, the UDP checksum provides the only way to guarantee that data has arrived intact and should be used.

The *CHECKSUM* field is interesting because it provides a check on more than just the UDP datagram. To compute the checksum, UDP prepends a *pseudo header* to the UDP datagram, suffixes an octet of zeros to pad the datagram to an exact multiple of 16 bits, and computes the checksum over the entire object. The octet used for padding and the pseudo header are *not* transmitted with the UDP datagram, nor are they included in the length. UDP uses the same checksum algorithm as IP. It treats the pseudo header, UDP header, data, and padding octet as a sequence of 16-bit integers (in network standard byte order). To compute a checksum, the software first accumulates a 16-bit one's complement sum. It then takes the 16-bit complement of the sum to produce the checksum. During checksum computation, the *CHECKSUM* field is assumed to contain zero.

The purpose of using a pseudo header is to verify that the UDP datagram has reached its correct destination. The key to understanding the pseudo header lies in realizing that the correct destination consists of a specific machine on the Internet and a specific protocol port within that machine. The UDP header itself specifies only the protocol port number. Thus, to verify the destination, UDP on the sending machine computes a checksum that covers the destination host address as well as the UDP datagram. At the ultimate destination, UDP software verifies the checksum using the destination Internet address obtained from the header of the IP datagram that carried the UDP message. If the checksums agree, then it must be true that the datagram has reached the desired destination host as well as the correct protocol port within that host.

The pseudo header used in the UDP checksum computation consists of 12 octets arranged as Figure 11.3 shows:

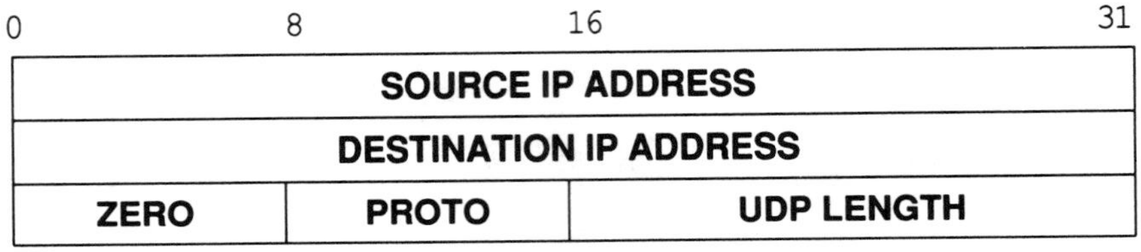

```
0                8               16                            31
┌──────────────────────────────────────────────────────────────┐
│                      SOURCE IP ADDRESS                         │
├──────────────────────────────────────────────────────────────┤
│                   DESTINATION IP ADDRESS                       │
├─────────────────┬───────────────┬──────────────────────────────┤
│      ZERO       │     PROTO     │          UDP LENGTH          │
└─────────────────┴───────────────┴──────────────────────────────┘
```

Figure 11.3 The 12 octets of the pseudo header used during UDP checksum computation.

The fields of the pseudo header labeled *SOURCE IP ADDRESS* and *DESTINATION IP ADDRESS* contain the source and destination Internet addresses that will be used when sending the UDP message. Field *PROTO* contains the IP protocol type code for UDP (17), and the field labeled *UDP LENGTH* contains the length of the UDP datagram. To verify the checksum, the receiver must extract these fields from the actual IP header, assemble them into the pseudo header format, and recompute the checksum.

11.5 UDP Encapsulation And Protocol Layering

UDP provides a first example of a protocol from the layer above the Internet layer. Conceptually, user processes access UDP, which uses IP to send and receive datagrams as Figure 11.4 shows.

Conceptual Layer

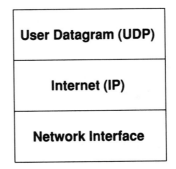

Figure 11.4 The conceptual layering of UDP above IP.

In practice, layering UDP above IP means that a complete UDP message, including the UDP header and data, is encapsulated in an IP datagram as it travels across the Internet as Figure 11.5 shows.

| IP header | Complete UDP datagram treated as data by IP |

Figure 11.5 A UDP datagram encapsulated in an IP datagram as it travels across the Internet.

For the protocols we have examined, encapsulation means that UDP prepends a header to the data that a user sends and passes it to IP. The IP layer prepends a header to what it receives from UDP. Finally, the network interface layer embeds the datagram in a frame before sending it from one machine to another. The format of the frame depends on the underlying network technology. Usually, network frames include an additional header.

On input, a packet arrives at the lowest layer of network software and begins its ascent through successively higher layers. Each layer removes one header before passing the message on, so that by the time the highest level passes data to the receiving process, all headers have been removed. Thus, the outermost header corresponds to the lowest layer of protocol, while the innermost header corresponds to the highest protocol layer. When considering how headers are inserted and removed, it is important to keep in mind the layering principle. In particular, observe that the layering principle applies to UDP, so the UDP datagram received from IP on the destination machine is identical to the datagram that UDP passed to IP on the source machine. Also, the data that UDP delivers to a user process on the receiving machine will be exactly the data that a user process passed to UDP on the sending machine.

The division of duties among various protocol layers is rigid and clear: the IP layer is responsible only for transferring data between hosts on the Internet, while the UDP layer is responsible only for differentiating among multiple sources or destinations *within* one host. Thus, only the IP header identifies the source and destination hosts; only the UDP layer identifies the source or destination ports within a host.

11.6 Layering And The UDP Checksum Computation

Observant readers will have noticed a seeming contradiction between the layering rules and the UDP checksum computation. Recall that the UDP checksum includes a pseudo header that has fields for the source and destination IP address. It can be argued that the destination IP address must be known to the user when sending a UDP datagram, and the user must pass it to the UDP layer. Thus, the UDP layer can obtain the destination IP address without interacting with the IP layer. However, the source IP address depends on the route IP chooses for the datagram, because the source address identifies the network interface over which the datagram is transmitted. Thus, UDP cannot know a source IP address unless it interacts with the IP layer.

We assume that UDP software asks the IP layer to compute the source and (possibly) destination IP addresses, uses them to construct a pseudo header, computes the checksum, discards the pseudo header, and then passes the UDP datagram to IP for transmission. An alternative approach that produces greater efficiency arranges to have the UDP layer encapsulate the UDP datagram in an IP datagram, fill in the source and destination IP header fields, compute the UDP checksum, and then pass the IP datagram to the IP layer, which fills in the remaining IP header fields.

Does the strong interaction between UDP and IP violate our basic premise that layering reflects separation of functionality? Yes. UDP has been tightly integrated with the IP protocol. It is clearly a compromise of the pure separation, made for entirely practical reasons. We are willing to overlook the layering violation because UDP does not add substantial new functionality to the Internet. Instead, it merely supplies a way for application programs to access and exploit the Internet connectionless delivery service. One of the exercises examines this issue from a different point of view, asking the reader to consider whether UDP should be separated from IP.

11.7 UDP Demultiplexing

We have seen that in many layers of the protocol hierarchy, the software must multiplex or demultiplex among multiple objects at the next layer. UDP software provides another example of demultiplexing. It accepts UDP datagrams from the IP software and demultiplexes based on UDP port, as Figure 11.6 shows.

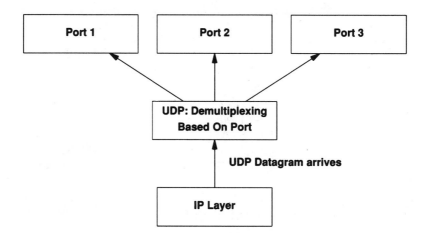

Figure 11.6 Example of demultiplexing one layer above IP. UDP uses the port number to select an appropriate destination for incoming datagrams.

11.8 Reserved And Available UDP Port Numbers

How should protocol port numbers be assigned? The problem is important because two machines need to agree on port numbers before they can interoperate. For example, when machine *A* wants to obtain a file from machine *B*, it needs to know what port the file transfer program on machine *B* uses. There are two fundamental approaches to port assignment. The first approach uses central authority. Everyone agrees to allow a central authority to assign port numbers as needed and to publish the list of all assignments. Then all software is built according to the list. This approach is sometimes called *universal assignment* and the port assignments specified by the authority are called *well-known port assignments*.

The second approach to port assignment uses dynamic binding. In the dynamic binding approach, ports are not globally known. Instead each program that needs a port is assigned one by the network software. To learn about the current port assignment on another machine, it is necessary to send a request that asks a question like, ''How do I reach the file transfer service.'' The target machine replies by giving the correct port number to use.

The Internet designers adopted a hybrid approach that assigns a few port numbers a priori, but leaves most available for local sites or application programs. The assigned port numbers have all but the low order 8 bits set to 0. Thus, only 255 ports can be assigned. The table in Figure 11.7 lists some of the currently assigned UDP port numbers:

Decimal	Keyword	Description
0		Reserved
1-4		Unassigned
5	RJE	Remote Job Entry
7	ECHO	Echo
9	DISCARD	Discard
11	USERS	Active Users
13	DAYTIME	Daytime
15	NETSTAT	Who is up or NETSTAT
17	QUOTE	Quote of the Day
19	CHARGEN	Character Generator
37	TIME	Time
39	RLP	Resource Location Protocol
42	NAMESERVER	Host Name Server
43	NICNAME	Who Is
53	DOMAIN	Domain Name Server
67	BOOTPS	Bootstrap Protocol Server
68	BOOTPC	Bootstrap Protocol Client
69	TFTP	Trivial File Transfer
75		any private dial out service
77		any private RJE service
79	FINGER	Finger
123	NTP	Network Time Protocol
133-159	Unassigned	
160-223	Reserved	
224-241	Unassigned	
247-255	Unassigned	

Figure 11.7 Examples of currently assigned UDP port numbers. To the extent possible, other protocols use these same port numbers.

11.9 Summary

Most computer systems permit multiple application programs to execute simultaneously. Using operating system jargon, we refer to each executing program as a *process*. The User Datagram Protocol, UDP, distinguishes among multiple processes within a given machine by allowing senders and receivers to add two 16-bit integer port numbers to each UDP message The port numbers identify the source and destination. Some UDP port numbers are reserved and honored throughout the net (e.g., port *69* is reserved for use by the Internet trivial file transfer protocol *TFTP*). Other port numbers are available for arbitrary application programs to use.

In the protocol layering scheme, UDP is one of the protocols that lies above the IP layer. Conceptually, the two layers are independent, but in practice there is a strong interaction between the two. The interaction is strong because we view UDP as a mechanism that provides user processes with access to the unreliable connectionless packet delivery service of the Internet.

FOR FURTHER STUDY

Tanenbaum [1981] contains a tutorial comparison of the datagram and virtual circuit models of communication. Ball *et. al.* [1979] describe message-based systems without discussing the message protocol. The UDP protocol described here is standard for the DARPA Internet and is defined by Postel [RFC 768].

EXERCISES

11.1   Try UDP in your local environment. Measure the average transfer speed with messages of 128, 256, 512, 1024, 2048, and 4096 bytes. Can you explain the results (hint: what is your network MTU)?

11.2   Why is the UDP checksum separate from the IP checksum? Would you object to a protocol that used a single checksum for the complete IP datagram including the UDP message?

11.3   Not using checksums can be dangerous. Explain how a single corrupted ARP packet broadcast by machine P can make it impossible to reach another machine, Q.

11.4   Should the notion of multiple destinations identified by protocol ports have been built into IP? Why, or why not?

11.5   *Name Registry.* Suppose you want to allow arbitrary pairs of processes to establish communication with UDP, but you do not wish to assign them fixed UDP port numbers. Instead, you would like potential correspondents to be identified by a character string of 64 or fewer characters. Thus, a process on machine A might want to communicate with the "funny-special-long-id" program on machine B (you can assume that a process always knows the Internet address of the host with which it wants to communicate). Meanwhile, a process on machine C wants to communicate with the "comer's-own-program-id" on machine A. Show that you only need to assign one UDP port to make such communication possible by designing software on each machine that allows (a) a local process to pick an unused UDP port id over which it will communicate, (b) a local process to register the 64-character name to which it responds, and (c) a foreign process to use UDP to establish communication using only the 64-character name and destination Internet address.

11.6   Implement name registry software from the previous exercise.

11.7   What is the chief advantage of using preassigned UDP port numbers? The chief disadvantage?

11.8   What is the chief advantage of using protocol ports instead of process identifiers to specify the destination within a machine?

11.9   UDP provides unreliable datagram communication because it does not guarantee delivery of the message. Devise a reliable datagram protocol that uses timeouts and acknowledgements to guarantee delivery. How much does reliability cost?

12

Reliable Stream Transport Service (TCP)

12.1 Introduction

Previous chapters have explored the unreliable connectionless packet delivery service that forms the basis for all communication in the Internet and the IP protocol that defines it. This chapter introduces the second most important and well known Internet service, reliable stream delivery, and the TCP protocol that defines it. We will see that TCP adds substantial functionality to the protocols already discussed, but that its implementation is also substantially more complex.

Although TCP is presented here as part of the Internet protocol suite, it is an independent, general purpose protocol that can be used with other delivery systems. For example, because TCP makes very few assumptions about the underlying network, it is possible to use it over a single network like an Ethernet, as well as over a complex Internet. In fact, TCP has been so popular that one of the International Standards Organization reliable stream protocols, TP-4, has been derived from it.

12.2 The Need For Stream Delivery

At the lowest level, computer communication networks provide unreliable packet delivery. Packets can be lost or destroyed when transmission errors interfere with data, when network hardware fails, or when networks become too heavily loaded to accommodate the load presented. Networks that route packets dynamically can deliver them out of order, delivery them after substantial delay, or deliver duplicates. Furthermore, underlying network technologies may dictate the optimal packet size or pose other constraints needed to achieve efficient transfer rates.

At the highest level, application programs often need to send large volumes of data from one computer to another. Using an unreliable connectionless delivery system for large volume transfers becomes tedious and annoying, and it requires programmers to build error detection and recovery into each application program. Because it is difficult to design, understand, or modify software that correctly provides reliability, few application programmers have the necessary technical background. As a consequence, one goal of network protocol research has been to find a general purpose solution to the problem of providing reliable stream delivery, making it possible for experts to build a single instance of stream protocol software that all application programs use. Having a single, general purpose protocol helps isolate application programs from the details of networking, and makes it possible to define a uniform interface for the stream transfer service.

12.3 Application Interface To The Reliable Delivery Service

The interface between application programs and the Internet stream delivery service can be characterized by 5 features:

* *Stream Orientation*. When two application programs (processes) transfer large volumes of data, we think of the data as a *stream* of bits, divided into 8-bit *octets* or *bytes*. The stream delivery service on the destination machine passes to the receiver exactly the same sequence of octets that the sender passed to it on the source machine.

* *Virtual Circuit Connection*. Making a stream transfer is analogous to placing a telephone call. Before transfer can start, both the sending and receiving application programs interact with their respective operating systems, informing them of the desire for a stream transfer. Conceptually, one machine places a "call" which must be accepted by the other. Protocol software modules in the two operating systems communicate by sending messages across the Internet, verifying that the transfer is authorized, and that both sides are ready. Once all details have been settled, the protocol modules inform the application programs that a *connection* has been established and that transfer can begin. During transfer, protocol software on the two machines continue to communicate to verify that data is received correctly. If the communication fails (e.g., because network hardware along the path between the machines fails), both machines detect the failure and report it to the appropriate application program. We use the term *virtual circuit* to describe such connections because although application programs view the connection as a dedicated hardware circuit, the reliability is an illusion provided by the stream delivery service.

* *Buffered Transfer*. Application programs send a data stream across the virtual circuit by repeatedly passing the operating system bytes from the stream. When transmitting data, each application uses whatever size pieces it finds convenient, which can be as small as a single byte. At the receiving end, the protocol software delivers bytes from the data stream in exactly the same order they were sent, making them available to the receiving application program as soon as they have been received and verified. The proto-

col software is free to divide the stream into packets independent of the pieces the application program transfers. To make transfer more efficient and to minimize network traffic, implementations usually collect enough data from a stream to fill a reasonably large datagram before transmitting it across the Internet. Thus, even if the application program generates the stream one byte at a time, transfer across the Internet may be quite efficient.

For those applications where data should be delivered even though it does not fill a buffer, the stream service provides a *push* mechanism that applications use to force transfer. At the sending side, a push forces protocol software to transfer all data that has been generated without waiting to fill a buffer. When it reaches the receiving side, the push causes TCP to make the data available to the application without delay. A push only guarantees that all data will be transferred; it does not provide record boundaries. Thus, even when delivery is forced, the protocol software may choose to divide the stream in unexpected ways.

● *Unstructured Stream.* It is important to understand that the Internet stream service does not honor structured data streams. For example, there is no way for a payroll application to have the stream service mark boundaries between employee records, or to identify the contents of the stream as being payroll data. Application programs using the stream service must understand stream content and agree on stream format before they initiate a connection.

● *Full Duplex Connection.* Connections provided by the Internet stream service allow concurrent transfer in both directions. Such connections are called *full duplex*. From the point of view of an application process, a full duplex connection consists of two independent streams flowing in opposite directions, with no apparent interaction. The stream service allows an application process to terminate flow in one direction while data continues to flow in the other direction. The advantage of a full duplex connection is that the underlying protocol software can send control information for one stream back to the source in datagrams carrying data in the opposite direction. Such *piggybacking* reduces network traffic.

12.4 Providing Reliability

We have said that the Internet reliable stream delivery service guarantees to deliver a stream of data sent from one machine to another without duplication or data loss. The question arises, "How can protocol software provide reliable transfer if the underlying communication system offers only unreliable packet delivery?" The answer is complicated, but most reliable protocols use a single fundamental technique known as *positive acknowledgement with retransmission.* The technique requires a recipient to communicate with the source, sending back an *acknowledgement* message every time it receives data. The sender keeps a record of each packet it sends and waits for an acknowledgement before sending the next packet. The sender also starts a timer when it sends a packet and *retransmits* a packet if the timer expires before an acknowledgement arrives.

Figure 12.1 shows how the simplest positive acknowledgement protocol transfers data.

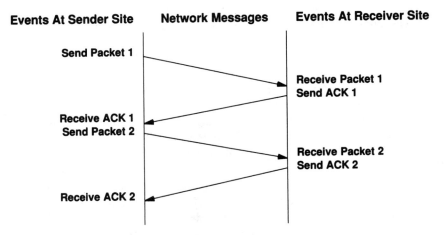

Figure 12.1 A protocol using positive acknowledgement with retransmission in which the sender awaits an acknowledgement for each packet sent. Vertical distance down the figure represents increasing time and diagonal lines across the middle represent network packet transmission.

In the figure, events at the sender and receiver are shown on the left and right. Diagonal lines crossing the middle show the transfer of one message across the network.

Figure 12.2 uses the same format diagram as Figure 12.1 to show what happens when a packet is lost or corrupted. The sender starts a timer after transmitting a packet. When the timer expires, the sender assumes the packet was lost and retransmits it.

The final reliability problem arises when an underlying packet delivery system duplicates packets. Duplicates can also arise when networks experience high delays that cause premature retransmission. Solving duplication requires careful thought because both packets or acknowledgements can be duplicated. Usually, reliable protocols detect duplicate packets by assigning each packet a sequence number and requiring the receiver to remember which sequence numbers it has received. To avoid confusion caused by delayed or duplicated acknowledgements, positive acknowledgement protocols send sequence numbers back in acknowledgements, so the receiver can correctly associate acknowledgements with packets.

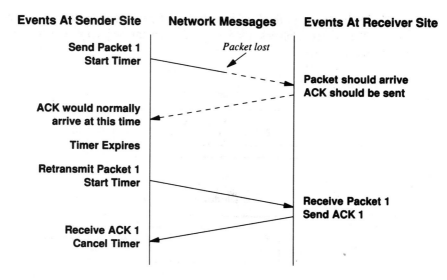

Figure 12.2 Timeout and retransmission that occurs when a packet is lost. The dotted lines show the time that would be taken by the transmission of a packet and its acknowledgement, if the packet were not lost.

12.5 The Idea Behind Sliding Windows

Before examining the Internet stream service, we need to explore an additional concept that underlies stream transmission. The concept, known as a *sliding window*, makes stream transmission efficient. To understand the motivation for sliding windows, recall the sequence of events that Figure 12.1 depicts. To achieve reliability, the sender transmits a packet and then waits for an acknowledgement before transmitting another. As the Figure shows, data only flows between the machines in one direction at any time, even if the network is capable of simultaneous communication in both directions. The network will be completely idle during times that machines delay responses (e.g., while machines compute routes or checksums). If we imagine a network with high transmission delays, the problem becomes clear:

> *A simple positive acknowledgement protocol wastes a substantial amount of network bandwidth because it must delay sending a new packet until it receives an acknowledgement for the previous packet.*

The sliding window technique is a more complex form of positive acknowledgement and retransmission than the simple method discussed above. Sliding window protocols use network bandwidth better because they allow the sender to transmit multiple packets before waiting for an acknowledgement. The easiest way to envision sliding window operation is to think of a sequence of packets to be transmitted as Figure 12.3 shows. The protocol places a small *window* on the sequence and transmits all packets that lie inside the window.

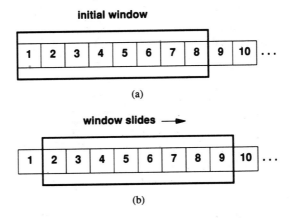

Figure 12.3 (a) A sliding window protocol with eight packets in the window, and (b) The window sliding so that packet *9* can be sent when an acknowledgement has been received for packet *1*. Only unacknowledged packets are retransmitted.

We say that a packet is *unacknowledged* if it has been transmitted but no acknowledgement has been received. Technically, the number of packets that can be unacknowledged at any given time is constrained by the *window size* and is limited to a small, fixed number. For example, in a sliding window protocol with window size *8*, the sender is permitted to transmit *8* packets before it receives an acknowledgement.

As Figure 12.3 shows, once the sender receives an acknowledgement for the first packet inside the window, it "slides" the window along and sends the next packet. The window continues to slide as long as acknowledgements are received.

The performance of sliding window protocols depends on the window size and speed at which the network accepts packets. Figure 12.4 shows an example of the operation of a sliding window protocol when sending three packets. Note that the sender transmits all three packets before receiving any acknowledgements.

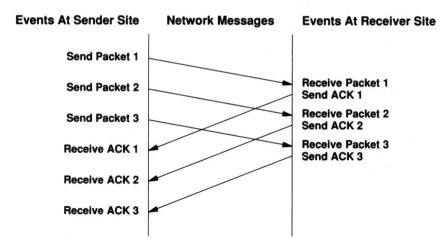

Figure 12.4 An example of three packets transmitted using a sliding window
protocol. The key concept is that the sender can transmit all packets in the window without waiting for an acknowledgement.

With a window size of *1*, a sliding window protocol is exactly the same as our simple positive acknowledgement protocol. By increasing the window size, it is possible to
eliminate network idle time completely. That is, in the steady state, the sender can
transmit packets as fast as the network can transfer them. The main point is:

*Because a well tuned sliding window protocol keeps the network com-
pletely saturated with packets, it obtains substantially higher
throughput than a simple, positive acknowledgement protocol.*

Conceptually, a sliding window protocol always remembers which packets have
been acknowledged and keeps a separate timer for each unacknowledged packet. If a
packet is lost, the timer expires and the sender retransmits that packet. When the sender
slides its window, it moves past all acknowledged packets. At the receiving end, the protocol software keeps an analogous window, accepting and acknowledging packets as they
arrive. Thus, the window partitions the sequence of packets into three sets: those packets to the left of the window have been successfully transmitted, received, and acknowledged; those packets to the right have not yet been transmitted; and those packets
that lie in the window are being transmitted. The lowest numbered packet in the window
is the first packet in the sequence that has not been acknowledged.

12.6 The Transmission Control Protocol

Now that we understand the principle of sliding windows, we can examine the reliable stream service provided by the Internet. The service is defined by the *Transmission Control Protocol*, or *TCP*. The reliable stream service is so important that the entire protocol suite is often referred to as TCP/IP. It is important to understand that:

TCP is a communication protocol, not a piece of software.

The difference between a protocol and the software that implements it is analogous to the difference between the definition of a programming language and a compiler. As in the programming language world, the distinction between definition and implementation sometimes becomes blurred. People encounter TCP software much more frequently than they encounter the protocol specification, so it is natural to think of a particular implementation as the standard. Nevertheless, the reader should try to distinguish between the two.

Exactly what does the TCP protocol provide? TCP is complex, so there is no simple answer. The protocol specifies the format of the data and acknowledgements that two computers exchange to achieve a reliable transfer, as well as the procedures the computers use to ensure that the data arrives correctly. It specifies how TCP software distinguishes among multiple destinations on a given machine, and how communicating machines recover from errors like lost or duplicated packets. The protocol also specifies how two machines initiate a TCP stream transfer and how they agree when it is complete.

It is also important to understand what the protocol does not include. Although the TCP specification describes how application programs use TCP in general terms, it does not dictate the details of the interface between an application program and TCP. That is, the protocol documentation discusses the operations TCP supplies, but it does not specify the exact procedures or arguments to those procedures that implement the operations. The reason for leaving the application program interface unspecified is flexibility. In particular, because programmers usually implement TCP in the computer's operating system, they need to employ whatever interface the operating system supplies. Allowing the implementor flexibility makes it possible to have a single TCP protocol specification that can be used to build software for a variety of machines.

Because the TCP protocol assumes little about the underlying communication system, TCP can be used with a variety of packet delivery systems including the Internet IP datagram delivery service. For example, TCP can be implemented to use dialup telephone lines, a local area network, a high speed fiber optic network, or a lower speed long haul network. In fact, the large variety of delivery systems TCP can use is one of its strengths.

12.7 TCP Ports And Connections

Like the User Datagram Protocol (UDP) presented in Chapter 11, TCP resides above IP in the Internet protocol layering scheme. Figure 12.5 shows the conceptual organization.

Conceptual Layering

Reliable Stream (TCP)	**User Datagram (UDP)**
Internet (IP)	
Network Interface	

Figure 12.5 The conceptual layering of UDP and TCP above IP. TCP provides a reliable stream service, while UDP provides an unreliable datagram delivery service. Application programs access both.

TCP allows multiple application programs on a given machine to communicate concurrently and it demultiplexes incoming TCP traffic among application programs. Like the User Datagram Protocol, TCP incorporates abstract objects called *ports* that identify the ultimate destination within a machine. Each port is assigned a small integer used to identify it†. Because port number assignments are local to a given machine and unique within that machine, the ultimate destination for TCP traffic is uniquely specified by giving both a destination host Internet address as well as a TCP port number on that host.

Unlike UDP, TCP is a connection oriented protocol that needs two endpoints to make communication meaningful. Before TCP traffic can pass across the Internet, application programs at both ends of the connection must agree that the connection is desired. To do so, the application program on one end performs a *passive open* function by contacting its operating system and indicating that it will accept an incoming connection. At that time, the operating system assigns a port number for one end of the connection. The application program at the other end must then contact its operating system using an *active open* request to establish a connection. The two TCP modules communicate to verify that the connection is established. Once a connection has been created, the TCP software modules at each end can begin passing data.

---

†Both TCP and UDP use integer port identifiers starting at *1*. There is no confusion between them because each incoming IP datagram identifies the protocol being used as well as the port number.

12.8 Segments, Streams, And Sequence Numbers

TCP views a data stream as a sequence of octets or bytes that it divides into *segments* for transmission. Usually, each segment travels across the Internet in a single IP datagram.

TCP uses a specialized sliding window mechanism to solve two important problems: efficient transmission and flow control. Like the sliding window protocol described earlier, the TCP window mechanism makes it possible to send multiple packets before an acknowledgement arrives. Doing so increases total throughput because it keeps the network busy. The TCP form of a sliding window protocol also solves the end-to-end *flow control* problem, by allowing the receiver to restrict transmission until it has sufficient buffer space to accommodate more data.

The TCP sliding window mechanism operates at the byte level, not at the packet level. Bytes of the data stream are numbered sequentially, and a sender keeps three pointers associated with every connection that define a sliding window as Figure 12.6 illustrates. The first pointer marks the left of the sliding window, separating bytes that have been sent and acknowledged from bytes yet to be sent. A second pointer marks the right of the sliding window and defines the highest byte in the sequence that can be sent before more acknowledgements are received. The third pointer marks the boundary inside the window that separates those bytes that have already been sent from those bytes that have not been sent. The protocol software sends all bytes in the window without delay, so the boundary inside the window usually moves from left to right quickly.

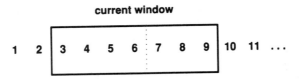

Figure 12.6 An example of the TCP sliding window. Octets through 2 have been sent and acknowledged, octets 3 through 6 have been sent but not acknowledged, octets 7 though 9 have not been sent but will be without delay, and octets 10 and higher cannot be sent until the window moves.

We have described how the sender's TCP window slides along and mentioned that the receiver must maintain a similar window to piece the stream together again. It is important to understand, however, that because TCP connections are full duplex, two transfers proceed simultaneously over each connection, one in each direction. We think of the transfers as completely independent because at any time data can flow across the connection in one direction, or in both directions. Thus, TCP software maintains two windows for each connection, one slides along the data stream being sent, while the other slides along as data is received.

12.9 Variable Window Size And Flow Control

One difference between the TCP sliding window protocol and the simplified sliding window protocol presented earlier occurs because TCP allows the window size to vary over time. Each acknowledgement, which specifies how many bytes have been received, contains a *window advertisement* that specifies how many additional bytes of data the receiver is prepared to accept. We think of the window advertisement as specifying the receiver's current buffer size. In response to an increased window advertisement, the sender increases the size of its sliding window and proceeds to send octets that have not been acknowledged. In response to a decreased window advertisement, the sender decreases the size of its window and stops sending bytes beyond the boundary. TCP software should not contradict previous advertisements by shrinking the window past previously acceptable positions in the byte stream. Instead, smaller advertisements accompany acknowledgements, so the window size changes at the time it slides forward.

The advantage of using a variable size window is that it provides flow control as well as reliable transfer. If the receiver's buffers begin to become full, it cannot tolerate more packets, so it sends a smaller window advertisement. In the extreme case, the receiver advertises a window size of zero to stop all transmissions. Later, when buffer space becomes available, the receiver advertises a nonzero window size to trigger the flow of data again.

Having a mechanism for flow control is essential in an Internet environment, where machines of various speeds and sizes communicate through networks and gateways of various speeds and capacities. There are really two independent flow control problems. First, Internet protocols need end-to-end flow control between the source and ultimate destination. For example, when a minicomputer communicates with a large mainframe, the minicomputer needs to regulate the influx of data, or protocol software would be overrun quickly. Thus, TCP must implement end-to-end flow control to guarantee reliable delivery. Second, Internet protocols need a flow control mechanism that allows intermediate machines like gateways to control a source that sends more traffic than they can tolerate. We observe that because TCP combines sliding windows with flow control, it solves only the end-to-end flow control problem. However, TCP does not solve the second flow control problem, but must rely on intermediate machines to use ICMP *source quench* messages (a less precise mechanism) to solve it.

12.10 TCP Segment Format

The unit of transfer between the TCP software on two machines is called a *segment*. Segments are exchanged to establish connections, to transfer data, to send acknowledgements, to advertise window size, and to close connections. Because TCP uses piggybacking, an acknowledgement traveling from machine *A* to machine *B* may travel in the same segment as data traveling from machine *A* to machine *B*, even though the acknowledgement refers to data sent from *B* to *A*‡. Figure 12.7 shows the TCP segment format.

---

‡In practice, piggybacking does not usually occur unless the recipient delays acknowledgements. See Appendix 1 for more details.

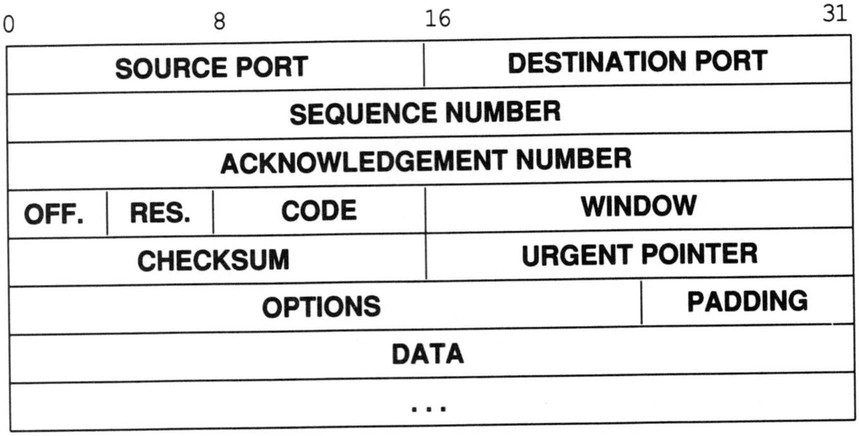

SOURCE PORT			DESTINATION PORT	
SEQUENCE NUMBER				
ACKNOWLEDGEMENT NUMBER				
OFF.	RES.	CODE	WINDOW	
CHECKSUM			URGENT POINTER	
OPTIONS				PADDING
DATA				
. . .				

Figure 12.7 The format of a TCP segment with a TCP header followed by data. Segments are used to establish connections as well as to carry data and acknowledgements.

Each segment is divided into two parts, a header followed by data. The header is often called the *TCP header*. The *SOURCE PORT* and *DESTINATION PORT* fields in the TCP header contain the TCP port numbers that identify the application programs at the ends of the connection. The *SEQUENCE NUMBER* identifies the position in the sender's byte stream of the data in the segment. The *ACKNOWLEDGEMENT NUMBER* field identifies the position of the highest byte that the source has received. Note that the sequence number refers to the stream flowing in the same direction as the segment, while the acknowledgement number refers to the stream flowing in the opposite direction as the segment.

The *offset* field (*OFF*) contains an integer that specifies the offset of the data portion of the segment. It is needed because the *OPTIONS* field varies in length, depending on which options have been included. Thus, the size of the TCP header varies depending on the options selected. The field marked *RES*. is reserved for future use.

Some segments carry only an acknowledgement while some carry data. Others carry requests to establish or close a connection. TCP software uses the 6-bit field labeled *CODE* to determine the purpose and contents of the segment. The six bits tell how to interpret other fields in the header according to the following table.

Bit (left to right)	Meaning
URG	Urgent pointer field is valid
ACK	Acknowledgement field is valid
PSH	This segment requests a push
RST	Reset the connection
SYN	Synchronize sequence numbers
FIN	Sender has reached end of its byte stream

TCP software advertises how much data it is willing to accept every time it sends a segment by specifying its buffer size in the *WINDOW* field. Window advertisements provide another example of piggybacking because they accompany all segments including those carrying data as well as those carrying only an acknowledgement.

TCP allows the sender to specify that some data is *urgent*, meaning that it should be delivered as quickly as possible. The protocol specifies that when urgent data is found, the receiving TCP should notify whatever application program is associated with the connection to go into ''urgent'' mode. After all urgent data has been received, TCP tells the application program to return to normal operation. Typically, urgent data contains messages other than normal data. For example, urgent traffic might include keyboard interrupt signals. Such traffic is often referred to as *out of band* traffic.

The exact details of how TCP informs the application program about urgent data depend on the computer's operating system, of course. The mechanism used to mark urgent data consists of the URG code bit and the *URGENT POINTER* field. When the URG bit is set to *1*, the urgent pointer specifies a position in the byte stream where urgent data ends.

TCP software uses the *OPTIONS* field to communicate with the TCP software at the other end of the connection. In particular, the TCP software at one end of a connection can specify a *maximum segment size* that it is willing to receive. It may be especially important to allow receivers to specify a maximum segment size when a small computer (i.e., a computer with little buffer space available) receives data from a large computer.

Choosing a good maximum segment size can be difficult because performance can be poor for either extremely large segments sizes or extremely small sizes. On one hand, when segment size decreases, network utilization decreases. To see why, recall that TCP segments travel encapsulated in IP datagrams which are encapsulated in physical network frames. Thus, each segment has at least 40 octets of TCP and IP header in addition to the data, so datagrams carrying one octet of data use at most 1/40 of the underlying network bandwidth for user data. On the other hand, extremely large segment sizes also produce poor performance. Large segments result in large datagrams which are fragmented for transmission across the Internet. Unlike datagrams, fragments are not independent; all fragments must arrive or they must all be retransmitted. If the probability of losing a packet is nonzero, increasing segment size above the fragmentation threshold decreases throughput.

12.11 TCP Checksum Computation

The *CHECKSUM* field in the TCP segment header contains a 16-bit integer checksum used to verify the integrity of the TCP segment header as well as the data. To compute the checksum, TCP software on the sending machine prepends a *pseudo header* to the segment, appends enough bytes containing zero to pad the segment to a multiple of 16 bits, and computes the checksum over the entire result. TCP does not count the padded zeros in the length, nor does it transmit them. Also, it assumes the checksum field itself is zero for purposes of the checksum computation. As with other checksums, TCP uses 16-bit arithmetic and takes the one's complement of the one's complement sum. At the receiving site, TCP software performs the same computation to verify that the segment arrived intact.

The purpose of using a pseudo header is exactly the same as in UDP. It allows the receiver to verify that the segment has reached its correct destination, which includes both a host Internet address as well as a protocol port number. Figure 12.8 shows the format of the pseudo header used in the checksum computation.

0	8	16	31
SOURCE IP ADDRESS			
DESTINATION IP ADDRESS			
ZERO	PROTO	TCP LENGTH	

Figure 12.8 The format of the pseudo header used in TCP checksum computations. At the receiving site, this information is extracted from the IP datagram that carried the segment.

In the pseudo header, the *PROTO* field specifies type TCP, and the *TCP LENGTH* field specifies the total length of the TCP segment. At the receiving end, information used in the pseudo header is extracted from the Internet datagram that carried the segment.

12.12 Acknowledgements And Retransmission

Because TCP sends data in variable length segments, acknowledgements refer to a position in the stream, and not to packets or segments. Each acknowledgement specifies one greater than the highest byte position that has been received. Thus, the sender receives continuous feedback from the receiver as it progresses through the stream. We can summarize this important idea:

Acknowledgements always specify the number of the next byte that the receiver expects to receive.

The TCP acknowledgement scheme is called *cumulative* because it reports how much of the stream has accumulated. Cumulative acknowledgements have both advantages and disadvantages. One advantage is that acknowledgements are both easy to generate and unambiguous. Another advantage is that lost acknowledgements do not necessarily force retransmission. A major disadvantage is that the sender does not receive information about all successful transmissions, but only about a single position in the stream that has been received.

To understand why lack of information about all successful transmissions makes the protocol inefficient, think of a window that spans *5000* bytes starting at position *101* in the stream, and suppose the sender has transmitted all data in the window by sending five segments. Suppose further that the first segment is lost, but all others arrive intact. The receiver continues to send acknowledgements, but they all acknowledge receiving through byte *100*, the highest contiguous byte number correctly received. There is no way for the receiver to tell the sender that most of the data for the current window arrived. When a timeout occurs at the sender's side, the sender must choose between two potentially inefficient schemes. It may choose to retransmit all five segments instead of the one missing segment. Of course, when the retransmitted segment arrives, the receiver will have correctly received all data from the window, and will acknowledge that bytes through *5100* have been received. However, that acknowledgement may not reach the sender quickly enough to prevent the unnecessary retransmission of other segments from the window.

If the sender follows accepted implementation policy and retransmits only the first unacknowledged segment, it must wait for the acknowledgement before it can decide what and how much to send. Thus, it reverts to a simple positive acknowledgement protocol and loses the advantages of having a large window.

12.13 Timeout And Retransmission

One of the most important ideas in TCP is embedded in the way it handles timeout and retransmission. Like other reliable protocols, TCP expects the destination to send acknowledgements whenever it successfully receives more of the data stream. Every time it sends a segment, TCP starts a timer and waits for an acknowledgement. If the timer expires before data in the segment has been acknowledged, TCP assumes that the segment was lost or corrupted and retransmits it.

To understand why the TCP retransmission algorithm differs from the algorithm used in many network protocols, we need to remember that TCP is intended for use in an Internet environment. In an Internet, the path between a pair of machines may traverse a single high speed network, or it may wind across multiple intermediate networks through multiple gateways. Thus, it is impossible to know a priori how quickly acknowledgements will return to the source. More important the delay at each gateway depends on traffic, so the time required to transmit a segment and receive an acknowledgement varies dramatically from one instant to another. Figure 12.9, which shows measurements of round trip times across the Internet for 100 consecutive packets, illustrates the problem.

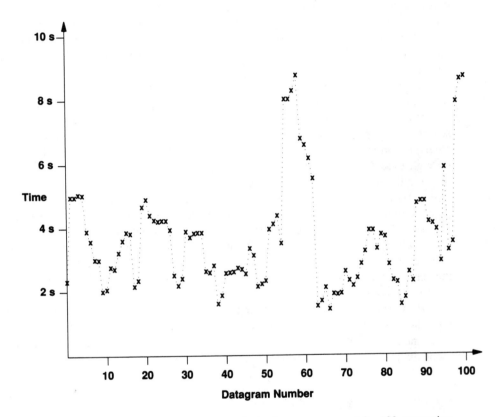

Figure 12.9 A plot of Internet round trip times as measured for 100 successive IP datagrams.

TCP accommodates varying Internet delays by using an adaptive algorithm. To collect the data needed for an adaptive algorithm, TCP records the time at which each segment is sent, and the time at which an acknowledgement arrives for the data in that segment. From the two times, TCP computes an elapsed time known as the *round trip time*. Whenever it measures a new round trip time, TCP adjusts its notion of the average round trip time for the connection. Usually, TCP software keeps the average round trip time as a weighted average and uses new round trip times to change the average slowly. For example, one averaging technique uses a constant weighting factor, q, where $0 \le q < 1$, to weight the old average against the latest round trip time:

$$W\_aver = (q * W\_aver) + ((1-q) * New\_Round\_Trip\_Time)$$

Choosing a value for *q* close to *1* makes the weighted average immune to changes that last a short time (e.g., a single segment that encounters long delay). Choosing a value for *q* close to *0* makes the weighted average respond to changes in delay very quickly. Usually, *q* is chosen closer to *1* to keep a single delay from affecting TCP dramatically. In practice, more sophisticated techniques allow TCP to respond more quickly to increases in delay.

We can summarize these ideas as follows:

> *To accommodate the varying delays encountered in an Internet environment, TCP needs to use an adaptive retransmission algorithm that monitors delays and adjusts its timeout parameter accordingly.*

12.14 Response To Congestion

It may seem that TCP software could be designed by considering the interaction between the two endpoints of a connection and the communication delays between them. In practice, however, TCP must also react to *congestion* in the Internet. Congestion is a condition of severe delay caused by an overload of datagrams at one or more switching points (e.g., at a gateway). When congestion occurs, delays increase and the queue of datagrams the gateway is waiting to switch grows. We must remember that each gateway has finite storage capacity and that datagrams compete for that storage (i.e., in a datagram based internet, there is no preallocation of resources to individual TCP connections). In the worst case, the total number of datagrams arriving at the congested gateway grows until the gateway reaches capacity and starts to drop datagrams.

When congestion occurs, TCP must respond by reducing transmission rates. Gateways can use techniques like the ICMP source quench to inform hosts that congestion has occurred, but transport level protocols can detect congestion automatically by observing increases in round trip delay. The point is that a poorly designed TCP aggravates congestion by ignoring increased delay and retransmitting segments frequently while a well designed TCP helps alleviate congestion.

12.15 Establishing A TCP Connection

To establish a connection, TCP uses a three-way handshake. In the simplest case, the handshake proceeds as Figure 12.10 shows.

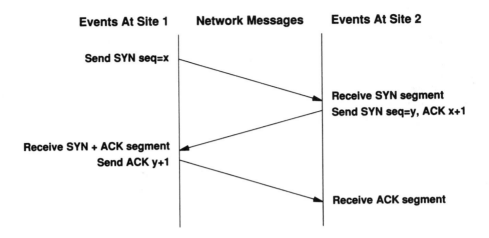

Figure 12.10 The sequence of messages in a three-way handshake. The SYN segments carry initial sequence number information.

The first segment of a handshake can be identified because it has the SYN† bit set in the code field. The second message has both the SYN bit and ACK bits set, indicating that it acknowledges the first SYN segment as well as continuing the handshake. The final handshake message is only an acknowledgement and is merely used to inform the destination that both sides agree that a connection has been established.

Usually, the TCP software on one machine waits passively for the handshake and the TCP software on another machine initiates it. However, the handshake is carefully designed to work even if both machines attempt to initiate a connection simultaneously. Thus, a connection can be established from either end or from both ends simultaneously. Once the connection has been established, data can flow in both directions equally well. There is no master or slave.

The three-way handshake is both necessary and sufficient for correct synchronization between the two ends of the connection. To understand why, remember that TCP builds on an unreliable packet delivery service so messages can be lost or delayed. Thus, the protocol must use a timeout mechanism and retransmit lost requests. Trouble arises if retransmitted requests arrive while the connection is being established, or when retransmitted requests are delayed until after a connection has been established, used, and terminated. A three-way handshake (plus the rule that TCP ignores additional requests for connection after a connection has been established) solves these problems.

The three-way handshake accomplishes two important functions. It guarantees that both sides are ready to transfer data (and that they know they are both ready), and it allows both sides to agree on initial sequence numbers. Sequence numbers are sent and acknowledged during the handshake. Each machine chooses an initial sequence number that it will use to identify bytes in the stream it is sending. Sequence numbers need not start at *1*; in fact, they should not (one of the exercises examines problems that can arise

---

†SYN stands for *synchronization*; it is pronounced ''sin''.

if they do). Of course, it is important that both sides agree on an initial number, so byte numbers used in acknowledgements agree with those used in data segments.

To see how machines can agree on sequence numbers for two streams after only three messages, recall that each segment contains both a sequence number field and an acknowledgement field. The machine that initiates a handshake, call it A, passes its initial sequence number, x, in the first SYN sequence field of the first segment of the three-way handshake. The second machine, B, receives the SYN, records the sequence number, and replies by sending its initial sequence number in the sequence field as well as an acknowledgement that specifies B expects byte $x+1$. In the final message of the handshake, A "acknowledges" receiving from B all bytes through y. In all cases, acknowledgements follow the convention of using the *next* byte number expected.

We have described how TCP usually carries out the three-way handshake by exchanging segments that contain a minimum amount of information. Because of the protocol design, it is possible to send data along with the initial sequence numbers in the handshake segments. In such cases, the TCP software must hold the data until the handshake completes. Once a connection has been established, the TCP software can release data being held and deliver it to a waiting application program quickly. The reader is referred to the protocol specification for the details.

12.16 Closing a TCP Connection

Recall that TCP connections are full duplex and that we view them as containing two independent stream transfers, one going in each direction. When an application program tells TCP that it has no more data to send, TCP will close the connection in that direction. To close its half of a connection, the sending TCP finishes transmitting the remaining data and then sends a segment with the FIN bit set. The receiving TCP acknowledges the FIN segment and informs the application program that no more data is available (e.g., using the operating system's end-of-file mechanism).

Once a connection has been closed in a given direction, TCP refuses to accept more data for that direction. Meanwhile, data can continue to flow in the opposite direction until the sender closes it. When both directions have been closed, the connection is deleted.

12.17 TCP Connection Reset

An application program closes a connection when it finishes using it. Thus, closing is considered a normal part of use, analogous to reaching the end of a data file. Sometimes abnormal conditions arise that force an application program or the network software to break a connection. TCP provides a reset operation for such abnormal disconnections.

One side of the connection initiates a reset by sending a segment with the RST bit in the *CODE* field set to *1*. The other side responds to a reset segment immediately by aborting the connection. It also informs the application program that a reset occurred. An abort means that transfer in both directions ceases immediately, and resources such as buffers are released.

12.18 Forcing Data Delivery

We have said that TCP is free to divide the stream of data into segments for transmission without regard to the size of transfer application programs use. The chief advantage of allowing TCP to choose a division is efficiency. It can accumulate enough bytes in a buffer to make segments reasonably long, reducing the high overhead that occurs when segments contain only a few data bytes.

Although buffering improves network throughput, it can interfere with some applications. Consider using a TCP connection to pass characters from an interactive terminal to a remote machine. The user expects instant response to each keystroke. If TCP buffers the data, response may be delayed.

To accommodate interactive users, TCP provides a *push* operation that an application program can use to force delivery of bytes currently in the stream without waiting for the buffer to fill. The push operation does more than force TCP to send a segment. It also requests TCP to set the *PSH* bit in the segment code field, so the data will be delivered to the application program on the receiving end. Thus, when sending data from an interactive terminal, the application uses the push function after each keystroke. Similarly, application programs can force output to be sent and displayed on the terminal promptly by calling the push function after writing a character or line.

In addition to the *push* function, TCP provides an *urgent pointer* facility that allows a sender to inform the receiver that data further along the stream is urgent and should be processed quickly. For example, imagine a TCP connection being used for traffic between an interactive terminal and a computer. Characters that stop and restart output (e.g., control-s and control-q) might be considered urgent because the receiver should process them immediately.

12.19 Reserved TCP Port Numbers

Like UDP, TCP combines static and dynamic port binding, using a set of *well-known port assignments* for commonly invoked programs (e.g., electronic mail), but leaving most port numbers available for the operating system to allocate as programs need them. Figure 12.11 lists some of the currently assigned TCP ports.

Decimal	Keyword	Description
0		Reserved
1-4		Unassigned
5	RJE	Remote Job Entry
7	ECHO	Echo
9	DISCARD	Discard
11	USERS	Active Users
13	DAYTIME	Daytime
15	NETSTAT	Who is up or NETSTAT
17	QUOTE	Quote of the Day
19	CHARGEN	Character Generator
20	FTP-DATA	File Transfer Protocol (data)
21	FTP	File Transfer Protocol
23	TELNET	Terminal connection
25	SMTP	Simple Mail Transport Protocol
37	TIME	Time
39	RLP	Resource Location Protocol
42	NAMESERVER	Host Name Server
43	NICNAME	Who Is
53	DOMAIN	Domain Name Server
67	BOOTPS	Bootstrap Protocol Server
68	BOOTPC	Bootstrap Protocol Client
69	TFTP	Trivial File Transfer
75		any private dial out service
77		any private RJE service
79	FINGER	Finger
95	SUPDUP	SUPDUP Protocol
101	HOSTNAME	NIC Host Name Server
102	ISO-TSAP	ISO-TSAP
113	AUTH	Authentication Service
117	UUCP-PATH	UUCP Path Service
123	NTP	Network Time Protocol
133-159	Unassigned	
160-223	Reserved	
224-241	Unassigned	
247-255	Unassigned	

Figure 12.11 Examples of currently assigned TCP port numbers. To the extent possible, protocols like UDP use the same numbers.

It should be pointed out that although TCP and UDP port numbers are independent, the designers have chosen to use the same integer port numbers for any service that is accessible from both UDP and TCP. For example, a domain name server can be accessed either with TCP or with UDP. In either protocol, port number *53* has been reserved for servers in the domain system.

12.20 Summary

The Transmission Control Protocol, TCP, defines a key service provided by the Internet, namely, reliable stream delivery. TCP provides a full duplex connection between two machines, allowing them to exchange large volumes of data efficiently.

Because it uses a sliding window protocol, TCP can make efficient use of a network. Because it makes few assumptions about the underlying delivery system, TCP is flexible enough to operate over a large variety of delivery systems. Because it provides flow control, TCP allows systems of widely varying speeds to communicate.

The basic unit of transfer used by TCP is a segment. Segments are used to pass control information (e.g., to allow TCP software on two machines to establish connections or break them) or data. The segment format permits a machine to piggyback acknowledgements for data flowing in one direction by including them in the segment headers of data flowing in the opposite direction.

TCP implements flow control by having the receiver advertise the amount of data it is willing to accept. It also supports out of band messages using a facility that sends urgent data and forced delivery using a push mechanism.

FOR FURTHER STUDY

The standard for TCP can be found in Postel [RFC 793]. Clark [RFC 813] describes TCP window management, Clark [RFC 816] describes fault isolation and recovery, and Postel [RFC 879] reports on TCP maximum segment sizes. Nagle [RFC 896] comments on congestion in TCP/IP networks. Tomlinson [1975] considers the three-way handshake in more detail. Mills [RFC 889] reports measurements of Internet round-trip delays. Karn and Partridge [1987] discuss estimation of round-trip times. Jain [1986] describes timer-based congestion control in a sliding window environment.

EXERCISES

12.1   TCP uses a finite field to contain stream sequence numbers. Study the protocol specification to find out how it allows an arbitrary length stream to pass from one machine to another.

12.2   The text notes that one of the TCP options permits a receiver to specify the maximum segment size it is willing to accept. Why does TCP support an option to specify maximum segment size when it also has a window advertisement mechanism?

12.3   Under what conditions of delay, bandwidth, load, and packet loss will TCP retransmit significant volumes of data unnecessarily?

12.4   Lost TCP acknowledgements do not necessarily force retransmissions. Explain why.

12.5   Experiment with local machines to determine how TCP handles machine restart. Establish a connection (e.g., a remote login) and leave it idle. Wait for the destination machine to crash and restart, and then force the local machine to send a TCP segment (e.g., by typing characters to the remote login).

12.6   Imagine an implementation of TCP that discards segments that arrive out of order, even if they fall in the current window. That is, the imagined version only accepts segments that extend the byte stream it has already received. Does it work? How does it compare to a standard TCP implementation?

12.7   What are the arguments for and against automatically closing idle connections?

12.8   If two application programs use TCP to send data but only send one character per segment (e.g., by using the PUSH operation), what is the maximum percent of the network bandwidth they will have for their data?

12.9   Suppose an implementation of TCP uses initial sequence number *1* when it creates a connection. Explain how a system crash and restart can confuse a remote system into believing that the old connection remained open.

12.10 Look at the round-trip time estimation algorithm suggested in the ISO TP-4 protocol specification and compare it to the TCP algorithm discussed in this chapter. Which would you prefer to use?

12.11 Find out how implementations of TCP must solve the *overlapping segment problem*. The problem arises because the receiver must receive only one copy of all bytes from the data stream even if the sender transmits two segments that partially overlap one another (e.g., the first segment carries bytes 100 through 200 and the second carries bytes 150 through 250).

13

The Core Gateway System (GGP)

13.1 Introduction

Previous chapters have concentrated on the network level services the Internet offers and the details of protocols that provide those services. This chapter turns to another aspect of the Internet, the architecture of the Internet gateway system. It begins with a simplified view of the gateway system, discussing how gateways obtain routes in general, and examining the interconnection of gateways in the DARPA Internet in particular. While this chapter focuses on the gateways that are operated by the Internet Network Operations Center (INOC), the next two chapters continue the discussion by exploring how Internet gateways owned by other groups fit into the architecture, and how they communicate among themselves and with gateways operated by the INOC.

13.2 The Origin Of Gateway Routing Tables

Recall from Chapter 3 that Internet gateways provide the active interconnections among networks. Each gateway attaches to two or more physical networks and routes IP datagrams among them, accepting datagrams that arrive over one network interface, and routing them out over another interface. Except for destinations on directly attached networks, hosts pass all IP traffic to gateways which route the datagrams on toward their final destinations. A datagram travels from gateway to gateway until it reaches a gateway that attaches directly to the same network as the final destination. Thus, the Internet gateway system forms the architectural basis for the Internet and handles all traffic except for direct delivery from one host to another.

Chapter 8 described the IP routing algorithm that hosts and gateways follow and showed how it uses a table of routes to make routing decisions. Each entry in the routing table specifies the network portion of a destination address and gives the address of the next machine along a path used to reach that network. Like hosts, gateways directly deliver datagrams to destinations on networks to which the gateway directly attaches.

Although we have seen the basics of routing, we have not said how hosts or gateways obtain the information for their routing tables. The issue has two parts: initialization and update. Each gateway must establish an initial set of routes when it starts, and it must update the table as routes change (e.g., when a network interface fails). Initialization depends on the operating system. In some systems, the gateway reads an initial routing table from secondary storage at startup, keeping it resident in main memory. In others, the operating system begins with an empty table which must be filled in by executing explicit commands (e.g., commands obtained from a startup command script). Finally, some operating systems start by deducing an initial set of routes from the set of addresses for the networks to which the machine attaches and contacting a neighboring machine to ask for its routes.

Once an initial routing table has been built, a gateway must accommodate changes in routes. In small, slowly changing internetworks, managers can modify gateway routes by hand. In rapidly changing environments like the Internet, however, manual update is impossibly slow. Automated methods are needed.

Before we can understand the automatic routing table update protocols used in Internet gateways, we need to review an important underlying idea. The next section does so, providing the necessary conceptual foundation. Later sections discuss the architecture of the Internet gateway system and the protocol gateways use to exchange routing information.

13.3 Routing With Partial Information

The principal difference between gateways and typical hosts is that hosts usually know little about the structure of the Internet. Hosts do not have complete knowledge of all possible destination addresses, or even of all possible destination networks. They depend on default entries in their routing tables to send to a nearby gateway all datagrams for which they have no specific route. The point is that:

> *Hosts can route packets successfully even if they only have partial routing information because they can rely on gateways.*

Can gateways also route packets with only partial information? Yes, but only under certain circumstances. To understand the criteria, imagine the Internet to be a foreign country crisscrossed with dirt roads that have directional signs posted at intersections. Imagine that you have no map, cannot ask directions because you cannot speak the local language, have no ideas about visible landmarks, but you need to travel to a village named *Sussex*. You leave on your journey, following the only road out of town and begin to look for directional signs. The first sign reads:

Norfolk to the left; Hammond to the right; others straight ahead.†

After several more signs, you finally find one that reads:

Essex to the left; Sussex to the right; others straight ahead.

You turn to the right, follow several more signs, and emerge on a road that leads to Sussex.

Our imagined travel is analogous to a datagram traversing the Internet, and the road signs are analogous to gateway routing tables. Without a map or other navigational aids, travel is completely dependent on road signs, just as packet routing in the Internet depends entirely on routing tables. Clearly, it is possible to navigate even though each road sign contains only partial information.

The central question concerns correctness. As a traveler, you might ask, "How can I be sure that following signs will lead to my final destination?" The answer depends on the topology of the road system and the contents of the signs, but the fundamental idea is that when taken as a whole, the information on the signs is both consistent and complete. A few examples will explain ways that consistency can be achieved.

If each village has exactly one road leading to it, and all those roads meet at a central point, the sign at that central intersection must contain information about all possible destinations. At the other extreme, we can imagine an arbitrary set of roads with signs at all intersections listing all possible destinations. Neither of these extremes works well for the Internet gateway system. On one hand, no machine is fast enough to serve as a central switch through which all traffic passes. On the other hand, having information about all possible destinations in all gateways is impractical because it requires propagating large volumes of information whenever a change occurs or whenever administrators need to check consistency. Thus, we seek a solution that allows an Internet site to manage local gateways autonomously, adding new network interconnections and routes without changing distant gateways.

The compromise selected by Internet designers consists of having a small, central set of gateways that keep complete information about all possible destinations, and a larger set of outlying gateways that keep partial information. In terms of our analogy, it is like designating a small set of centrally located intersections to have signs that list all destinations, and allowing the outlying intersections to list only local destinations. As long as the default route at each outlying intersection points to one of the central intersections, travelers will eventually reach their destination. The advantage of using partial information in outlying gateways is that it permits local administrators to manage local structural changes without affecting other parts of the Internet. The disadvantage is that it introduces the potential for inconsistency. In the worst case, an error in an outlying gateway can make distant routes unreachable.

---

†Fortunately, signs are printed in English.

We can summarize these ideas:

The routing tables in a given gateway contain partial information about possible destinations in the Internet. Routing based on partial information allows sites autonomy in making local routing changes but introduces the possibility of inconsistencies that may make some destinations unreachable from some sources.

In gateways, routing inconsistencies arise from errors in the algorithms that compute routing tables, incorrect data supplied to those algorithms, or from errors that occur while transmitting the results to other gateways. Protocol designers look for ways to limit the impact of errors, with the objective being to keep all routes consistent at all times. If routes become inconsistent for some reason, the protocols gateways use should be robust enough to detect and correct the errors quickly. Most important, the protocols should be designed to constrain the effect of errors.

13.4 Core And Noncore Gateways

Loosely speaking, Internet gateways can be partitioned into two groups, a small set of *core gateways* controlled by the Internet Network Operations Center (INOC), and a larger set of *noncore gateways* controlled by individual groups. The core system is designed to provide reliable, consistent, authoritative routes for all possible destinations; it is the glue that holds the Internet together and makes universal interconnection possible. By fiat, each site assigned an Internet network address must arrange to advertise that address to the core system. The core gateways communicate among themselves, so they can guarantee that the information they share is consistent. Because a central authority monitors and controls the core gateways, they are highly reliable.

To fully understand the core gateway system, it is necessary to remember that the Internet evolved with a wide-area network, the ARPANET, already in place. When the Internet experiments began, designers thought of the ARPANET as a main backbone on which to build. Thus, a large part of the motivation for the core gateway system came from the desire to connect local networks to the ARPANET. Figure 13.1 illustrates this view.†

Suppose that the Internet consisted entirely of local area networks attached to the ARPANET through gateways, and imagine routing packets if the gateways contained only partial information. A packet could cross the ARPANET several times flowing from one gateway to another until it reached a gateway that had a route to the final destination. To avoid unnecessary trips across the ARPANET the designers arranged for core gateways to exchange routing information so that each would have complete information about all possible destinations.

---

†The terms *stub gateway* and *nonrouting gateway* have also been applied to gateways that connect local area networks to the ARPANET.

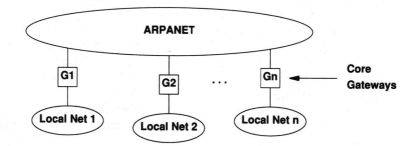

Figure 13.1 The core gateway system viewed as a set of routers that connect local area networks to the ARPANET. Hosts on the local networks pass all nonlocal traffic to the closest core gateway.

Although the simplistic architecture shown in Figure 13.1 is easy to understand, it is impractical for two reasons. First, not all the gateways connecting the ARPANET to other networks will fall under the administrative control of the central authority that manages the core. Second, because core gateways all interact to ensure consistent routing information, the architecture does not scale up well. We will return to this problem in Chapter 14 after we examine the protocols that the core system uses to exchange routing information.

13.5 Gateway-To-Gateway Protocol (GGP)

The original core gateways used a protocol known as the *Gateway-to-Gateway Protocol (GGP)* to exchange routing information. GGP messages travel in IP datagrams like UDP messages or TCP segments, and each GGP message has a fixed format header that identifies the message type and the format of the remaining fields. Because only core gateways participate in GGP, and because core gateways are controlled by the INOC, outsiders cannot interfere with the exchange.

The core system is arranged to permit new core gateways to be added without modifying existing gateways. When a new gateway is added to the core system, it is assigned one or more core *neighbors* with which it communicates. The neighbors are already members of the core and will actively propagate new routing information they obtain to the rest of the core. Thus, the new gateway only needs to propagate information about networks it can reach to its neighbors; they will update their routing tables and propagate the information further.

The routing information gateways exchange consists of a set of pairs, *(N,D)*, where *N* is a network, and *D* is a *distance* that gives the cost of reaching that network. We say that a gateway *advertises* the networks it can reach and its cost for reaching them. The distance metric allows a receiver to compare advertised costs with its current costs and compute new shortest path routes to all networks. Once the receiver updates its routes, it advertises the new costs to its neighbors. The information will eventually propagate throughout the core.

Distances are usually measured in *gateway hops*. A gateway is defined to be zero hops from directly connected networks, one hop from networks that are reachable through one other gateway, and so on. Thus, in the Internet, the *number of hops* or the *hop count* along a path from a given source to a given destination refers to the number of gateways that a datagram encounters along that path. It should be obvious that using hop counts to calculate shortest paths does not always produce desirable results. For example, a path with hop count *3* that crosses three Ethernets may be substantially faster than a path with hop count *2* that crosses two slow speed serial lines. Many gateways use artificially high hop counts for routes across slow networks. Much research is being done on other possible metrics like delay.

13.6 GGP Message Formats

There are four types of GGP messages, each with its own format. The first octet contains a code that identifies the message *type*. Figure 13.2 shows the format of one GGP message type, the messages core gateways exchange to learn about routes. Recall that the information consists of pairs of network and distance values. To keep messages small, networks are grouped together by distance, and the message contains a sequence of sets, where each set contains a distance value followed by a list of all networks at that distance.

The value *12* in the field labeled *TYPE* specifies that this message is a *routing update* message, distinguishing it from other GGP message types. The 16-bit *SEQUENCE NUMBER* is used to validate GGP messages; both sender and receiver must agree on the sequence number before the receiver will accept messages. The field labeled *UPDATE* is treated as a binary value that specifies whether the sender needs an update from the receiver. Because GGP groups networks by distance, the field labeled *NUM. DISTANCES* specifies how many distance groups are present in this update.

The last part of a GGP routing update message contains a set of networks grouped by distance. Each group starts with two 8-bit fields that specify a distance value and a count of networks at that distance. If the count specifies *n* networks at a given distance, exactly *n* network IP addresses must occur before the next group header. To conserve space, only the network portion of the IP address is included, so network numbers may be 1, 2, or 3 octets long. The receiver must look at the first bits of the network identifier to determine its length.

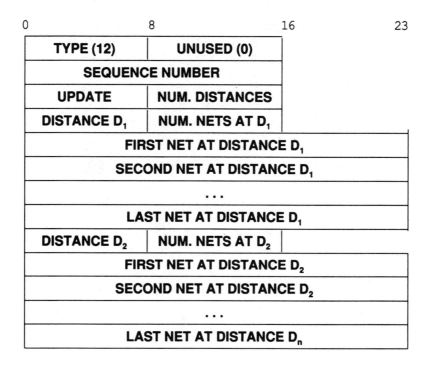

Figure 13.2 The format of GGP routing update messages. A core gateway sends such a message to advertise destination networks it knows how to reach. Network numbers contain either 1, 2, or 3 octets, depending on whether the network is class *A*, *B*, or *C*.

When a gateway receives a routing update message, it sends a GGP *acknowledgement* message back to the sender, using a positive acknowledgement if the routing update was acceptable, and a negative acknowledgement if an error was detected. Figure 13.3 illustrates the format of GGP acknowledgements.

```
0               8               16                              31
┌───────────────┬───────────────┬───────────────────────────────┐
│     TYPE      │  UNUSED (0)   │           SEQUENCE            │
└───────────────┴───────────────┴───────────────────────────────┘
```

Figure 13.3 The format of GGP acknowledgement messages. Type *2* identifies the message as a positive acknowledgement, while type *10* identifies the message as a negative acknowledgement.

In positive acknowledgement messages, the field labeled *SEQUENCE* specifies a sequence number that the receiver is acknowledging. In negative acknowledgements, the *SEQUENCE* field gives the sequence number that the receiver last received correctly.

In addition to routing update messages, the GGP protocol includes messages that allow one gateway to test whether another is responding. A gateway sends an *echo request* message to a neighbor, which requests that the recipient respond by sending back an *echo reply* message. Figure 13.4 shows the echo message formats.

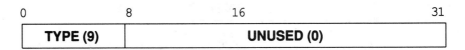

Figure 13.4 The format of GGP echo request or reply messages. Type *8* identifies the message as an echo request, while type *0* identifies the message as an echo reply.

Finally, GGP defines a *network interface status* message that allows a gateway to test a local network interface. Figure 13.5 shows the format of interface status messages.

```
0              8              16                          31
+--------------+-----------------------------------------+
|   TYPE (9)   |              UNUSED (0)                  |
+--------------+-----------------------------------------+
```

Figure 13.5 The format of GGP interface status messages. A gateway sends such messages to itself to verify that its connection to a network is operational.

13.7 Alternatives To GGP

The main disadvantage of GGP is that it does not scale well. In essence, gateways running GGP implement a distributed shortest-path computation that must converge after every change in network topology. If the computation does not converge, routing updates may keep the system in oscillation, with some routes flipping between two equal length paths. Furthermore, because the routing update messages contain an entry for every possible network, their size is proportional to the total number of networks in the Internet. Finally, GGP has a pragmatic disadvantage – it is a closed system available only within the core. Thus, while noncore gateways can send datagrams to the core to be routed, they cannot use GGP to obtain information for their routing tables.

Later versions of the core gateway code that run on Butterfly processors† use a Shortest Path First (SPF) algorithm. The idea is to replicate a complete database of network topology and connectivity in every gateway and to run a shortest path computation locally. Because the computation is local, it is both efficient and guaranteed to converge.

---

†The butterfly is a multiprocessor computer that has a special purpose, high speed interconnection among processors, designed to support packet switching. It is manufactured by Bolt, Beranek, and Newman, Inc. The transition to a new core system that uses Butterflys should be complete by the end of 1988.

Also, because each machine contains the database of all links, gateways only need to propagate information about the distance to their neighbors, which makes routing update messages smaller than those used by GGP.

13.8 Summary

Because an Internet is a loosely coupled system without central control, routing can be a problem. Hosts and most gateways contain only partial information. To ensure that all networks remain reachable with high reliability, the Internet includes a core gateway system that consists of a small set of gateways controlled by the Internet Network Operations Center. Core gateways contain complete information about networks in the Internet, and they exchange information with other core gateways periodically.

We examined the details of GGP, one protocol used to propagate routing update information throughout the core, and saw that gateways use it to send network reachability information to neighbors. Each routing update can be viewed as an advertisement that lists the set of reachable networks along with the gateway's cost to reach that network. Because GGP bases costs on a metric that measures gateway hops, a low cost path does not necessarily mean the path has the least delay or highest capacity. Thus, some gateways state artifically high costs for some paths.

One disadvantage of GGP is that it performs a distributed shortest path computation that may not converge. Another disadvantage is that GGP routing update messages grow large as the number of networks increases. Ultimately, GGP may be replaced by an algorithm that performs a shortest path computation locally.

FOR FURTHER STUDY

The definition of the core gateway system and GGP protocol in this chapter come from Hinden and Sheltzer [RFC 823]. The next chapters report on alternatives.

EXERCISES

13.1   Suppose a gateway discovers it is about to route an IP datagram back out the same network interface over which the datagram arrived. What should it do? Why?

13.2   After reading RFC 823, explain what an Internet gateway does in the situation described in the previous question.

13.3   Should core gateways use default routes? Why or why not?

13.4   Imagine students experimenting with a gateway that attaches a local area network to the Internet. They want to advertise their network to the core gateway system, but if they accidentally advertise zero length routes to arbitrary networks (e.g., the ARPANET), real Internet traffic would be diverted to their gateway. How can the core protect itself from illegal data while still accepting updates from such "untrusted" gateways?

13.5   Which ICMP messages does a gateway generate?

13.6   How do core gateways determine whether a designated neighbor is "up" or "down?" Hint: consult RFC 823.

13.7   Suppose two core gateways each advertise the same cost, k, to reach a given network, N. Describe the circumstances under which routing through one of them may take fewer hops than routing through the other one.

13.8   How does a gateway know that an incoming datagram carries a GGP message?

14

Autonomous Systems and Confederations (EGP)

14.1 Introduction

The previous chapter introduced the core gateway system and reviewed the GGP protocol that core gateways use to exchange routing information. This chapter extends our understanding of the Internet gateway system architecture. It discusses the concepts of autonomous systems and autonomous confederations and shows the protocols that a group of networks and gateways, operating under autonomous authority, use to propagate network reachability information to the core.

14.2 Adding Complexity To The Architectural Model

As we said, the core gateway system evolved at a time when the ARPANET was already in place, and part of the motivation for it was to provide connections between local area networks and the ARPANET (see Figure 13.1). If the Internet consisted of only the ARPANET plus one local area network at each ARPANET site, no further structure would be needed. Each gateway would know the single local network to which it attached and could learn about all other networks by exchanging messages with other gateways. Unfortunately, the Internet is not nearly that simple. First, even if each site had only one network, the core system would be inadequate because it cannot grow arbitrarily large. Second, many sites have multiple local area networks interconnected by local gateways. After examining the consequences of each of these ideas, we will learn how a single mechanism accommodates both.

So far, we have been thinking of the core system as a central routing mechanism to which noncore gateways can send datagrams for delivery. Having fewer core gateways than sites, however, means that we must change our view of the core or routing will be nonoptimal. To see why, consider the example in Figure 14.1

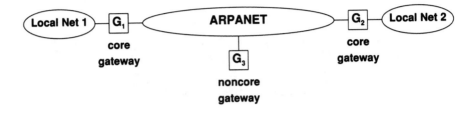

Figure 14.1 The extra hop problem. Noncore gateways must learn routes from core gateways to have optimal routing.

In the figure, core gateways G_1 and G_2 connect to networks *1* and *2*, respectively. Because they exchange routing information, they both know how to reach both networks. Suppose noncore gateway G_3 thinks of the core as a delivery system and chooses one of the core gateways, say G_1, to deliver all datagrams destined for networks to which it has no direct connection. G_3 sends datagrams for network *2* across the ARPANET to its chosen core gateway, G_1, which must then send them back across the ARPANET to gateway G_2. The optimal route, of course, requires G_3 to send datagrams destined for network *2* directly to G_2. Notice that the choice of core gateway makes no difference. Only destinations that lie beyond the chosen gateway have optimal routes; all destinations that lie beyond other gateways require an extra hop.

We call the routing anomaly illustrated in Figure 14.1 the *extra hop problem*. Solving it requires us to change our view of the core:

> *Treating the core system as a central router introduces an extra hop for most traffic. A mechanism is needed that allows noncore gateways to learn routes from core gateways so they can choose optimal routes.*

Allowing sites to have mulitple networks and gateways means that the core does not attach to all networks directly, so an additional mechanism is needed to allow the core system to learn about them. Consider, for example, the set of networks and gateways shown in Figure 14.2. We might imagine such an interconnection on a university campus, where each network corresponds to a single building or to a single department.

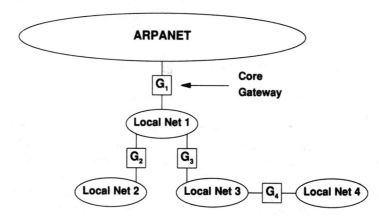

Figure 14.2 An example of multiple networks and gateways at a single AR-
PANET site. A mechanism is needed to pass reachability information about additional local networks to the core system.

Suppose the site has just installed local network *4* and has obtained an Internet address
for it. Also assume that the gateways G_2, G_3, and G_4 have routes for all four local networks as well as default routes that pass other traffic to the core gateway, G_1. Machines
directly attached to local network *4* can communicate with one another, and any machine
on that network can route packets out to Internet sites. However, because gateway G_1 attaches only to local network *1*, it does not know about local network *4*. We say that,
from the point of view of the core system, local network *4* is *hidden* behind local network
1. The important point is:

> *Because the Internet allows complex structure at each site, the core
> system does not attach directly to all networks. A mechanism is needed
> that allows noncore gateways to inform the core about hidden net-
> works.*

Keep in mind that in addition to providing the core with information about hidden networks, we need a mechanism that allows noncore gateways to obtain routing information
from the core. Ideally, a single mechanism should solve both problems. Building such a
mechanism can be tricky. The subtle issues are responsibility and capability. Exactly
where does responsibility for informing the core reside? If we decide that one of the
gateways should inform the core, which one is capable of doing it? Look again at the example. Gateway G_4 is the gateway most closely associated with local network *4*, but it
lies *1* hop away from the nearest core gateway. Thus, G_4 must depend on gateway G_3 to
route packets to network *4*. The point is that G_4 cannot guarantee reachability of local
network *4* on its own. Gateway G_3 lies zero hops from the core and can guarantee to pass
packets, but it does not directly attach to local network *4*. So, it seems incorrect to grant

G_3 responsibility for network *4*. Solving this dilemma will require us to introduce a new concept. The next sections discuss the concept and a protocol built around it.

14.3 Autonomous System Concept

The puzzle over which gateway should communicate reachability information to the core system arises because we have only considered the mechanics of the Internet and not the administrative issues. Interconnections, like those in the example of Figure 14.2, that arise when a site has a complex local structure, should not be thought of as multiple independent networks connected to the Internet, but as a single site that has multiple networks under its control. Because the networks and gateways fall under a single administrative authority, that authority can guarantee that internal routes remain consistent and viable. Furthermore, the administrative authority can choose one of its machines to serve as the machine that will apprise the core system about network reachability. In the example from Figure 14.2, because gateways G_2, G_3, and G_4 fall under control of one administrative authority, that authority can arrange to have G_3 advertise reachability for networks *2*, *3*, and *4* (the core system already knows about network *1* because a core gateway attaches directly to it).

For purposes of routing, a group of networks and gateways controlled by a single administrative authority is called an *autonomous system*. Gateways within an autonomous system are free to choose their own mechanisms for discovering, propagating, validating, and checking consistency of routes. Note that, under this definition, the core gateways form an autonomous system. We have seen that core gateways use GGP to communicate among themselves; the next chapter reviews other protocols that machines in autonomous systems can use to propagate routing information.

Conceptually, the autonomous system idea is a straightforward and natural generalization of the architecture, depicted by Figure 14.2, with autonomous systems replacing local area networks. Figure 14.3 illustrates the idea.

To make networks that are hidden inside autonomous systems reachable throughout the Internet, each autonomous system must agree to advertise network reachability to other autonomous systems. Although advertisements can be sent to any autonomous system, it is crucial that each autonomous system propagate information to a core gateway. Usually, one gateway in the autonomous system takes responsibility for advertising routes and interacts directly with one of the core gateways. It is possible, however, to have several gateways each advertise for a subset of the networks.

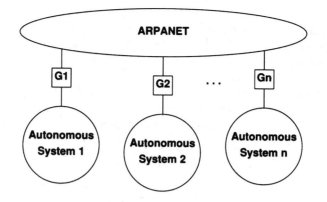

Figure 14.3 The Internet architecture with autonomous systems at ARPANET
sites. Each autonomous system consists of multiple networks and
gateways under a single administrative authority.

It may seem that our definition of an autonomous system is vague, but in practice,
the boundaries between autonomous systems must be precise to allow automated algorithms to make routing decisions. For example, an autonomous system owned by a corporation may choose not to route packets through an autonomous system owned by
another even though they connect directly. To make it possible for automated routing algorithms to distinguish among autonomous systems, each is assigned an *autonomous system number* by the same central authority that is charged with assigning all Internet network addresses. When two gateways exchange network reachability information, the
messages carry the autonomous system identifier that the gateway represents.

We can summarize these ideas:

> *The Internet treats a site that has a complex set of networks and gate-
> ways operating under one administrative authority as single auto-
> nomous system. An autonomous system must collect reachability infor-
> mation for its networks internally and choose machine(s) to pass that
> reachability information to other autonomous systems. In particular,
> every autonomous system must pass reachability information to core
> gateways.*

The next section presents the details of the protocol gateways use to advertise network
reachability. Later sections return to architectural questions to discuss an important restriction on routing. They also show how the Internet model can be extended.

14.4 Exterior Gateway Protocol

Two gateways that exchange routing information are said to be *exterior neighbors* if they belong to two different autonomous systems, and *interior neighbors* if they belong to the same autonomous system. The protocol exterior gateways use to advertise reachability information to other autonomous systems is called the *exterior gateway protocol* or *EGP*. EGP is especially important because autonomous systems use it to advertise reachability information to the core system.

Figure 14.4 illustrates how exterior neighbors use EGP.

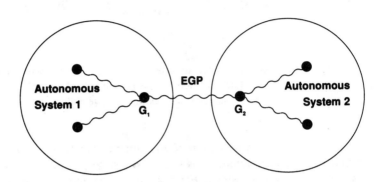

Figure 14.4 Two exterior gateways G_1 and G_2 using EGP to advertise reachability to each other's autonomous system once they have collected the information from within their autonomous systems. As the name implies, *exterior* gateways are usually close to the outer "edge" of an autonomous system.

EGP has three main features. First, it supports a *neighbor acquisition* mechanism that allows one gateway to request another to agree that the two should communicate reachability information. We say that the first gateway *acquires* an *EGP peer* or an *EGP neighbor*. EGP peers are neighbors only in the sense that they will exchange routing information; there is no notion of geographic proximity. Second, a gateway continually tests whether its EGP neighbors are responding. Third, EGP neighbors periodically exchange network reachability information by passing *routing update messages*.

14.5 EGP Message Header

To accommodate the three basic functions, EGP defines nine messages as the following table shows:

EGP Message	Description
Acquisition Request	Requests gateway become a neighbor (peer)
Acquisition Confirm	Positive response to acquisition request
Acquisition Refuse	Negative response to acquisition request
Cease Request	Requests termination of neighbor relation
Cease Confirm	Confirmation response to cease request
Hello Request	Requests neighbor to respond if alive
I-Heard-You	Response to hello message
Poll Request	Requests network routing update
Routing Update	Network reachability information
Error	Response to incorrect message

All EGP messages begin with a fixed header that identifies the message type. Figure 14.5 shows the EGP header format.

```
0               8               16                       31
+---------------+---------------+-------------+-----------+
|   VERSION     |     TYPE      |    CODE     |  STATUS   |
+---------------+---------------+-------------+-----------+
|         CHECKSUM              |  AUTONOMOUS SYSTEM NUM.  |
+------------------------------+--------------------------+
|    SEQUENCE NUMBER           |
+------------------------------+
```

Figure 14.5 The fixed header that precedes every EGP message.

The header field labeled *VERSION* contains an integer that identifies the version of EGP used to format the message. Receivers check the version number to verify that their software is using the same version of the protocol as the message. Field *TYPE* identifies the type of the message, with the *CODE* field used to distinguish among subtypes. The *STATUS* field contains message-dependent status information.

EGP uses a checksum to verify that the message arrives intact. EGP uses the same checksum algorithm as IP, treating the entire EGP message as a sequence of 16-bit integers and taking the one's complement of the one's complement sum. When performing the computation, field *CHECKSUM* is assumed to contain zeros, and the message is padded to a multiple of 16 bits by adding zeros.

The field labeled *AUTONOMOUS SYSTEM NUM.* gives the assigned number of the autonomous system of the gateway sending the message, and the *SEQUENCE NUMBER* field contains a number that the sender uses to synchronize messages and replies. A gateway establishes an initial sequence value when acquiring a neighbor and increments the sequence number each time it sends a message. The neighbor replies with the last sequence number it received, allowing the sender to match responses to transmissions.

14.6 EGP Neighbor Acquisition Messages

A gateway sends *neighbor acquisition* messages to establish communication with another gateway. Note that EGP does not specify why or how one gateway chooses another gateway as its neighbor. We assume that such choices are made by the organizations responsible for administering the gateways, and not by the protocol software.

In addition to the standard header with a sequence number, neighbor acquisition messages contain initial values for a time interval to be used for testing whether the neighbor is alive (called a *hello interval*) and a *polling interval* that controls the maximum frequency of routing updates. The sender supplies a polling interval of *n* to specify that the receiver should not poll more often than every *n* seconds†. The original sender can change the polling interval dynamically as time passes. Furthermore, the polling intervals that peers use can be asymmetric, allowing one peer to poll more frequently than another. Figure 14.6 shows the format of acquisition messages and responses.

0	8	16	31
VERSION	TYPE (3)	CODE	STATUS
CHECKSUM		AUTONOMOUS SYSTEM NUM.	
SEQUENCE NUMBER		HELLO INTERVAL	
POLL INTERVAL			

Figure 14.6 EGP neighbor acquisition message format. Fields beyond the header specify initial parameters used by the protocol.

The *CODE* field identifies the specific message as the following table shows:

Code	Meaning
0	Acquisition Request
1	Acquisition Confirm
2	Acquisition Refuse
3	Cease Request
4	Cease Confirm

14.7 EGP Neighbor Reachability Messages

EGP permits two forms of testing whether a neighbor is alive. In active mode, gateways test neighbors by periodically sending *Hello* messages along with *poll* messages and waiting for responses. In passive mode, a gateway depends on its neighbor to periodically send *hello* or *poll* messages. A gateway operating in passive mode uses information from the *status field* of a reachability message (see below) to deduce whether

---

†In practice, most implementations use the polling interval as the exact frequency at which they send poll requests.

the peer is alive and whether the peer knows it is alive. Usually both gateways in a pair operate in active mode.

Separating the calculation of neighbor reachability from routing information exchanges is important because it leads to lower network overhead. Because network routing information does not change as frequently as the status of individual gateway machines, it need not be passed frequently. Furthermore, neighbor reachability messages are small and require little computation overhead, while routing exchange messages are large and require much computation. Thus, by separating the two tests, neighbors can be tested frequently without incurring much computational or communication overhead. Figure 14.7 shows that neighbor reachability requests consist of only the EGP message header.

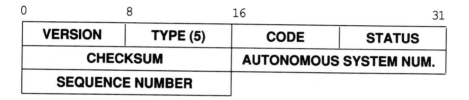

Figure 14.7 EGP neighbor reachability message format. Code *0* specifies a Hello request message, while code *1* specifies an I-Heard-You response.

Because it is possible for Hello messages or I-Heard-you responses to be lost in transit, EGP uses a form of the k-out-of-n rule to determine whether a peer has changed from "up" to "down." The best way to think of the algorithm is to imagine a gateway sending a continuous sequence of Hello messages and receiving I-Heard-You responses, and think of a window spanning the last n exchanges. At least k of the last n exchanges must fail for the gateway to declare its neighbor down, and at least j must succeed for the gateway to declare that the neighbor is up, once it has been declared down. The protocol standard suggests values for j and k that imply two successive messages must be lost (received) before EGP will declare the peer down (up).

The hysteresis introduced by j and k have an important effect on the overall performance of EGP. As with any routing algorithm, EGP should not propagate unnecessary changes. The reason is simple: changes do not stop after a gateway propagates them to its EGP peer. The peer may propagate them to other gateways as well. Minimizing changes is crucial when the core system is involved because the core gateways use a distributed shortest path computation that requires many exchanges before the data in all gateways becomes consistent. If exterior gateways propagate new reachability information whenever an update is lost, they will keep the core in continual transition.

14.8 EGP Poll Request Messages

The *poll request* and *poll response* messages allow a gateway to obtain reachability information. Figure 14.8 shows the message formats.

0	8	16	31
VERSION	TYPE (2)	CODE (0)	STATUS
CHECKSUM		AUTONOMOUS SYSTEM NUM.	
SEQUENCE NUMBER		RESERVED	
IP SOURCE NETWORK			

Figure 14.8 EGP poll message format. Code *0* specifies a Hello request message, while code *1* specifies an I-Heard-You response.

The field labeled *IP SOURCE NETWORK* specifies a network common to the autonomous systems to which both gateways belong. The routing update message will contain routes that have distances measured with respect to gateways on the specified IP source network.

It may be difficult to understand why EGP chooses to make a polling request specify a network. There are two reasons. First, recall that a gateway connects to two or more physical networks. If an application on the gateway implements EGP, it may not know over which interface EGP requests arrive. Thus, it may not know to which network the request refers. Second, gateways that run EGP often collect information for an entire autonomous system. When advertising network reachability, they must specify pairs of destination network and gateway to use to reach that destination. The gateway that should be used to reach a destination depends on where traffic enters the autonomous system. Thus, the network mentioned in the polling request specifies the point at which packets will enter the autonomous system. Figure 14.9 illustrates the idea of a common network used as a base for reachability information.

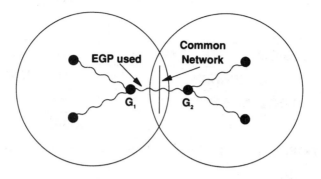

Figure 14.9 Gateways in two autonomous systems using EGP to communicate
network reachability information. Reachability messages specify
gateways on a network common to both systems and destinations
reachable via those gateways.

14.9 EGP Routing Update Messages

An exterior gateway sends a *routing update* message to convey information about
reachable networks to its EGP neighbor. Usually, the gateway has collected the information and is making that information available to a gateway in another autonomous system. In principle a gateway running EGP could report two types of reachability to a peer.
The first type consists of destination networks that are reachable entirely within the
gateway's autonomous system. The second type consists of destination networks that the
gateway has learned about, but which lie beyond the gateway's autonomous system
boundary.

It is important to understand that EGP does not permit an arbitrary gateway to advertise reachability to an arbitrary destination network. The restriction limits gateways to
advertising only those destinations for which it is an authority. That is:

> *EGP restricts noncore gateways to advertise only those networks
> reachable entirely from within the gateway's autonomous system.*

This rule, sometimes called the *EGP third party restriction* is intended to control the propagation of information and allow each autonomous system to choose exactly how it advertises reachability. For example, if each university campus forms an autonomous system, a gateway on a given university campus might collect information about networks
on that campus and advertise them to the core, but it would not advertise routes to networks on other campuses. Naturally, the restriction does not apply to the core system.

Figure 14.10 illustrates the format of routing update messages.

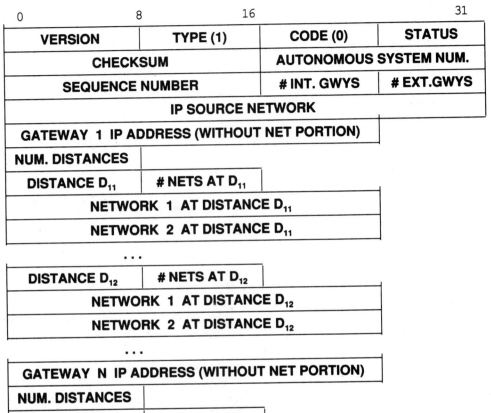

Figure 14.10 EGP routing update message format. All routes are given relative to a specified network. The message lists gateways on that network and the cost of reaching destinations through each. Network addresses contain *1, 2,* or *3* octets.

The fields labeled *# INT. GWYS* and *# EXT. GWYS* give the number of interior and exterior gateways appearing in the message. Distinguishing between interior and exterior gateways allows the recipient to know whether distances are comparable. Unfortunately, it is impossible to make such a distinction based on gateway addresses alone and there is no provision in the message for such a distinction. In practice, EGP implementations ovecome the problem by sending separate update messages for interior and exterior gateways. The field labeled *IP SOURCE NETWORK* gives the network from which all reachability is measured.

In a sense, EGP routing update messages are a generalization of GGP routing update messages because they accommodate multiple gateways instead of a single gateway. Thus, the fields of the routing update message following the *IP SOURCE NETWORK* form a sequence of blocks, where each block gives reachability information for one of the gateways on the source network. A block begins with the IP address of a gateway. The networks reachable from that gateway are listed along with their distance. Just like GGP, EGP groups networks into sets based on "distance." For each distance, there is a count of networks at that distance followed by the list of network addresses. After the list of all networks at a given distance, the pattern is repeated for all distance values.

14.10 The Key Restriction Of EGP

We have already seen that EGP restricts noncore gateways, allowing them to advertise only those destination networks reachable entirely within the gateway's autonomous system. However, there is a more fundamental limitation imposed on EGP:

> *EGP does not interpret any of the distance metrics that appear in routing update messages.*

The rules specify that a value of *255* means the network is unreachable, but other values are only comparable if they refer to gateways in the same autonomous system. In essence, EGP uses the distance field to specify whether a path exists; the value cannot be used to compute the shorter of two routes unless those routes are both contained within a single autonomous system.

We can now see why a gateway in one autonomous system should not advertise reachability to networks in another autonomous system (i.e., why the third party rule exists). The essential observation is this: when the gateway learned of a network in another autonomous system, it did not obtain a universally accepted measure of distance. Therefore, it should not pass that measure on to the core. Advertising reachability with EGP is equivalent to saying "my autonomous system provides *the* path to this network." There is no way for the gateway to say "my autonomous system provides a high cost path to this network."

Looking at interpretation of distances another way allows us to realize that EGP cannot be used as a routing algorithm. In particular, even if a gateway learns about two different routes to the same network, it cannot know which is shorter. Without routing information, we must be careful to advertise only the route we want traffic to follow. As a result, there will only be one path from the core to any network. We can summarize:

> *Because EGP only propagates reachability information, it restricts the topology of any Internet using EGP to a tree structure in which a single core gateway system forms the root, and there are no loops among other autonomous systems connected to it.*

The key point here is that the current Internet architecture uses a centralized core gateway system, and it cannot change until EGP changes.

The restriction on EGP that produces a tree structure results partially from the historical evolution of an Internet based around the ARPANET. Although it may seem innocuous, the restriction has some surprising consequences:

1. Universal connectivity fails if the core gateway system fails. Of course, it is unlikely the entire core will fail simultaneously, but there have been interesting examples of minor failures. In particular, on several occasions the rapid growth of the Internet resulted in table overflows in core gateways, preventing EGP from successfully installing routes to new networks. Those network addresses that could not be installed in the core tables remain unreachable from many parts of the Internet.

2. The core gateway system can have only one active connection to a given autonomous system. That is, at any given instant, all traffic routed from the core to networks in the autonomous system will traverse one path, even if multiple physical connections are present. Also note that the core will only use one return path even if the autonomous system divides outgoing traffic among two or more paths, making delay and throughput between a pair of machines asymmetric, and making the network difficult to debug.

3. EGP does not support load sharing on gateways between arbitrary autonomous systems. If two autonomous systems have multiple gateways connecting them, one would like to balance the traffic equally between all gateways. EGP allows autonomous systems to divide the load by network (e.g., to partition themselves into multiple subsets and have multiple gateways advertise partitions), but it does not support load sharing.

4. As a special case of point 3, EGP is inadequate for routing among long haul networks that have multiple interconnection points to the ARPANET. For example, the NSFnet or Cypress networks, described in Chapter 2, must designate a single path from the core to machines on a given network, even though there are multiple physical connections between the networks.

5. It is difficult to switch to alternate physical paths if one fails, especially when the paths cross two or more autonomous systems. Because EGP does not interpret distances, third parties cannot advertise routes and rely on the core to switch to an alternate if one fails. Instead, responsiblility for selecting the least cost route falls to the exterior gateways that advertise reachability.

14.11 Problems Addressed In EGP2/EGP3

EGP has several weaknesses, many of which are trivial technicalities. The weaknesses must be repaired before EGP can support the rapidly expanding Internet environment. Some problems are addressed by a new version of the protocol called *EGP2*, *EGP3*, or humorously referred to as *Son Of EGP*. The most pressing problem EGP3 solves concerns the size of update messages. Recall from Figure 14.10 that update messages contain long lists of networks. For large autonomous systems, those with many gateways and many networks, the size of a single EGP routing update message can be too large for some networks or gateways to handle. In the past, not all gateways handled fragmentation and reassembly, so it was sometimes impossible to transfer routing update messages. The new version of the protocol allows the sender to divide routing updates into multiple messages.

14.12 Decentralization Of The Internet Architecture

Two important architecture questions remain unanswered. The first focuses on centralization: how can the Internet architecture be modified to remove dependence on the (centralized) core gateway system? The second concerns levels of trust: can the Internet architecture be expanded to allow closer cooperation (trust) between some autonomous systems than between others?

Removing the dependence on the core system will not be easy. The Internet continues to evolve, but its centralized roots are evident in many protocols. As more software is built using existing protocols, inertia increases and change becomes more difficult and expensive. More important, unlike many autonomous systems, the core is reliable and supported by a professional staff. Finally, as the size of the Internet grows, so does the volume of routing information that gateways must keep. A mechanism must be found to limit the information needed by each node, or the update traffic will inundate the network.

14.13 The Autonomous Confederation Concept

Extending the notions of trust between autonomous systems is complex. The easiest step is to group autonomous systems hierarchically. Imagine, for example, three autonomous systems in three separate academic departments on a large university campus. It is natural to group these three together into one *autonomous confederation*. The motivation for hierarchical grouping comes primarily from the notion of trust. Gateways within an autonomous confederation trust one another with a high level of confidence. Thus, they are able to relax the usual EGP constraint that prohibits loops in the connection topology while still being able to guarantee that no routing loops occur.

To implement the autonomous confederation concept requires only minor changes to EGP. New versions of EGP must agree to use an artificial scaling factor when reporting hop counts, allowing counts to be increased when passed across the boundary from one autonomous confederation to another. The technique, loosely called *metric transformation*, partitions distance values into three categories. For example, suppose gateways within an autonomous system use distance values less than 128. We could make the rule that when passing distance information across an autonomous system boundary within a single autonomous confederation, the distances must be transformed into the range of 128 to 191. Finally, we could make the rule that when passing distance values across the boundary between two autonomous confederations, the values must be transformed into the range of 192 to 255. The effect of such transformations is obvious: for any given destination network, any path that lies entirely within the autonomous system is guaranteed to have lower cost than a path that strays outside the autonomous system. Furthermore, among all paths that stray outside the autonomous system, those that remain within the autonomous coonfederation have lower cost than those that cross autonomous confederation boundaries. The key advantages of metric transformations are that it uses an extant protocol, EGP, still allows an autonomous system to choose its own distance metrics, but allows some interpretation of distances between autonomous systems.

14.14 Summary

The Internet is composed of a set of autonomous systems, where each autonomous system consists of gateways and networks under one administrative authority. Autonomous systems use the Exterior Gateway Protocol to advertise routes to other autonomous systems. Specifically, autonomous systems must advertise reachability to the core gateway system for all destinations to be reachable from all sources. We saw that EGP supports three basic functions: neighbor (peer) acquisition, testing reachability of neighbors, and advertising network reachability to neighbors.

The Internet architecture consists of a central, connected piece (built around the AR-PANET and NSFnet backbone), with autonomous systems connected to the center in a tree structure topology. The core gateway system is part of the central piece, while the ''fringe'' consists of local area networks that have only a single connection to the rest of the Internet. Moving from a centralized architecture to a completely distributed one will require substantial changes in protocols like EGP.

FOR FURTHER STUDY

Mills [RFC 904] contains the formal EGP protocol specification. An early version of EGP was given in Rosen [RFC 827], which also discusses the restriction to tree structured topologies. Additional background can be found in the NSF gateway requirements document [RFC 888] and Mills [RFC 975]. Braden and Postel [RFC 1009] discuss requirements for Internet gateways and outline some of the problems with EGP (also see the predecessor, in RFC 985). Finally, Kirton [RFC 911] describes the widely used implementation of EGP that runs under Berkeley 4.3 BSD UNIX.

EXERCISES

14.1   If your site connects to the Internet, find out which machine(s) advertise routes to the core gateway system.

14.2   Implementations of EGP use a "hold down" mechanism that causes the protocol to delay accepting an *acquisition request* from a neighbor for a fixed time following the receipt of a *cease request* message from that neighbor. Read the protocol specification to find out why.

14.3   For the networks in Figure 14.2, which machine(s) should run EGP? Why?

14.4   The formal specification of EGP includes a finite state machine that explains how EGP operates. Why does a *confirm* message take the EGP finite state machine from the *acquisition* state to the *down* state, instead of from the *acquisition* state to the *up* state?

14.5   What happens if a gateway in an autonomous system sends EGP routing update messages to the core, claiming to be the gateway used to reach every destination?

14.6   Can two autonomous systems establish a routing loop by sending EGP updates messages to one another?

14.7   Should gateways treat EGP separately from their own routing tables? For example, should a gateway ever advertise reachability if it has not installed a route to that network in its routing table? Why or why not?

15

Interior Gateway Protocols (RIP, HELLO, GATED)

15.1 Introduction

The previous chapter introduced the autonomous system concept and examined the Exterior Gateway Protocol that a gateway uses to advertise networks within its system to other autonomous systems including the core. This chapter completes our overview of the Internet gateway system by examining how a gateway in an autonomous system learns about other networks within its autonomous system.

15.2 Static Vs. Dynamic Interior Routes

Two gateways within an autonomous system are said to be *interior* to one another. For example, two LSI-11 core gateways are interior to one another because the core forms a single autonomous system. Two gateways on a university campus are considered interior to one another as long as machines on the campus are collected into a single autonomous system.

How can one gateway in an autonomous system learn about networks in that autonomous system, so it can advertise them to other systems? The simplest scheme is manual. The administrator keeps a table of networks and updates the table whenever a new network is added to, or deleted from, the autonomous system. The disadvantages of a manual system are obvious; manual systems cannot accommodate rapid growth or rapid change.

To automate the task of keeping network reachability information accurate, interior gateways usually communicate with one another, exchanging either network reachability data or network routing information from which reachability can be deduced. Once the reachability information for an entire autonomous system has been assembled, one of the gateways in that autonomous system can advertise it to other autonomous systems using EGP.

Unlike exterior gateway communication, for which EGP provides a widely accepted standard, no single protocol has emerged for use within an autonomous system. Part of the reason for diversity comes from diverse topologies and technologies used in autonomous systems. Part of the reason stems from the lack of an early standard that was both functionally adequate and well defined. As a result, a handful of protocols have become popular; most autonomous systems use one of them to propagate reachability information internally. Each of the protocols has advantages and disadvantages.

Because there is no single standard, we use the term *interior gateway protocol* or *IGP* as a generic description that refers to any algorithm that interior gateways use when they exchange network reachability and routing information. For example, the core gateways form a somewhat specialized autonomous system that uses GGP as its Interior Gateway Protocol. Some autonomous systems use EGP as their IGP, although this seldom makes sense for small autonomous systems that span local area networks with broadcast capability.

Figure 15.1 illustrates an autonomous system using an IGP to propagate reachability among interior gateways.

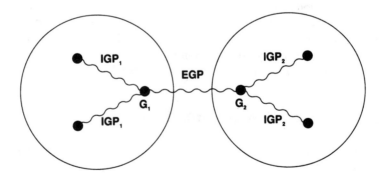

Figure 15.1 Conceptual view of two autonomous systems using EGP to communicate between exterior gateways and each using its own IGP to communicate within the system. In practice, EGP specifies distances with respect to a common network.

In the figure, *IGP₁* refers to the interior gateway protocol within autonomous system *1*, and *IGP₂* refers to the protocol used within autonomous system *2*. The figure also illustrates an important idea:

A single gateway may use two different reachability protocols simul-
taneously, one for communication outside its autonomous system and
another for communication within its autonomous system.

In particular, gateways that run EGP to advertise reachability, usually also need to run an IGP to obtain information from within their autonomous system.

15.3 Routing Information Protocol (RIP)

The most widely used IGP is the *Routing Information Protocol* (RIP), better known by the name of a program that implements it, *routed*†. The *routed* software was original-ly designed at the University of California at Berkeley to provide consistent routing and reachability information among machines on their local network. It relies on physical network broadcast to make routing exchanges quickly. It was never intended to be used on large, long haul networks (although it now is).

Based on earlier internetworking research done at Xerox Corporation's Palo Alto Research Center (PARC), *routed* implements a protocol derived from the Xerox *NS Routing Information Protocol*, but generalizes it to cover multiple families of networks.

Despite minor improvements over its predecessors, the popularity of RIP as an IGP does not arise from its technical merits. Instead, it has resulted because Berkeley distri-buted *routed* software along with their popular 4.X BSD UNIX systems. Thus, many In-ternet sites adopted and installed *routed* and started using RIP without even considering its technical merits or limitations. Once installed and running, it became the basis for lo-cal routing, and research groups adopted it for larger networks. For example, the Cypress network, described in Chapter 2, uses RIP to propagate network reachability among all its machines.

Perhaps the most startling fact about RIP is that it was built and widely distributed with no formal standard. Most implementations have been derived from the Berkeley code, with interoperability limited by the programmer's understanding of undocumented details and subtleties. As new versions appear, more problems arise.

The underlying RIP protocol is straightforward. It arranges to have gateways broad-cast their current routing database to neighbors periodically. As with GGP and EGP, the message lists each destination along with a distance to that destination measured in gate-way hops. Unlike EGP, the RIP hop count is reported relative to the sender's active rout-ing table. That is, RIP messages do not list a gateway nor do they list networks relative to a specific gateway.

A RIP implementation must handle three kinds of errors that the protocol does not explicitly cover. First, because the protocol does not detect routing loops, the implemen-tation must either assume participants can be trusted or take precautions to prevent such loops. Second, the protocol uses a hop count of *15* to denote infinity. Thus, an imple-mentation of RIP must either avoid or use alternative protocols for cases where hop counts approach *15*. (Indeed, the small limit on hop counts makes RIP unsuitable for

---

†The name comes from the UNIX convention of attaching "d" to the names of daemon processes; it is pronounced "route d".

large networks.) Third, the algorithm used by RIP creates a so called *slow convergence* or *count to infinity* problem in which inconsistencies arise, because routing update messages propagate slowly across the network. (Choosing *15* as the value of infinity helps limit slow convergence.)

Inconsistency is not unique to RIP. It happens with any routing protocol in which messages carry only pairs of destination network and distance to that network. To understand the problem consider a set of gateways depicted in Figure 15.2.

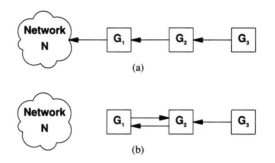

Figure 15.2 The slow convergence problem. In (a) each gateway has a route to network N. In (b) the route to N has vanished, but G_2 and G_3 still advertise it.

Part (a) of the figure shows three gateways that have a route to network N, as well as a correct distance to that network. In part (b) the connection between gateway G_1 and network N has failed. G_1 examines the information it has collected and finds that G_2 has a length *1* route to gateway N. Therefore, G_1 calculates that it now takes *2* hops to reach N, changes its routing tables, and begins to route traffic destined for N to G_2. A routing loop results. In the next round of routing exchanges, G_2 learns that G_1 now has a length *2* route to N, so it calculates a new length for the route to N. In the third round, G_1 increments its length, continuing the count to infinity.

For the example in Figure 15.2, it is possible to solve the slow convergence problem by using a technique known as *split horizon update*. When using split horizons, a gateway records the interface over which it received a particular route and does not propagate its higher cost route back over that interface. In the example, gateway G_2 would not advertise its length *1* route back to gateway G_1, so when G_1 loses connectivity to network N, it would stop advertising a route. After a few rounds of routing updates, all machines would agree that the network is unreachable. However, splitting the horizon does not cover all topologies as one of the exercises suggests.

Another way to think of the slow convergence problem is in terms of information flow. If a gateway advertises a short route to some network, all receiving gateways respond quickly to install that route. When a gateway finds that a destination is unreachable, it does not propagate the information directly. Instead, it considers alternatives, chooses the best available, and propagates that information. It cannot know if the alternative depended on the route that just disappeared. A short epigram captures the idea and explains the phenomenon:

Good news travels quickly; bad news travels slowly.

One technique used to solve the slow convergence problem uses a *hold down*. Hold down forces a participating gateway to ignore information about a network for a fixed period of time following receipt of a message that claims the network is unreachable. Typically, the hold down period is set to 60 seconds. The idea is to wait long enough to ensure that all machines receive the bad news and not to mistakenly accept a message that is out of date. It should be noted that all machines participating in a RIP exchange need to use identical notions of hold down, or routing loops can occur. The disadvantage of a hold down technique is that if routing loops occur, they will be preserved for the duration of the hold down period. More important, the hold down technique preserves all incorrect routes during the hold down period, even when alternatives exist.

The use of broadcast, potential for routing loops, and use of hold down to prevent slow convergence can make RIP extremely inefficient in a wide area network. Broadcasting always takes substantial bandwidth. Having all machines broadcast periodically means that the traffic increases as the number of gateways increases. The potential for routing loops can also be deadly when line capacity is limited. Once lines become saturated by looping packets, it may be difficult or impossible for gateways to exchange the routing messages needed to break the loops. Also, in a wide area network, hold down periods are so long that the timers used by higher level protocols can expire and lead to broken connections. Despite these well known problems, many groups continue to use RIP as an IGP in wide area networks.

15.4 RIP Message Format

RIP messages can be broadly classified into two types: routing messages and debugging messages used to control tracing. We will ignore debugging messages and discuss only routing messages.

All RIP messages consist of a fixed header followed by an optional list of network reachability. Figure 15.3 shows the message format:

0	8	16	31

COMMAND	VERSION	RESERVED	
FAMILY OF NET 1		NET 1 ADDR., OCTETS 1 - 2	
NET 1 ADDRESS, OCTETS 3 - 6			
NET 1 ADDRESS, OCTETS 7 - 10			
NET 1 ADDRESS, OCTETS 11 - 14			
DISTANCE OF NETWORK 1			
FAMILY OF NET 2		NET 2 ADDR., OCTETS 1 - 2	
NET 2 ADDRESS, OCTETS 3 - 6			
NET 2 ADDRESS, OCTETS 7 - 10			
NET 2 ADDRESS, OCTETS 11 - 14			
DISTANCE OF NETWORK 2			

. . .

Figure 15.3 The format of RIP routing messages that contain a sequence of pairs where each pair consists of a network address and distance to that network.

In the figure, field *COMMAND* specifies the contents of the packet as a request for routing information (*1*) or a response (*2*). Usually, gateways broadcast unsolicited response packets periodically.

Field *VERSION* contains the protocol version number and is used by the receiver to verify it will interpret the message correctly.

The RIP message format is not limited to the Internet; it can be used with multiple network protocol families. The field labeled *FAMILY OF NET i* identifies the protocol family under which the network address should be interpreted, using integers assigned to address families under 4.X BSD UNIX.

The generality of RIP is also evident in the way it transmits network addresses. As Figure 15.3 shows, each network reported by RIP can have an address of up to 14 octets. Of course, Internet addresses need only 4, so the remaining octets are unused.

The final field of each entry in a RIP routing update, labeled *DISTANCE OF NET i*, contains an integer count of the distance of the specified network. Distances are measured in gateway hops, as in GGP. RIP retains the convention that distance count *15* means infinity. Thus, RIP is limited to autonomous systems that are small enough to report distances using small integers.

15.5 HELLO Protocol As An IGP

Using GGP, or RIP as an interior gateway protocol limits routing to a metric based on hop count. Often, hop counts provide only a crude measure of network response or capacity that does not produce optimal routes. Furthermore, computing routes on the basis of minimum hop counts has the severe disadvantage that it makes routing relatively static because routes cannot respond to changes in network load.

The HELLO protocol provides an example of an IGP that uses a routing metric based on network delay instead of hop count. HELLO is especially important to the Internet because it is the IGP used among LSI-11 "fuzzball" gateways that form the NSFnet backbone. Other autonomous systems in the Internet use it as well.

HELLO provides two functions: it synchronizes the clocks among a set of machines, and it allows each machine to compute shortest delay paths to destinations. Thus, HELLO messages carry timestamp information as well as routing information. The basic idea behind HELLO is simple: each machine participating in the HELLO exchange maintains a table of its best estimate of the clock in neighboring machines. Before transmitting a packet, a machine adds its timestamp by copying the current clock value into the packet. When a packet arrives, the receiver computes the current delay on the link. To do so, the receiver subtracts the timestamp on the incoming packet from its estimate for the current clock in the neighbor. Periodically, machines poll their neighbors to reestablish estimates for clocks.

HELLO messages also allow participating machines to compute new routes. The algorithm works much like RIP but uses delay instead of hop count. Each machine periodically sends its neighbor a table of estimated delay for all other machines. Suppose machine *A* sends machine *B* a routing table that specifies destinations and delays. *B* examines each entry in the table. It then reroutes traffic to *A* for all destinations that have delay from *B* much higher than the delay from *A* plus the delay required to reach *A*. That is, *B* sends traffic to *A* as long as taking that path shortens delay.

As in any routing algorithm, HELLO cannot change routes too rapidly, or it would become unstable. Instabilities in routing algorithms produce a two-stage oscillation effect in which traffic switches back and forth between alternate paths. In the first stage, the machines find a lightly loaded path and abruptly switch their traffic onto it, only to find that it becomes completely overloaded. In the second stage, the machines switch traffic away from the overloaded path, only to find that it becomes the least loaded path, and the cycle continues. Such oscillations do occur. To avoid them, implementations of HELLO choose to change routes only when the difference in delays is large.

Figure 15.4 shows the HELLO message format. The protocol is more complex than the message format shows because it distinguishes local network connections from those multiple hops away, times out stale entries in its routing tables, and uses local identifiers for hosts instead of full Internet addresses.

0	8	16	24	31

CHECKSUM		DATE		
TIME				
TIMESTAMP		DISP	HOSTS (n)	
DELAY$_1$		OFFSET$_1$		
DELAY$_2$		OFFSET$_2$		

. . .

DELAY$_n$		OFFSET$_n$		

Figure 15.4 The format of HELLO messages. Each message carries an entry
for the date and time as well as a timestamp that the protocol uses
to estimate network delays.

Field *CHECKSUM* contains a checksum over the message, field *DATE* contains the local
date of the sender, and field *TIME* contains the local time according to the sender's
clock, whereas the *TIMESTAMP* field is used in round trip computation.

The field labeled *HOSTS* specifies how many entries follow in the list of hosts and
the field labeled *DISP* points into the list to mark the block of entries used for the local
network. Each entry contains two fields, *DELAY* and *OFFSET*, that give the delay to
reach a host, and the sender's current estimate of the offest between the host's clock and
the sender's clock.

15.6 Combining RIP, Hello, And EGP

We have already observed that a single gateway may use both an IGP to gather routing information within its autonomous system and EGP to advertise routes to other autonomous systems. In principle, it should be easy to construct a single piece of software
that combines the two protocols, making it possible to gather routes and advertise them
without human intervention. In practice, technical and political obstacles make doing so
complex.

Technically, IGP protocols, like RIP and Hello, are routing protocols that build new
routes for a machine based on messages received from other machines in its autonomous
system, while EGP works in addition to the gateway's usual routing tables. Thus, the
UNIX program that implements RIP, *routed*, changes routing tables in the operating system directly, trusting those machines that use it to pass correct data.

Politically, gateways using EGP to advertise reachability must take care to only propagate those routes it is authorized to advertise, or it may affect other parts of the Internet. For example, if one machine in an autonomous system happens to propagate a distance *0* route to, let's say Purdue University, when it has no such route, RIP will install

the route in other machines and start passing Purdue traffic to the gateway that made the error. As a result, it may be impossible for machines in the autonomous system to reach Purdue. If EGP propagates such errors outside the autonomous system, it may become impossible to reach Purdue from some parts of the Internet.

Written at Cornell University, the UNIX program *gated*† combines RIP, Hello, and EGP along with a set of rules that constrains how it advertises routes to exterior gateways. *Gated* accepts RIP or Hello messages and modifies the local machine routing tables just like the *routed* program, and it advertises routes from within its autonomous system using EGP. The rules allow the systems administrator to specify exactly which networks *gated* may and may not advertise and how to report distances to those networks. Thus, although *gated* is not an IGP, it plays an important role in gateway routing because it demonstrates that it is feasible to build an automated mechanism linking an IGP with EGP without sacrificing protection.

Gated performs another useful task by implementing metric transformations. Recall from Chapter 14 that the proposed extensions to EGP allow autonomous systems to make intelligent routing decisions as long as all gateways using EGP agree to a loose interpretation of distance metrics. In particular, the gateways within an autonomous system must agree to use distance values below a fixed threshold, say 128. Whenever an exterior gateway advertises reachability outside its autonomous system but inside its autonomous confederation, it must transform the distance metrics into a higher range, say 128-191. The transformation tends to keep traffic within an autonomous system by artifically raising the cost to route outside. Finally, gateways transform distances into an even higher range, say 192-255, when passing them across an autonomous confederation boundary to encourage traffic to remain within an autonomous confederation, if possible. Because *gated* provides the interface between its autonomous system and other autonomous systems, it can implement such transformations easily.

15.7 Routing With Partial Information

We began our discussion of Internet gateway architecture by discussing the concept of partial information. Hosts can route with only partial information because they rely on gateways. It should now be clear that not all gateways have complete information. Most autonomous systems have a single gateway that forms a bridge, connecting the autonomous system to the rest of the Internet. Gateways within the autonomous system know about destinations within that autonomous system, but they route all other traffic to the bridge.

Routing with partial information becomes obvious if we examine a gateway's routing tables. Gateways in the core system have a complete set of routes to all possible destinations; they do not use default routing. In fact, if a destination network address does not appear in the core tables, only two possibilities exist: either the address is not a valid Internet address, or the address is valid but currently unreachable (e.g., because the only gateway leading to that address has failed). Noncore gateways do not usually have a complete set of routes; they rely on a default route to handle network address they do not

---

† pronounced ''gate d'' from ''gate daemon''

understand.

Using default routes for most noncore gateways has two consequences. First, it means that local routing errors can go undetected. For example, if a machine in an autonomous system incorrectly routes a packet to a core gateway instead of a local gateway, the core will route it back to the autonomous system (perhaps sending an ICMP redirect). Thus connectivity may be preserved even if routing is incorrect. The problem may not seem severe for small autonomous systems that have high speed interconnections, but in a wide area network with relatively slow speed lines, incorrect routes can be deadly. Second, on the positive side, having default routes means that the IGP routing update messages will be much smaller than the routing updates the core system uses.

15.8 Summary

Before a gateway in an autonomous system can advertise reachability, it needs to learn about the networks in that system. Manual lists of networks suffice only for small, slowly changing autonomous systems; most require automated procedures that discover routes. Protocols for such procedures are called Interior Gateway Protocols, or IGPs.

We examined three IGPs: GGP, used by the core gateway system, HELLO, used by fuzzball gateways on the NSFnet backbone, and RIP, used by the UNIX program *routed*. Finally, we saw that the *gated* program provides an interface between an interior gateway protocol like RIP and the exterior gateway protocol, EGP, automating the process of gathering routes from within an autonomous system and advertising them to another autonomous system.

FOR FURTHER STUDY

As the text points out, there is no good documentation for RIP except for the code from the *routed* program. The HELLO protocol is documented in Mills [RFC 891]. Mills and Braun [1987] discusses the problems of converting between delay and hop-count metrics. Mark Fedor of the Cornell Theory Center wrote *gated*.

EXERCISES

15.1   What possible network families does RIP support? Hint: read the networking section of the 4.3 BSD UNIX Programmer's Manual.

15.2   Consider a large autonomous system using an interior gateway protocol like HELLO that bases routes on delay. What difficulty does this autonomous system have in advertising reachability to other autonomous systems?

15.3   An autonomous system can be as small as a single local area network or as large as multiple long haul networks. Why does the variation in size make it difficult to find a standard IGP?

15.4   Characterize the circumstances under which the split horizon technique will prevent slow convergence.

15.5   Consider an autonomous system composed of several local area networks running RIP as an IGP. Find an example that shows how a routing loop can result if the code does not provide "hold down" after receiving information that a network is unreachable.

15.6   Under what circumstances will a hop count metric produce better routes than a metric that uses delay?

15.7   Can you imagine a situation in which an autonomous system chooses *not* to advertise all its networks? Hint: think of a university.

15.8   In broad terms, we could say that RIP distributes its own routing table, while EGP distributes a table of known networks and gateways used to reach them (i.e., a gateway can send an EGP advertisement for a network without installing a route to that network in its own routing table). What are the advantages of each approach?

15.9   Consider a function used to convert between delay and hop-count metrics. Can you find properties of such functions that are sufficient to prevent routing loops. Are your properties necessary as well? (Hint: look at the paper by Mills and Braun).

16

Transparent Gateways and Subnet Addressing

16.1 Introduction

Previous chapters discussed addressing in an internetwork, presented the basic forms of addresses used in the Internet, and showed how gateways learn about network addresses. This chapter examines an extension of the original scheme called subnet addressing that allows a site to use a single Internet network address for multiple physical networks. It considers the motivation for subnet addressing, as well as the details of the scheme that is an Internet standard.

16.2 Review Of Relevant Facts

Chapter 4 discussed addressing in internetworks and presented the fundamentals of the scheme used throughout the Internet. We said that 32-bit Internet addresses are carefully assigned, so the Internet addresses of all hosts on a given physical network share a common prefix. In the original Internet addressing scheme, designers thought of the common prefix as defining the network portion of an Internet address and the remainder as a host portion. The consequence of importance to us is:

> In the original Internet addressing scheme, each physical network is assigned a unique network address; hosts on the network have the network address embedded in their individual addresses.

The chief advantage of dividing an Internet address into two parts is that it reduces the size of routing tables required in gateways. Instead of keeping one routing entry per destination host, a gateway can keep one entry per network and examine only the network portion of a destination address when making routing decisions.

Recall that the Internet accommodates widely diverse network sizes by having three classes of addresses. Networks assigned class *A* addresses partition the 32 bits into an 8-bit network portion and a 24-bit host portion. Class *B* addresses partition the 32 bits into 16-bit network and host portions, while class *C* partitions the address into a 24-bit network portion and an 8-bit host portion.

Also recall the Internet architecture, described in Chapters 13, 14, and 15. Loosely speaking, the Internet can be thought of as a central core gateway system with a set of autonomous systems attached to it. For routing purposes, topology is restricted to a tree structure in which each autonomous system advertises its networks to the core.

16.3 Minimizing Network Numbers

The Internet addressing scheme seems to handle all possibilities, but it has a minor weakness. How did the weakness arise? What did the Internet designers fail to envision? The answer is simple: growth. The designers planned for tens of networks and hundreds of hosts. Because they worked in a world of expensive mainframe computers, they did not foresee tens of thousands of small networks of personal computers that would suddenly appear a decade later.

A large number of trivial networks stresses the entire Internet plan because it means (1) immense administrative overhead is required merely to manage network addresses, and (2) the routing tables in gateways are extremely large. The second problem is important because it means that when gateways use protocols like GGP and EGP to exchange their routing table information, the computational effort required in the gateway is large, as is the load on the network. So the problem becomes how to minimize the number of assigned network addresses without destroying the original addressing scheme.

To minimize network addresses, the same Internet address must be shared by multiple physical networks. Of course, the routing procedures must be modified, and all machines that connect to those networks must understand the conventions used.

The idea of sharing one network address among multiple physical networks is not new and has taken several forms. We will examine three: transparent gateways, proxy ARP, and Internet standard subnets.

16.4 Transparent Gateways

The *transparent gateway* scheme is based on the observation that networks like the ARPANET, which have class *A* Internet addresses, can be extended through a simple trick illustrated in Figure 16.1.

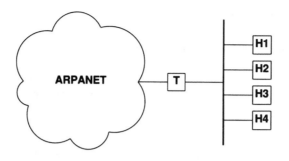

Figure 16.1 Transparent gateway *T* extending the ARPANET to multiple hosts at a site. Each host appears to have an Internet address on the ARPANET.

The trick consists of arranging for the ARPANET to multiplex several host connections through a single host port. As Figure 16.1 shows, a special purpose gateway connects one ARPANET host port to a local area network. The local area network does not have its own Internet address; hosts attached to it are assigned ARPANET addresses as if they connected directly to the ARPANET. A transparent gateway demultiplexes packets that arrive from the ARPANET by sending them to the appropriate host either by using a table of addresses or by decoding some part of the Internet address.

To make demultiplexing efficient, transparent gateways often divide the Internet address into multiple parts and encode information in unused parts. For example, the AR-PANET is a class *A* network with Internet address $10.0.0.0$. Each packet switch node (PSN) on the ARPANET is assigned a unique integer address. Internally, the ARPANET treats any 4-octet Internet address of the form $10.p.u.i$ as four separate octets that specify the network (10), a specific port on the destination PSN (p), and a destination PSN (i). Octet u is uninterpreted. Thus, ARPANET addresses $10.2.5.37$ and $10.2.9.37$ refer to the same host connection. A transparent gateway connected to PSN 37 port 2 can examine the u octet to decide which real host should receive the datagram. The ARPANET itself need not be aware of the multiple hosts that lie beyond the PSN.

Transparent gateways have advantages and disadvantages when compared to conventional gateways. One advantage is that they require fewer network addresses. Another is that they can support load balancing. That is, if two transparent gateways connect to the same local area network, traffic to hosts on that network can be split between them. By comparison, conventional gateways can only advertise one route to a given network.

One disadvantage of transparent gateways is that they only work with networks that have a large address space from which to choose host addresses. Thus, they work best with class *A* networks, and they do not work well with class *C* networks. Another disadvantage is that because they are not conventional gateways, they do not provide all the same services as standard gateways. In particular, transparent gateways may not participate fully in ICMP.

16.5 Proxy ARP

The terms *proxy ARP*, *promiscuous ARP*, and *the ARP hack* refer to a second technique used to map a single Internet network address onto multiple physical addresses. The technique, which only applies to networks that use ARP to bind Internet addresses to physical addresses, can best be explained with an example. Figure 16.2 illustrates the situation.

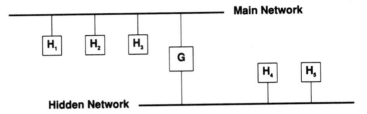

Figure 16.2 Proxy ARP technique (the ARP hack) used to allow one network address to be shared between two physical nets. Gateway *G* answers ARP requests on each network for hosts on the other network, giving its hardware address and then routing packets correctly when they arrive. In essence, *G* lies about Internet-to-physical address bindings.

In the figure, two networks share a single IP network address. Imagine that the network labeled *main network* was the original network, and that the second, labeled *hidden network* was added later. The gateway connecting the two networks, *G*, knows which hosts lie on which physical network and uses ARP to maintain the illusion that only one network exists. To make the illusion work, *G* keeps the location of hosts completely hidden, allowing all other machines on the network to communicate as if directly connected. In our example, when host H_1 needs to communicate with host H_4, it does so by invoking ARP to map H_4's Internet address into a physical address and then sending the datagram directly to that physical address. *G* captures the ARP request from H_1, decides that the machine in question lies on the other physical network, and responds to the ARP request by sending its own physical hardware address. H_1 receives the ARP response, installs the mapping in its ARP table and then uses the mapping to send datagrams destined for H_4 to *G*. *G* must forward datagrams destined for H_4 over the hidden network. To allow hosts on the hidden network to reach hosts on the main network, *G* performs the proxy ARP service on that network as well.

Gateways using the proxy ARP technique are taking advantage of an important feature of the ARP protocol, namely, trust. ARP is based on the idea that all machines cooperate and that any response is legitimate. Hosts install mappings obtained through ARP without checking their validity and without maintaining consistency. It may happen that the ARP table maps several Internet addresses to the same physical address, but that does not violate the protocol specification.

The chief advantage of proxy ARP is that it can be added to a single gateway on a network without disturbing the routing tables in other hosts or other gateways on that network. Thus, proxy ARP completely hides the details of physical connections.

The chief disadvantage of proxy ARP is that it does not work for networks unless they use ARP for address resolution. Furthermore, it does not generalize to more complex network topology (e.g., multiple gateways interconnecting two physical networks), nor does it support a reasonable form of routing.

16.6 Subnet Addresses

The third technique used to allow a single network address to span multiple physical networks is called *subnet addressing*, or *subnet routing*. Subnetting is the most widely used of the three techniques because it is the most general and because it has been standardized.

The easiest way to understand subnet addressing is to imagine that a site has a single class *B* IP network address assigned to it, but it has two or more physical networks. Only local gateways know that there are two physical nets and how to route traffic among them; the core gateways route all traffic as if there is a single network. Figure 16.3 shows an example.

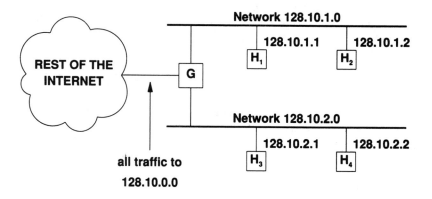

Figure 16.3 A site with two physical networks using subnet addressing to span them with a single class *B* network address. Gateway *G* accepts all traffic for net 128.10.0.0 and chooses a physical network based on the third octet of the address.

In the example, the site is using the single class *B* network address *128.10.0.0* for two networks. All Internet gateways, except for *G*, treat destinations on that network equally. Once a packet reaches *G*, it must be sent across the correct physical network to its destination. To make the choice of physical network efficient, the local site has chosen to assign machines on one physical network addresses of the form *128.10.1.X*, and to assign machines on the other physical network addresses of the form *128.10.2.X*, where *X* represents a small integer used to identify a specific host. To choose a physical network, *G* examines the third octet of the destination address and routes datagrams with value *1* to the network labeled *128.10.1.0* and those with value *2* to the network labeled *128.10.2.0*.

Conceptually, adding subnets only changes the interpretation of IP addresses slightly. Instead of dividing the 32-bit Internet address into a network portion and a host portion, subnetting divides the address into a *network portion* and a *local portion*. The interpretation of the network portion remains the same as for networks that do not use subnetting. Reachability to the network must be advertised to the core, and all traffic destined for that network will follow the advertised route. The interpretation of the local portion of an address is left up to the site (within the constraints of the formal standard for subnet addressing). To summarize:

> *We think of a 32-bit Internet address as having an Internet portion and a local portion, where the Internet portion identifies a site, possibly with multiple physical networks, and the local portion identifies a host at that site.*

The example of Figure 16.3 showed subnet addressing with a class *B* address that had a 2-octet Internet portion and a 2-octet local portion. To make routing among the physical networks efficient, the site in our example chose to use one octet of the local portion to identify a physical network and chose to use the other octet of the local portion to identify a host on that network, as Figure 16.4 shows.

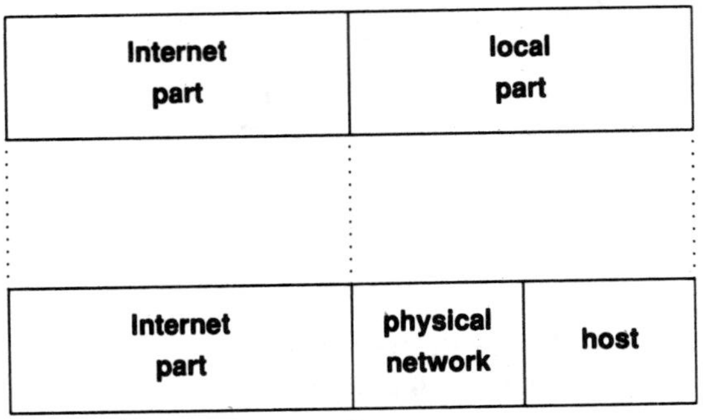

Figure 16.4 Interpretation of 32-bit Internet addresses for the subnet scheme shown in Figure 16.3. The local portion is divided into two parts that identify a physical network and a host on that network.

The result is a form of *hierarchical routing* in which the top level of the routing hierarchy (i.e., the core gateway system) uses the first two octets when routing, and the next level (e.g., the local site) uses an additional octet. Finally, the lowest level (i.e., routing across one physical network) uses the entire address.

Hierarchical routing is not new; many systems have used it before. The best example is the U.S. telephone system where a 10-digit phone number is divided into a 3-digit area code, 3-digit exchange, and 4-digit connection. The advantage of using hierarchical addressing is that it accommodates large growth because it means a given gateway does not need to know as much detail about distant destinations as it does about local ones. One disadvantage is that choosing a hierarchical structure is difficult, and it often becomes difficult to change a hierarchy once it has been established.

16.7 Flexibility In Subnet Addressing

The Internet standard for subnet addressing recognizes that not every site will have the same hierarchical addresses; it allows sites flexibility in choosing how to assign hierarchical addresses. To understand why such flexibility is desirable, imagine a site with five networks interconnected, as Figure 16.5 shows. Suppose the site has a single class *B* network address that it wants to use for all physical networks. How should the address be divided to make routing efficient?

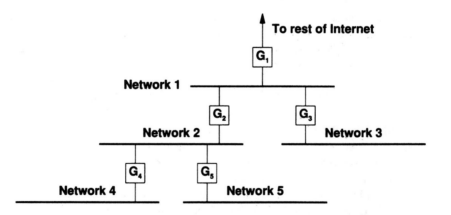

Figure 16.5 A site with five physical networks arranged in three "levels." The simplistic division of addresses into physical net and host parts may not be optimal for such cases.

In our example, the site will choose a partition of the local part of the Internet address based on how it expects to grow. Dividing the 16-bit local part into an 8-bit network identifier and an 8-bit host identifier (as shown in Figure 16.4) allows up to 256 networks with up to 256 hosts per network. Using 3 bits to identify a physical network and 13 bits to identify a host on that network allows 8 networks with up to 8192 hosts per network.

No single partition of the local part of the address will work for all sites because some have many networks, while others have many hosts. Furthermore, it may be that even within one site, some groups have many networks, while others have many hosts on a few networks. To allow maximum autonomy, the Internet standard allows the subnet partition to be selected on a per-network basis. Once a partition has been selected for a particular network, machines attached to that network are expected to use it. If they do not, packets can be lost or misrouted. We can summarize:

> *To allow maximum flexibility in choosing how to partition subnet ad-*
> *dresses, the Internet standard permits subnet interpretation to be*
> *chosen independently for each physical network. Once a subnet parti-*
> *tion has been selected, all machines on that network must honor it.*

16.8 Implementation Of Subnets With Masks

We have implied that choosing a subnet addressing scheme is synonymous with choosing how to partition the local portion of an Internet address into physical net and host part. Indeed, most sites that use subnet addresses do exactly that, but subnet addressing allows more complex assignments as well. The standard specifies that a site using subnet addressing must choose a 32-bit *subnet mask* for each network. Bits in the subnet mask are set to *1*, if the network treats the corresponding bit in the Internet address as part of the network address, and *0*, if it treats the bit as part of the host identifier. For example, the 32-bit subnet mask

$$11111111 \quad 11111111 \quad 11111111 \quad 00000000$$

specifies that the first three octets identify the network and the fourth octet identifies a host on that network. It is assumed that the subnet mask has *1*s for all bits that correspond to the Internet portion of the address (e.g., the subnet mask for a class *b* network will include the first two octets).

The interesting twist in subnet addressing arises because the standard does not restrict subnet masks to select contiguous bits of the address. For example, a network might be assigned the mask

$$11111111 \quad 11111111 \quad 00011000 \quad 01000000$$

which selects the first two octets, two bits from the third octet, and one bit from the fourth. Although such flexibility makes it possible to arrange interesting assignments of addresses to machines, it makes understanding routing tables tricky. Thus, most sites prefer fixed, contiguous subnet masks, and usually use the same mask throughout an entire set of physical nets that share an Internet address.

16.9 Routing In The Presence Of Subnets

The standard IP routing algorithm must be modified to work with subnet addresses. Obviously, all machines that have a subnet address need to use the modified algorithm, which is called *subnet routing*. What may not be obvious is that other hosts and gateways at the site may also need to use subnet routing. To see why, consider the example set of networks shown in Figure 16.6.

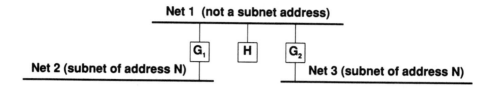

Figure 16.6 An example site with three networks where nets *2* and *3* are subnets of a single Internet address, *N*. Host H must use subnet routing even though net *1* does not have a subnet address.

In the figure, physical networks *2* and *3* have been assigned subnet addresses of a single Internet address, *N*. Although host *H* does not directly attach to a network that has a subnet address, it must use subnet routing to decide whether to send packets destined for network *N* to gateway G_1 or gateway G_2. It could be argued that *H* can send to either gateway and let them handle the problem, but that solution means not all traffic will follow a shortest path. In larger examples, the difference between an optimum and nonoptimum path can be significant.

In theory, there is a simple rule that determines when machines need to use subnet routing:

> *To achieve optimal routing, a machine* M *must use subnet routing for an Internet address* N, *unless there is a single path* P *that is a shortest path between* M *and every physical network that is a subnet of* N.

Unfortunately, the theoretical possibilities do not help much in assigning subnets. First, we know that shortest paths change if hardware fails or if routing algorithms redirect traffic around congestion. Such dynamic changes make it difficult to use the subnet rule except in trivial cases. Second, the subnet rule fails to consider the architectural boundaries of autonomous systems or the difficulties involved in propagating subnet masks. It is impossible to propagate subnet routes beyond the boundary of an autonomous system because current network reachability protocols like EGP do not provide for it. Realistically, it becomes extremely difficult to propagate subnet information beyond a given physical network. Therefore, sites that use subnet addresses, usually choose to keep subnets as simple as possible (e.g., hierarchical) and require all machines to participate in subnet routing.

16.10 The Subnet Routing Algorithm

Like the standard IP routing algorithm, the subnet routing algorithm bases its decisions on a table of routes. In the standard algorithm, per-host routes and default routes are special cases; the table is used for all others. Each table entry contains a pair of

(network address, next gateway)

where the *network address* field specifies the Internet address of a destination network, and the *next gateway* field specifies the address of the next gateway to which to send datagrams for that network. The standard routing algorithm compares the Internet portion of a destination address to the *network address* field of each entry in the routing table until a match is found. Because the *next gateway* field is constrained to specify a machine that is reachable over a directly connected network, only one table lookup is ever needed.

The standard algorithm knows how an address is partitioned into Internet portion and local portion because the first two bits encode the address type (class *A*, *B*, or *C*). With subnets, it is not possible to decide which bits correspond to the network and which to the host from the address alone. Instead, the modified routing table used with subnets maintains that information in the routing table, where each entry contains one additional field that specifies the subnet mask used with the network in that entry:

(subnet mask, network address, next gateway)

When choosing routes, the modified algorithm uses the subnet mask to extract bits of the destination address for comparison with the table entry. That is, it performs a bit-wise Boolean *and* of the full 32-bit destination Internet address and the *subnet mask* field from an entry, and it then checks to see if the result equals the value in the *network address* field of that entry. If so, it routes the datagram to the address specified in the *next gateway* field† of the entry.

16.11 Unified Routing Algorithm

Observant readers may have noticed that the subnet routing algorithm can subsume all the special cases of the standard algorithm. It can handle routes to individual hosts, default routes, and routes to directly connected networks using the same masking technique it uses for subnets. In addition, masks can handle routes to conventional networks (i.e., networks not using subnet addressing). The flexibility comes from the ability to combine arbitrary 32-bit values in the *subnet mask* fields and arbitrary 32-bit addresses in the *network address* field. For example, to install a route for a single host, one uses a subnet mask of all *1*s and network address equal to the host's IP address. To install a default route, one uses a subnet mask of all *0*s and a network address of all *0*s. To install a route to a standard, nonsubnet class *B* network, one specifies a mask with two octets of *1*s and two octets of *0*s.

_____

†as in the standard routing algorithm, the next gateway must be reachable by a directly connected network.

16.12 Maintenance Of Subnet Masks

How do subnet masks get assigned and propagated? Chapter 9 answered the second part of the question by showing that a host can obtain the subnet mask for a given network by sending an ICMP *subnet mask request* to a gateway on that network. The request can be broadcast if the host does not know the specific address of a gateway. However, there is no standard protocol for propagating the information from one gateway to another.

The first part of the question is more difficult to answer. Of course, each site is free to choose subnet masks for its networks. The difficulty arises because it is possible to assign masks that lead to ambiguous routes. Or worse, it is possible to make valid assignments that become invalid if more hosts are added to the networks. There are no easy rules, so most sites make conservative choices. Typically, they select contiguous bits from the local portion of an address to identify a network and often use the same partition for all local networks at the site.

16.13 Broadcasting To Subnets

Broadcasting becomes more difficult in a subnet architecture. Recall that in the Internet addressing scheme, a host address of all *1*s specifies broadcast to all hosts on the specified network. From the point of view of an observer outside a subnet network, broadcasting still makes sense as long as the gateways that know about the subnets propagate the packet to all physical networks. Within the set of subnetted networks, it becomes possible to broadcast to a specific subnet (i.e., to broadcast to all hosts on a physical network that has been assigned one of the subnet addresses). More complex subnet address assignments (e.g., those where individual networks divide the subnet address differently) may or may not allow broadcasting to selected subsets of physical networks that make up a subnet. The reader is referred to the appropriate RFCs for more details.

16.14 Summary

The original Internet address scheme assigns a unique 32-bit address to each physical network and requires Internet gateways to keep routing tables proportional to the number of gateways. We examined three techniques that have been invented to allow sites to share one Internet address among multiple physical networks. The first uses transparent gateways to extend host addresses from one network to several hosts on other networks. The second, called proxy ARP, arranges for a local gateway to impersonate computers on another physical network by answering ARP messages sent to them. It is useful only on networks that use ARP for address resolution. The third technique, called subnet addressing, allows a site to share a single Internet address among multiple physical networks, as long as all the hosts and gateways on those networks cooperate. Subnetting requires hosts to use a modified routing algorithm in which table entries contain a subnet mask. The algorithm can be viewed as a generalization of the original routing algorithm because it handles special cases like default routes or host-specific routes.

FOR FURTHER STUDY

The standard for subnet addressing comes from Mogul [RFC 950]; Clark [RFC 932], Karels [RFC 936], Gads [RFC 940], and Mogul [RFC 917] all contain early proposals for subnet addressing schemes. Mogul [RFC 932] discusses broadcasting in the presence of subnets. Postel [RFC 925] considers the use of proxy ARP for subnets. Carl-Mitchell and Quarterman [RFC 1027] discusses using proxy ARP to implement transparent subnet gateways.

EXERCISES

16.1 If gateways using proxy ARP use a table of host addresses to decide whether to answer ARP requests, the gateway table must be changed whenever a new host is added to one of the networks. Explain how to assign IP addresses so hosts can be added without changing tables. Hint: think of subnets.

16.2 Can transparent gateways be used with local area networks like the Ethernet?

16.3 Show that proxy ARP can be used with three physical networks that are interconnected by two gateways.

16.4 Consider a fixed subnet partition of a class *B* network number that will accommodate at least 76 networks. How many hosts can be on each network?

16.5 Does it ever make sense to subnet a class *C* network address? Why or why not?

16.6 Design a subnet address scheme for your organization assuming you have one class *B* address to use.

16.7 Is it reasonable for a single gateway to use both proxy ARP and subnet addressing? If so, explain how. If not, explain why.

16.8 Argue that any network using proxy ARP is vulnerable to ''spoofing'' (i.e., an arbitrary machine can impersonate any other machine).

16.9 Can you devise a (nonstandard) implementation of ARP that supports normal use but prohibits proxy ARP?

16.10 One vendor decided to add subnet addressing to its IP software by allocating a single subnet mask and a single IP network address. The vendor modified its standard IP routing software to make the subnet check a special case. Find a simple example in which this implementation cannot work correctly.

16.11 Characterize the (restricted) situations in which the subnet implementation discussed in the previous exercise will work correctly.

16.12 Read the standard to find out more about broadcasting in the presence of subnets. Can you characterize subnet address assignments that allow one to specify a broadcast address for all possible subsets?

16.13   The standard allows an arbitrary assignment of subnet masks for networks that comprise a subnetted Internet address. Should the standard restrict subnet masks to cover contiguous bits in the address? Why or why not?

16.14   Carefully consider default routing in the presence of subnets. What can happen if a packet arrives destined for a nonexistant subnet?

16.15   Compare architectures that use subnet addressing and gateways to interconnect multiple Ethernets to an architecture that uses bridges. Under what circumstances is one architecture preferable to the other?

17

Client-Server Model Of Interaction

17.1 Introduction

Early chapters presented the details of Internet technology, including the protocols that provide basic services. The four previous chapters described the architecture of the DARPA Internet and the protocols gateways use to exchange routing information. Now that we understand the basic technology, we can examine examples of application programs that profit from the cooperative use of the Internet. While the examples are both practical and interesting, they do not comprise the main point. Instead, focus rests on the patterns of interaction among the communicating application programs. The primary pattern of interaction among cooperating applications is known as the *client-server* paradigm. It forms the basis of most network communication. It is fundamental because it helps us understand the foundation on which distributed algorithms are built. This chapter considers the relationship between client and server, paving the way for later chapters that illustrate the client-server pattern with further examples.

17.2 The Client-Server Model

The term *server* applies to any program that offers a service that can be reached over the network. Servers accept requests that arrive over the network, perform their service, and return the result to the requester. Usually, each request arrives in a single internet packet.

An executing program becomes a *client* when it sends a request to a server and waits for a response. Because the client-server model is a convenient and natural extension of interprocess communication on a single machine, it is easy to build programs that use it to interact.

Servers can perform simple or complex tasks. For example, a *time-of-day server* merely returns the current time whenever a client sends it a packet. A *file server* receives requests to perform operations that store or retrieve information from a file; the server performs the operation and returns the result.

Usually, servers are implemented as application level programs, called *processes* on some systems. Such programs can execute on any computing system that supports Internet communication. Thus, the server for a particular service may execute on a timesharing system along with other programs, or it may execute on a personal computer. Multiple servers may offer the same service, and they may execute on the same machine or on multiple machines. In fact, it is common to replicate copies of a given server onto physically independent machines to increase reliability. If a machine's primary purpose is to support a particular server program, the term ''server'' may be applied to the machine as well as to the server program. Thus, one hears statements like ''machine *A* is the file server.''

17.3 A Simple Example: UDP Echo Server

The simplest form of client-server interaction uses unreliable datagram delivery to convey messages from the client to the server and back. Consider, for example, a *UDP echo server*. The mechanics are straightforward as Figure 17.1 shows. At the server site, a UDP *echo server process* begins by negotiating with its operating system for permission to use the UDP port id reserved for *echo*. We call this the UDP *echo port*. Once it has obtained permission, the echo server process enters an infinite loop that has three steps: (1) wait for a datagram to arrive at the echo port, (2) reverse the source and destination addresses† (including source and destination Internet addresses as well as UDP port ids), and (3) return the datagram to its original sender. At some other site, a program becomes a UDP *echo-client* when it allocates an unused UDP port id, sends a UDP message to the UDP server, and awaits the reply. The client expects to receive back exactly the same data as it sent.

The UDP echo service illustrates two important points that are generally true about client-server interaction. The first concerns the difference between the lifetime of servers and clients:

> *A server starts execution before interaction begins and (usually) continues to accept requests and send responses without ever terminating. A client is any program that makes a request and awaits a response; it (usually) terminates after using a server a finite number of times.*

---

†One of the exercises suggests considering this step in more detail.

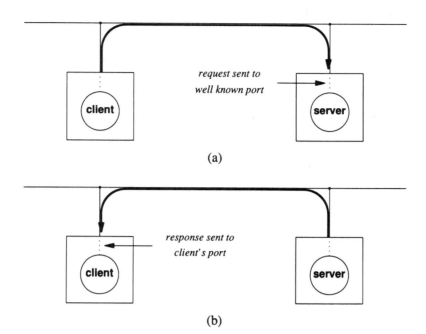

(a)

(b)

Figure 17.1 UDP echo as an example of the client-server model. In (a) the
client sends a request to the server at a known destination IP address and at a well known UDP port, and in (b) the server returns
a response. Clients use any UDP port that is available.

The second point is more technical. It concerns the use of reserved and nonreserved port
identifiers:

> *A server waits for requests at a well known port that has been reserved
> for the service it offers. A client allocates an arbitrary, unused, non-
> reserved port for its communication.*

In a client-server interaction, only one of the two ports needs to be reserved. Assigning a
unique port identifier to each service makes it easy to build both clients and servers.

Who would use an echo service? Certainly not an average user. However, systems
programmers who design, implement, measure, or modify network protocol software
often use echo servers in testing. Echo servers can also be used to determine if it is possible to reach a remote machine.

17.4 Time And Date Service

The echo server is extremely simple, and little code is required to implement either the server or client side (provided that the operating system offers a reasonable way to access the underlying Internet protocols). Our second example, a time server, shows that even simple client-server interaction can provide useful services. The problem it solves is that of setting a computer's time-of-day clock. The time of day clock is the hardware device that maintains the current date and time, making it available to programs. Once set, the time of day clock keeps time as accurately as a wristwatch.

Many systems solve the problem by asking a programmer to type in the time and date when the system boots. The system increments the clock periodically (e.g., every second). When an application program asks for the date or time, the system consults the internal clock and formats the time of day in human readable form. We can use a server to set the clock by arranging for one machine to run a time-of-day server, and having other machines contact the server when they boot.

17.4.1 Representation for the Date and Time

How should an operating system maintain the date and time-of-day? One useful representation stores the time and date as the count of seconds since an epoch date. For example, the UNIX operating system uses the zeroth second of January 1, 1970 as its epoch date. The Internet protocols also define an epoch date and report times as seconds past the epoch. For the Internet, the epoch is defined to be the zeroth second of January 1, 1900 and times are kept in 32-bit integers, a representation that accommodates all dates in the near future.

Keeping the date as the time in seconds since an epoch makes the representation compact and allows easy comparison. It ties together the date and time of day and makes it possible to measure time by incrementing a single binary integer.

17.4.2 Local and Universal Time

What should we choose as the epoch, and exactly what time zone does the count represent? When two systems communicate across large geographic distances, using the local time zone from one or the other becomes difficult; they must agree on a standard time zone to keep values for date and time comparable. Thus, in addition to defining a representation for the date and choosing an epoch, the Internet time server standard specifies that all values are given with respect to a single time zone. The time zone is Greenwich Mean Time, now called *universal coordinated time*, or *universal time*.

The interaction between client and server that offers time service works much like the echo server. At the server side, the server application obtains permission to use the reserved port assigned to time servers, waits for a UDP message directed to that port, and responds by sending a UDP message that contains the current time in a 32-bit integer. We can summarize:

Sending a datagram to a time server is equivalent to making a request for the current time; the server responds by returning a UDP message that contains the current time.

17.5 The Complexity of Servers

In our examples so far, servers are fairly simple because they are sequential. That is, the server processes one request at a time. After accepting a request, the server forms a reply and sends it before going back to see if another request has arrived. We implicitly assumed that the operating system will queue requests that arrive for a server while it is busy, and that the queue will not become too long because the server has only a trivial amount of work to do.

In practice, servers are usually much more difficult to build than clients because they need to accommodate multiple concurrent requests, even if a single request takes considerable time to process. For example, consider a file transfer server responsible for copying a file to another machine on request. Typically, the server performs the following five steps:

Open port
> The server opens the well-known port at which it can be reached.

Wait for client
> The server waits for a new client to send a request.

Choose port
> The server allocates a new local protocol port for this request and informs the client.

Spawn process
> The server starts an independent, concurrent process (a copy of the server) to handle this request. Note that the new process no longer needs to accept random requests from the well-known server port.

Continue
> The server returns to the *wait* step and continues accepting new requests while the independent process handles the current request.

In addition to handling concurrent requests, servers have responsibility for enforcing authorization and protection rules. Server programs often execute with highest privilege because they need to read system files, keep logs, and access protected data. Thus, they cannot blindly honor requests. Instead, each server is responsible for enforcing the system access and protection policies.

Finally, servers must protect themselves against malformed requests or against requests that will cause the server program itself to abort. Often, it is difficult to foresee potential problems. For example, one project at Purdue University designed a file server that allowed student operating systems to access files on a UNIX timesharing system.

Students discovered that requesting the server to open a file named */dev/tty* caused the server to abort because UNIX associates that name with the terminal to which a program is attached. The server, created at system startup, had no such terminal. Once the server program aborted, none of the machines could access files until a systems programmer restarted it.

We can summarize all these points:

> *Servers are usually more difficult to build than clients because, even though they can be implemented with application level programs, servers must enforce all the access and protection policies of the computer system on which they run, and they must protect themselves against all possible errors.*

17.6 RARP Server

So far, all our examples of client-server interaction require the client to know the complete address of the server. The RARP protocol from Chapter 6 provides an example of client-server interaction with a slightly different twist. Recall that when a diskless machine boots, it uses RARP to find its Internet address. Instead of having the client communicate directly with a server, RARP clients broadcast their requests. One or more machines executing RARP server processes respond, each returning a packet that answers the query.

There are two significant differences between a RARP server and a UDP echo or time server. First, RARP packets travel across the physical network in hardware packets, not in IP datagrams. Thus, the RARP server must be on the same physical network as the sender. Second, the echo and time servers can be built as application programs as long as the operating system supplies access to the UDP, but it must provide access to raw hardware packets for the RARP server to be written as an application program.

17.7 Alternatives To The Client-Server Model

What are the alternatives to client-server interaction, and when might they be attractive? This section gives at least one answer to those questions.

In the client-server model, processes usually act as clients when they need information, but it is sometimes important to minimize such interactions. The ARP protocol from Chapter 5 gives one example. It uses a modified form of client-server interaction to obtain physical address mappings. Machines use ARP cache answers to improve the efficiency of later queries. Caching improves the performance of client-server interaction in cases where the recent history of queries is a good indicator of future use.

Although caching improves performance, it does not change the essence of client-server interaction. The essence lies in our assumption that processing must be driven by demand. We have assumed that a program executes until it needs information and then acts as a client to obtain the needed information. Taking a demand-driven view of the world is natural and arises from experience. Caching helps alleviate the cost of obtaining information by lowering the retrieval cost for all except the first process that makes a request.

How can we lower the cost of information retrieval for the first request? In a distributed system, it may be possible to have concurrent background activities that collect and propagate information *before* any particular program requests it, making retrieval costs low even for the initial request. More important, precollecting information can allow a given system to continue executing even though other machines or the networks connecting them fail.

Precollection is the basis for the 4.3 BSD UNIX *ruptime* command. When invoked, *ruptime* reports the CPU load and time since system startup for each machine on the local network. Background activities broadcast information about the local machine periodically, collect information about other machines, and place it in a file. Because each machine has a copy of the latest information on hand, the client never needs to access the network. It reads the information from secondary storage and arranges it in a readable form.

The chief advantage of having information collected locally before the client needs it lies in speed. The *ruptime* command responds immediately when invoked without waiting for messages to traverse the network. A secondary benefit occurs because the client can find out something about machines that are no longer operating. In particular, for machines that stop responding, the client can report how long the machine has been off-line.

Precollection has one major disadvantage: it uses processor time and network bandwidth even when no one cares about the data being collected. For example, the ruptime broadcast and collection continues running throughout the night, even when no one is logged in to read the information. If only a few machines connect to a given network, precollection cost is insignificant. It can be thought of as an innocuous background activity. For networks with many hosts, however, the large volume of broadcast traffic generated by precollection makes it too expensive. In particular, the cost of reading and processing broadcast messages becomes high. Thus, precollection is not among the most popular techniques.

17.8 Summary

Processes that use network communication often fall into a pattern of use called the client-server model. Server processes await requests and perform an action based on the request. The action may include sending a response. Clients usually formulate a request, send it to the server, and then await a reply.

We have seen examples of clients and servers and found that some of them send requests directly, while others communicate by broadcasting requests. Broadcast is especially useful on a local network when a machine does not know the address of a server.

We also noted that if servers use Internet protocols like UDP, they can accept and respond to requests across the Internet. If they communicate using physical frames and physical hardware addresses, they are restricted to a single physical network.

Finally, we considered an alternative to the client-server paradigm that used precollection of information to avoid delays. An example of precollection came from a machine status service.

FOR FURTHER STUDY

UDP echo service is defined in Postel [RFC 862]. The *ruptime* command is only one part of the 4.3BSD UNIX *rwho* mechanism. Feinler *et. al.* [1985] specifies many standard DARPA Internet server protocols not discussed here, including discard, character generation, day and time, active users, and quote of the day.

EXERCISES

17.1   Build a UDP echo client that sends a datagram to a specified echo server, awaits a reply, and compares it to the original message.

17.2   Carefully consider the manipulation of IP addresses in a UDP echo server. Under what conditions is it incorrect to create new IP addresses by reversing the source and destination IP addresses?

17.3   As we have seen, servers can be implemented by separate application programs or by building server code into the protocol software in an operating system. What are the advantages and disadvantages of having a user program (process) per server?

17.4   Suppose you do not know the IP address of a local machine running a UDP echo server, but you know that it responds to port 7. Is there an IP address you can use to reach it?

17.5   Build a client for the UDP time service.

17.6   Which of the techniques from Chapter 16 allow one to have a RARP server on a separate physical network from its client?

17.7   What is the chief disadvantage of having all machines broadcast their status periodically?

17.8   Examine the format of data broadcast by the 4.3 BSD ruptime system. What information is available to the client in addition to machine status?

18

The Domain Name System

18.1 Introduction

So far we have used 32-bit integers called Internet Protocol Addresses (IP addresses) to identify machines. Although such addresses provide a convenient, compact representation for specifying the source and destination in packets sent across the Internet, users prefer to assign machines pronounceable, easily remembered names.

This chapter considers a scheme for assigning meaningful high-level names to a large set of machines, and it discusses a mechanism that maps between high-level machine names and IP addresses. It considers both the translation from high-level names to IP addresses and the translation from IP addresses to high-level machine names. The naming scheme is interesting for two reasons. First, it has been used to assign machine names throughout the Internet. Second, the implementation of the name mapping mechanism provides a large scale example of the client–server paradigm described in the previous chapter because it uses a geographically distributed set of servers to map names to addresses.

18.2 Names For Machines

The earliest computer systems forced users to understand numeric addresses for objects like system tables and peripheral devices. Timesharing systems advanced computing by allowing users to invent meaningful symbolic names for both physical objects (e.g., peripheral devices) and abstract objects (e.g., files). A similar pattern has emerged in computer networking. Early systems supported point-to-point connections between computers and used low-level hardware addresses to specify machines. Internetworking introduced universal addresses, as well as protocol software to map universal addresses into low-level hardware addresses. When users became aware of multiple machines in their computing environment, they wanted to use meaningful, symbolic names to identify them.

Early machine names reflected the small environment in which they were chosen. It was quite common for a site with a handful of machines to choose names based on the machines' purpose. For example, machines often had names like *research*, *production*, *accounting*, and *development*. Users find such names appealing and prefer to use them instead of the more cumbersome hardware address.

Although the distinction between *address* and *name* is intuitively appealing, it is artificial. Any *name* is merely an identifier that consists of a sequence of characters chosen from a finite alphabet. Names are only useful if the system can efficiently map them to the object they denote. Thus, we think of an Internet addresses as a *low-level name*, and we say that users prefer *high-level names* for machines.

The form of high-level names is important because it determines how names are translated to lower-level names or bound to objects, as well as how name assignments are authorized. When only a few machines interconnect, choosing names is easy, and any form will suffice. On the Internet, where tens of thousands of machines interconnect, choosing symbolic names becomes difficult. For example, when the Computer Science Department at Purdue University connected to the Internet in 1980, it chose the name *purdue* to identify the connected machine. The list of potential conflicts contained only a few dozen names. By mid 1986, the official list of hosts on the Internet contained 3100 officially registered names and 6500 official aliases. Although the list was growing rapidly, most sites had additional machines (e.g., personal computers) that were not registered.

18.3 Flat Namespace

The original set of machine names used in the Internet formed a *flat namespace* in which each name consisted of a sequence of characters without any further structure. In the original scheme, a central site, the Internet Network Information Center, administered the namespace and determined whether a new name was appropriate (i.e., it prohibited obscene names or names that conflicted with existing names).

The chief advantage of a flat namespace is that names are convenient and short; the chief disadvantage of a flat namespace is that it cannot generalize to large sets of machines for both technical and administrative reasons. First, because names are drawn from a single set of identifiers, the potential for conflict increases as the number of sites increases. Second, because authority for adding new names must rest at a single site, the administrative workload at that site increases as the number of sites increases. To understand the severity of the problem, imagine a rapidly growing Internet with thousands of sites, each of which has hundreds of individual personal computers and workstations. Every time someone acquires and connects a new personal computer, its name must be approved by the central authority. Third, because the name-to-address bindings change frequently, the cost of maintaining correct copies at each site is high and increases as the number of sites increases. Alternatively, if the name database resides at a single site, traffic to that site increases as the number of sites increases.

18.4 Hierarchical Names

How can a naming system accommodate a large, rapidly expanding set of names without requiring a central site to administer them? The answer lies in decentralizing the naming mechanism by delegating authority for parts of the namespace and distributing responsibility for mapping between names and addresses. The Internet now uses such a scheme. Before examining the details of the Internet scheme, we will consider the motivation and intuition behind it.

The partition of a namespace must be made in such a way that it supports efficient name mapping and guarantees autonomous control of name assignment. Optimizing only for efficient mapping can lead to solutions that retain a flat namespace and reduce traffic by dividing the names among multiple mapping machines. Optimizing only for administrative ease can lead to solutions that make delegation of authority easy but name mapping expensive or complex.

To understand how the namespace should be divided, think of the internal structure of large organizations. At the top, the chief executive has overall responsibility. Because the chief executive cannot oversee everything, the organization may be partitioned into divisions, with an executive in charge of each division. The chief executive grants each division autonomy within specified limits. More to the point, the executive in charge of a particular division can hire or fire employees, assign offices, and delegate authority, without obtaining direct permission from the chief executive.

Besides making it easy to delegate authority, the hierarchy of a large organization introduces autonomous operation. For example, when average office workers need information like telephone numbers of new employees, they begin by asking local clerical workers (who may have to contact clerical workers in other divisions). The point is that although authority always passes down the corporate hierarchy, information can flow across the hierarchy from one office to another.

18.5 Delegation Of Authority For Names

A hierarchical naming scheme works like the management of a large organization. The namespace is *partitioned* at the top level, and authority for names in the subdivisions is passed to a designated agent. For example, we might choose to partition the namespace based on *site name* and to delegate to each site responsibility for maintaining names within its partition. The topmost level of the hierarchy partitions the namespace and delegates authority for the partitions; it need not be bothered by changes within one partition.

The syntax of hierarchically assigned names often reflects the hierarchical delegation of authority used to assign them. As an example, consider a namespace with names
of the form

local . site

where *site* is the name of a site authorized by the central authority, *local* is the part of a
name controlled by the site, and the period† character (".") is a delimiter used to
separate them. When the topmost authority approves adding a new site, X, it adds X to
the list of valid sites and delegates to site X authority for all names that end in '$.X$'.

18.6 Subset Authority

In a hierarchical namespace, authority may be further subdivided at each level. In
our example of partition by sites, the site itself may consist of several administrative
groups, and the site authority may choose to subdivide its namespace among the groups.
The idea is to keep subdividing the namespace until each subdivision is small enough to
be manageable.

Syntactically, subdividing the namespace introduces another subdivision to the
name. For example, adding a *group* subdivision to names already partitioned by site produces the following name syntax:

local . group . site

Because the topmost level delegates authority, group names do not have to agree between
sites. A university site might choose group names like *engineering*, *science*, and *arts*,
while a corporate site might choose group names like *production*, *accounting*, and *per-
sonnel*.

The U.S. Telephone system provides another example of hierarchical naming syntax. The 10 digits of a phone number have been partitioned into a 3-digit *area code*, 3-
digit *exchange*, and 4-digit *subscriber number* within the exchange. Each exchange has
authority for assigning subscriber numbers within its piece of the namespace. Although
it is possible to group arbitrary subscribers into exchanges and to group arbitrary exchanges into area codes, the assignment of telephone numbers is not capricious; they are
carefully chosen to make it easy to route phone calls across the telephone network.

The telephone example is important because it illustrates a key distinction between
the hierarchical naming scheme used in the Internet and other hierarchies: partitioning
the set of machines owned by an organization along lines of authority does not necessarily imply partitioning by physical location. For example, it could be that at some university, a single building houses the mathematics department, as well as the computer science
department. It might even turn out that although the machines from these two groups fall
under completely separate administrative domains, they connect to the same physical network. It also may happen that a single group owns machines on several physical networks. For these reasons, the Internet naming scheme allows arbitrary delegation of au-

---

†In domain names, the period delimiter is pronounced "dot."

thority for the hierarchical namespace without regard to physical connections. The concept can be summarized:

> *In the Internet, hierarchical machine names are assigned according to the structure of organizations that obtain authority for parts of the namespace, not according to the structure of the physical network interconnections.*

Of course, at many sites the organizational hierarchy corresponds with the structure of physical network interconnections. At a large university, for example, most departments that have computers also have their own local area network. If the department is assigned part of the naming hierarchy, all the machines that have names in its part of the hierarchy will also connect to a single physical network.

18.7 Internet Domain Names

The Internet machine name hierarchy is called the *domain name* system, and it has two, conceptually independent aspects. The first is abstract: the name syntax and rules for delegating authority over names. The second is concrete: the implementation of a system that efficiently maps names to addresses. This section considers the name syntax; later sections examine the implementation.

The Internet uses a hierarchical naming scheme known as *domain names*. As in our earlier examples, a domain name consists of a sequence of subnames separated by a delimiter character, the period. In our examples we said that individual sections of the name might represent sites or groups, but the domain system simply calls each section a *label*. Thus, the domain name

cs.*purdue*.*edu*

contains three *labels*: *cs*, *purdue*, and *edu*. Any suffix of labels in a domain name is called a *domain*. Thus, in the above example the lowest level domain is *cs*.*purdue*.*edu*, an abbreviation for the Computer Science Department; the second level domain is *purdue*.*edu* (for Purdue University); and the top level domain is *edu* (for educational institution). As the example shows, domain names are written with the local most label first and the topmost domain last.

The Internet authority that has ultimate responsibility for the namespace has chosen to partition the top level into the domains listed in Figure 18.1.

Domain Name	Meaning
COM	Commercial organizations
EDU	Educational institutions
GOV	Government institutions
MIL	Military groups
NET	Major networks support centers
ORG	Organizations other than those above
ARPA	Temporary ARPANET domain
country code	Countries other than USA

Figure 18.1 The top-level Internet domains and their meaning.

When a foreign country wants to participate in the domain naming system, the central authority assigns it a new top-level domain consisting of its international standard 2-letter country identifier. When an organization in the United States wants to participate in the domain naming system, the central authority assigns it a subdomain under one of the existing top-level domains.

Another example may help clarify the authority structure. The machine named *xinu* in the Computer Science Department at Purdue University has the official domain name

xinu.cs.purdue.edu

The name was approved and registered by the system staff in the Computer Science Department. They had previously obtained authority to manage the subdomain *cs.purdue.edu* from the university administrator, who had obtained permission to manage the subdomain *purdue.edu*. The Internet authority retains control of the *edu* domain, so new universities can only be added with their permission. Similarly, the university administrators at Purdue University retain authority for the *purdue.edu* subdomain, so new departments or machines may only be added with their permission.

A domain name may name a machine, a subdomain, or even a user. Thus, in our example, it is possible to have a machine named

gwen.purdue.edu

even though

cs.purdue.edu

is a subdomain. We can summarize this important point:

One cannot distinguish the names of subdomains from the names of machines using only the domain name syntax.

18.8 Mapping Domain Names To Addresses

In addition to the rules for name syntax and delegation of authority, the Internet domain name scheme includes an efficient, reliable, general purpose, distributed system for mapping names to addresses. The system is distributed in the technical sense, meaning that a set of servers operating at multiple sites cooperatively solve the mapping problem. It is efficient in the sense that most names can be mapped locally; only a few require Internet traffic. It is general purpose because it is not restricted to machine names (although we will use that example for now). Finally, it is reliable in that no single machine failure will prevent the system from operating correctly.

The Internet scheme for mapping names to addresses consists of independent, cooperative systems called *name servers*. A name server is a server program that supplies name-to-address translation, mapping from domain names to Internet addresses. Often, server software executes on a dedicated processor, and the machine itself is called the name server. The client software, called a *name resolver*, uses one or more name servers when translating a name.

Conceptually, all Internet domain name servers are arranged in a tree structure that corresponds to the naming hierarchy as Figure 18.2 shows.

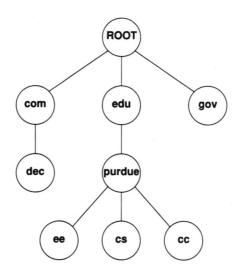

Figure 18.2 The conceptual arrangement of domain name servers in a tree that corresponds to the hierarchy of name authority. Each node represents a name server that handles names for a single subdomain.

The root of the tree is a server that recognizes the top level domain. At the next level of the conceptual tree, a set of name servers each recognize one of the top level subdomains (e.g., *edu*). At the third level of the tree, name servers recognize subdomains under the top level domains (e.g., *purdue* under *edu*). The conceptual tree continues with one server at each level for which a subdomain has been defined.

Links in the conceptual tree do not indicate physical connections. Instead, they show which other name servers a given server knows and contacts. Because links follow the subdivision of authority, a link in the tree from a node labeled *x*, down to a node labeled *y*, means that *y* is a subdomain of *x*. Before authority can be granted for a subdomain, the organization requesting it must establish a domain name server so it can be linked into the tree.

18.9 Domain Name Resolution

Although the conceptual tree makes understanding the relationship between servers easy, it hides several subtle details. Looking at the resolution algorithm will help explain them.

Conceptually, domain name resolution proceeds top-down, starting with the root name server and proceeding to servers located at the leaves of the tree. There are two ways to use the domain name system: by contacting name servers one at a time or asking the name server to perform the complete translation. In either case, the client software forms a domain name query that contains the name to be resolved, a declaration of the type of the name, the type of mapping desired, and a code that specifies whether the name server should translate the name completely.

When a domain name server receives a query, it checks to see if the name lies in the subdomain for which it is an authority. If so, it translates the name to an address according to its database and appends an answer to the query before sending it back to the client. If the name server cannot resolve the name completely, it checks to see what type of interaction the client specified. If the client requested complete translation (*recursive resolution* in domain name terminology), the server contacts a domain name server that can resolve the name and returns the answer to the client. If the client requested non-recursive resolution, the name server cannot supply an answer. It generates a reply that specifies the name server the client should contact next to resolve the name.

How does a resolver find a name server at which to begin the search? How does a name server find other name servers that can answer questions when it cannot? The answers are simple. A resolver must know how to contact at least one name sever. To ensure that a domain name server can reach others, the domain system requires that each server know the address of at least one root server†. In addition, a server may know the address of a server for the domain immediately above it (called the *parent*). The domain name servers use a well-known protocol port for all communication, so clients know how to reach a server if they know the IP address of the machine in which the server executes. There is no standard way for hosts to locate the machine on which the local name server runs; that is left to the system designer. In some systems, the address of the machine that supplies domain name service is bound into application programs at compile time, while in others, the address is configured into the operating system at startup. In others, the administrator places the address of a server in a file on secondary storage.

---

†For reliability, there are multiple physical copies of each node in the domain server tree.

18.10 Efficient Translation With Caching

Although it may seem natural to resolve queries by working down the tree of name servers, it can lead to inefficiencies for three reasons. First, most name resolution refers to local names, those found within the same subdivision of the namespace as the machine from which the request originates. Tracing a path through the hierarchy to contact the local authority would be inefficient. Second, if each name resolution always started by contacting the topmost level of the hierarchy, the machine at that point would become overloaded. Third, failure of machines at the topmost levels of the hierarchy would prevent name resolution, even if the local authority could resolve the name. The telephone number hierarchy mentioned earlier helps explain. Although telephone numbers are assigned hierarchically, they are resolved in a bottom-up fashion. Because the majority of telephone calls are local, they can be resolved by the local exchange without searching the hierarchy. Furthermore, calls within a given area code can be resolved without contacting sites outside the area code. When applied to domain names, these ideas lead to a two-step name resolution mechanism that preserves the administrative hierarchy but permits efficient translation.

The two-step name resolution mechanism uses the local server before searching the hierarchy. We have said that most queries to name servers refer to local names. Thus, to keep the cost of resolution low, resolution begins with the local name server. The cost of lookup for nonlocal names can be extremely high, however, if a resolver must send each query through the name server system to the server that has authority for the name. Thus, to improve the overall performance of the name server system, it is necessary to lower the cost of lookup for nonlocal names.

Internet name servers use *name caching* to optimize search costs. Each server maintains a cache of recently used names as well as a record of where the mapping information for that name was obtained. When a client asks the server to resolve a name, the server first checks to see if it has authority for the name according to the standard procedure. If not, the server checks its cache to see if the name was resolved recently. Servers report cached information to clients, but mark it as a *nonauthoritative* binding, and give the domain name of the server, S, from which they obtained the binding. The local server also sends along additional information that tells the client the binding between S and an Internet address. So the client receives an answer quickly, but the information may be out-of-date. If efficiency is important, the client will choose to accept the nonauthoritative answer and proceed. If accuracy is important, the client will choose to contact the authority and verify that the binding between name and address is still valid.

Caching works well in the domain name system because name to address bindings change infrequently. However, they do change. If servers cached information the first time it was requested and never changed it, entries in the cache could become incorrect. To keep the cache correct, servers timeout each entry and dispose of entries that exceed a reasonable time. When the server is asked for the information after it has removed the entry from the cache, it must go back to the authoritative source and obtain the binding again. More important, servers do not apply a single fixed timeout to all entries, but allow the authority for an entry to configure its timeout. Whenever an authority responds to a request, it includes a *Time To Live* (TTL) value in the response that specifies how long the server expects the binding to remain true. Thus, authorities can reduce network overhead by specifying long timeouts for entries that they expect to remain unchanged, while improving correctness by specifying short timeouts for entries that they expect to change frequently.

Caching is important in hosts as well as local domain name servers. Many timesharing systems run a complex form of resolver code that attempts to provide even more efficiency than the server system. The host downloads the complete database of names and addresses from a local domain name server at startup, maintains its own cache of recently used names, and uses the server only when names are not found. Naturally, a host that maintains a copy of the local server database must check with the server periodically to obtain new mappings and it must also timeout entries from its cache. However, most sites have little trouble maintaining consistency because domain names change so infrequently.

Keeping a copy of the local server's database in each host has several advantages. Obviously, it makes name resolution on local hosts extremely fast because it means the host can resolve names without any network activity. It also means that the local site has protection in case the local name server fails. Finally, it reduces the computational load on the name server, and makes it possible for a given server to supply names to more machines.

18.11 Domain Server Message Format

Looking at the details of messages exchanged between clients and domain name servers will help clarify how the system operates from the view of a typical application program. The client formats a message that contains one or more questions and sends it to the server. Each question is essentially a domain name for which the client seeks an Internet address. The server responds by returning a similar message that contains answers to the questions for which the server has bindings, as well as information about other name servers that the client can contact for questions that the server cannot answer directly. Figure 18.3 shows the message format.

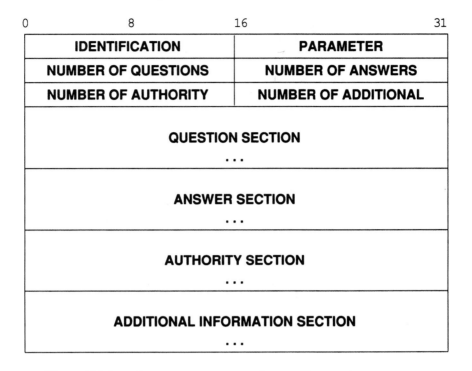

Figure 18.3 Domain name server message format. The question, answer, authority, and additional information sections are variable length.

As Figure 18.3 shows, each message begins with a fixed header that contains a unique *IDENTIFICATION* that the client uses to match responses to queries. In the header, the field labeled *PARAMETER* specifies the operation requested and a response code, as shown in Figure 18.4 below.

The fields labeled *NUMBER OF* each give a count of entries in the corresponding field that occurs later in the message. For example, the field labeled *NUMBER OF QUESTIONS* gives the count of entries that appear in the *QUESTION SECTION* of the message. The *QUESTION SECTION* contains queries for which answers are desired. The client fills in only the question section; the server returns the questions and answers in its response. Each question consists of a *QUERY DOMAIN NAME* followed by *QUERY TYPE* and *QUERY CLASS* fields, as Figure 18.5 shows.

Bits of PARAMETER	Meaning

0	Operation:
	  0 Query
	  1 Response

1-4	Query Type:
	  0 Standard
	  1 Inverse
	  2 Completion 1 (now obsolete)
	  3 Completion 2 (now obsolete)

5	Set if answer authoritative
6	Set if message truncated
7	Set if recursion desired
8	Set if recursion available
9-11	Reserved

12-15	Response Type:
	  0 No error
	  1 Format error in query
	  2 Server failure
	  3 Name does not exist

Figure 18.4 The meaning of bits of the *PARAMETER* field in a domain name server message. Bits are numbered left to right starting at 0.

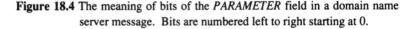

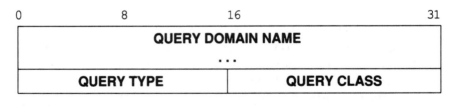

Figure 18.5 The format of entries in the question section of a domain name server message. Clients fill in the questions; servers return them along with answers.

The *QUERY TYPE* encodes the type of the question (e.g., whether the question refers to a machine name or mail address). The *QUERY CLASS* field allows domain names to be used for arbitrary objects because Internet names are only one possible class. It should be noted that, although the diagram in Figure 18.5 follows the convention of showing formats in 32-bit multiples, the query domain name field may contain an odd number of octets. No padding is used. Therefore, messages to or from domain name servers may contain an odd number of octets.

In a domain name server message, each of the answer, authority, and additional information sections consists of a set of *resource records* that describe domain names and mappings. Each resource record describes one name. Figure 18.6 shows the format.

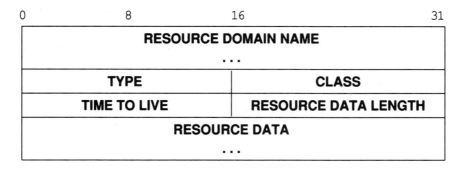

Figure 18.6 The format of resource records used in later sections of messages returned by domain name servers.

The *RESOURCE DOMAIN NAME* field contains a domain name to which this resource record refers. It may be an odd length. The *TYPE* field specifies the type of the data included in the resource record. The *TIME TO LIVE* field contains an integer that specifies the number of seconds information in this resource record can be cached. It is used by clients who have requested a name binding and may want to cache the results. The last two fields contain the results of the binding, with the *RESOURCE DATA LENGTH* field specifying the count of octets in the *RESOURCE DATA* field.

18.12 Compressed Name Format

Domain name servers often return multiple answers to a query and, in many cases, suffixes of the domain names overlap. To conserve space in the reply packet, the name servers compress names by storing only one copy of each domain name. When following a domain name, the client software must check each segment of the name to see whether it consists of a literal string (in the standard format of a 1-byte count followed by the characters that make up the name) or a pointer to a literal string. When it encounters a pointer, the client must follow the pointer to a new place in the message to find the remainder of the name.

Pointers always occur at the beginning of segments and are encoded in the count byte. If the top 2 bits of the 8-bit segment count field are 1s, the client must take the next 14 bits as an integer pointer. If the top two bits are zero, the next 6 bits represent a count of the characters that follow.

18.13 Abbreviation Of Domain Names

The telephone number hierarchy illustrates another useful feature of local resolution, viz., *name abbreviation*. Abbreviation provides a method of shortening names when the resolving process can supply part of the name automatically. Normally, a subscriber omits the area code when dialing a local telephone number. The resulting digits form an abbreviated name assumed to lie within the same area code as the subscriber's phone. Abbreviation also works well for machine names. Given a name like *xyz* the resolving process can assume it lies in the same local authority as the machine on which it is being resolved. Thus, the resolver can supply missing parts of the name automatically. For example, within the Computer Science Department at Purdue, the abbreviated name

xinu

is equivalent to the full domain name

xinu . cs . purdue . edu

We said that the client takes responsibility for the expansion of such abbreviations, but it should be emphasized that such abbreviations are not part of the domain name system itself. Programs that depend on abbreviations may not work correctly outside the environment in which they were built. We can summarize:

> *The Internet domain name system only maps full domain names into addresses; abbreviations are not part of the domain name system itself, but are introduced by client software to make local names convenient for users.*

18.14 Inverse Mappings

We said that the domain name system can provide mappings other than machine name to Internet address. *Inverse queries* allow the client to ask a server to map "backwards" by taking an answer and generating the question that would produce that answer. Of course, not all answers have a unique question. Even when they do, a server may not be able to answer it. Although inverse queries have been part of the domain system since it was first specified, they are generally not used. The chief problem is that there is often no way to find the server that can resolve the inverse query without searching the entire set of servers.

18.15 Pointer Queries

One form of inverse mapping is so obviously needed that the domain system supports a special domain and a special form of question called a *pointer query* to answer it. In a pointer query, the question presented to a domain name server specifies an Internet address encoded as a printable string in the form of a domain name (i.e., text separated by periods). A pointer query requests the name server to return the correct domain name for the machine with the specified Internet address. Pointer queries are especially useful for diskless machines because they allow the system to obtain a high-level name given only an Internet address. (We have already seen in Chapter 6 how a diskless machine obtains its Internet address.)

Pointer queries are not difficult to generate. If we think of the Internet address written in dotted-decimal form, it has the following format:

$$aaa.bbb.ccc.ddd$$

To form a pointer query, the client rearranges the dotted decimal representation of the address into a string of the form:

$$ddd.ccc.bbb.aaa.in\text{-}addr.arpa$$

The new form is a name in the special *in-addr.arpa* domain. The local name server may not be the authority for either the *arpa* domain or the *in-addr.arpa* domain, so it may need to contact other name servers to complete the resolution. To make the resolution of pointer queries efficient, the root domain servers maintain a database of Internet addresses along with information about domain name servers that can resolve each address.

18.16 Extensions To Other Types Of Names

We have mentioned that the domain name system can be used for translating mailbox names to hosts as well as for translating host names to Internet addresses. The domain system is quite general in that it can be used for arbitrary hierarchical names. For example, one might decide to store the names of available computational services along with mappings from service name to the telephone number of a person to call to find out about that service. Or one might store names of protocol products along with mappings to the name and address of vendors that offered such products.

To accommodate additional mappings, all data in the domain system has a *type* assigned to it. Most data is of type *IN*, meaning that it consists of the name of a host attached to the Internet along with the host's Internet address. The second most useful domain type, known as *MX*, is assigned to names used in electronic mail. When sending a request, a client must specify the type; servers always specify the type of a response in the resource records they return. Thus, it is possible to have a single domain server participate in two or more conceptually separate hierarchies simultaneously because the requests and responses specify the type of the mapping.

18.17 Obtaining Authority For A Subdomain

Before an institution is granted authority for a second-level domain, it must agree to operate a domain name server that meets Internet standards. Of course, a domain name server must obey the protocol standards that specify message formats and the rules for responding to requests. The server must also know the addresses of servers that handle each subdomain (if any exist) as well as the address of its parent in the tree of servers.

In practice, the domain system is much more complex than we have outlined. In most cases, a single physical server may handle more than one level of the naming hierarchy as long as the levels all lie under a common point in the naming hierarchy. For example, a single name server at Purdue University handles both the second-level domain *purdue.edu* as well as the third-level domain *cs.purdue.edu*. The set of names managed by a given name server forms a *zone of authority*. Another practical complication arises because servers must be able to handle many requests, even though some requests take a long time to resolve. Usually, servers support concurrent activity, allowing work to proceed on later requests while earlier ones are being processed. Handling requests concurrently is especially important when the server receives a recursive request that forces it to send the request on to another server for resolution.

Server implementation is also complicated because the standard requires the information in every domain name server to be replicated in at least one additional domain name server that shares no single common point of failure with the original. Avoiding common points of failure means that the two name servers cannot even obtain electrical power from the same source. To meet the requirements, a site must find another site that agrees to operate a backup name server. Of course, the parent name server knows how to locate both the primary and backup name servers for a given name, and it can direct queries to the backup name server if the primary name server is unavailable.

18.18 Summary

Hierarchical naming systems allow delegation of authority for names, making it possible to accommodate an arbitrarily large set of names without overwhelming a central site with administrative duties. Although name resolution is separate from delegation of authority, it is possible to create hierarchical naming systems in which resolution is an efficient process that proceeds from the local server even though delegation of authority always flows from the top of the hierarchy downward.

We examined the Internet domain name system, an example of a distributed, hierarchical naming scheme. Domain name servers map high-level domain names to Internet addresses and Internet addresses to domain names. Clients begin by trying to resolve names locally. When the local server cannot resolve the name, the client must choose to work through the tree of name servers iteratively or request the local name server to do it recursively. Finally, we saw that the domain name system also supports binding from Internet addresses to high-level names.

FOR FURTHER STUDY

Mockapetris [RFC 1034] discusses Internet domain naming in general, giving the overall philosophy, while Mockapetris [RFC 1035] provides a protocol standard for domain naming. Older versions appeared in Mockapetris [RFC 822, 823, and 973]. Postel and Reynolds [RFC 920] state the requirements that an Internet domain name server must meet. Stahl [RFC 1032] gives administrators guidelines for establishing a domain, and Lottor [RFC 1033] provides guidelines for operating a domain name server. Finally, Partridge [RFC 974] relates domain naming to electronic mail addressing.

EXERCISES

18.1   Machine names should not be bound into the operating system at compile time. Explain why.

18.2   Would you prefer to use a machine that obtained its name from a remote file or from a name server? Why?

18.3   Why should each name server know the Internet address of its parent instead of the domain name of its parent?

18.4   Devise a naming scheme that tolerates changes to the naming hierarchy. As an example, consider that two large companies each have an independent hierarchy and they merge. Can you arrange to have all previous names still work correctly?

18.5   Read the standard and find out when the domain name system uses *MX* records.

18.6   The Internet domain naming system can also accommodate mailbox names. Find out how.

18.7   The standard suggests that when a program needs to find the domain name associated with an Internet address, it should send an inverse query to the local server first and use domain *in-addr.arpa* only if that fails. Why?

18.8   How would you accommodate abbreviations in the Internet domain naming scheme? Sketch name servers for two departments at each of two universities as well as a top level name server. Explain how each server would treat each type of abbreviation.

18.9   Obtain the official description of the Internet domain name system and build a client program.

18.10   Extend the exercise above to include a pointer query. Try looking up the domain name for address *128.10.2.1* .

19

Application Level Services

19.1 Introduction

This chapter continues our exploration of Internetworking by considering important high level Internet services like electronic mail and the protocols that support them. These services form an integral part of the Internet. They determine how users perceive the Internet and demonstrate the advantages of Internet technology.

We will learn that high level services provide increased communication functionality and allow users to interact with one another as well as with remote machines. We will see that such services are implemented with application level programs, and we will learn how they depend on the network level services described in previous chapters. Finally, we will review the network services that users are likely to encounter and relate them to the protocols we have studied.

19.2 Remote Interactive Computing

We have already seen how the client–server model can provide specific computational services like a time of day service to multiple machines. Reliable stream protocols like TCP make it possible to imagine interactive use of remote machines as well. For example, we can imagine building a server that provides a remote text editing service. We would need a server that accepted requests to edit a file and a client to make a request. To invoke the remote editor service, a user would execute the client program. The client would establish a TCP connection from the local machine to the server and it would then begin sending keystrokes to the server and reading screen output that the server sent back.

How can remote interactive computing be generalized? The problem with using one server for each computational service is that machines quickly become clogged with server processes. We can eliminate most specialized servers and provide more generality by allowing the user to establish a login session on the remote machine and then execute commands. With a *remote login* facility, users have access to all the commands available on the remote system, and system designers need not provide specialized servers.

Of course, providing remote login may not be simple. Most extant timesharing systems were designed before networks became popular, so they expect login sessions only from directly connected terminals. Adding a remote login server will probably require modifying the machine's operating system. On some systems, building interactive client software may be difficult. Consider, for example, systems that assign special meaning to some keystrokes. If the local system interprets Control–C to mean ''abort the currently executing command process,'' it may be impossible to pass Control–C to the remote machine. But if the client chooses to pass Control-C to the remote site, it may be impossible to abort the local client process.

Despite the technical difficulties, system programmers have managed to build remote login server software for most operating systems and to construct application programs that act as a client. Often, the client software overrides the local interpretation of all keys except one, allowing the user to interact with the remote machine exactly as one would from a locally connected terminal. The single key execption provides a way for the user to abort the client program and return to normal local processing. In addition, some remote login protocols recognize a set of *trusted hosts*, permitting remote login from such hosts without verifying passwords.

19.3 Internet TELNET Protocol

The Internet protocol suite includes a simple remote terminal protocol called *TEL-NET*. TELNET allows a user at one site to establish a TCP connection to a login server at another, and then it passes keystrokes from the local machine directly to the remote machine. Although TELNET is not sophisticated compared to some remote terminal protocols, it is widely available on the Internet. Usually, TELNET client software allows the user to specify a remote machine by Internet address as well as by domain name. Because it accepts Internet addresses, TELNET can be used with hosts even if the name-to-address binding cannot be established (e.g., when domain naming software is being debugged).

TELNET offers three basic services. First, it defines a *network virtual terminal* that provides an interface to remote systems against which client programs are built. Second, it includes a mechanism that allows the client and server to negotiate options and it provides a set of standard options (e.g., an option controls whether data passed across the connection is binary or ascii text). Finally, TELNET treats boths ends of the connection symmetrically. So, instead of forcing one end to connect to a user's terminal, TELNET allows either end of the connection to be a program.

Figure 19.1 illustrates how application level processes implement TELNET. As the figure shows, when a user invokes TELNET, an application program on the user's machine becomes the client. It contacts the server at a well-known TCP port and establishes a connection over which they will communicate. The client accepts keystrokes from the user's terminal and sends them to the server, while concurrently accepting characters that the server sends back and displaying them on the user's terminal. The server must accept a TCP connection and then relay data between the TCP connection and the local operating system.

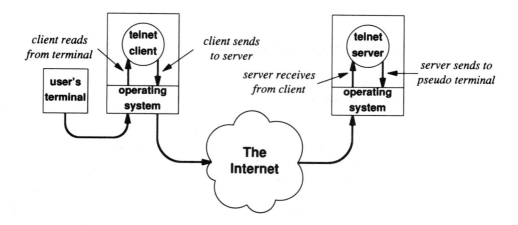

Figure 19.1 The path of data in a TELNET remote terminal session as it travels from the user's terminal to the remote operating system. Adding a TELNET server to a timesharing system usually requires modifying the operating system.

In practice, the server is more complex than the figure shows because it must handle multiple, concurrent connections. Usually, a single server process waits for new connections and spawns a new program to handle each connection. Thus, the "telnet server," shown in Figure 19.1, is only the small piece of the server system that handles a single connection. The figure does not show processes handling other connections nor does it show the original server that listens for new requests.

We use the term *pseudo terminal*† to describe the operating system entry point that allows a running program like the TELNET server to simulate a terminal. It is impossible to build a TELNET server unless the operating system supplies such a facility.

Arranging for the TELNET server to be an application level program has advantages and disadvantages. The most obvious advantage is that it makes modification and control of the server easier than if the code were embedded in the operating system. The obvious disadvantage is inefficiency. Each keystroke travels from the user's terminal through the operating system to the client program, from the client program back through the operating system and across the Internet to the server machine. After reaching the

---

†UNIX calls the entry point a *pseudo tty* because terminal devices are called *ttys*.

destination machine, the data must travel up through the server's operating system to the server application program and, finally, from the server application program back into the server's operating system at a pseudo terminal entry point. Meanwhile, output travels back from the server to the client over the same path.

Readers who understand operating systems will appreciate that for the implementation shown in Figure 19.1, every keystroke requires the machines to switch process context several times. In some systems, an additional context switch is required because the operating system on the server's machine must pass characters from the pseudo terminal back to another application program (e.g., a command interpreter). Although context switching is expensive, the scheme is practical because users do not type at high speed.

19.4 Rlogin (4.3 BSD UNIX)

The 4.3 BSD UNIX system includes a remote login service, *rlogin*, that understands trusted hosts. It allows system administrators to choose a set of machines over which login names and file access protections are globally shared and to establish equivalences among user logins. Users can control access to their account by authorizing remote login based on remote host and remote user name. Thus, it is possible for a user to have login name *X* on one machine and *Y* on another, and still be able to remotely login from one of the machines to the other without typing a login name or password each time.

Having automatic authorization makes remote login facilities useful for general purpose programs as well as human interaction. One variant of the 4.3 BSD *rlogin* command, *rsh*, invokes a command interpreter on the remote UNIX machine and passes the command line arguments to the command interpreter, skipping the login step completely. The format is

rsh machine command

Thus, typing

rsh merlin ps

on any of the machines in the Computer Science Department at Purdue University executes the *ps* command on machine *merlin* (with UNIX's standard input and standard output connected across the network to the user's terminal). The user sees the output as if logged into machine *merlin*. Because the user can arrange to have *rsh* invoke remote commands without prompting for a password, it can be used in programs as well as from the keyboard.

Because protocols like *rlogin* understand both the local and remote computing environments, they communicate between them better than general purpose remote login protocols like TELNET. For example, *rlogin* understands the UNIX notions of *standard input*, *standard output*, and *standard error*, and uses TCP to connect them to the remote machine. Thus, it is possible to type

```
rsh merlin ps > xxx
```

and have output from the remote command redirected† into file *xxx*. *Rlogin* also understands terminal control functions like flow control characters (typically Control–S and Control–Q). It arranges to stop output immediately without waiting for the delay required to send them across the network to the remote host. Finally, rlogin exports as much of the user's environment to the remote machine as possible, including information like the user's terminal type. As a result, remote login sessions appear to behave almost exactly like local login sessions.

19.5 File Transfer

The term *file transfer* means copying a file from one machine to another. It is among the most frequently used network operations. Because files can be large objects, file transport is an operation that can generate much network traffic. Given a reliable end-to-end transport protocol like TCP, file transfer might seem trivial. However, the transfer of bytes from one machine to another can only be accomplished after files have been identified and the transfer has been authorized.

Even though a process at one machine must initiate the transfer, many file transfer protocols permit transfer in either direction. That is, the client may send a file to the server's machine or request a file from the server's machine. To make such a transfer, users invoking the client must identify themselves and obtain access permissions. Local permission is handled by the local operating system (e.g., permissions are granted at login based on login id and password). Users accessing remote files must also identify themselves to the server which is responsible for authenticating the client before it allows file transfer. The server also may need to check and enforce permissions on individual files or directories.

Remote authorization can be difficult, especially in an insecure network. File transfer protocols that have clients send unencrypted passwords over a network are susceptible to eavesdroppers who, once they have discovered the password, will have access to all the files it protects. One way to simplify a family of protocols is to solve the authorization problem once and build other protocols on top of it.

19.6 Internet File Transfer Protocol (FTP)

The Internet protocol suite includes a file transfer protocol, *FTP*. FTP allows authorized users to log into a remote system, identify themselves, list remote directories, copy files to or from the remote machine, and execute a few simple commands remotely (e.g., to obtain help with the remote machine file name syntax). In addition, FTP understands a few basic file formats and can convert among popular representations (e.g., between EBCDIC and ASCII character sets). Although FTP allows direct, interactive use by humans, the protocol is designed to be used by programs. Many FTP implementations provide statistics on transfer rates and diagnostic aids like packet tracing.

---

†The "greater than" symbol is the usual UNIX syntax for directing the output of a command into a file.

FTP is more complex than TELNET for three reasons. First, it allows a user to access multiple machines in a single "session." Second, it maintains separate TCP connections for control and data transfer. Third, it uses the TELNET protocol for its control connection. The main advantage of TELNET is that it provides an authentication system that allows users to identify themselves to the remote system.

In the simplest case, FTP operates between a pair of machines. Figure 19.2 illustrates the connections between the client and server.

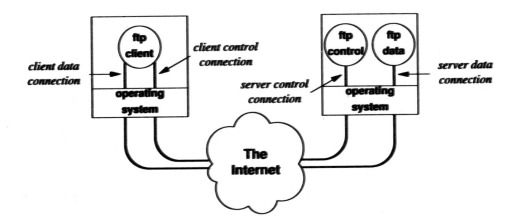

Figure 19.2 The simplest use of FTP. The client contacts the server, establishes a separate TCP connection for data transfer, and transfers the file.

As the figure shows, the client forms two connections to the server, one is used to pass control information (e.g., to send the name of a file and the operation desired), while the other is used to transfer the file itself.

Although the exact implementation of an FTP server depends on the operating system, many follow a pattern. At the server site, a single application process, S, runs in background waiting for a connection at the well-known FTP port. When a client opens a connection to the well-known port, process S starts a new FTP control process, N, to handle the incoming connection and goes back to waiting for another client to contact it. Process N communicates with the client over the "control connection," as shown in Figure 19.2. It forces the client to supply a login id and password before allowing any transfer. FTP uses the control connection to allow clients to list remote directories, set the mode for transfer, and specify the names of files to be transferred. Finally, after the user has logged in and the client has requested a transfer, process N starts an additional process, D, to handle the data transfer. D opens a second TCP connection to the client, to be used only for data transfer. Once the data transfer completes, process D closes the connection and terminates. The client resumes interacting with N and may request another transfer.

Not all systems follow the procedure outlined above, of course. The facilities available in some systems make it easier to have the client start an additional process to handle data transfer just like the server starts an additional process. Others require additional processes to validate login ids and passwords. For the simple case, however, the exact number of processes is irrelevant.

FTP is a sophisticated protocol that can do much more than transfer files from a server to a client. For example, FTP can handle third party transfers. To do so, a client must open control connections to servers on two remote machines, call them A and B. The client must have permission to transfer a file from A and permission to transfer a file to B. It asks the server on A to transfer the file to B. The server on A forms a direct TCP connection to the server on B and transfers the data across it. The client retains control of the transfer but does not participate in moving data.

19.7 Internet Trivial File Transfer Protocol

A second Internet file transfer protocol provides inexpensive, unsophisticated service known as the *Trivial File Transfer Protocol*, or *TFTP*. TFTP is intended for applications where complex interactions among clients and servers are not needed. Because TFTP is restricted to simple file transfers, it is much smaller than FTP.

Small size is important in many applications. For example, manufacturers of diskless workstations can encode TFTP in read-only memory (ROM) chips and use it to obtain an initial memory image when the machine is powered on. The program in ROM is called the system *bootstrap*. The advantage of using TFTP is that it allows bootstrapping code to use the same underlying Internet protocols that the running system uses.

Unlike FTP, TFTP does not use a reliable stream service. It runs on top of UDP or any unreliable packet delivery system. It uses timeout and retransmission to ensure that data arrives. The sending side transmits a file in fixed size (*512* byte) blocks and awaits an acknowledgement for each block before sending the next. The receiver acknowledges each block.

The rules for TFTP are simple. The first packet sent requests a file transfer and establishes the interaction between client and server. Blocks of the file are numbered consecutively starting at *1*. Each data packet contains the number of the block it carries, and each acknowledgement contains the number of the block being acknowledged. A block of less than *512* bytes signals the end of file. It is possible to send an error message, either in the place of data or an acknowledgement; errors terminate the transfer.

Retransmission in TFTP is unusual because it is symmetric. Each side implements a timeout and retransmission. If the side sending data times out, it retransmits the last data block. If the side sending acknowledgements times out, it retransmits the last acknowledgement. Having both sides participate in retransmission helps ensure that transfer will not fail after a single packet loss.

Although TFTP contains little except the minimum needed for transfer, it does support multiple file types. One interesting part of TFTP allows it to be integrated with electronic mail (see next section). A client can specify to the server that it will send a file that should be treated as mail (with the "file name" taken to be the identifier of a mailbox to which the server should deliver the message).

19.8 Electronic Mail

Most users first encounter computer networks when they send or receive electronic mail to or from a remote site. Indeed, many users never use a network except for electronic mail. Mail is popular because it offers a fast, convenient method of transferring information. It can accommodate small notes or large voluminous memos, with a single mechanism. It should not surprise you to learn that more users send files with electronic mail than with file transfer programs.

Mail delivery is a new concept because it differs fundamentally from other uses of networks that we have discussed. In all our examples, network protocols send packets directly to destinations, using timeout and retransmission for individual segments if no acknowledgement returns. In the case of electronic mail, however, the system must provide for instances when the remote machine or the network connections have failed. The user does not want to wait for the remote machine before continuing work, nor does the user want to have the transfer abort if the remote machine is not available.

To handle delayed delivery, mail systems use a technique known as *spooling*. When the user "sends" a mail message, the system places a copy in its private storage (spool) area along with identification of the sender, recipient, destination machine, and time of deposit. The system then initiates background transfer.

The background mail process maps the destination machine name to an Internet address and attempts to deliver the message by contacting the mail server on the destination machine. If it succeeds, the background process copies the message to the destination system's spool area and removes the local copy. If it fails, the background process records the time it tried and terminates. The mail system periodically sweeps through the spool area, checking for undelivered mail. When the system finds the message, or when some other user deposits mail, it attempts delivery again. If the software finds that a mail message cannot be delivered after an extended time (e.g., 3 days), it returns the mail message to the sender.

19.9 Mailbox Names And Aliases

There are two important ideas hidden in our description of mail delivery. First, users specify recipients by giving a pair of *destination machine* name and *mailbox address* on that machine. Second, the names used in such specifications are independent of other names assigned to machines. Usually, mailbox addresses are the same as the user's login id, and destination machine names are the same as the machine's domain name, but that is not necessary. It is possible to assign a mailbox to a position of employment (e.g., making the mailbox identifier *department-chair* refer to whomever currently chairs the department). The domain name system supports a database and query type for mail destinations, making it possible to decouple mail destination from the usual domain names used for machines.

Most systems provide an alias mechanism that allows the local site to map mail identifiers to a set of one or more mail addresses. After the user composes a message and names a recipient, the mail interface program consults the local aliases to replace the recipient with the mapped version before passing the message to the delivery system. Recipients for which no mapping has been specified remain unchanged. Similarly, the underlying mail system uses the mail aliases to map incoming recipient addresses.

Having aliases increases mail system functionality and convenience substantially. It allows a single human to have multiple mail identifiers, including nick names and positions. It allows a site to associate groups of recipients with a single identifier. Using aliases, it is possible to establish a mail *exploder* that accepts one incoming message and sends it to a large set of recipients. Not all the recipients on a list need to be local. Although it is uncommon, it is possible to have a mailing list at site, Q, with none of the recipients from the list located at Q. Expanding a mail alias into a large set of recipients is a popular technique used throughout the Internet.

19.10 The Relationship Of Internetworking And Mail

Many commercial computer systems support electronic mail even though they do not connect to the Internet. How do such systems differ from the Internet mail system? There are two crucial differences. First, the Internet makes possible universal delivery service. Second, electronic mail systems built on an Internet are inherently more reliable than those built from arbitrary networks. The first idea is easy to understand. The Internet makes possible universal mail delivery because it provides universal interconnection among machines. In essence, all machines attached to the Internet behave as if attached to a single, vendor independent network. With the basic network services in place, devising a standard mail exchange protocol becomes easier.

The second claim, that having an Internet makes mail delivery more reliable than other mechanisms, needs explanation. The key idea here is that the Internet provides end-to-end connectivity. That is, mail software on the sending machine acts as a client, contacting a server on the ultimate destination. Only after the client successfully transfers a mail message to the server does it remove the message from the local machine. Thus, direct, end-to-end delivery enforces the following principle:

> *Mail systems that use end-to-end delivery can guarantee that each mail message remains in the sender's machine until it has been successfully copied to the recipient's machine.*

With such systems, the sender can always determine the exact status of a message by checking the local mail spool area.

The alternative form of electronic mail delivery uses *mail gateways†*, sometimes called *mail bridges*, or *mail relays*, or *intermediate mail stops* to transfer messages. In

---

†Readers should not confuse the concept of *mail gateway* with the concept of *Internet gateway* discussed earlier.

such systems, the sender's machine does not contact the recipient's machine directly but sends mail across one or more intermediate machines that forward it on.

The main disadvantage of using mail gateways is that they introduce unreliability. Once the sender's machine transfers a message to the first intermediate machine, it discards the local copy. Thus, while the message is in transit, neither the sender nor the recipient have a copy. Failures at intermediate machines may result in message loss without informing either the sender or recipient. Message loss can also result if the mail gateways route mail incorrectly. Another disadvantage of mail gateways is that they introduce delay. A mail gateway can hold messages for minutes, hours, or even days if it cannot forward them on to the next machine. Again, senders cannot determine where messages have been delayed, why they have not arrived, or how long the delay will last. The important point is that the sender and recipient must depend on machines over which they may have no control.

If mail gateways are less reliable than end-to-end delivery, why are they used? The chief advantage of mail gateways is interoperability. They provide connections among standard Internet mail systems and nonstandard mail systems, as well as between the Internet and networks that do not support Internet protocols. Suppose, for example, that company X has a large internal network, and that employees use electronic mail, but that the network software they use does not support TCP/IP. Although it may be infeasible to make the company's network part of the Internet, it might be easy to place a mail gateway between the company's private network and the Internet, and to devise software that accepts mail messages from the local network and forwards them to the Internet.

While the idea of mail gateways may seem somewhat clumsy, electronic mail has turned into such an important tool that users who do not have Internet access depend on them. CSNET provides an interesting example of mail gateway service. Started as an organization to help computer scientists obtain access to each other's research, CSNET members currently include universities, corporations, and sites in foreign countries. CSNET operates a mail gateway service that allows subscriber sites to send and receive mail across the Internet using only a dial-up modem. To do so, subscribers obtain mail system software from CSNET and install it on their machines. The mail gateway polls subscriber sites regularly using a dialup telephone connection, leaves mail that it has for the site, and picks up outgoing mail. The mail gateway, which connects directly to the Internet, sends the outgoing mail using standard techniques.

CSNET's mail delivery service illustrates that mail gateways can be a very effective way for users at non-Internet sites to communicate. Well over 95% of the CSNET mail traffic is delivered in under 24 hours. A given site is able to improve its service by paying for more frequent dial-up connections. Thus, although the service is not as direct as end-to-end delivery, it can still be useful.

19.11 Internet Standard For Electronic Mail Service

Recall that the goal of the Internet effort is to provide for interoperability across the widest range of computer systems and networks. To extend the interoperability of electronic mail, the Internet divides the standards into two sets. One set of standards specifies the format for mail messages†. The other specifies standards for exchange of electronic mail between two computers. Keeping the two standards for electronic mail separate makes it possible to build mail gateways that connect to the Internet on one side and to some other vendor's mail delivery system on the other, while still using the same message format for both.

As anyone who has used electronic mail knows, each memo is divided into two parts: a header and a body. The Internet standard for mail messages specifies the exact format of mail headers as well as the semantic interpretation of each header field; it leaves the format of the body up to the sender. In particular, the standard specifies that headers contain readable text, divided into lines that consist of a keyword followed by a colon followed by a value. For example, a header line that begins *to:* contains the electronic mail address of the recipient. A line that begins *from:* contains the electronic mail address of the sender. A line that begins *reply-to:* specifies an address to which replies should be addressed (it allows the sender to specify that replies should be sent to something other than the sender's usual address).

The mail message format is chosen to make it easy to process. Keeping the mail header format straightforward allows it to be used on a wide range of systems (including personal computers). Using only readable text avoids the problem of selecting a standard binary representation.

Anyone familiar with electronic mail knows that mail address formats seem chaotic. Thus, it can be difficult to determine a correct electronic mail address. Within the Internet, addresses have a simple, easy to remember form:

local-part @ domain-name

where the *domain-name* is the Internet domain name of a machine to which the mail should be delivered, and *local-part* is the address of a mailbox on that machine. For example, within the Internet, the author's electronic mail address is:

comer @ purdue.edu

However, mail gateways make addresses complex. Someone outside the Internet must either address the mail to their nearest mail gateway or have software that automatically does so. For example, someone outside the Internet using the CSNET mail relay machine might address the author as:

comer % purdue.edu @ relay.cs.net

Once the mail reaches *relay.cs.net*, that machine takes the *local-part* and uses that as a

---

†Mail systems experts often refer to the mail message format as "822" or "733" because RFC 822 contains the standard (RFC 733 was a former standard).

destination address. In this example, we are assuming that the relay machine maps the percent sign ''%'' into a commercial at sign ''@.''

The reason addresses become so complex when they include non-Internet sites is that the electronic mail address mapping function is local to each machine. Thus, some mail gateways require the local part to contain addresses of the form:

user % domain-name

while others require

user : domain-name

and still others use completely different forms. We can summarize the problem:

> *Because each mail gateway determines the exact details of how it interprets and maps electronic mail addresses, there is no standard for addresses that cross mail gateway boundaries.*

19.12 Internet Simple Mail Transfer Protocol (SMTP)

In addition to message formats, the Internet specifies a standard for the exchange of mail between machines that attach to it. The standard transfer protocol is known as *SMTP*, the *Simple Mail Transfer Protocol*. As you might guess, SMTP is simpler than an earlier *Mail Transfer Protocol, MTP*. The SMTP protocol focuses specifically on how the underlying mail delivery system passes messages across a link from one machine to another. It does not specify how the mail system accepts mail from a user or how the user interface presents the user with incoming mail. Also, SMTP does not specify how mail is stored or how frequently the mail system attempts to send messages.

SMTP is surprisingly simple. Communication between a client and server consists of readable text. Although SMTP rigidly defines the command format, a transcript of interactions between a client and server is easily read by humans. Initially, the client establishes a reliable stream connection to the server and waits for the server to send a *220 READY FOR MAIL* message. (If the server is overloaded, it may delay sending the *220* message temporarily.) Upon receipt of the *220* message, the client sends a *HELO†* command, where the end of a line marks the end of the command. The server responds by identifying itself. Once communication has been established, the sender can transmit one or more mail messages, terminate the connection, or request the server to turn roles of sender and receiver around so messages can flow in the opposite direction. The receiver must acknowledge each message. It can also abort the entire connection or abort the current message transfer.

Mail transactions begin with a *MAIL* command that gives the sender identification as well as a *FROM:* field that contains the address to which errors should be reported. A recipient resets its data structures to make it ready to receive a new mail message and replies to a *MAIL* command by sending the response *250*. Response *250* means that all is

---

†*HELO* is an abbreviation for ''hello.''

well. The full response consists of the text *250 OK*. Placing numbers at the beginning of each response makes them easier to parse.

After a successful *MAIL* command, the sender issues a series of *RCPT* commands that identify recipients of the mail message. The receiver must acknowledge each *RCPT* command by sending *250 OK* or by sending the error message *550 No such user here*.

After all *RCPT* commands, the sender issues a *DATA* command. The receiver responds with message *354 Start mail input* and specifies a sequence of characters used to terminate mail messages. The termination sequence consists of 5 characters: carriage return, line feed, period, carriage return, and line feed.

An example will make the SMTP exchange clear. Suppose user Smith at host Alpha.EDU sends a message to users Jones, Green, and Brown at host Beta.GOV. The SMTP client software on host Alpha.EDU contacts the SMTP server software on host Beta.GOV and begins the following exchange shown in Figure 19.3.

```
R: 220 Beta.GOV Simple Mail Transfer Service Ready
S: HELO Alpha.EDU
R: 250 Beta.GOV

S: MAIL FROM:<Smith@Alpha.EDU>
R: 250 OK

S: RCPT TO:<Jones@Beta.GOV>
R: 250 OK

S: RCPT TO:<Green@Beta.GOV>
R: 550 No such user here

S: RCPT TO:<Brown@Beta.GOV>
R: 250 OK

S: DATA
R: 354 Start mail input; end with <CR><LF>.<CR><LF>
S: ...sends body of mail message...
S: ...continues for as many lines as message contains
S: <CR><LF>.<CR><LF>
R: 250 OK

S: QUIT
R: 221 Beta.GOV Service closing transmission channel
```

Figure 19.3 Example of SMTP transfer from Alpha.EDU to Beta.GOV. Lines that begin with ''S:'' are transmitted by the sender (Alpha), while lines that begin ''R:'' are transmitted by the receiver. In the example, machine Beta.GOV does not recognize intended recipient Green.

Once a client has finished sending all the mail message it has for a particular destination, the client may issue the *TURN*† command to turn the line around. If it does, the receiver responds *250 OK* and assumes control of the line. With the roles reversed, the side that was originally a server sends back any waiting mail messages or merely issues a *QUIT* command to terminate the session.

SMTP is much more complex than we have outlined here. For example, if a user has moved, the server may know about the user's new mailbox address. SMTP allows the server to choose to inform the client about the new address so the client can use it in the future. When informing the client about a new address, the server may choose to forward the mail that triggered the message or it may request that the client take the responsibility for forwarding.

19.13 Protocol Dependencies

The chart in Figure 19.4 shows dependencies among the major protocols we have discussed. Each enclosed polygon corresponds to one protocol and resides directly above the polygons representing protocols that it uses. For example, the mail protocol, SMTP, depends on TCP, which depends on IP. Both ARP and RARP appear in the diagram, even though not all machines or network technologies use them. In particular, RARP is seldom used except for diskless machines.

On most systems, application programs are limited. They can access any of the protocols that form the top level in Figure 19.4, but nothing below the TCP/UDP level. However, some systems provide special purpose mechanisms that allow an application program to interact with lower protocol layers. For example, having access to ICMP echo request and reply service is especially helpful to programmers building Internet software or network managers responsible for Internet operation and maintenance.

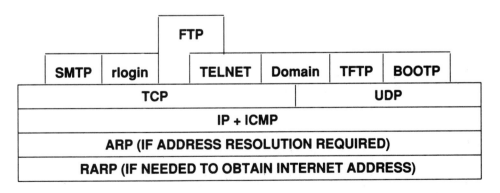

Figure 19.4 Dependencies among higher level Internet protocols. A protocol uses those protocols that lie directly below it. Application programs can use all protocols above IP.

---

†In practice, few mail servers use the *TURN* command.

19.14 Summary

Much of the rich functionality associated with the Internet results from a variety of high level services supplied by application programs. The high level protocols these programs use build on the basic services: unreliable datagram delivery and reliable stream transport. They usually follow the client-server model in which servers operate at known protocols ports so clients know how to contact them.

The highest levels of protocols provide user services like file and mail transfer and remote login. The chief advantages of having an Internet on which to build such services are that it provides universal connectivity and simplifies the application protocols. In particular, when used by two machines that attach to the Internet, services like electronic mail can guarantee that the client program on the source machine communicates directly with the server on the destination machine.

FOR FURTHER STUDY

Many high-level protocols have been proposed, but only a few are in common use. Edge [1979] compares end-to-end protocols with the hop-by-hop approach. Saltzer, Reed, and Clark [1984] argue for having the highest level protocols perform end-to-end acknowledgement and error detection.

Quarterman and Hoskins [1986] discusses how mail gateways connect various networks. Partridge [1986] provides a more theoretical treatment of the problem.

The protocols described in this chapter are all specified in Internet RFCs. Postel [RFC 821] describes the Simple Mail Transfer Protocol and gives many examples. The exact format of mail messages is given by Crocker [RFC 822]. Partridge [RFC 974] discusses the relationship between mail routing and the Internet domain name system. Sluizer [RFC 780] defines the older MTP protocol. Horton [RFC 976] proposes a standard for the UNIX UUCP mail system.

Postel [RFC 854] contains the TELNET remote login protocol specification. It was preceded by over three dozen RFCs that discuss TELNET options, weaknesses, experiments, and proposed changes, including Postel [RFC 764] that contains an earlier standard.

Postel [RFC 959] contains the FTP protocol standard. Like TELNET, over three dozen RFCs comment on FTP, propose modifications, or define new versions of the protocol. Among them, Lottor [RFC 913] describes a Simple File Transfer Protocol. The Trivial File Transfer Protocol described here comes from Sollins [RFC 783]; Finlayson [RFC 906] describes its use in bootstrapping computer systems.

In a series of papers, Mills proposes protocols for clock synchronization and reports on experiments [RFCs 956, 957, and 958].

EXERCISES

19.1   Experiment with both TELNET and rlogin. What are the noticeable differences?

19.2   Despite the large volume of notes written about TELNET, it can be argued that the protocol is still not well defined. Experiment by using TELNET to reach a machine and then
invoking TELNET to reach a second machine. Does your implementation handle the *line
feed* and *carriage control* characters properly?

19.3   Why should file transport protocols compute a checksum on the file data they receive even
when using a reliable end-to-end stream transfer protocol like TCP?

19.4   Find out whether FTP computes a checksum for files it transfers.

19.5   Outline a method that uses TFTP to bootstrap a diskless machine. Be careful. Exactly
what Internet addresses does it use?

19.6   Implement a TFTP client.

19.7   Some mail systems force the user to specify a sequence of machines through which the
message should travel to reach its destination. The mail protocol in each machine merely
passes the message on to the next machine. List three disadvantages of such a scheme.

19.8   Experiment with FTP or an equivalent protocol to see how fast you can transfer a file
between two reasonably large systems across an Ethernet. Try the experiment when the
network is busy and when it is idle. Explain the result.

19.9   What is a remote procedure call?

19.10   Folklore says that operating systems come and go while protocols last forever. Test this
axiom by surveying your local computing site to see whether the operating system or communication protocols have changed more frequently.

19.11   Build TELNET client software.

19.12   Find out if your computing systems allow you to invoke SMTP directly.

19.13   Build an SMTP client and use it to deliver a mail message.

19.14   See if you can send mail through the CSNET mail gateway and back to yourself.

19.15   Make a list of mail address forms that your site handles and write a set of rules for parsing
them.

19.16   Find out how the Berkeley UNIX *sendmail* program can be used to implement a mail gateway.

20

Internet Research And Engineering Problems

20.1 Introduction

With thousands of users at hundreds of sites depending on the Internet as part of their daily work environment, it might seem that the Internet is nothing more than a stable, production facility. It has passed the early stage of development in which every user was also an expert and entered a stage in which few users understand the technology. Despite its appearance, the Internet is not static. It changes as new groups interconnect their networks and find new ways to use the facilities. It also changes as researchers discover ways to solve networking problems and as engineers find ways to improve the underlying mechanisms. In short, the technology evolves.

The purpose of this chapter is to consider the evolutionary process and characterize some of the current research and engineering efforts. We are looking for patterns, not merely facts. Our goal is to understand the work well enough to be able to classify it into broad categories and to assess how it might impact the Internet. Whether the projects we review become integral parts of the Internet technology in the next years or decades is unimportant; the objective here is to provide the reader with some intuition about the scope of research and engineering projects associated with the Internet at a given point in time. While some of these issues will surely fade, others will rise. The motion is never ending.

20.2 The Forces Stimulating Evolution

In a broad sense, four types of change stimulate the evolution of the Internet technology, as Figure 20.1 illustrates. No single thrust dominates the technology.

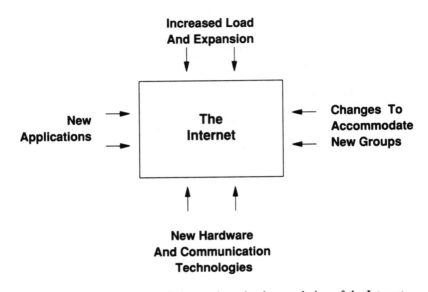

Figure 20.1 The four types of change that stimulate evolution of the Internet technology.

Increased load and expansion. As the user population grows, load increases. Of course, new users arrive when new sites are added to the Internet. Surprisingly, load can also increase when groups at existing Internet sites suddenly start using the facilities. In any case, load can increase faster than the population because as individuals gain access to the Internet, they can stimulate new interactions among existing users. As a result of load, engineers and researchers seek ways to obtain better service from existing facilities.

New technologies. Like most technically oriented groups, researchers working on the Internet maintain a keen interest in new technologies. As new minicomputers became available, Internet researchers used them as packet switches and gateways. Besides conventional packet switching networks that use leased communication lines, Internet research has studied point to point satellite communication, multiple station synchronized satellite communication, and communication using packet radio networks. More recently, Internet researchers have studied voice and video conferencing. Thus, researchers have used new technologies to expand the Internet and improve its capacity to meet increased load. More important, Internet research has produced innovative technology (e.g., the Butterfly multiprocessor used as Internet gateways).

Changes to accommodate new groups. Adding new groups of users differs from merely adding new sites or increasing the load because it results in new administrative authorities. Changes in the authority produce changes in administrative policies and mandate new mechanisms to enforce the new policies. As we have seen, both the architecture of the Internet gateway system and the protocols it uses need to change in fundamental ways to move away from a centralized structure. Many of the research and engineering efforts focus on finding ways to accommodate new administrative groups.

New applications. One of the most exciting frontiers of research, new applications often demand facilities or service that the Internet cannot provide. They stimulate researchers to reconsider both the assumptions underlying Internet architecture and protocols as well as the details of the services the Internet provides.

Although we have listed the four types of stimuli separately, it should be obvious that they interact. A new communication technology may make it possible to support an entirely new set of applications, which, in turn, may entice an entirely new group of users to become interested in joining the Internet. Or it may happen that the need to support increased load stimulates research that yields a new communication technology. Thus, it can be difficult to know which ideas came first.

Despite the difficulty in attributing a given idea to one of the four areas listed above, it will be instructive to do so because it helps us understand the ideas and motivations. The next sections each present one category and list several example research and engineering questions in it.

20.3 Accommodating Expansion And Increased Load

Perhaps the most important short-term problem Internet engineers face is success. The Internet was designed and built as a research prototype. Early estimates suggested the Internet should support dozens of networks and hundreds of host computers. By 1987, the size had reached hundreds of active networks and tens of thousands of hosts. But numbers alone do not accurately reveal the problem: the rate of growth changed dramatically from the slow, steady pace of early years to a sudden explosion in connectivity. One observation from the late summer of 1987 suggested the growth rate had reached 15% per month.

The engineering and research questions underlying rapid expansion are complex and we can only list a few. We begin with routing issues.

> *Question: will the current Internet routing mechanisms operate with substantially more hosts and networks, and if not, what must be done to accommodate an order of magnitude growth?*

Recall that the current routing model requires at least some gateways to have tables proportional to the number of IP network addresses. Knowing that routing tables would exceed the addressing capability of the old LSI-11 computers used for core gateways, Internet engineers have adopted a new generation of hardware that will accommodate much larger tables. Transition to the new hardware should be complete by the end of 1988.

New hardware alone will not solve all the routing problems. As we have seen, exterior gateways using EGP to advertise network reachability have a more serious problem because EGP requires the list of all networks being advertised to fit into a single IP datagram. One of the Internet engineering efforts is focused on designing a new version of EGP that removes the single packet limitation.

The subnet routing and transparent gateway schemes described in Chapter 16 have been invented to help solve the expansion problem. If every site used subnet addressing, the size of core gateway tables would grow more slowly, making it possible to use current technology longer. Thus, work on subnetting will continue until it becomes a well understood and integral part of all IP implementations.

Other researchers are considering more dramatic changes to the Internet addressing and routing scheme that remove dependency on the core system. One idea is called *landmark routing*, with the name coming from an analogy to the way humans navigate. We think of each gateway as having a measure of importance determined by the span of its knowledge base. Gateways that only know about directly connected networks are least important; those that know about networks within a large radius of themselves are quite important. The important gateways are known as landmarks. Under the landmark scheme, host addresses must include both a nearby landmark as well as a specific network and host identifier. When routing, a gateway can route easily to destinations within its radius of information using only the network and host identifier. To route to distant destinations, the gateway uses the landmark information.

One advantage of a landmark addressing and routing scheme is that it places gateways in a hierarchy that can be extended to accommodate growth. Another advantage is that because each gateway makes a completely independent decision about each packet, the initial gateway does not have to select the ultimate route. The initial gateway picks a landmark and routes the packet on toward it. As the packet approaches the landmark, it passes through gateways that may know about the destination network (because it lies close to them). As soon as a gateway knows a better path, it forwards the packet down that path. Thus, even though landmarks are used as targets, they do not have to process all traffic that enters their region from distant sources.

Increases in load imply increases in the number of individual users. A problem arises because it becomes difficult to locate information about a given individual. When the Internet began, the Network Information Center published a directory of all users along with their postal and electronic mail addresses. With a user population growing rapidly, printed directories are hopelessly inadequate. The central question has become:

> *How can we automate mechanisms for storing and locating information about individual users?*

It is easy to see how to build client and server software that allows one to access an on-line database of user names, addresses, and telephone numbers. The NIC has such a database, as does CSNET. Unfortunately, centralized facilities have two major drawbacks: the information becomes out of date quickly because users do not take an active interest in updating their entries and the central server is a bottleneck through which all traffic must pass (a central server also causes the entire system to fail if it is unavailable).

It is more challenging to design a system that can expand indefinitely, allows fairly broad database queries (e.g., to find all users with first name "peter"), and keeps the information current. The problem is known as the *white pages problem*, the name being a reference to the white pages of a U.S. telephone book. Internet researchers are building a prototype white pages service that uses an architecture built around hierarchically organized, distributed servers. The architecture is not unlike that of the domain name system, but the problem is much different because it admits a wider range of queries.

A related problem occurs because a mechanism is needed that allows users to locate Internet services. In the beginning, it was possible to send out mail or even draft an RFC requesting information about which hosts offered which services. As the Internet expands, manual schemes become hopelessly inadequate. This problem, known as the *yellow pages problem*, can be summarized:

> *How can we automate mechanisms for storing and locating information*
> *about services offered by hosts in the Internet?*

Researchers are examining automated ways to allow hosts to advertise services that are available and to locate services on other hosts. The ultimate goal is to have a system in which any user can find desired computational services quickly and invoke those services with little overhead. Again, the problem differs from the domain name lookup problem because multiple hosts offer a given service and because services change more quickly than host names.

Expansion also affects the way we manage the Internet and the networks that comprise it. Early management schemes consisted of cooperation among researchers who built and used Internet software. The gateways came from very few vendors who each devised whatever monitoring or control software they thought was needed. If a particular host or protocol implementation caused problems, researchers cooperated to identify the problem and then simply discussed it with whoever was responsible for the offending host. Since those early days, the Internet has grown in complexity as well as size. Now, many vendors manufacture gateways, protocols, and application software. Many systems programmers install, modify, and maintain Internet protocol software. Clearly, automated methods are needed to manage the Internet.

To understand the Internet management problem well, we must remember that at the lowest level the Internet uses a best-effort, datagram delivery service. Connectionless delivery means all traffic uses common resources like gateways and servers without preallocation. The result is that when a system misbehaves, it can affect others. The management question becomes:

*How can we create automated, vendor independent mechanisms that
will allow network managers to monitor and control traffic in the Internet as well as its constituent networks?*

One final problem deserves special attention because it has been a constant theme of
Internet work. Although expansion and increased load often provide immediate incen-
tives to work on it, the problem is more fundamental:

*How can we improve protocols, including message formats and the
underlying algorithms, or the implementations of protocols?*

The problem is notable not only because it is constantly on the minds of Internet
researchers, but because there have been outstanding successes. Recently, for example,
work on TCP retransmission timer computations has produced new implementations that
achieve ten times the throughput of early implementations.

20.4 New Applications

The birth of any new technology stimulates creative people to find new ways to use
it. The Internet is no exception. As soon as users become comfortable with the technology, they begin to apply it to their everyday tasks. They imagine new uses of the existing
technology and dream of how slightly more advanced technology can make their work
even easier. There are more new applications driving the Internet than we can hope to
cover here. So, instead of a survey, we will concentrate on a handful of research projects. These projects have been selected because they illustrate both innovation and utility.

Readers who lack first hand experience with existing Internet facilities may find
new applications difficult to appreciate. To make sure everyone begins from a common
point of view, we will spend a short time reviewing an existing service, electronic mail,
and the way people with Internet access use it. While the discussion presents one point
of view, that of a scientist, most of the activities described are common to most professional jobs.

Electronic mail forms an integral part of most Internet users' professional environment. People who have access to the Internet environment quickly begin to depend on
electronic mail as their primary form of business communication. For experienced users,
it is difficult to imagine a world without it. Scientists, for example, use electronic mail to
exchange technical papers and scientific data, to debate technical ideas, to announce new
results to colleagues, to schedule national meetings, to submit research proposals, and to
replace most telephone conversations. Besides using electronic mail for interactions
among distant parties, the scientist uses it to contact local groups like the business office
or purchasing agent. The advantages are obvious: while electronic communication provides a written record, it is much faster than postal delivery. By integrating local and re-

mote communication, the scientist is able to have a uniform environment for conducting business. Unlike a telephone, electronic mail does not require the two correspondents to rendezvous at exactly the same time. Finally, electronic mail allows a user to define sets of colleagues so memos can be distributed to a group as easily as to an individual.

As an example, consider scientists working together on a project. They distribute periodic reports of progress and conduct technical discussions by electronic mail. When they do decide to meet face to face, the person who volunteers to make local arrangements collects information about arrival and departure times and informs the groups about travel and hotel accommodations by electronic mail. The chairperson distributes a meeting agenda by electronic mail and collects suggestions for additions or changes. After the meeting, the secretary mails minutes of the meeting to the chairperson for approval and, once the chairperson approves, distributes minutes to the entire group. Finally the scientists use electronic mail to send summaries of progress to funding agencies.

For people with access to the Internet, such communication is not fantasy. It is part of their everyday work environment. The point here is that Internet users depend on electronic mail the way most professionals depend on a telephone. It has been integrated into their working environment and has made major changes in the way they conduct daily business.

Now that we understand the current state of communication by electronic mail and how it is used in the Internet, we can appreciate the excitement generated by some of the new research projects. The question driving all of these investigations is:

> *How can we make substantial improvements in electronic communication while retaining all the features that have made electronic mail so popular and successful?*

The answers require imagination and engineering skill because we are seeking mechanisms that go far beyond current capabilities and yet remain economical enough for most users to obtain. We will discuss five areas of research that pose different answers.

Integrated text and graphics. There is an obvious and immediate need for standards that will allow participants to send more than simple text messages. Several research and engineering projects are examining ways to integrate graphics into electronic mail. The goal is to make it easy for users to send line drawings or images along with text. Although research prototypes have been built that demonstrate feasibility, the goal is to make such facilities available using commercially available hardware. Researchers are looking for ways to represent images without making them hardware dependent. The objective is to define an abstraction for images that makes it possible to have a compact representation (to make transmission across the Internet efficient) while still accommodating a wide variety of underlying hardware displays (to make mapping onto any given hardware efficient and easy).

Voice mail. A second interesting area of research focuses on the question of how to integrate spoken voice with electronic mail. Novice users often express disappointment in electronic mail because they cannot convey emotion (e.g., tone of voice) along with messages. Some users send textual clues to alleviate the problem (e.g., the sideways smiley face ":-)" to indicate humor), but even such clues do not solve the problem completely. The result is that electronic memos or replies can be misinterpreted. While the lack of inflection can make electronic mail frustrating, users like the ability to read electronic mail at their leisure instead of being interrupted by telephone calls. So, the question becomes, "how can one record voice and send it along with electronic mail?"

Although digitized voice storage has been well understood for many years, new technologies make possible low cost digitizing and playback equipment. Thus, adding digital voice to electronic mail has become more interesting. The success of current research projects will make it possible to have digitizing and playback equipment widely available across the Internet.

Integrated telephone services. Once mechanisms and standards are in place for voice storage, it becomes natural to interconnect computers and telephones. We can imagine an automated system that works like an answering machine except that it digitizes the incoming message, so it can be sent through electronic mail. A user traveling in a distant city could arrange to have the telephone server answer the phone, digitize phone messages, forward them to the user, and then accept responses from the user along with instructions that cause the server to return the call and play the recorded response.

Video mail. Once electronic mail includes graphics and digitized voice, it seems natural to ask whether video can be included as well. Powerful workstations have appeared that allow one to display real time video in a window on their bit mapped display, so the hardware technology exists. Storing and transporting video requires substantially more resources than voice because video uses much higher bandwidth. Some research projects are looking for ways to compress the amount of bandwidth needed for real time video, while others are examining how users react to slow speed video.

Because applications like video cannot be added to the existing Internet without changing the performance, some researchers are experimenting to see how well current protocols perform with new applications. One interesting project conducted at MIT has turned the experiment around and considered what new protocols are needed to support the efficient transfer of large bulk data across the Internet. The protocol being developed is called *NETBLT*†. A preliminary version has already become an official Internet protocol.

NETBLT tries to achieve better throughput by controlling the rate at which packets enter the Internet. The idea comes from the observation that when bursts of traffic clog communication paths, the burst results in many lost packets that require retransmission. NETBLT tries to avoid unnecessary retransmissions as well.

Teleconferencing. The logical extension of integrating voice and video with electronic mail is a real-time voice and video delivery service. If such a delivery service were available, it could be used for *teleconferencing*, in which a geographically diverse set of users conduct business by having video and voice display of each other.

Internet researchers have already used the WIDEBAND network to hold video conferences in which groups at two sites conducted a joint business meeting. Although such experiments demonstrate exciting possibilities, they also show fundamental limits of the Internet protocols. Indeed, for teleconferencing to work well, special purpose protocols must be used as well as special purpose communication links. Thus, one of the main questions becomes:

---

†NETBLT is pronounced "net blit."

How can the Internet adapt its protocols to accommodate new applications that need high bandwidth communication paths?

20.5 New Hardware And Communication Technologies

The advent of a new communication technology always stimulates curiosity. When that technology promises to increase communication bandwidth several orders of magnitude, while simultaneously decreasing the error rate, then it becomes revolutionary. One communication technology with those properties is collectively called *fiber optics*. Fiber can be used to interconnect two computers, to build local area networks, to build metropolitan area networks, or to provide high capacity trunk connections in wide area networks.

Fiber technology comes at a crucial time for the Internet, just as the demand for higher capacity interconnection has begun to exceed the capacity of existing backbone networks. With fiber, it is possible to substantially increase bandwidth of interconnections. The motivation is to improve performance of existing applications as well as to allow new applications that are not now possible. Thus, researchers and engineers ask two questions:

What minor changes are needed to allow existing Internet protocols to use higher speed backbone interconnections effectively? What major changes or additions must be made to Internet protocols to accommodate new applications that need higher throughput than is now possible?

The NETBLT protocol research discussed above provides an example of how researchers are attacking the second question. Related research has focused on special protocols that obtain high throughput when using satellite links. The Internet includes both point to point satellite connections (SATNET) as well as a synchronized, multistation satellite system (WIDEBAND) that uses a slotted reservation protocol. The latter has sufficient bandwidth to deliver video and voice traffic (i.e. it can support teleconferencing).

The most dramatic consequence of increased communication bandwidth is its effect on packet switching technology. To understand why, consider one of the packet switches in a network that uses *DS1 speed*† leased line interconnections. Imagine incoming traffic from a single leased line that operates at 100% capacity. The amount of computation required in the packet switch is proportional to the number of packets switched. Thus, the packet switch must do more computation per unit time if packet sizes are small (because more of them arrive per unit time).

How fast must a packet switch operate to handle a DS1 line? Consider switching IP datagrams that carry TCP segments. Recall that such datagrams have an IP header followed by a TCP segment header, followed by data. As a result, the smallest datagram

---

†DS1 speed lines operate at 1.544 Mbps and are often called *T1* lines after a standard low level protocol commonly used with them.

(e.g., those that carry one octet of TELNET data) is approximately 40 octets long. Dividing the line speed by 40 octets of 8 bits per octet shows that the packet switch must handle approximately 4800 packets per second. Of course, a packet switch must handle traffic in at least two directions simultaneously and should be able to accommodate multiple leased line connections. Thus, a general purpose packet switch needs a total switching capacity above 10000 packets per second.

Most current packet switches have only a single CPU. The fastest single CPU systems are capable of switching an aggregate of between 2000 and 5000 packets per second, clearly not enough for DS1 speed lines. DS1 speed is only the beginning, however, because fiber optics can handle speeds of tens of gigabits per second. Accommodating such speeds requires entirely new packet switching technologies. The question becomes:

> *How can new processing technologies make it possible to switch packets at speeds comparable with the transmission speeds provided by fiber optic interconnects?*

Several Internet research projects are investigating packet switching, with the most interesting concentrating on designs that eventually avoid electronics and use only optical switches. It is interesting to note that the advent of such switches may eventually force changes in IP because in its present form, gateways must read and change the IP header when switching the datagram.

20.6 Changes To Accommodate New Groups

New groups joining the Internet stimulate change in two ways. First, they bring demands for new services that support their desired interface or applications. Second, they add new administrative constraints. The issue raised by both types of demands is simply:

> *How can the Internet change to accommodate the technical needs of new groups of users while simultaneously allowing all groups to retain some autonomy in administrative matters?*

Recent work on ways to accommodate personal computer users provides an example of how the Internet adapts to new technical ideas. The Network Basic Input Output Service, *NetBIOS*, defines the standard many small computers use for network access. Internet engineers have developed a standard that specifies how NetBIOS operations can be supported in an Internet environment. The work, already adopted as an Internet standard, specifies the semantics for each NetBIOS operation by explaining how the operation maps onto the Internet protocols and address scheme.

Another example of ways that the Internet accommodates new technical ideas can be found in its use of international protocol standards. The principals have agreed that, as soon as possible, the Internet will migrate from its current TCP/IP protocols to equivalent protocols being defined by the International Standards Organization (ISO). Of course, no one wants to adopt new protocols before they have been tested and proved useful. The point is, merely, that in cases where minor differences exist between the technology used by the Internet and the rest of the community, the Internet changes to accommodate the community.

Sometimes, the community does not agree to a single standard. Even if agreement is reached in principle, it may take many years for everyone to migrate to the new standard. In those cases, researchers and engineers work to find ways to include new technical ideas under the Internet umbrella. For example, the new ISO standard for electronic mail, called *X.400* may eventually replace other electronic mail standards. Because many mail electronic systems are already in place, the migration to X.400 may take several years. Until the change is compete, Internet engineers are looking for ways that allow old mail systems to interoperate with new X.400 mail systems.

Other groups of users want to build applications that make extensive use of *transaction processing*. Transaction processing follows the client-server model, but does not need the overhead of reliable stream delivery. Instead, it uses a request-response style of interaction best supported by reliable datagram delivery.

To understand the need for reliable datagram processing, consider a set of remote machines that gather data and send transactions to update or query a central database. Such processing is common in commercial banking, where remote, automated teller machines accept requests for deposit or withdraw. The entire transaction between the server that supplies the database and the remote machines making requests can easily be carried out with a single message and a single response. However, the messages must be delivered reliably.

Building reliable datagram service is not as easy as it sounds. Remember that we want the protocols to work over an Internet where delays can be high and can vary from transaction to transaction. The User Datagram Protocol (UDP) does not provide any end-to-end reliability whatsoever. Many application programmers use UDP with simplistic, fixed length timeout mechanisms that do not adapt to the delays found in an Internet environment. The question arises:

> *Can we devise a single, general purpose protocol that supports reliable datagram transfer in an Internet environment while retaining the efficiency of current datagram protocols?*

One of the current Internet research projects is exploring such a protocol. It has resulted in a preliminary draft specification and prototype implementation. Early measurements show that the protocol, known as *VMTP*, performs well, adapts to Internet delays, and supports a wide variety of applications. If the results continue to be positive, VMTP may become an Internet standard on which transaction processing systems can be built.

An example of ways the Internet changes to adapt to the administrative needs of new groups can be seen most clearly in the evolution of the Internet gateway system. We have already seen that expanding the Internet beyond a single administrative domain makes a single core gateway system inadequate. A single core system cannot be used as a central routing mechanism because the load would be too high and because it introduces the extra hop problem. Even if the core serves only as a repository of routing information, the current architecture cannot be expanded arbitrarily because the core will become overrun with internal routing update messages or external EGP traffic.

Beyond the changes needed to accommodate increased load, the core must accommodate multiple autonomous systems that have their own administrative control. Permitting such control means discarding the single core authority that arbitrates routes. In the old system, a single administrative group monitored the core gateways. They could detect conflicting reachability updates and take action to notify the groups responsible. Ultimately, the administrators controlling the core could isolate groups that did not follow established policies by refusing to pass routing information to them. Without a single, central administration, control of routing becomes more difficult. It relies on cooperation and trust among autonomous systems.

Before researchers can devise mechanisms that handle routing without a central core, they must devise a trust model. A model is needed that explains the conditions under which two systems trust one another and also explains the consequences of trust violations. The basic trade-off is between efficiency and danger. Increased trust allows a gateway to obtain more efficient routes but exposes the gateway to the peril of routing errors. Once a model is well understood, mechanisms can be built that allow parties to trust some autonomous systems more than they trust others, and to understand, when making such choices about trust, exactly what they are risking.

One project exploring a simple trust model has produced a proposed extension to EGP called the *Dissimilar Gateway Protocol*, or *DGP*. DGP recognizes that some pairs of autonomous systems may choose to trust one another completely while other pairs have little trust. It provides formulas for computing distance measures that allow a gateway to artificially inflate distances reported by autonomous systems it does not trust. It also includes notions of metric transformation that allow multiple autonomous systems to each use their own distance metric (e.g., one system bases its routing on network delay while another bases its routing on the conventional hop count).

20.7 Summary

The Internet is not a static entity. It includes an active, ongoing research effort that keeps the technology stretching and evolving. The stimulus for change occurs as increased use forces improvements to maintain service, as new applications demand more from the underlying technology, as new technologies make it possible to provide new services, and as new groups extend the architectural and functional basis. We examined a few of the many research and engineering problems that arise because the Internet is growing and adapting to new applications, technologies, and groups of users. We discussed a few of the many engineering and research projects aimed at solving those problems.

FOR FURTHER STUDY

Arnon [RFC 1019] discusses representations for mathematical equations. Mills and Braun [1987] describe some of the problems created by NSFnet. Reynolds *et al* [October 1985] discusses multi-media experiments. Crowley *et al* [June 1987] focuses on a multi-media mail system that integrates graphics, voice, and text. In a series of reports on internet management, Partridge and Trewitt define the problem and show how the HEMS and HEMP protocols can be used to help solve it [RFC 1021, 1022, 1023, and 1024]. Finally, Clark *et al* [1987] describe the NETBLT protocol and Lambert [RFC 1030] reports the results of experiments with it.

Much of the research described in this chapter is not in print at the time of publication. The continuing series of RFCs usually contains the earliest published record of Internet problems and research results. Also see Lynch and Jacobson [1987] for timely discussions.

Appendix 1

4.3 BSD UNIX Interface to Internet Protocols

Operating System Interface to Protocols

So far, we have concentrated on discussing the principles and concepts that underly the Internet protocols without specifying the interface between the protocol software and application programs. There are two reasons for postponing the discussion of interfaces. First, because Internet protocol software usually resides in the computers' operating system, some of the details of the interface depend on the operating system instead of the protocols. Second, because there is no single best mechanism that interfaces application programs to Internet protocols, it is inappropriate to tie the discussion of protocols to a method of using them.

This appendix reviews one example of an interface between application programs and underlying protocols. The example we have chosen comes from the 4.3 BSD UNIX operating system. The reader should keep in mind that our goal is merely to give one concrete example, not to prescribe how interfaces should be designed. Thus, the operations listed here do not comprise a standard in any sense.

The UNIX I/O Paradigm And Network I/O

Developed in the late 1960s and early 1970s, UNIX was originally designed as a timesharing system for single processor computers. It is a process-oriented system in which application programs execute as user level processes. An application program interacts with the operating system by making *system calls*. From the programmer's point of view, system calls look and behave exactly like other procedure calls. They take arguments and return one or more results. Arguments can be values (e.g., an integer count) or pointers to objects in the application program (e.g., a buffer to be filled with characters).

The UNIX input and output (I/O) commands, derived from those in Multics and earlier systems, follow a paradigm sometimes referred to as *open-close-read-write*. Before a user process can perform I/O operations, it calls *open* to specify the file or device to be used and obtains permission. The call to *open* returns a small integer *file descriptor*† that the process uses for I/O operations on the opened file or device. Once an object has been opened, the user process makes one or more calls to *read* or *write* to transfer data. *Read* transfers data from the device to the user process; *write* transfers data from the user process to the device. Both *read* and *write* take three arguments that specify the file descriptor to use, the address of a buffer, and the count of bytes to transfer to or from the device. After all transfer operations are complete, the user process calls *close* to inform the operating system that it has finished using an object (the operating system automatically closes all open objects if the process terminates without calling *close*).

Adding Network I/O to UNIX

Originally, UNIX designers cast all I/O operations in the open-close-read-write paradigm described above. The scheme included I/O for character-oriented devices like CRT terminals, and block-oriented devices like disks and data files. The group adding network protocols to UNIX decided that because network protocols are more complex than conventional I/O devices, interaction between user processes and network protocols must be more complex than interactions between user processes and conventional I/O devices. In particular, the interface to protocols must allow programmers to create both server code that awaits connections passively as well as client code that forms connections actively. Furthermore, application programs sending datagrams may wish to specify the destination address along with each datagram instead of binding destinations with *open*. To handle all these cases, the designers chose to abandon the traditional UNIX open-close-read-write paradigm and add several new operating system calls as well as new library routines. Adding network protocols to UNIX increased the complexity of the I/O interface substantially.

Further complexity arises in the UNIX protocol interface because designers attempted to build a general mechanism that accommodates all possible protocols. For example, the generality makes it possible to have protocol software for both the DARPA Internet protocols (TCP/IP) as well as the Xerox internet protocols (XNS), and to allow application programs to use them both. As a consequence, the application program cannot merely supply an address and expect the operating system to interpret it as an Internet address. The application must explicitly specify that the address refers to the DARPA Internet.

---

†The term ''file descriptor'' arises because in UNIX all devices are mapped into the file system name space. Thus, in most cases, files and devices are indistinguishable.

The Socket Abstraction

The basis for network I/O in 4.3 BSD UNIX centers on an abstraction known as the *socket*. We think of a socket as a generalization of the UNIX file access mechanism that provides an endpoint for communication. As with file access, application programs request the operating system to create a socket when one is needed. The system returns a small integer that the application program uses to reference the newly created socket. The chief difference between file descriptors and sockets is that the operating system binds a file descriptor to a specific file or device when the application calls *open*, but it can create sockets without binding them to specific destination addresses. The application can choose to supply a destination address each time it uses the socket (e.g., when sending datagrams), or it can choose to bind the destination address to the socket and avoid specifying the destination repeatedly (e.g., when making a TCP connection).

Whenever it makes sense, sockets perform exactly like UNIX files or devices, so they can be used with traditional operations like *read* and *write*. For example, once two application programs create sockets and open a TCP connection between them, one program can use *write* to send a stream of data and the other program can use *read* to receive it. To make it possible to use primitives like *read* and *write* with both files and sockets, the operating system allocates descriptors so they do not conflict.

Creating A Socket

The *socket* system call creates sockets on demand. It takes three integer arguments and returns an integer result:

$$result = socket(af, type, protocol)$$

Argument *af* specifies the protocol family to be used with the socket. That is, it specifies how to interpret addresses when they are supplied. Current families include the DARPA Internet (AF_INET), Xerox Corporation PUP internet (AF_PUP), Apple Computer Incorporated Appletalk network (AF_APPLETALK), and UNIX file system (AF_UNIX) as well as many others.

Argument *type* specifies the type of communication desired. Possible types include reliable stream delivery service (SOCK_STREAM) and connectionless datagram delivery service (SOCK_DGRAM), as well as a raw type (SOCK_RAW) that allows privileged programs to access low level protocols or network interfaces. Two additional types have been planned but not implemented.

Although the general approach of separating protocol families and types may seem sufficient to handle all cases easily, it does not. First, it may be that a given family of protocols does not support one of the types of service. For example, the UNIX family has an interprocess communication mechanism called the *pipe* that uses a reliable stream delivery service, but it has no mechanism for sequenced packet delivery. Thus, not all combinations of protocol family and type of service make sense. Second, some protocol families have multiple protocols that support one type of service. For example, it may be that a single protocol family has two connectionless datagram delivery services. To accommodate multiple protocols within a family, the socket call has a third argument that can be used to select a specific protocol. To use the third argument, the programmer must understand the protocol family well enough to know the type of service each protocol supplies.

Because the designers tried to capture many of the conventional UNIX operations in their socket design, they needed a way to simulate the UNIX pipe mechanism. Pipes differ from standard network operations because the calling process creates both endpoints for the communication simultaneously. To accommodate pipes, the designers added a *socketpair* system call that takes the form:

socketpair(af, type, protocol, sarray)

Socketpair has one more argument than the *socket* procedure, *sarray*. The additional argument gives the address of a 2-element integer array. *Socketpair* creates two sockets simultaneously and places the two socket descriptors in the two elements of *sarray*. Readers should understand that *socketpair* is not meaningful when applied to the DARPA Internet protocol family (it has been included here merely to make our description of the interface complete).

Socket Inheritance And Termination

UNIX uses the *fork* system call to create new processes. As with file descriptors, newly created processes inherit a copy of all open sockets when the process is created. Internally, the operating system keeps a reference count associated with each socket, so it knows how many processes can access it. Both the old and new processes have the same access rights and both can access the socket. Thus, it is the responsibility of the programmer to ensure that the two processes use the shared socket meaningfully.

When a process finishes using a socket it calls *close*. *Close* has the form:

close(socket)

where argument *socket* specifies the descriptor of a socket to close. When a process terminates for any reason, the system closes any sockets that remain open. Internally, a call to *close* decrements the reference count for a socket and destroys the socket when the count reaches zero.

Specifying A Local Address

Initially, a socket is created without any association to local or destination addresses. For the Internet protocols, this means no local protocol port number has been assigned. In many cases, application programs do not care about the local address they use and are willing to allow the protocol software to choose one for them. However, server processes that operate at a well-known port must be able to specify that port to the system. Once a socket has been created, a server uses the *bind* system call to establish a local address for it. *Bind* has the following form:

bind(socket, localaddr, addrlen)

Argument *socket* is the integer descriptor of the socket to be bound. Argument *localaddr* is a structure that specifies the local address to which the socket should be bound, and argument *addrlen* is an integer that specifies the length of the address measured in bytes. Instead of giving the address merely as a sequence of bytes, the designers chose to use a fixed structure for addresses. The structure, generically named *sockaddr*, begins with a 2-byte field that identifies the protocol family and is followed by up to 14 bytes of information specific to that family. In practice, the socket address structure is a union of structures for all possible address families. For example, addresses for the Internet protocol family are represented by structure *sockaddr_in*, with the 2-byte protocol family set to value AF_INET followed by a 2-byte protocol port number and a 4-byte Internet address. The Internet address structure does not use the remaining 8 bytes available in the generic address structure.

Not all possible bindings are valid. For example, the caller might request a local protocol port that is already in use by another program, or it might request an invalid local Internet address. In such cases, the bind call fails and returns an error message.

Connecting Sockets To Destination Addresses

Initially, a socket is created in the *unconnected state*, which means that the socket is not associated with any foreign destination. The system call *connect* binds a permanent destination to a socket, placing it in the *connected state*. An application program must call *connect* to establish a connection before it can transfer data through a reliable stream socket. Sockets used with connectionless datagram services need not be connected before they are used, but doing so makes it possible to transfer data without specifying the destination each time.

The *connect* system call has the form:

connect(socket, destaddr, addrlen)

Argument *socket* is the integer descriptor of the socket to connect. Argument *destaddr* is a structure that specifies the destination address to which the socket should be bound and argument *addrlen* specifies the length of the destination address measured in bytes.

The semantics of *connect* depend on the underlying protocols. Selecting the reliable stream delivery service in the Internet family means choosing TCP. In such cases, *connect* builds a TCP connection with the destination and returns an error if it cannot. In the case of connectionless service, *connect* does nothing more than store the destination address locally.

Sending Data Through A Socket

Once an application program has established a socket, it can use the socket to transmit data. There are five possible operating system calls from which to choose: *send, sendto, sendmsg, write,* and *writev. Send, write,* and *writev* only work with connected sockets because they do not allow the caller to specify a destination address. The differences between the three are minor. *Write* takes three arguments:

write(descriptor, buffer, length)

When used with the Internet, argument *descriptor* contains an integer socket descriptor (*write* can also be used with file descriptors). Argument *buffer* contains a sequence of bytes to be sent, and argument *length* specifies the number of bytes. The call to *write* blocks until the data can be transferred (e.g., it blocks if internal system buffers for the socket are full).

The system call *writev* works like *write* except that it uses a ''gather write'' form, making it possible for the application program to write a message without copying the message into contiguous bytes. *Writev* has the form:

writev(descriptor, iovector, vectorlen)

Argument *iovector* gives the address of a structure of type *iovec* that contains a sequence of pointers to blocks of bytes that form the message. Argument *vectorlen* specifies the number of entries in *iovector*. The reader is referred to the UNIX documentation for the details of structure *iovec*.

The *send* system call has the form:

send(socket, message, length, flags)

where argument *socket* specifies the socket to use, argument *message* gives the address of the sequence of bytes to be sent, argument *length* specifies the number of bytes to be sent, and argument *flags* controls the transmission. One value for *flags* allows the sender to specify that the message should be sent out-of-band on sockets that support such a notion. When using TCP, for example, out-of-band message correspond to urgent data.

Another value for *flags* allows the caller to request that the message be sent without using local routing tables. The intention is to allow the caller to take control of routing, making it possible to write network debugging software. Not all sockets support such a request.

System calls *sendto* and *sendmsg* allows the caller to send a message through an unconnected socket because they both require the caller to specify a destination. *Sendto*, which takes the destination address as an argument, has the form:

sendto(socket, message, length, flags, destaddr, addrlen)

The first four arguments are exactly the same as those used with the *send* system call. The final two arguments specify a destination address and give the length of that address. Argument *destaddr* gives the address of a *sockaddr* structure as defined above.

A programmer may choose to use system call *sendmsg* in cases where the long list of arguments required for *sendto* makes the program inefficient or difficult to read. *Sendmsg* has the form:

sendmsg(socket, messagestruct, flags)

where argument *messagestruct* is a structure that contains the message to be sent, its length, the destination address, and its length. This call is especially useful because there is a corresponding input operation (described below) that produces a message structure in exactly the same format.

Receiving Data Through A Socket

Analogous to the five different output operations, 4.3 BSD UNIX offers five system calls that a process can use to receive data through a socket: *read, readv, recv, recvfrom,* and *recvmsg*. The conventional UNIX input operation, *read,* can only be used when the socket is connected. It has the form:

read(descriptor, buffer, length)

where *descriptor* gives the integer descriptor of a socket or file descriptor from which to read data, *buffer* specifies the address in memory at which to store the data, and *length* specifies the maximum number of bytes to read.

An alternative form, *readv,* allows the caller to use a "scatter read" style of interface that places the incoming data in noncontiguous locations. *Readv* has the form:

readv(descriptor, iovector, vectorlen)

Argument *iovector* gives the address of a structure of type *iovec* that contains a sequence of pointers to blocks of memory into which the incoming data should be stored. Argument *vectorlen* specifies the number of entries in *iovector*. The reader is referred to the UNIX documentation for the details of structure *iovec*.

In addition to the conventional input operations, three additional system calls provide for network message input. Processes call *recv* to receive data from a connected socket. It has the form:

recv(socket, buffer, length, flags)

Argument *socket* specifies a socket descriptor from which data should be received. Argument *buffer* specifies the address in memory into which the message should be placed and argument *length* specifies the length of the buffer area. Finally, argument *flags* allows the caller to control the reception. Among the possible values for the *flags* argument is one that allows the caller to look ahead by extracting a copy of the next incoming message without removing the message from the socket.

The system call *recvfrom* allows the caller to specify to receive from an unconnected socket. It includes additional arguments that allow the caller to specify the destination from which data should be received. The form is:

recvfrom(socket, buffer, length, flags, fromaddr, addrlen)

The two additional arguments, *fromaddr* and *addrlen* are pointers to a socket address structure and an integer. The operating system uses *fromaddr* to record the address of the message sender and uses *fromlen* to record the length of sender's address. Notice that the output operation *sendto*, discussed above, takes an address in exactly the same form as *recvfrom* generates. Thus, sending replies is easy.

The final system call used for input, *recvmsg*, is analogous to the *sendmsg* output operation. *Recvmsg* operates like *recvfrom*, but requires fewer arguments. Its form is:

recvmsg(socket, messagestruct, flags)

where argument *messagestruct* gives the address of a structure that holds the address for incoming message as well as locations for the sender's address. The structure produced by *recvmsg* is exactly the same as the structure used by *sendmsg*, making them operate well as a pair.

Obtaining Local And Remote Socket Addresses

We said that newly created processes inherit the set of open sockets from the process that created them. Sometimes, the newly created process needs to determine the address of the destination to which a socket connects. A process may also wish to determine the local address of a socket. Two system calls provide such information: *getpeername* and *getsockname* (despite their names, both deal with what we think of as "addresses").

A process calls *getpeername* to determine the address of the peer to which a socket connects. It has the form:

getpeername(socket, destaddr, addrlen)

Argument *socket* specifies the socket for which the address is desired. Argument *destaddr* is a pointer to a structure of type *sockaddr* that will receive the socket address. Finally, argument *addrlen* is a pointer to an integer that receives the length of the address. *Getpeername* only works with connected sockets.

System call *getsockname* returns the local address associated with a socket. It has the form:

getsockname(socket, localaddr, addrlen)

As expected, argument *socket* specifies the socket for which the local address is desired. Argument *locaddr* is a pointer to a structure of type *sockaddr* that will contain the address, and argument *addrlen* is a pointer to an integer that will contain the length of the address.

Obtaining And Setting Socket Options

In addition to binding a socket to a local address or connecting it to a destination address, the need arises for a mechanism that permits application programs to control the socket. For example, when using protocols that use timeout and retransmission, the application program may want to obtain or set the timeout parameters. It may also want to control the allocation of buffer space, determine if the socket allows transmission of broadcast, or control processing of out-of-band data. Rather than add new system calls for each new control operation, the designers decided to build a single mechanism. The mechanism has two operations: *getsockopt* and *setsockopt*.

System call *getsockopt* allows the application to request information about the socket. A caller specifies the socket, the option of interest, and a location at which to store the requested information. The operating system examines its internal data structures for the socket and passes the requested information to the caller. The call has the form:

getsockopt(socket, level, optionid, optionval, length)

Argument *socket* specifies a socket for which information is needed. Argument *level* identifies whether the operation applies to the socket itself or to the underlying protocol being used. Argument *optionid* specifies a single option to which the request applies. The pair of arguments *optionval* and *length* specify two pointers. The first gives the address of a buffer into which the system places the requested value and the second gives the address of an integer into which the system places the length of the option value.

System call *setsockopt* allows an application program to set a socket option using the same set of values obtained with *getsockopt*. The caller specifies a socket for which the option should be set, the option to be changed, and a value for the option. The call to *setsockopt* has the form:

setsockopt(socket, level, optionid, optionval, length)

where the arguments are like those for *getsockopt* except that the *length* argument contains the length of the option being passed to the system. The caller must supply a legal value for the option as well as a correct length for that value. Of course, not all options apply to all sockets. The correctness and semantics of individual requests depend on the current state of the socket and the underlying protocol being used.

Specifying A Queue Length For A Server

One of the options that applies to sockets is used so frequently, a separate system call has been dedicated to it. To understand how it arises, consider a server. The server creates a socket, binds it to a well-known protocol port, and waits for requests. If the server uses a reliable stream delivery or if computing a response takes nontrivial amounts of time, it may happen that a new request arrives before the server finishes responding to an old request.

The system call *listen* allows servers to prepare a socket for incoming connections. In terms of the underlying protocols, *listen* puts the socket in a passive mode ready to accept connections. When the server invokes *listen*, it also informs the operating system that the protocol software should enqueue multiple simultaneous requests that arrive at a socket. The form is:

listen(socket, qlength)

Argument *socket* gives the descriptor of a socket that should be prepared for use by a server, and argument *qlength* specifies the length of the request queue for that socket. After the call, the system will enqueue up to *qlength* requests for connections. If the queue is full when a request arrives, the operating system will refuse the connection by discarding the request. Listen applies only to sockets that have selected reliable stream delivery service.

How A Server Accepts Connections

As we have seen, a server process uses the system calls *socket*, *bind*, and *listen* to create a socket, bind it to a well-known protocol port, and specify a queue length for connection requests. Note that the call to *bind* associates the socket with a well-known protocol port, but that the socket is not connected to a specific foreign destination. In fact, the foreign destination must specify a wild card allowing the socket to receive connection requests from an arbitrary client.

Once a socket has been set up, the server needs to wait for a connection. To do so, it uses system call *accept*. A call to *accept* blocks until a connection request arrives. It has the form:

$$newsock = accept(socket, addr, addrlen)$$

Argument *socket* specifies the descriptor of the socket on which to wait. Argument *addr* is pointer to a structure of type *sockaddr*, and *addrlen* is a pointer to an integer. When a request arrives, the system fills in *addr* with the address of the client that has placed the request and sets *addr* to the length of the address. Finally, the system creates a new socket that has its destination connected to the requesting client and returns the new socket descriptor to the caller. The original socket still has a wildcard foreign destination and it still remains open.

When a connection arrives, the call to *accept* returns. The server can either handle requests iteratively or concurrently. In the iterative approach, the server handles the request itself, closes the new socket, and then calls *accept* to obtain the next connection request. In the concurrent approach, after the call to accept returns, the server forks a new process to handle the request. The new process inherits a copy of the new socket, so it proceeds to service the request and then exits. The original server process must close its copy of the new socket and then call *accept* to obtain the next connection request.

The concurrent design for servers may seem confusing because multiple processes will be using the same local protocol port number. The key to understanding the mechanism lies in the way underlying protocols treat protocol ports. For example, recall that in TCP a pair of endpoints define a connection. Thus, it does not matter how many processes use a given local protocol port number as long as they connect to different destinations. In the case of a concurrent server, there is one process per client and one additional process that accepts connections. The main server process has a wildcard for the destination, allowing it to connect with an arbitrary foreign site. Each remaining processes has a specific foreign destination. When a TCP segment arrives, it will be sent to the socket connected to the segment's source. If no such socket exists, the segment will be sent to the socket that has a wildcard for its foreign destination. Furthermore, because the socket with a wildcard foreign destination does not have an open connection, it will only honor TCP segments that request a new connection.

Servers That Handle Multiple Services

The 4.3 BSD interface provides another interesting possibility for server design because it allows a single process to wait for connections on multiple sockets. The system call that makes such organization possible is called *select*, and it applies to I/O in general, not just to communication over sockets. Select has the form:

nready = select(ndesc, indesc, outdesc, excdesc, timeout)

In general, a call to *select* blocks waiting on one of a set of file descriptors to become ready. Argument *ndesc* specifies how many descriptors should be examined (the descriptors checked are always *0* through *ndesc*-1). Argument *indesc* is a pointer to a bit mask that specifies the file descriptors to check for input, argument *outdesc* is a pointer to a bit mask that specifies the file descriptors to check for output, and argument *excdesc* is a pointer to a bit mask that specifies the file descriptors tp check for exception conditions. Finally, if argument *timeout* is nonzero, it is the address of an integer that specifies how long to wait for a connection before returning to the caller. A zero value forces the call to block until a descriptor becomes ready. Because the *timeout* argument contains the address of the timeout integer and not the integer itself, a process can request zero delay by passing the address of an integer that contains zero (i.e., a process can poll to see if I/O is ready).

A call to *select* returns the number of file descriptors from the specified set that are ready for I/O. It also changes the bit masks to which *indesc*, *outdesc*, *excdesc* point, to inform the application which of the selected file descriptors are ready. Thus, before calling *select*, the caller must turn on those bits that correspond to descriptors to be checked. Following the call, all bits that remain set to *1* correspond to a ready file descriptor.

Obtaining And Setting The Internal Host Identification Number

Each 4.3 BSD UNIX system maintains a unique 32-bit integer, called a *hostid*, that identifies the machine. Host ids are related to the Internet because, by convention, machines use the 32-bit Internet address of one of their main network interfaces as their hostid. The hostid is usually stored in network standard byte order.

A user process can request the host id, and a privileged process can set the hostid (usually, the host id is set only at system startup). The operating system calls that manage the host id are: *sethostid* and *gethostid*. Any process can call *gethostid* to obtain the 32-bit id. The call takes the form of a function:

hostid = gethostid()

where *hostid* is a long (32-bit) integer.

The corresponding call privileged programs use to set the host id has the form:

sethostid(hostid)

Argument *hostid* is a long integer that contains the new host id.

Obtaining And Setting The Host Names

The 4.3 BSD UNIX operating system maintains an internal host name. For machines on the Internet, the internal name is usually chosen to be the domain name for the machine's main network interface. The *gethostname* system call allows user processes to access the host name, and the *sethostname* system call allows privileged processes to set the host name. *Gethostname* has the form:

gethostname(name, length)

Argument *name* gives the address of an array of bytes where the name is to be stored, and argument *length* is an integer that specifies the length of the *name* array. To set the host name, a privileged process makes a call of the form:

sethostname(name, length)

Argument *name* gives the address of an array where the name is stored, and argument *length* is an integer that gives the length of the name.

Obtaining And Setting The Internal Host Domain

The operating system maintains a string that specifies the naming domain under which the machine falls. When a site obtains authority for part of the domain name space, it invents a string that identifies its piece of the space and uses that string as the name of the domain. For example, machines in the domain

cs.purdue.edu

have names taken from the arthurian legend. Thus, one finds machines like *merlin*, *arthur*, *guenevere*, and *lancelot*. The domain itself has been named *camelot*, so the operating system on each host in the group must be informed that it resides in the *camelot* domain. To do so, a privileged processes uses system call *setdomainname*, which has the form:

setdomainname(name, length)

Argument *name* gives the address of an array of bytes that contains the name of a domain, and argument *length* is an integer that gives the length of the name.

User processes call *getdomainname* to retrieve the name of the domain from the system. It has the form:

getdomainname(name, length)

where argument *name* specifies the address of an array where the name should be stored, and argument *length* is an integer that specifies the length of the array.

4.3 BSD UNIX Network Library Calls

In addition to the system calls described above, 4.3 BSD UNIX offers a set of library routines that perform useful functions related to networking. The difference between system calls and library routines is that system calls pass control to the computer's operating system, while library routines are like other procedures that the programmer binds into a program.

Many of the 4.3 BSD UNIX library routines provide database services that allow a process to determine the names of machines and network services, protocol port numbers, and other related information. For example, one set of library routines provides access to the database of network services. We think of entries in the services database as 3-tuples, where each 3-tuple contains the (human readable) name of a network service, the protocol that supports the service, and a protocol port number for the service. Library routines exist that allow a process to obtain information from the entry given any piece.

The next sections examine each group of library routines, explaining their purpose and providing information about how they can be used.

Network Byte Order Conversion Routines

Recall that machines differ in the way they store integer quantities and that the Internet defines a machine independent standard for byte order. 4.3 BSD UNIX provides four library procedures that convert between the local machine byte order and the network standard byte order. To make programs portable, they must be written to call the conversion routines every time they copy an integer value from the local machine to a network packet, or when they copy a value from a network packet to the local machine.

All four conversion routines are functions that take a value as an argument and return a new value with the bytes rearranged. For example, to convert a short (2-byte) integer from network byte order to the local host byte order, a programmer calls *ntohs* (network to host short). The format is:

$$localshort = ntohs(netshort)$$

Argument *netshort* is a 2-byte (16-bit) integer in network standard byte order and the result, *localshort*, is in local host byte order.

Unix calls 4 byte (32 bit) integers *long*s. Function *ntohl* (network to host long) converts 4-byte longs from network standard byte order to local host byte order. Programs invoke it as a function, supplying a long integer in network byte order as an argument:

$$locallong = ntohl(netlong)$$

Two analogous functions allow the programmer to convert from local host byte order to network byte order. Function *htons* converts a 2-byte (short) integer in the host's local byte order to a 2-byte integer in network standard byte order. Programs invoke it as a function:

$$netshort = htons(localshort)$$

The final conversion routine, *htonl*, converts long integers to network standard byte order. Like the others, it is a function:

$$netlong = htonl(locallong)$$

It should be obvious that the conversion routines preserve the following mathematical relationships:

$$netshort = htons(ntohs(netshort))$$

and

$$localshort = ntohs(htons(localshort))$$

Similar relationships hold for the long integer conversion routines.

Internet Address Manipulation Routines

Because many programs translate between 32-bit Internet addresses and the corresponding dotted decimal notation, the 4.3 BSD library includes utility routines that perform the translation. Procedure *inet_addr* and *inet_network* each translate from dotted decimal format to a 32-bit Internet address. They have the form:

$$address = inet\_addr(string)$$

and

$$address = inet\_network(string)$$

where argument *string* gives the address of an ascii string that contains the number expressed in a dotted decimal format. The dotted decimal form can have 1 to 4 segments of digits separated by periods (dots). If all 4 appear, each corresponds to a single byte of the resulting 32-bit integer. If less than 4 appear, the last segment is expanded to fill remaining bytes.

Procedure *inet_ntoa* performs the inverse of *inet_addr* by mapping a 32-bit integer to an ascii string in dotted decimal format. It has the form:

$$str = inet\_ntoa(internetaddr)$$

where argument *internetaddr* is a 32-bit Internet address and *str* is the address of the resulting ascii version.

Often programs that manipulate Internet addresses must combine a network address with the local address of a host on that network. Procedure *inet_makeaddr* performs such a combination. It has the form:

internetaddr = inet_makeaddr(net, local)

Argument *net* is a 32-bit Internet network address, and argument *local* is the integer representing a local address on that network.

Procedures *inet_inaof* and *inet_netof* provide the inverse of *inet_makeaddr* by separating the network and local portions of an Internet address. They have the form:

net = inet_netof(internetaddr)

and

local = inet_inaof(internetaddr)

where argument *internetaddr* is a 32-bit Internet address.

Accessing The Domain Name System

A set of five library procedures comprise the 4.3 BSD UNIX interface to the Internet domain name system. Application programs that call these routines become clients of one domain name system, sending one or more servers requests and receiving responses.

The general idea is that a program makes a query, sends it to a server, and awaits an answer. Because many options exist, the routines have only a few basic parameters and use a global structure, *res*, to hold others. For example, one field in *res* enables debugging messages while another controls whether the code uses UDP or TCP for queries. Most fields in *res* begin with reasonable defaults, so the routines can be used without changing it.

A program calls *res_init* before using other procedures. The call takes no arguments:

res_init()

Res_init reads a file that contains information like the name of a machine that runs the domain name server and stores the results in global structure *res*.

Procedure *res_mkquery* forms a domain name query and places it in a buffer in memory. The form of the call is:

res_mkquery(op, dname, class, type, data, datalen, newrr, buffer, buflen)

The first seven arguments correspond directly to the fields of a domain name query. Argument *op* specifies the requested operation, *dname* gives the address of a character array that contains a domain name, *class* is an integer that give the class of the query, *type* is an integer that gives the type of the query, *data* gives the address of an array of data to be included, and *datalen* is an integer that give the length of the data. In addition to the library procedures, UNIX provides application programs with definitions of symbolic constants for important values. Thus, programmers can use the domain name system without understanding the details of the protocol. The last two arguments, *buffer* and *buflen*, specify the address of an area into which the query should be placed and the integer length of the buffer area, respectively. Finally, in the current implementation, argument *newrr* is unused.

Once a program has formed a query, it calls *res_send* to send it to a name server and obtain a response. The form is:

res_send(message, msglen, answer, anslen)

Argument *message* is a pointer to a buffer that holds the message to be sent (presumably, the application called procedure *res_mkquery* to form the message). Argument *msglen* is an integer that specifies the length. Argument *answer* gives the address in memory into which a response should be written and argument *anslen* is an integer that specifies the length of the answer area.

In addition to routines that make and send queries, the 4.3 BSD library contains two routines that translate domain names between conventional ascii and the compressed format used in queries. Procedure *dn_expand* expands a compressed domain name into a full ascii version. It has the form:

dn_expand(msg, eom, compressed, full, fullen)

Argument *msg* give the address of a domain name message that contains the name being expanded, with *eom* specifying the end-of-message limit beyond which the expansion cannot go. Argument *compressed* is a pointer to the first byte of the compressed name. Argument *full* is a pointer to an array into which the expanded name should be written and argument *fullen* is an integer that specifies the length of the array.

Generating a compressed name is more complex than expanding a compressed name because compression involves eliminating common suffixes. When compressing names, the client must keep a record of suffixes that have appeared previously. Procedure *dn_comp* compresses a full domain name by comparing suffixes to a list of previously used suffixes and eliminating the longest possible suffix. A call has the form:

dn_comp(full, compressed, cmprlen, prevptrs, lastptr)

Argument *full* gives the address of a full domain name. Argument *compressed* points to an array of bytes that will hold the compressed name, with argument *cmprlen* specifying the length of the array. The argument *prevptrs* is the address of an array of pointers to previously compressed suffixes, with *lastptr* pointing to the end of the array. Normally, *dn_comp* compresses the name and updates the *prevptrs* if a new suffix has been used.

Procedure *dn_comp* can also be used to translate a domain name from ascii to the internal form without compressing (i.e., without removing suffixes). To do so, one invokes it with the *prevptrs* argument set to *NULL* (i.e., zero).

Obtaining Information About Hosts

Library procedures exist that allow a process to retrieve information about a host given either its Internet domain name or its Internet address. When used on a machine that has access to a domain name server, the library procedures make the process a client of the domain name system by sending a request to a server and waiting for a response. When used on systems that do not have access to the domain name system (e.g., a host not on the Internet), the routines obtain the desired information from a database kept on secondary storage.

Procedure *gethostbyname* takes a domain name and returns a pointer to a structure of information for that host. A call takes the form:

ptr = gethostbyname(namestr)

Argument *namestr* is a pointer to a character string that contains a domain name for the host. The value returned, *ptr*, points to a structure that contains the following information: the official host name, a list of aliases that have been registered for the host, the host address type (i.e., whether the address is an Internet address), the address length, and a list of one or more addresses for the host. More details can be found in the UNIX Programmer's Manual.

Procedure *gethostbyaddr* produces the same information as *gethostbyname*. The difference between the two is that *gethostbyaddr* accepts a host address as an argument:

ptr = gethostbyaddr(addr, len, type)

Argument *addr* is a pointer to a sequence of bytes that contain a host address. Argument *len* is an integer that gives the length of the address, and argument *type* is an integer that specifies the type of the address (e.g., that it is an Internet address).

Three support procedures allow a user process to read the nameserver database sequentially. The client passes procedure *sethostent* a nonzero argument to establish a connection to the nameserver and start at the beginning of the database. The client then retrieves one entry at a time and finally closes the connection. The call to *sethostent* takes the form:

sethostent(nonzero)

The client calls a related routine, *endhostent*, to close the connection:

endhostent()

To retrieve the next entry from the database, the client calls *gethostent*. It has the form:

$$ptr = gethostent()$$

Like the first two host access routines described above, *gethostent* returns a pointer to a structure with information about a host. Each successive call returns information for a different host. The code for *sethostent* creates a TCP connection to the nameserver, which remains open until the call to *endhostent* closes it. Once a connection has been closed, the client can call *sethostent* to create a new connection and start again at the beginning of the database.

Obtaining Information About Networks

Hosts running 4.3 BSD UNIX keep a simple database of networks in the Internet. The network library routines include five routines that allow a process to access the network database. Procedure *getnetbyname* obtains and formats the contents of an entry from the database given the domain name of a network. A call has the form:

$$ptr = getnetbyname(name)$$

where argument *name* is a pointer to a string that contains the name of the network for which information is desired. The value returned is a pointer to a structure that contains fields for the official name of the network, a list of registered aliases, an integer address type, and a 32-bit network address number.

A process calls library routine *getnetbyaddr* when it needs to search for information about a network given its address. The call has the form:

$$ptr = getnetbyaddr(netaddr, addrtype)$$

Argument *netaddr* is a 32-bit network address, and argument *addrtype* is an integer that specifies the type of *netaddr*.

Like the host information routines, the network routines allow sequential access of the database. Procedure *setnetent* allows the calling process to open the database and move to the beginning. A call has the form:

$$setnetent(stayopen)$$

If the integer argument *stayopen* is nonzero, it causes the database to remain open after calls to routines that search for an entry.

Procedure *getnetent* allows a process to retrieve entries sequentially, one at a time. It has the form:

$$ptr = getnetent()$$

and returns the same structure as other retrieval requests.

Finally, procedure *endnetent* allows a process to close the connection to database. A call has the form:

$$endnetent()$$

Obtaining Information About Protocols

Five library routines provide access to the database of protocols available on a machine. Each protocol has an official name, registered aliases, and an official protocol number. Procedure *getprotobyname* allows a caller to obtain information about a protocol given its name:

$$ptr = getprotobyname(name)$$

Argument *name* is a pointer to an ascii string that contains the name of the protocol for which information is desired. The procedure returns a pointer to a structure that has fields for the official protocol name, a list of aliases, and a unique integer value assigned to the protocol.

Procedure *getprotobynumber* allows a process to search for protocol information using the protocol number as a key:

$$ptr = getprotobynumber(number)$$

Finally, procedure *getprotoent* allows a process to access the database sequentially:

$$ptr = getprotoent()$$

As with other database routines, utility routines control access to the database. Procedure *setprotoent* opens and rewinds the protocol database file. If integer argument *stayopen* is nonzero, the file will remain open between successive retrieval requests:

$$setprotoent(stayopen)$$

Procedure *endprotoent* closes the database file:

$$endprotoent()$$

Obtaining Information About Network Services

Recall from Chapter 12 that the Internet reserves some UDP and TCP protocol port numbers. For example, TCP port *43* is reserved for the *whois* service. *Whois* allows a client on one machine to contact a server on another and obtain information about a user that has an account on the server's machine. The entry for *whois* in the services database specifies the service name, *whois*, the protocol, *TCP*, and the protocol port number *43*. Five Library routines exist that obtain information about services and protocol ports they use.

Procedure *getservbyname* maps a named service onto a port number:

$$ptr = getservbyname(name, proto)$$

Argument *name* specifies the address of a string that contains the name of the desired service, and integer argument *proto* specifies the protocol with which the service is to be used. Typically, protocols are limited to TCP and UDP. The value returned is a pointer to a structure that contains fields for the name of the service, a list of aliases, an identification of the protocol with which the service is used, and an integer protocol port number assigned for that service.

Procedure *getservbyport* allows the caller to obtain an entry from the service database given the port number assigned to it. A call has the form:

$$ptr = getservbyport(port, proto)$$

Argument *port* is the integer protocol port number assigned to the service, and argument *proto* specifies the protocol for which the service is desired.

As with other databases, a process can access the service database sequentially. To do so, it calls *getservent*:

$$ptr = getservent()$$

Each call returns the next entry in the database.

Procedure *setservent* opens and rewinds the database. It has the form:

$$setservent(stayopen)$$

where a nonzero value for integer argument *stayopen* specifies that the database should not be closed after retrievals.

A process calls procedure *endservent* to close the database.

An Example Client

The following C programming example illustrates the 4.3BSD operating system interface to TCP/IP. It is a very simple implementation of a *whois* client and server. As defined in RFC 954, the *whois* service allows a client on one machine to obtain information about a user on a remote system. In this implementation, the client is an application program that a user invokes along with two arguments: the name of a remote machine and the name of a user on that machine about whom information is desired. The client calls *gethostbyname* to map the remote machine name into an Internet address and calls *getservbyname* to find the well-known port for the *whois* service. Once it has mapped the host and service names, the client creates a socket, specifying that the socket will use reliable stream delivery (i.e., TCP). The client then binds the socket to the *whois* protocol port on the specified destination machine.

```
/* whoisclient.c - main */

#include <stdio.h>
#include <sys/types.h>
#include <sys/socket.h>
#include <netinet/in.h>
#include <netdb.h>


/*------------------------------------------------------------------
 * Program:     whoisclient
 *
 * Purpose:     UNIX application program that becomes a client for the
 *              Internet "whois" service.
 *
 * Use:         whois hostname username
 *
 * Author:      Barry Shein, Boston University
 *
 * Date:        January, 1987
 *
 *------------------------------------------------------------------
 */
main(argc,argv) int argc; char **argv;  /* std UNIX argument declaration*/

{
    int s;                              /* socket descriptor          */
    int len;                            /* length of received data    */
    struct sockaddr_in sa;              /* Internet socket addr. struct.*/
    struct hostent *hp ;                /* result of host name lookup */
    struct servent *sp ;                /* result of service lookup   */
```

```
char buf[BUFSIZ] ;                      /* buffer to read whois info   */
char *myname;                           /* pointer to name of this pgm */
char *host;                             /* pointer to remote host name */
char *user;                             /* pointer to remote user name */

myname = argv[0];
/*
 * Check that there are two command line arguments
 */
if(argc != 3) {
  fprintf(stderr,"Usage: %s host username\n",myname);
  exit(1);
}
host = argv[1];
user = argv[2];
/*
 * Look up the specified hostname
 */
if((hp = gethostbyname(host)) == NULL) {
  fprintf(stderr,"%s: %s: no such host?\n",myname,host);
  exit(1);
}
/*
 * Put host's address and address type into socket structure
 */
bcopy((char *)hp->h_addr,(char *)&sa.sin_addr,hp->h_length);
sa.sin_family = hp->h_addrtype;
/*
 * Look up the socket number for the WHOIS service
 */
if((sp = getservbyname("whois","tcp")) == NULL) {
  fprintf(stderr,"%s: No whois service on this host\n",myname);
  exit(1);
}
/*
 * Put the whois socket number into the socket structure.
 */
sa.sin_port = sp->s_port;
/*
 * Allocate an open socket
 */
if((s = socket(hp->h_addrtype,SOCK_STREAM,0)) < 0) {
  perror("socket");
  exit(1);
```

```
}
/*
 * Connect to the remote server
 */
if(connect(s,&sa,sizeof sa) < 0) {
  perror("connect") ;
  exit(1) ;
}
/*
 * Send the request
 */
if(write(s,user,strlen(user)) != strlen(user)) {
  fprintf(stderr,"%s: write error\n",myname);
  exit(1);
}
/*
 * Read the reply and put to user's output
 */
while((len = read(s,buf,BUFSIZ)) > 0)
  write(0, buf, len);
close(s);
exit(0);
}
```

An Example Server

The example server is only slightly more complex than the client. It listens on the well-known "whois" port and returns information to any clients that request it. The information is taken from the UNIX password file on the server's machine.

```
/* whoisserver.c - main */

#include <stdio.h>
#include <sys/types.h>
#include <sys/socket.h>
#include <netinet/in.h>
#include <netdb.h>
#include <pwd.h>


/*-------------------------------------------------------------------
 * Program:     whoisserver
 *
 * Purpose:     UNIX application program that acts as a server for
```

```
 *                    the "whois" service on the local machine.  It listens
 *                    on well-known WHOIS port (43) and answers queries from
 *                    clients.  This program requires super-user privilege to
 *                    run.
 *
 * Use:               whois hostname username
 *
 * Author:            Barry Shein, Boston University
 *
 * Date:              January, 1987
 *
 *-------------------------------------------------------------------
 */

#define BACKLOG          5          /* # of requests we're willing to queue */
#define MAXHOSTNAME     32          /* maximum host name length we tolerate */

main(argc,argv) int argc; char **argv;  /* std UNIX argument declaration*/
{
  int s, t;                         /* socket descriptors                    */
  int i;                            /* general purpose integer               */
  struct sockaddr_in sa, isa;       /* Internet socket address structure     */
  struct hostent *hp;               /* result of host name lookup            */
  char *myname;                     /* pointer to name of this program       */
  struct servent *sp;               /* result of service lookup              */
  char localhost[MAXHOSTNAME+1];/* local host name as character string   */

  myname = argv[0];
  /*
   * Look up the WHOIS service entry
   */
  if((sp = getservbyname("whois","tcp")) == NULL) {
    fprintf(stderr,"%s: No whois service on this host\n",myname);
    exit(1);
  }
  /*
   * Get our own host information
   */
  gethostname(localhost,MAXHOSTNAME);
  if((hp = gethostbyname(localhost)) == NULL) {
    fprintf(stderr,"%s: cannot get local host info?\n",myname);
    exit(1);
  }
  /*
```

```
 * Put the WHOIS socket number and our address info
 * into the socket structure
 */
sa.sin_port = sp->s_port;
bcopy((char *)hp->h_addr,(char *)&sa.sin_addr,hp->h_length);
sa.sin_family = hp->h_addrtype;
/*
 * Allocate an open socket for incoming connections
 */
if((s = socket(hp->h_addrtype,SOCK_STREAM,0)) < 0) {
  perror("socket");
  exit(1);
}
/*
 * Bind the socket to the service port
 * so we hear incoming connections
 */
if(bind(s,&sa,sizeof sa,0) < 0) {
  perror("bind");
  exit(1);
}
/*
 * Set maximum connections we will fall behind
 */
listen(s,BACKLOG);
/*
 * Go into an infinite loop waiting for new connections
 */
for(;;) {
  i = sizeof isa ;
  /*
   * We hang in accept() while waiting for new customers
   */
  if((t = accept(s,&isa,&i)) < 0) {
    perror("accept");
    exit(1);
  }
  whois(t);            /* perform the actual WHOIS service */
  close(t);
 }
}
/*
 * Get the WHOIS request from remote host and format a reply.
 */
```

```
whois(sock) int sock;
{
  struct passwd *p;
  char buf[BUFSIZ];
  int i;

  /*
   * Get one line request
   */
  if((i = read(sock,buf,BUFSIZ)) <= 0)
    return;
  buf[i] = ' ';          /* Null terminate */
  /*
   * Look up the requested user
   * and format reply
   */
  if((p = getpwnam(buf)) == NULL)
    strcpy(buf,"User not found\n");
  else
    sprintf(buf,"%s: %s\n",p->pw_name,p->pw_gecos);
  /*
   * Return reply
   */
  write(sock,buf,strlen(buf));
  return;
}
```

Appendix 2

Hints And Suggestions For Implementors

Introduction

This appendix contains a list of hints intended for people who are implementing Internet protocol software. The items vary in level of detail and importance from those that describe a general, philosophical approach to those that focus on some small detail often missed or misunderstood. It is impossible to provide an exhaustive description of each problem, its consequences, or its solution. Instead, our intent is to present implementors with the (sometimes unwritten) lessons learned from experience.

To help the reader gain some perspective, the hints have been divided into broad categories. Within each category, hints have been ordered to make sequential reading sensible; the reader should not infer anything about the importance of ideas from the ordering. Despite the careful partitioning, much overlap exists. Thus, the reader might be admonished to apply the first hint to this appendix itself: read the entire list of hints before rushing off to follow one of them.

General Approach

- *Study everything before implementing anything.* Although protocol software is separated into conceptual layers, the layers interact closely. Designing a given layer without understanding the functional requirements of other layers leads to unexpected mismatches.

● *Plan for full generality.* It is tempting to think of starting small and generalizing later, but that seldom works well. For example, when building a diskless workstation, it is tempting to limit the design to a single network connection or to assume that the workstation will use a single file server. However, such assumptions lead to designs that cannot be expanded easily.

● *Plan for change.* As long as the Internet remains a research project, change will continue.

● *Plan on multiple protocols at each level.* It is tempting to assume that only the application level will have multiple protocols and that there is no reason for more protocols at the level of TCP or IP. However, we know that the migration to ISO TP-4/IP will require systems to adapt to new transport protocols. If the initial design is robust, such transitions will be much easier.

● *Avoid context switching.* The high cost of context switching limits throughput in systems that switch process context many times as they handle packets. Thus, designers should avoid designs that place each protocol in an application program because such designs require a context switch every time data passes to or from the protocol.

● *Avoid copying.* When implementing layered protocol software, find an efficient data structure that allows packets to pass between layers of protocol software without being copied. Copying simply costs too much. One alternative to copying, developed at BBN for the BSD UNIX implementation of TCP/IP, uses a linked list data structure called *mbuf*s. When sending a packet, each layer of protocol allocates an additional *mbuf* from the free list, adds it to the beginning of the linked list for the packet being sent, and places the header for that protocol in the new mbuf. When the linked list reaches a device driver, the driver can copy it into contiguous storage for transmission (or use gather-write if the device supports it). Thus, only one copy of a packet is needed, independent of the number of layers of protocol software.

● *Avoid small buffers.* Experiments have shown that storing a large packet as a long chain of small buffers (e.g., mbuf structures described above) produces substantially higher processing cost than storing the same packet in large buffers. Furthermore, in most machines, the cost of using a large buffer to store a small packet is trivial.

● *Build debugging code from the start.* Give network experts a way to monitor the network or the protocol software itself. Sealed black boxes are frustrating and unpleasant to use.

● *Use domain names.* Early Internet software used a local disk file to map host names onto Internet addresses. Doing so required machines to obtain copies of a host name file from the Network Information Center. However, this method is hopelessly inadequate and should not be considered for new implementations. Use the on-line domain name system instead.

● *Always accept a dotted decimal address in place of a name.* It is especially important when debugging to be able to specify the address of a specific network interface (as opposed to the name of a machine which software maps into one of its IP addresses). As a rule, checking for dotted decimal form first produces noticeably faster performance.

• *Adhere to standards.* Implementors often think they can improve on protocols or take advantage of unused or uninterpreted header fields. The temptation is especially strong when a vendor assumes customers will only use that vendor's products and will only have a small, isolated local area network. But breaking standards is always a mistake. Eventually, someone will try to use the software to interoperate with other vendor's products and other networks. There are three specific examples of standards that should be pointed out: standard network byte order, the standard (all 1's) broadcast address, and standard subnet addressing.

• *Be careful of MIL standards.* The documents describing MIL standards for DDN protocols are not identical to the RFCs. Several contain typos.

• *Do not assume that the best-known implementations are the best.* Well-known implementations do not always perform well or adhere to the standards. In particular, the 4.2BSD UNIX implementation of TCP/IP protocols contained bugs, inefficiencies, and standards violations. Yet, it was ported to many systems so faithfully that they exhibit exactly the same bugs.

• *Check the RFC that describes Official Protocols.* The list of official protocols contains reports of problems and clarifications of RFC documents. Check the latest version before implementing a protocol.

Operating System Interface

• *Plan for multiple application programs to use the network protocols.* This advice is obvious for large, time-sharing systems, but also applies to small, single-user machines because even an individual may wish to invoke two concurrent programs that use the Internet (e.g., to transfer a file in background while sending electronic mail). Limiting network access to a single application program severely limits the system functionality.

• *Make simple communication easy.* The interaction between an application program and the operating system can be complicated because the program needs to specify the type of communication service desired, destination address, and possibly even the protocol family to be used. However, few programs exercise all possible options. Most have simple communication requirements. Thus, the system should make it easy to handle common tasks.

• *Plan access to all levels of protocols.* It is a mistake to isolate application programs from lower level protocols because it means that all network monitoring and control code must reside in the operating system. Instead, one should plan on allowing access to low level protocols so that authorized network administrators can send and receive packets without recompiling the operating system (and without rebooting the machine).

TCP

● *Avoid the silly window syndrome.* RFC 813 describes how the window mechanism in TCP can lead to a steady state in which the receiver acknowledges a small segment by advertising a small increase in available window size, causing the sender to transmit another small segment. This is a fundamental problem that arises because TCP ties flow control to window size. A large window is needed for high throughput even though the receiver wants to reduce flow temporarily. The solution, also discussed in RFC 813, consists of introducing hysteresis by having either the sender or receiver (or both) delay further transmission until a reasonable size window exists.

● *Avoid the Cypress syndrome.* Cypress causes a problem with many implementations of TCP because it introduces one or more slow speed links on the path between machines. We observe that during file transfer, throughput sometimes drops to one half the line capacity because TCP transmits each segment twice. The problem occurs when the network is reliable, but delays across a slow speed line cause the retransmission timer to expire before the ACK arrives. After TCP transmits a segment the second time, the ACK from the original transmission arrives. TCP incorrectly associates the ACK with the second transmission (because ACKs identify only the data received, not the datagram that carried the segment), retains the low estimate of round trip delay, and the cycle repeats with the next segment transmitted. One way to detect the problem is to count extra ACKs and adjust the round trip estimate upwards if the count exceeds a fixed threshold. Another technique is to count retransmissions and increase the round trip estimate if they exceed a threshold. It has been proved that Karn's algorithm solves the problem as does Jacobsen's dynamic estimate of variance scheme.

● *Use smaller segment size instead of relying on IP fragmentation.* Fragmentation is fundamentally inferior to smaller segment size in the following way. When a gateway fragments a datagram, it copies the IP sequence number onto all fragments and sends them on their way. The receiver must collect all fragments from a given datagram in order to reassemble it. If any fragment is lost, the receiver discards the complete datagram. Consider a large TCP segment that is fragmented in transmission. If any one of the fragments is lost, the datagram carrying the segment is considered lost and must be retransmitted. If a fragment of the retransmitted segment is lost, the segment must be retransmitted a second time. All the fragments from one datagram must arrive intact for successful transmission. If the sending TCP software used a smaller segment size and transmitted the same data as many small segments, the receiver would save all those pieces that arrived successfully.

● *Do not assume that push marks boundaries in the stream.* The TCP push function is used to force delivery but does not guarantee that the receiver will obtain data in the same quantities that the sender pushes. That is, push should not be interpreted as a record mark.

● *Be careful of urgent pointer.* The urgent data pointer points to the last octet of urgent data (not to the first octet of nonurgent data).

• *Connections can be idle.* The specification says that TCP does not automatically close idle connections, nor does it periodically check to see if the peer is alive.

• *Accept segments out of order.* TCP implementations that "cheat" by only accepting segments in order (i.e., implementations that do not correctly implement a sliding window) incur a severe performance penalty and are discouraged.

• *Use the Nagle heuristic to handle small packets.* Found in RFC 896, along with a discussion of TCP problems, the Nagle heuristic admonishes the sending TCP to delay transmission of additional small segments until outstanding data has been acknowledged. For example, in a TELNET session where a user types characters into a slow network, the sending TCP would send the first character in a segment as soon as it arrives, but then queue incoming characters until the acknowledgement for the first character arrives.

• *Do not delay acknowledgements.* Some implementations of TCP attempt to decrease TCP overhead by delaying acknowledgements so they can travel piggyback in a segment that carries data in the opposite direction. The argument has been made that delaying ACKs works especially well for TELNET because one expects the server to echo (send back) each character shortly after it arrives. However, studies have shown that such delays can lower throughput and can confuse the client's round trip estimate algorithms. Delaying acknowledgements also interferes with the Nagle heuristic (see above).

• *Use better round-trip estimations.* Work by V. Jacobson, and P. Karn have produced algorithms that give much better estimates of round-trip times than the original algorithm suggested in RFC 791. In addition, Jain's scheme helps TCP respond to congestion.

• *Remember the performance margin.* Because TCP acknowledgements refer to stream position and not to individual segments, performance does not degrade in exact proportion to packet loss. In particular, if a given connection loses n percent of the packets passed across it, the throughput of TCP running across that connection will be strictly less than $100 - n$ percent. Another way of looking at this implies that packet loss will have a dramatic effect on TCP performance.

IP

• *Implement ICMP.* ICMP is a required part of IP. Trying to add it on after IP software has been built is a mistake.

• *Plan on multi-homed hosts.* Implementations of IP designed for a single network interface do not extend gracefully to multiple network interfaces. However, users cannot seem to resist connecting machines to multiple physical networks. Thus, designers should plan for multi-homed hosts.

• *Choose a strategy for nonstandard broadcast addresses.* This is simply practical advice based on the observation that some vendors insist on using nonstandard broadcast addresses (e.g., all 0's). At the very least, one should avoid using the all 0's address; one might even consider accepting nonstandard broadcast addresses as well as standard broadcast addresses.

• *Plan to handle the multi-homed address problem.* Multi-homed hosts have a set of network interfaces and a set of IP addresses for them. Even if a datagram is addressed to the host, the destination IP address may not match the IP address of the interface on which it arrives. IP must correctly decide that the datagram has reached its destination.

• *Distinguish between network interfaces and IP addresses.* Incoming packets have both an interface on which they arrive and a destination address. For debugging and routing, it is important to keep both pieces of information. Of special concern is routing in the presence of subnets.

• *Be aware of the source mismatch problem.* Source mismatch occurs when machine *A* sends a datagram to multi-homed machine *B* using a destination address I_1, but *B* routes back to *A* over a different network and lists I_2 as its IP source. Machine *A* cannot match the source address of the return datagram to the destination address of the datagram it sent.

• *Be careful of broadcasting in the presence of subnets.* At the very least, read the pertinent RFCs on this subject. Broadcasting on subnets can be tricky.

• *Beware of default routes, especially with subnet addressing.* Default routes are both powerful and dangerous. In particular, default routes used in gateways that attach to networks with subnet addresses can cause routing loops for datagrams addressed to nonexistent subnets.

• *Provide for interaction with lower layers of protocol software.* As a specific example, consider the interaction between IP and ARP. When IP routes a datagram, it passes the datagram to a network interface for transmission or, if it has no route for the host, reports "host unreachable" to the sender. If the interface is an Ethernet and ARP must be used, failure of ARP to resolve the address should result in the same "host unreachable" error condition.

• *Never lie about an IP source address.* In theory, a multi-homed host can use any of its IP addresses as the source address in an IP datagram. However, using an address that differs from the address of the interface over which the datagram is being sent, means that return traffic will not follow the same path as traffic going out and invites source mismatch problems.

• *Tie IP processing to routing algorithms.* As a common example, consider a system running the *gated* routing program. In such systems, IP should not time-out routes (i.e., remove them) without telling *gated*.

• *Avoid fragmentation, if possible.* Fragmentation is an all-or-nothing proposition because there are no selective acknowledgements. The receiver must receive all fragments or discard the entire datagram. Thus, it is preferable to divide transmission into smaller datagrams at the source than to rely on fragmentation.

• *Be aware of the MTU problem.* Because machines on the Internet cannot know the path a datagram will follow, they cannot know the maximum size datagram that can be transferred without fragmentation. However, upper level protocols should at least be able to obtain information about the MTU for directly attached networks. The accepted scheme is to use the local network MTU for local traffic and an MTU of 576 for nonlocal traffic.

• *Conserve IP sequence numbers.* IP has a 16-bit sequence number field and requires hosts to stamp each outgoing IP datagram with a unique sequence number that the receiver uses when reassembling the datagram from fragments. The idea is that the contents of this field must be unique among all datagrams sent by a host. Usually, because only a handful of datagrams from a specific host remain alive in the Internet, and because their maximum lifetime is measured in tens of seconds, there is no problem with duplicate sequence numbers. However, implementors should be aware that reassembly will fail if two datagrams have the same sequence number. Thus, using only part of the address space is discouraged.

ICMP

• *Implement echo request and echo reply early.* Having an IP-level echo protocol is essential for testing routes and reachability.

• *Allow user level processes to interact with ICMP.* ICMP defines only a message protocol and not a comprehensive algorithm for reacting to messages. Because many implementations use application programs like *gated* to handle routing, such programs need to receive the information that arrives via ICMP. For example, *gated* would work better if it received a copy of all ICMP redirect messages.

• *Plan mechanisms that inform higher level protocols when errors occur.* Information like "destination network unreachable" is much more helpful to a user than the more generic "cannot connect."

GGP/EGP/IGP

• *User be warned.* There are few implementations of these protocols, and most do not function well. EGP is the worst offender. In addition to mistakes in the implementation, many arguments have been made that show the protocols themselves are deficient.

• *Use active mode on both sides of EGP.* EGP implementations tend to avoid declaring passive mode connections down even if the network suffers substantial packet loss (although, in principle, the protocol parameters can be changed to make it detect loss). As a result, keeping both sides active works better.

Gateways

• *Building gateways is complex.* Although it may seem that a simple extension to the IP routing algorithm is sufficient to handle routing in a gateway, gateways are not simple at all. Read the literature before starting, including IEN 109, RFC 1009.

• *Do not use timesharing machines as gateways.* General purpose systems can add more delay than dedicated machines and are less robust (crash more frequently). In addition, network traffic can load the machine.

● *Assume a significant number of incorrect addresses.* Incorrect addresses are common. Make sure gateways can handle them correctly (including subnet addresses) and efficiently.

● *Do not keep IP datagrams forever.* RFC 970 discusses why gateways should not keep arbitrarily long queues of datagrams even if storage is available. In essence, keeping old datagrams loads the network with useless traffic. For example, when network delays increase, a given gateway may accumulate several copies of a single datagram that have been retransmitted. Attempting to send them only adds to the congestion and guarantees that the network will not recover.

● *Do not reset the TTL when fragmenting.* It is a mistake for gateways to reset the time to live field when fragmenting a datagram (even though at least one popular implementation does so). Each fragment should be given a copy of a datagram's TTL field.

● *Beware of default routes in gateways.* Default routes can be especially dangerous if a gateway uses automatic routing software (e.g., EGP) to change other routes.

Appendix 3

A Guide To RFCs

Introduction

Most of the written information about the Internet, including its architecture, protocols, and history, can be found in a series of reports known as *Request For Comments* or *RFC*s. An informal, loosely coordinated set of notes, RFCs are unusually rich in information and color. Before we consider the more serious aspects of RFCs, it is fitting that we take a few minutes to pay attention to the colorful side. A good place to begin is with Cerf's *'Twas the Night Before Start-up* (RFC 968), a humorous parody that describes some of the problems encountered when starting a new network. Knowing not to take itself too seriously has pervaded the Internet effort. Anyone who can remember both their first Internet meeting, filled with networking jargon, and Lewis Carroll's *Jabberwocky*, filled with strangely twisted English, will know exactly why D. L. Covill put them together in *ARPAWOCKY* (RFC 527). Anyone that has read Knuth's *The Art Of Computer Programming* may chuckle over RFC 473 asking where on the ARPANET one could execute MIX programs. We can imagine Pickens filled with pride when responding with RFC 485, *MIX and MIXAL at UCSB*. The University of California at Santa Barbara wasn't alone in offering MIX to the world. Walden showed so in RFC 494, which provides a list of all hosts on the network that supported MIX programming.

Other RFCs seem equally frivolous. Interspersed amid the descriptions of ideas that would turn out to dramatically change networking, we find notes like RFC 416, written in early November, 1972: *The ARC System will be Unavailable for Use During Thanksgiving Week*. It says exactly what you think it says. If notes like that do not seem insignificant, think about the sixty-six RFCs listed as *never issued*. They were all assigned a number and had an author, but none ever saw the light of day. All that remains are the holes in the numbering scheme, preserved as little reminders of ideas that vaporized or work that remains incomplete.

Even after the silly, lighthearted, and useless RFCs have been removed, the remaining documents do not conform to most standards for scientific writing. Unlike scholarly scientific journals that concentrate on identifying papers of important archival interest, screening them carefully, and filing them for posterity, RFCs provide a record of ongoing conversations among the principals involved in designing, building, measuring, and using the ARPANET and, later, the Internet. The reader understands at once that RFCs include the thoughts of researchers on the leading edge of technological innovation, not the studied opinions of scholars who have completely mastered a subject. The authors are not always sure of the consequences of their proposals, or even of the contents, but they clearly realize the issues are too complex to understand without community discussion.

Despite the inconsistencies in RFCs that sometimes make them difficult for beginners to understand, the RFC mechanism has evolved and now works extremely well. Because they are available electronically, information is propagated to the community quickly. Because they span a broad range of interests, practitioners as well as designers contribute. Because they record informal conversations, they capture discussions and not merely final conclusions. Even the disagreements and contradictory proposals are useful in showing what the designers considered before settling on a given protocol (and readers interested in the history of a particular idea or protocol can use RFCs to follow it from its inception to its current state).

How To Obtain An RFC Over The Internet

RFCs are available electronically from the Internet Network Information Center. The Internet domain name for the host that provides the archive is:

SRI-NIC.ARPA

To obtain a copy of the text file for an RFC directly from the archive, you must use the Internet File Transfer Protocol (FTP) on a computer attached to the Internet. After invoking FTP on your local computer system, you need to supply retrieval commands. Issue the *user* command to identify yourself to the FTP server and supply a user name *guest* and password *anonymous* when asked. Once the server recognizes you, use the *get* command to retrieve a file named

<rfc>rfc$N$.txt

where N is the number of the RFC desired. For example, to obtain a copy of RFC 822, retrieve file

<rfc>rfc822.txt

The file you retrieve will contain ASCII text with a form feed character separating pages and newline (line feed) characters separating lines. Except for the newline and form feed characters, the entire file contains printable text that can be rendered with a conventional line printer. No line drawings or other special graphics are included.

The following command script illustrates how one might use FTP to retrieve RFCs under 4.3 BSD UNIX:

```
-----------------------------------------------------------------------
#! /bin/sh
#
# rfc - 4.3 BSD UNIX (Bourne) shell script to obtain copies of RFCs,
#         keeping a local cache for subsequent requests.
#
# use: rfc number [number...]
#
PATH=/bin:/usr/bin:/usr/ucb
PUB=/usr/pub/RFC
for i
do      if test ! -r $PUB/$i -o $i = "-index"
        then echo Retrieving RFC $i from SRI-NIC.ARPA >&2
#
# invoke FTP under 4.3 BSD UNIX and feed it retrieval commands as input.
#
                ftp -n SRI-NIC.ARPA  >/dev/null 2>&1 <<!
user anonymous guest
get <rfc>rfc$i.txt $PUB/$i
quit
!
#
# Have obtained file; give copy to user if retrieval was successful.
#
        if test -r $PUB/$i
        then cat $PUB/$i
        else echo Could not retrieve RFC $i 1>&2
        fi
done
-----------------------------------------------------------------------
```

The script shown above does more than use FTP to retrieve an RFC. It leaves a copy of the RFC in directory /usr/pub/RFC. The advantage of keeping a local copy of an RFC is that subsequent requests are much faster than the first because they do not use FTP nor do they pass information across the Internet. If the script finds one of the requested RFCs in the cache, it merely presents the user with a copy. Note that the script does not look in the cache when retrieving the special file -index because the index contains a list of all RFCs that changes as new RFCs appear.

How To Obtain An RFC Through Electronic Mail

The CSNET Coordination and Information Center, located at Bolt, Beranek, and Newman Inc. in Cambridge Massachusetts, operates an information server that can respond to electronic mail messages. That is, you send electronic mail to a special address, a computer program reads the mail and consults its database of information, and the computer program sends the answer back in electronic mail. The address of the information server is:

info-server @ sh.cs.net

The database contains text documents for RFCs along with other information.

To obtain an RFC, you must mail the information server an electronic message that contains two lines. the first line specifies the keyword *REQUEST:* followed by the value *rfc*. The second specifies the keyword *TOPIC:* followed by the integer number of the RFC to retrieve. For example, to retrieve RFC 822, you send the mail message

REQUEST: rfc
TOPIC: 822

If you need more information on CSNET's info-server, you can send a request *help*. To obtain help with RFCs only, send a message in which the request is *rfc* and the topic is *help*.

How To Obtain A Paper Copy Of An RFC

People without access to any electronic networks can still obtain copies of RFCs from the Network Information Center. Their telephone number is 1-800-235-3155. Before calling, use this appendix to make a list of the RFCs needed.

Browsing Through RFCs

There are several indexes that can help one browse through RFCs. First, as we mentioned above, the file *<rfc>rfc-index.txt* contains an accurate list of all RFCs listed in reverse chronological order. It is kept at the archive along with text files for the RFCs. Anyone can obtain the index file using FTP or by mail; users who plan to browse through RFCs usually obtain the index first to verify that they know about the latest RFCs. Second, many RFCs contain summaries or indexes of other RFCs. For example, RFC 899 contains an index of all RFCs numbered 800 through 899, in reverse chronological order. Third, readers often need to know which RFC contains the latest version of some official Internet protocol or which protocols are official and which are unofficial. To accommodate such needs, people at the Information Sciences Institute of the University of

Southern California who are responsible for Internet protocols periodically publish a new RFC entitled *Official ARPA-Internet Protocols*. The official protocols RFC provides a list of all protocols that have been adopted as Internet standards and lists, as of the time of its publication, the number of the most recent RFC describing each protocol. The same group also publishes related information periodically in RFCs entitled *Internet Numbers*†. The Internet numbers RFCs contain values used by official protocols.

Despite these indexes, browsing through RFCs can be difficult, especially when the reader is searching for information pertinent to a given topic. Reading a chronological list of all RFCs becomes tedious, but there is no mechanism that allows one to find related groups of RFCs. To exacerbate the problem, information on a given topic may be spread across many years. Browsing through a chronological index of RFCs is particularly difficult because titles do not provide sufficient identification of the information in an RFC. (How could one guess that *Leaving Well Enough Alone* pertains to FTP?) Finally, having multiple RFCs with a single title (e.g., Internet Numbers) can be confusing because the reader cannot easily tell whether a document is out of date without checking the archive.

RFCs Arranged By Topic

The final section of this appendix contains some help in finding information in RFCs because it contains a list of the first 1000 RFCs arranged by topic. The topical arrangement comes from RFC 1000, which also provides an annotated, chronological list of all RFCs. Although long, RFC 1000 is highly recommended as a source of authoritative and valuable critique. Its introduction is especially fascinating. Recalling the origin of RFCs along with the origin of the ARPANET, it captures the spirit of adventure and energy that still characterizes the Internet.

---

†The *Internet Numbers* RFCs were formerly entitled *Assigned Numbers*.

RFCs Organized By Major Category And Subtopic
(As Found In RFC 1000)

1. Administrative

1a. Assigned Numbers (official values used by protocols)

997, 990, 960, 943, 923, 900, 870, 820, 790, 776, 770, 762, 758, 755, 750, 739, 717, 604, 503, 433, 349, 322, 317, 204, 179, 175, 167.

1b. List Of Official Internet Protocols

991, 961, 944, 924, 901, 880, 840, 694, 661, 617, 582, 580, 552.
774 - Internet Protocol Handbook Table of Contents

1c. Meeting Notes and Minutes

898 - Gateway Special Interest Group Meeting Notes
808, 805, 469 - Computer Mail Meeting Notes
910, 807 - Multimedia Mail Meeting Notes
585 - ARPANET Users Interest Working Group Meeting
549, 396, 282, 253 - Graphics Meeting Notes
371 - International Computer Communications Conference
327 - Data and File Transfer Workshop Notes
316 - Data Management Working Group Meeting Report
164, 131, 116, 108, 101, 082, 077, 066, 063, 037, 021 - Network Working
    Group Meeting

1d. Meeting Announcements and Group Overviews

828 - Data Communications: IFIP's International "Network" of Experts
631 - Call for Papers: International Meeting on Minicomputers and Data
    Communication
584 - Charter for ARPANET Users Interest Working Group
537 - Announcement of NGG Meeting
526 - Technical Meeting - Digital Image Processing Software Systems
504 - Workshop Announcement
483 - Cancellation of the Resource Notebook Framework Meeting
474, 314, 246, 232, 134 - Network Graphics Working Group
471 - Announcement of a (Tentative) Workshop on Multi-Site Executive
    Programs
461 - Telnet Meeting Announcement
457 - TIPUG
456 - Memorandum
454 - File Transfer Protocol Meeting Announcement

1e. Distribution Lists

1f. Policies Documents

1g. Request for Comments Administrative

999, 899, 800, 699 - Requests for Comments Summary

825 - Request for Comments on Requests for Comments

629 - Scenario for Using the Network Journal

628 - Status of RFC Numbers and a Note on Pre-assigned Journal Numbers

598, 200, 170, 160, 100, 084 - RFC Index

1h. Bibliographies

829 - Packet Satellite Technology Reference Sources

290 - Computer Network and Data Sharing: A Bibliography

243 - Network and Data Sharing Bibliography

1i. Other

637 - Change of Network Address for SU-DSL

634 - Change in Network Address for Haskins Lab

616 - Latest Network Maps

609 - Statement of Upcoming Move of NIC/NLS Service

590 - MULTICS Address Change

588 - London Node is Now Up

551 - NYU, ANL, and LBL Joining the Net

544 - Locating On-Line Documentation at SRI-ARC

543 - Network Journal Submission and Delivery

518 - ARPANET Accounts

511 - Enterprise Phone Service to NIC From ARPANET Sites

510 - Request for Network Mailbox Addresses

432 - Network Logical Map

423, 389 - UCLA Campus Computing Network Liaison Staff for ARPA
           Network

421 - A Software Consulting Service for Network Users

419 - MIT-DMS on Vacation

416 - The ARC System will be Unavailable for Use During Thanksgiving Week

405 - Correction to RFC 404

404 - Host Address Changes Involving Rand and ISI

403 - Desirability of a Network 1108 Service

386 - Letter to TIP Users - 2

384 - Official Site IDENTS for Organizations in the ARPA Networks

381 - Three Aids to Improved Network Operation

356 - ARPA Network Control Center

334 - Network Use on May 8

305 - Unknown Host Numbers

301 - BBN IMP No. 5 and NCC Schedule for March 4, 1972

2. ARPANET Host to Host Protocol

2a. Network Control Protocol (predecessor of TCP/IP)

2b. Initial Connection Protocol

3. Internet Level

3a. Internet Protocol (IP)

3b. Internet Control Message Protocol (ICMP)

3c. Gateway Protocols (GGP, EGP)

3d. Other

4. Host Level

4a. User Datagram Protocol (UDP)

4b. Transmission Control Protocol (TCP)

879 - The TCP Maximum Segment Size and Related Topics

872 - TCP-ON-A-LAN

817 - Modularity and Efficiency in Protocol Implementation

816 - Fault Isolation and Recovery

814 - Name, Addresses, Ports, and Routes

794 - Pre-Emption

793, 761, 675 - Transmission Control Protocol

721 - Out of Band Control Signals in a Host to Host Protocol

700 - A Protocol Experiment

4c. Transaction Protocols and Distributed Operating Systems

955 - Towards a Transport Service for Transaction Processing Applications

938 - Internet Reliable Transaction Protocol Functional and Interface Specification

908 - Reliable Data Protocol

722 - Thoughts on Interactions in Distributed Services

713 - MSDTP -- Message Services Data Transmission Protocol

712 - A Distributed Capability Computing System DCCS

708 - Elements of a Distributed Programming System

707 - A High-Level Framework for Network-Based Resource Sharing

684 - A Commentary on Procedure Calling as A Network Protocol

677 - The Maintenance of Duplicate Databases

674 - Procedure Call Documents--Version 2

672 - A Multi-Site Data Collection Facility

671 - A Note on Reconnection Protocol

645 - Network Standard Data Specification Syntax

615 - Proposed Network Standard Data Pathname Syntax

610 - Further Datalanguage Design Concepts

592 - Some Thoughts on System Design to Facilitate Resource Sharing

578 - Using MIT-MATHLAB MACSYMA From MIT-DMS Muddle - An Experiment in Automated Resource Sharing

515 - Specifications for Datalanguage, Version 0/9

500 - The Integration of Data Management Systems on a Computer Network

441 - Inter-Entity Communication - An Experiment

437 - Data Reconfiguration Service at UCSB

203 - Achieving Reliable Communication

076 - Connection-by-Name: User-Oriented Protocol

062 - A System for Interprocess Communication in a Resource Sharing Computer Network

061 - A Note on Interprocess Communication in a Resource Sharing Computer Network

051 - Proposal for a Network Interchange Language

031 - Binary Message Forms in Computer Networks

005 - DEL

001 - Host Software

4d. Other

998, 969 - NETBLT: A Bulk Data Transfer Protocol

988 - Host Extensions for IP Multicasting

979 - PSN End-to-End Functional Specification

966 - A Multicast Extension to the Internet Protocol

869 - Host Monitoring Protocol

741 - Specifications for the Network Voice Protocol NVP

643 - Cross Net Debugger

162 - NETBUGGER3

5. Application Level

5a. Telnet Protocol (TELNET)

854, 764 - Telnet Protocol Specification

818 - The Remote User Telnet Service

801 - NCP/TCP Transition Plan

782 - A Virtual Terminal Management Model

764 - Telnet Protocol Specification

728 - A Minor Pitfall in the Telnet Protocol

688 - Tentative Schedule for the New Telnet Implementation for the TIP

681 - Network Unix

600 - Interfacing an Illinois Plasma Terminal to the ARPANET

596 - Second Thoughts on Telnet Go-Ahead

595 - Some Thoughts in Defense of the Telnet Go-Ahead

593 - Telnet and FTP Implementation Schedule Change

576 - Proposal for Modifying Linking

570 - Experimental Input Mapping Between NVT ASCII and UCSB Online System

562 - Modifications to the Telnet Specification

559 - Comments on the New Telnet Protocol and Its Implementation

529 - A Note on Protocol Synch Sequences

513 - Comments on the New Telnet Specifications

495 - Telnet Protocol Specification

466 - Telnet Logger/Server for Host LL-67

461 - Telnet Meeting Announcement

452 - Telnet Command at Host LL

5b. Telnet Options

5c. File Transfer Protocol (FTP, TFTP, SFTP, SMTP)

5d. Domain Name System

5e. Mail and Message Systems (SMTP)

786 - Mail Transfer Protocol - ISI TOPS-20 MTP-NIMAIL Interface
785 - Mail Transfer Protocol - ISI TOPS-20 File Definitions
784 - Mail Transfer Protocol - ISI TOPS-20 Implementation
771 - Mail Transition Plan
763 - Role Mailboxes
757 - A Suggested Solution to the Naming, Addressing, and Delivery Problem
      for ARPANET Message Systems
754 - Out-of-Net Host Addresses for Mail
753 - Internet Message Protocol
751 - Survey of FTP Mail and MLFL
733 - Standard for the Format of ARPA Network Text Messages
724 - Proposed Official Standard for the Format of ARPA Network Messages
720 - Address Specification Syntax for Network Mail
706 - On the Junk Mail Problem
680 - Message Transmission Protocol
644 - On the Problem of Signature Authentication for Network Mail
577 - Mail Priority
574 - Announcement of a Mail Facility at UCSB
561 - Standardizing Network Mail Headers
555 - Responses to Critiques of the Proposed Mail Protocol
539, 524 - A Proposed Mail Protocol
498 - On Mail Service to CCN
491 - What is "Free"?
475 - On FTP and the Network Mail System
458 - Mail Retrieval via FTP
333 - A Proposed Experiment with a Message Switching Protocol
278, 224, 221, 196 - A Mail Box Protocol

5f. Facsimile and Bitmaps

809 - UCL Facsimile System
804 - Facsimile Formats
803 - Dacom 450/500 Facsimile Date Transcoding
798 - Decoding Facsimile Data From the Rapicom 450
797 - Bitmap Formats
769 - Rapicom 450 Facsimile File Format

5g. Graphics

965 - A Format for a Graphical Communication Protocol
553 - Draft Design for a Text/Graphics Protocol
493 - Graphics Protocol
401 - Conversion of NGP-0 Coordinates to Device Specific Coordinates

5h. Data Management

5i. Remote Job Entry (NETRJE, NETRJS)

283 - NETRJT - Remote Job Service Protocol for TIPS

105 - Network Specification for Remote Job Entry and Remote Job Output Retrieval at UCSB

5j. Time And Date

958, 957, 956 - Network Time Protocol

868 - Time Server Protocol

867 - Daytime Protocol

778 - DCNET Time Server Protocol

738 - Time Server

685 - Response Time in Cross-network Debugging

034 - Some Brief Preliminary Notes on the ARC Clock

032 - Some Thoughts on SRI's Proposed Real Time Clock

028 - Time Standards

5k. Other

978 - Voice File Interchange Protocol (VFIP)

972 - Password Generator Protocol

954, 812 - Whois Protocol

951 - Bootstrap Protocol

937, 918 - Post Office Protocol

931, 912 - Authentication Service

913 - Simple File Transfer Protocol

909 - Loader Debugger Protocol

891 - DCN Local Net Protocol

887 - Resource Location Protocol

866 - Active Users Protocol

865 - Quote of the Day Protocol

864 - Character Generator Protocol

863, 361, 348 - Discard Protocol

862, 361, 347 - Echo Protocol

821, 822 - Simple Mail Transfer Protocol

783 - Trivial File Transfer Protocol

767 - Document Formats

759 - Internet Message Protocol

742 - Finger Protocol

734 - SUPDUP Protocol

726 - Remote Controlled Transmission and Echoing Telnet Option

666 - Specification of the Unified User-Level Protocol

621 - NIC User Directories at SRI-ARC

569 - Network Standard Text Editor

470 - Change in Socket for TIP News Facility

451 - Tentative Proposal for a Unified User Level Protocol

098, 079 - Logger Protocol

029 - Note in Response to Bill English's Request for Comments

6. Program Documentation

6a. General

496 - A TNLS Quick Reference Card is Available

494 - Availability of MIX and MIXAL in the Network

488 - NLS Classes at Network Sites

485 - MIS and MIXAL at UCSB

431 - Update on SMFS Login and Logout

411 - New Multics Network Software Features

409 - TENEX Interface to UCSB's Simple-Minded File System

399 - SMFS Login and Logout

390 - TSO Scenario Batch Compilation and Foreground Execution

382 - Mathematical Software on the ARPA Network

379 - Using TSO at CCN

373 - Arbitrary Character Sets

350 - User Accounts for UCSB On-Line System

345 - Interest Mixed Integer Programming (MPSX on 360/91 at CCN)

321 - CBI Networking Activity at MITRE

317 - Official Host-Host Protocol Modification: Assigned Link Numbers

311 - New Console Attachments to the UCSB Host

251 - Weather Data

223 - Network Information Center Schedule for Network Users

217 - Specification Changes for OLS, RJE/RJOR, and SMFS

174 - UCLA-Computer Science Graphics Overview

122 - Network Specifications for UCSB's Simple-Minded File System

121 - Network On-Line Operators

120 - Network PL1 Subprograms

119 - Network FORTRAN Subprograms

074 - Specifications for Network Use of the UCSB On-Line System

7. Network Specific

7a. ARPANET

878, 851, 802 - The ARPANET 1822L Host Access Protocol

852 - The ARPANET Short Blocking Feature

789 - Vulnerabilities of Network Control Protocols: An Example

716 - Interim Revision to Appendix F of BBN 1822

7b. Internet Protocol On Networks

895 - A Standard for the Transmission of IP Datagrams over Experimental Ethernet Networks

894 - A Standard for the Transmission of IP Datagrams over Ethernet Networks

893 - Trailer Encapsulations

891 - Internet Protocol on DC Networks

877 - A Standard for the Transmission of IP Datagrams Over Public Data Networks

826 - Address Resolution Protocol

796 - Address Mappings

795 - Service Mappings

7c. Host Front End Protocols

929, 928, 705, 647 - Host-Front End Protocol

7d. Other

935 - Reliable Link Layer Protocols

916 - Reliable Asynchronous Transfer Protocol

914 - Thinwire Protocol

824 - The Cronus Virtual Local Network

8. Measurement

8a. General

573 - Data and File Transfer - Some Measurement Results

557 - Revelations in Network Host Measurements

546 - Tenex Load Averages for July 1973

462 - Responding to User Needs

415 - TENEX Bandwidth

392 - Measurement of Host Costs for Transmitting Network Data

352 - TIP Site Information Form

308 - ARPANET Host Availability Data

286 - Network Library Information System

274 - Establishing a Local Guide for Network Usage

214, 193 - Network Checkout

198 - Site Certification - Lincoln Labs

182 - Compilation of List of Relevant Site Reports

180 - File System Questionnaire

156 - Status of the Illinois Site (Response to RFC 116)

153 - SRI ARC-NIC Status

152 - SRI Artificial Intelligence Status Report

126 - Ames Graphics Facilities at Ames Research Center

112 - User/Server Site Protocol Network HOST Questionnaire

104 - Link 191

106 - USER/SERVER Site Protocol Network Host Questionnaire

8b. Surveys

971 - A Survey of Data Representation Standards

876 - Survey of SMTP Implementations

848 - Who Provides the "Little" TCP Services?

847 - Summary of Smallberg Surveys

844 - Who Talks ICMP, too? Survey of 18 February 1983

846, 845, 843, 842, 839, 838, 837, 836, 835, 834, 833, 832 - Who Talks TCP?

787 - Connectionless Data Transmission Survey/Tutorial

703, 702, 701, 679, 669 - Survey of New-Protocol Telnet Servers

565 - Storing Network Survey Data at the Datacomputer

545 - Of What Quality be the UCSB Resource Evaluators?

530 - A Report on the SURVEY Project

523 - SURVEY is in Operation Again

519 - Resource Evaluation

514 - Network Make-Work

464 - Resource Notebook Framework

460 - NCP Survey

459 - Network Questionnaire

450 - Multics Sampling Timeout Change

446 - Proposal to Consider a Network Program Resource Notebook

096 - An Interactive Network Experiment to Study Modes of Access to the
        Network Information Center

090 - CCN as a Network Service Center

081 - Request for Reference Information

078 - NCP Status Report: UCSB/Rand

8c. Statistics

996 - Statistics Server

618 - A Few Observations on NCP Statistics

612, 601, 586, 579, 566, 556, 538, 522, 509, 497, 482, 455, 443, 422, 413, 400,
        391, 378 - Traffic Statistics

603, 597, 376, 370, 367, 366, 362, 352, 344, 342, 332, 330, 326, 319, 315, 306,
        298, 293, 288, 287, 267, 266 - Network Host Status

550 - NIC NCP Experiment

388 - NCP Statistics

255, 252, 240, 235 - Site Status

9. Network Experience and Demonstrations

9a. General

10. Site Documentation

10a. General

11. Protocol Standards By Other Groups Of Interest To The Internet

11a. ANSI

11b. CCITT

11c. NRC

11d. ISO

995 - End System to Intermediate System Routing Exchange Protocol for Use in Conjunction with ISO 8473

994 - Final Text of DIS 8473, Protocol for Providing the Connectionless Mode Network Service

982 - Guidelines for the Specification of the Structure of the Domain Specific Part (DSP) of the ISO Standard NSAP Address

941 - Addendum to the Network Service Definition Covering Network Layer Addressing

926 - Protocol for Providing the Connectionless-Mode Network Services

905 - ISO Transport Protocol Specification (ISO DP 8073)

892 - ISO Transport Protocol

873 - The Illusion of Vendor Support

12. Never Issued

12a. Never Issued

014, 026, 092, 159, 201, 220, 244, 248, 257, 258, 259, 260, 261, 262, 272, 275, 277, 279, 284, 337, 341, 358, 375, 380, 383, 397, 424, 427, 428, 444, 465, 481, 484, 502, 507, 517, 536, 540, 541, 554, 558, 564, 572, 575, 583, 605, 639, 641, 646, 648, 649, 650, 664, 665, 668, 670, 673, 676, 682, 693, 709, 710, 711, 715, 723, 853.

Appendix 4

Glossary of Internet Terms and Abbreviations

Internet Terminology

Like most large enterprises, the Internet has a language all its own. A curious blend of networking jargon, protocol names, project names, and names of government agencies, the language is both difficult to learn and difficult to remember. To outsiders, discussions among the cognoscenti sound like meaningless babble laced with acronyms at every possible opportunity. Even after a moderate amount of exposure, readers may find that specific terms are difficult to understand. The problem is compounded because some terminology is loosely defined and because the sheer volume is overwhelming.

This glossary helps solve the problem by providing short definitions for terms used throughout the Internet. It is not intended as a tutorial for beginners. Instead, we focus on providing a concise reference to make it easy for those who are generally knowledgeable about networking to look up the meaning of specific terms or acronyms quickly. Readers will find it substantially more useful as a reference after they have studied the text than before.

A Glossary of Terms and Abbreviations
In Alphabetical Order

733

See 822.

822

The Internet standard format for electronic mail messages. Mail experts often refer to "822 messages." The name comes from RFC 822 that contains the specification. 822 format was previously known as 733 format.

1822

The (old) protocol that specifies how a host computer attached to the ARPANET sends and receives packets. In particular, the protocol describes the connection and interaction between a host computer and an ARPANET packet switch node. The name *1822* is taken from the number of the technical report by BBN that describes the protocol. The ARPANET may eventually replace all 1822 interfaces.

ACK

Abbreviation for *Acknowledgement*.

acknowledgement

A response sent by a receiver to indicate successful reception of information. Acknowledgements may be implemented at any level including the physical level (using voltage on one or more wires to coordinate transfer), at the link level (to indicate successful transmission across a single hardware link), or at higher levels (e.g., to allow an application program at the final destination to respond to an application program at the source).

active open

The operation that a client performs to establish a TCP connection with a server at a known address.

address mask

A bit mask used to select bits from an Internet address for subnet addressing. The mask is 32 bits long and selects the network portion of the Internet address and one or more bits of the local portion.

address resolution

Conversion of an Internet address into a corresponding physical address. Depending on the underlying network, resolution may require broadcasting on a local network. See ARP.

ANSI

(*American National Standards Institute*) A group that defines U.S. standards for the information processing industry. ANSI participates in defining network protocol standards.

ARP

(*Address Resolution Protocol*) The Internet protocol used to dynamically bind a high level Internet Address to a low level physical hardware address. ARP is only across a single physical network and is limited to networks that support hardware broadcast.

ARP hack

See *proxy ARP*.

ARPA

(*Advanced Projects Research Agency*) Former name of DARPA, the government agency that funded the ARPANET and, later, the DARPA Internet. The group within ARPA with responsibility for the ARPANET was IPTO (*Information Processing Techniques Office*), later ISTO (*Information Systems Technology Office*). Located at 1400 Wilson Blvd, Arlington, VA.

ARPANET

A pioneering long haul network funded by ARPA (later DARPA) and built by BBN. It served as the basis for early networking research as well as a central backbone during development of the Internet. The ARPANET consists of individual packet switch nodes interconnected by leased lines. Also see PSN, DARPA Internet.

ARQ

(*Automatic Repeat Request*) Any protocol that uses positive and negative acknowledgements with retransmission techniques to ensure reliability. The sender automatically repeats the request if it does not receive an answer.

authority zone

A part of the domain name hierarchy for which a single name server is the authority.

autonomous confederation

A set of autonomous systems grouped together because they trust network reachability/routing information obtained from one another more than they trust network reachability/routing information obtained from other autonomous systems.

autonomous system

A collection of gateways and networks that fall under one administrative entity and cooperate closely to propagate network reachability (and routing) information among themselves using an interior gateway protocol of their choice. Gateways within an autonomous system have a high degree of trust. At least one gateway in an autonomous system must advertise networks in that system to a core gateway using EGP.

baseband

Characteristic of any network technology like Ethernet that uses a single carrier frequency and requires all stations attached to the network to participate in every transmission. See broadband.

baud

Literally, the number of times per second the signal can change on a transmission line. Commonly, the transmission line uses only two signal states (e.g., two voltages), making the baud rate equal to the number of bits per second that can be transferred. The underlying transmission technique may use some of the bandwidth, so it may not be the case that users experience data transfers at the line's specified bit rate. For example, because asynchronous lines require 10 bit-times to send an 8-bit character, a 9600 bps asynchronous transmission line can only send 960 characters per second.

BBN

(*Bolt, Beranek, and Newman, Incorporated*) The Cambridge, MA company responsible for development, operation, and monitoring of the ARPANET and, later, Internet core gateway system, CSNET Coordination and Information Center (CIC), and NSFnet Network Service Center (NNSC). BBN works on DARPA research contracts and has contributed much to the Internet.

best-effort delivery

Characteristic of network technologies that do not provide reliability at link levels. Best-effort delivery systems work well with the Internet because the Internet protocols assume that the underlying network provides unreliable connectionless delivery. The combination of Internet protocols IP and UDP provides best-effort delivery service to application programs.

big-endian

A format for storage or transmission of binary data in which the most-significant byte (bit) comes first. The Internet's standard network byte order is big-endian. Also see *little-endian*.

BISYNC

(*BInary SYNchronous Communication*) An early, low level protocol developed by IBM and used to transmit data across a synchronous communication link. Unlike most modern link level protocols, BISYNC is byte-oriented, meaning that it uses special characters to mark the beginning and end of frames. BISYNC is often called BSC, especially in commercial products.

BITNET

(*Because It's Time NETwork*) A low cost, low speed network started at City University of New York, it connects over 200 universities and attaches to EARN in Europe. The technology consists of (mostly IBM) mainframe computers interconnected by 9600 bps leased lines. The fundamental paradigm is remote job entry: one machine sends a set of card images which the receiver treats as a remote job to be executed. When the job runs, it produces a new set of card images and sends them on to the next site, where they are treated as a remote job. BITNET provides services like electronic mail by building a remote job that invokes the mailer router program. At each node, the mailer examines the message, chooses a route, and encapsulates the message in a new job that it sends over the chosen route.

bps

(*bits per second*) A measure of the rate of data transmission.

bridge

A router that connects two or more networks and forwards packets among them. Usually, bridges operate at the physical network level. For example, an Ethernet bridge connects two physical Ethernet cables and forwards from one cable to the other exactly those packets that are not local. Bridges differ from repeaters because bridges store and forward complete packets while repeaters forward electrical signals.

broadband

Characteristic of any network technology that multiplexes multiple, independent network carriers onto a single cable (usually using frequency division multiplexing). For example, a single 100 mbps broadband cable can be divided into ten 10 mbps carriers, with each treated as an independent Ethernet. The advantage of broadband is less cable; the disadvantage is higher cost for equipment at connections. See baseband.

broadcast

A packet delivery system that delivers a copy of a given packet to all hosts that attach to it is said to broadcast the packet. Broadcast may be implemented with hardware (e.g., as in Ethernet) or with software (e.g., as in Cypress).

BSC

(*Binary Synchronous Communication*) See BISYNC.

catastrophic network event

See Ethernet meltdown.

CCITT

(*Consultative Committee on International Telephony and Telegraphy*) An international organization that sets standards for interconnection of telephone equipment. It defined the standards for X.25 network protocols (Note: in Europe, PTTs offer both voice telephone services and X.25 network services).

checksum

A small, integer value computed from a sequence of octets by treating them as integers and computing the sum. A checksum is used to detect errors that result when the sequence of octets is transmitted from one machine to another. Typically, protocol software computes a checksum and appends it to a packet when transmitting. Upon reception, the protocol software verifies the contents of the packet by recomputing the checksum and comparing to the value sent. Many Internet protocols use a 16-bit checksum computed with one's complement arithmetic with all integer fields in the packet stored in network byte order.

client-server

The model of interaction in a distributed system in which a program at one site sends a request to a program at another site and awaits a response. The requesting program is called a client; the program satisfying the request is called the server. It is usually easier to build client software than server software.

connection

The path between two protocol modules that provides reliable stream delivery service. In the Internet, a connection extends from a TCP module on one machine to a TCP module on the other.

connectionless service

Characteristic of the packet delivery service offered by most hardware and by the Internet Protocol (IP). The connectionless service treats each packet or datagram as a separate entity that contains the source and destination address. Usually, connectionless services can drop packets or deliver them out of sequence.

core gateway

One of a set of gateways operated by the Internet Network Operations Center (INOC) at BBN. Gateways in the core system exchange routing updates periodically to ensure that their routing tables remain consistent. The core forms a central part of Internet routing in that all groups must advertise paths to their networks to core gateways using the Exterior Gateway Protocol.

CRC

(*Cyclic Redundancy Code*) A small, integer value computed from a sequence of octets used to detect errors that result when the sequence of octets is transmitted from one machine to another. Typically, packet switching network hardware computes a CRC and appends it to a packet when transmitting. Upon reception, the hardware verifies the contents of the packet by recomputing the CRC and comparing to the value sent. Although more expensive to compute, a CRC detects more errors than a checksum that uses additive methods.

CSMA

(*Carrier Sense Multiple Access*) A characteristic of network hardware that operates by allowing multiple stations to contend for access to a transmission medium by listening to see if it is idle.

CSMA/CD

(*Carrier Sense Multiple Access with Collision Detection*) A characteristic of network hardware that uses CSMA access combined with a mechanism that allows the hardware to detect when two stations simultaneously attempt transmission. Ethernet is an example of a well-known network based on CSMA/CD technology.

CSNET

(*Computer Science NETwork*) A network offering mail delivery service using dialup telephone, as well as Internet connectivity using X25NET and Cypress. CSNET offers other services like a registry of members and an Internet domain name server for member institutions that cannot run their own. Initially funded by the National Science Foundation, CSNET is now self sufficient.

DARPA

(*Defense Advanced Projects Research Agency*) Formerly called ARPA. The government agency that funded research and experimentation with the ARPANET and, later, the DARPA Internet. The group within DARPA responsible for the ARPANET is ISTO (*Information Systems Techniques Office*), formerly IPTO (*Information Processing Techniques Office*). Located at 1400 Wilson Blvd, Arlington, VA.

DARPA Internet

See Internet.

datagram

see IP datagram.

DCA

(*Defense Communication Agency*) The government agency responsible for installation of Defense Data Network (e.g., ARPANET and MILNET) lines and PSNs. DCA writes contracts for operation of the DDN and pays for network services.

DCE

(*Data Communications Equipment*) Term X.25 protocol standards apply to switching equipment that forms a packet switched network to distinguish it from the computers or terminals that connect to the network. Also see DTE.

DDCMP

(*Digital Data Communication Message Protocol*) The link level protocol Digital Equipment Corporation uses in their network products. DDCMP operates over serial lines, delimits frames by a special character, and includes checksums at the link level. It is relevant to the Internet only because NSFnet runs DDCMP over its backbone lines.

DDN

(*Defense Data Network*) Used loosely to refer to the MILNET, ARPANET, and the TCP/IP protocols they use. More literally, it is the MILNET and associated parts of the Internet that connect military installations.

demultiplex

To separate from a common input into several outputs. Demultiplexing occurs at many levels. Hardware demultiplexes signals from a transmission line based on time or carrier frequency to allow multiple, simultaneous transmissions across a single physical cable. Internet protocol software demultiplexes incoming datagrams, sending each to the appropriate high level protocol module or application program.

domain

In the Internet, a part of the naming hierarchy. Syntactically, a domain name consists of a sequence of names (labels) separated by periods (dots).

dotted decimal notation

The syntactic representation for a 32-bit integer that consists of four 8-bit numbers written in base 10 with periods (dots) separating them. Many Internet application programs accept dotted decimal notation in place of destination machine names.

DSAB

(*Distributed Systems Architecture Board*) A group of approximately 12 researchers analogous to the IAB that explores distributed systems. Most members of the DSAB chair a task force responsible for investigating a problem or set of issues deemed important. The DSAB meets regularly to hear task force reports, discuss policies, and exchange information with agencies like DARPA and NSF. The DSAB and IAB are interlocking and share some task forces.

DTE

(*Data Terminal Equipment*) Term X.25 protocol standards apply to computers and/or terminals to distinguish them from the packet switching network to which they connect. Also see DCE.

EARN

(*European Academic Research Network*) A network using BITNET technology to connect universities and research labs in Europe. EARN interconnects with BITNET in the U.S. and allows electronic mail transfer as well as remote job entry.

Ethernet meltdown

An event that causes saturation or near saturation on an Ethernet. It usually results from illegal or misrouted packets and typically lasts only a short time. As an example, consider an IP datagram directed to a nonexistent host and delivered via hardware broadcast to all machines on the network. Gateways receiving the broadcast will send out ARP packets in an attempt to find the host and deliver the datagram.

EGP

(*Exterior Gateway Protocol*) The protocol used by a gateway in one autonomous system to advertise the Internet addresses of networks in that autonomous system to a gateway in another autonomous system. Every autonomous system must use EGP to advertise network reachability to the core gateway system.

EIA

(*Electronics Industry Association*) A standards organization for the electronics industry. Known for RS232C and RS422 standards that specify the electrical characteristics of interconnections between terminals and computers or between two computers.

encapsulation

The technique used by layered protocols in which a lower level protocol accepts a message from a higher level protocol and places it in the data portion of the low level frame. Encapsulation often means that packets traveling across a physical network have a sequence of headers in which the first header comes from the physical network frame, the next from the Internet Protocol, the next from the transport protocol, and so on.

epoch date

A point in history chosen as the date from which time is measured. The Internet uses January 1, 1900, Universal Time (formerly called Greenwich Mean Time) as its epoch date. Throughout the Internet, when programs exchange date or time of day they express time as the number of seconds past the epoch date.

Ethernet

A popular local area network technology invented at the Xerox Corporation Palo Alto Research Center. An Ethernet itself is a passive coaxial cable; the interconnections contain all active components. Ethernet is a best-effort delivery system that uses CSMA/CD technology. Xerox Corporation, Digital Equipment Corporation, and Intel Corporation developed and published the standard for 10 Mbps Ethernet. Originally, the coaxial cable specified for Ethernet was a 1/2 inch diameter heavily shielded cable. However, many office environments now use a lighter coaxial cable sometimes called *thinnet* or *cheapernet*. It is also possible to run Ethernet over shielded twisted pair cable.

EACK

(*Extended ACKnowledgement*) See SACK.

fair queueing

The best-known proposal for controlling congestion in gateways. Called "fair" because it restricts every host to an equal share of gateway bandwidth. Fair queueing is not completely satisfactory because it does not distinguish between small and large hosts or between hosts with few active connections and those with many.

FDDI

(*Fiber Distribution Data Interface*) An emerging standard for a network technology based on fiber optics that has been established by the American National Standards Institute (ANSI). FDDI specifies a 100 mbps data rate using 1300 nanometer light wavelength and limits networks to approximately 200 km in length, with repeaters every 2 km or less. The access control mechanism uses token ring technology.

FDM

(*Frequency Division Multiplexing*) The method of passing multiple, independent signals across a single medium by assigning each a unique carrier frequency. Hardware to combine signals is called a multiplexor; hardware to separate them is called a demultiplexor.

file server

A process running on a computer that provides access to files on that computer to programs running on remote machines. The term is often applied loosely to computers that run file server programs.

flat namespace

Characteristic of any naming in which object names are selected from a single set of strings (e.g., street names in a typical city). Flat naming contrasts with hierarchical naming in which names are divided into subsections that correspond to the hierarchy of authority that administers them (e.g., telephone numbers that are divided into area code, exchange, and subscriber).

flow control

Control of the rate at which hosts or gateways inject packets into a network or internet, usually to avoid congestion. Flow control mechanisms can be implemented at various levels. Simplistic schemes like ICMP source quench simply ask the sender to cease transmission until congestion ends. More complex schemes vary the transmission rate continuously.

fragment

One of the pieces that results when a Internet gateway divides an IP datagram into smaller pieces for transmission across a network that cannot handle the original datagram size. Fragments use the same format as datagrams; fields in the IP header declare whether a datagram is a fragment, and if so, the offset of the fragment in the original datagram. IP software at the receiving end must reassemble fragments into complete datagrams.

frame

Literally, a packet as it is transmitted across a serial line. The term derives from character oriented protocols that added special start-of-frame and end-of-frame characters when transmitting packets. We use the term throughout this book to refer to the objects that physical networks transmit, even if the network does not use traditional framing. (X.25 networks use the term to specifically refer to the format of data transferred between a host and a packet switch.)

FTP

(*File Transfer Protocol*) The Internet standard, high level protocol for transferring files from one machine to another. Usually implemented as application level programs, FTP uses the TELNET and TCP protocols. The server side requires a client to supply a login identifier and password before it will honor requests.

Fuzzball

Term applied to both a piece of gateway software and the Digital Equipment Corporation LSI-11 computer on which it runs. NSFnet uses fuzzballs as packet switches on its backbone network.

gated

(*GATEway Daemon*) A program that runs under 4.3 BSD UNIX on a gateway to allow the gateway to collect information from within one autonomous system using RIP, HELLO, or other interior gateway protocols, and to advertise routes to another autonomous system using the exterior gateway protocol, EGP.

gateway

A special purpose, dedicated computer that attaches to two or more networks and routes packets from one to the other. In particular, an Internet gateway routes IP datagrams among the networks to which it connects. Gateways route packets to other gateways until they can be delivered to the final destination directly across one physical network. The term is loosely applied to any machine that transfers information from one network to another, as in *mail gateway*.

GGP

(*Gateway to Gateway Protocol*) The protocol core gateways use to exchange routing information, GGP implements a distributed shortest path routing computation. Under normal circumstances, all GGP participants will reach a steady state in which the routing information at all gateways agrees.

hardware address

The low level addresses used by physical networks. Each type of network hardware has its own addressing scheme. For example, Ethernet uses 48-bit hardware addresses assigned by the vendor, while proNET-10 uses small integer hardware addresses assigned when a connection to the network is installed.

HDLC

(*High level Data Link Control*) A link level protocol standard by ISO. CCITT later adapted HDLC for its link access protocol (LAP) used with X.25 networks. HDLC is increasingly important to the Internet because PSN interfaces now use it to transfer frames between the host and PSN.

HELLO

The protocol used by a group of cooperative, trusting packet switches to allow them to discover minimal delay routes. It is important to the Internet primarily because fuzzballs on the NSFnet backbone use it.

HEMS

(*High-level Entity Management System*) A generalization of early host monitoring protocols that uses the Internet to send statistics to a central monitoring site. HEMS allows one to monitor and control a set of remote machines (e.g., a set of gateways). Also see HMP.

hierarchical routing

Routing that is based on a hierarchical addressing scheme. Most Internet routing is based on a 2-level hierarchy in which an Internet address is divided into a network portion and a host portion. Gateways use only the network portion until the datagram reaches a gateway that can deliver it directly. Subnetting introduces additional levels of hierarchical routing.

HMP

(*Host Monitoring Protocol*) A protocol still used by the Internet Network Operations Center to monitor computers. It is especially pertinent because the operations center uses HMP to monitor Internet gateways. Also see HEMS.

hop count

A measure of distance between two points in the Internet. A hop count of *n* means that *n* gateways separate the source and destination.

IAB

(*Internet Activities Board*) A group of approximately 12 researchers who provide much of the direction and focus for the Internet project. Most members of the IAB chair task forces responsible for investigating a problem or set of issues deemed important. The IAB meets regularly to hear task force reports, discuss policies, and exchange information with agencies like DARPA and NSF that support Internet research. See also DSAB.

ICMP

(*Internet Control Message Protocol*) An integral part of the Internet Protocol (IP) that handles error and control messages. Specifically, gateways and hosts use ICMP to send reports of problems about datagrams back to the original source that sent the datagram. ICMP also includes an echo request/reply used to test whether a destination is reachable and responding.

IEN

(*Internet Engineering Notes*) A series of notes developed in parallel to RFCs and available across the Internet from the INIC. IENs contain many of the early thoughts on the Internet.

IGP

(*Interior Gateway Protocol*) The generic term applied to any protocol used to propagate network reachability and routing information within an autonomous system. Although there is no Internet standard IGP, RIP is among the most popular.

IMP

(*Interface Message Processor*) Former name of packet switches used in the ARPANET. An IMP is now called a Packet Switched Node. See PSN.

INOC

(*Internet Network Operations Center*) One subgroup of the NOC at BBN that monitors and controls the Internet core gateway system and its interaction with the ARPANET. The INOC measures traffic flow, tests reachability, monitors routing tables, and controls downloading of the new gateway software.

International Standards Organization

See ISO.

internet

Physically, a collection of packet switching networks interconnected by gateways along with protocols that allow them to function logically as a single, large, virtual network. When written in upper case, Internet refers specifically to the DARPA Internet and the TCP/IP protocols it uses.

Internet

The collection of networks and gateways, including the ARPANET, MILNET, and NSFnet, that use the TCP/IP protocol suite and function as a single, cooperative virtual network. The Internet provides universal connectivity and three levels of network services: unreliable, connectionless packet delivery; reliable, full duplex stream delivery; and application level services like electronic mail that build on the first two. The Internet reaches many universities, government research labs, and military installations.

Internet address

The 32-bit address assigned to hosts that want to participate in the Internet using TCP/IP. Internet addresses are the abstraction of physical hardware addresses just as the Internet is an abstraction of physical networks. Actually assigned to the interconnection of a host to a physical network, an Internet address consists of a network portion and a host portion. The partition makes routing efficient.

Internet Engineering Notes

See IEN.

Internet Protocol

See IP.

interoperability

The ability of software and hardware on multiple machines from multiple vendors to communicate meaningfully. This term best describes the goal of Internetworking, namely, to define an abstract, hardware independent networking environment that makes it possible to build distributed computations that interact at the network transport level without knowing the details of underlying technologies.

IP

(*Internet Protocol*) The Internet standard protocol that defines the Internet datagram as the unit of information passed across the Internet and provides the basis for the Internet connectionless, best-effort packet delivery service. IP includes ICMP control and error message protocol as an integral part. The Internet protocol suite is often referred to as TCP/IP because IP is one of the two most fundamental protocols.

IP datagram

The basic unit of information passed across the Internet. An IP datagram is to the Internet as a hardware packet is to a physical network. It contains a source and destination address along with data.

ISDN

(*Integrated Services Digital Network*) The name of a proposed digital network that telephone carriers intend to provide. It will combine voice and digital network services through a single medium, making it possible to offer customers digital data services as well as voice connections. CCITT controls technical and protocol standards.

ISO

(*International Standards Organization*) An international body that drafts, discusses, proposes, and specifies standards for network protocols. ISO is best know for its 7-layer reference model that describes the conceptual organization of protocols. ISO is developing a suite of protocols like the Internet TCP/IP suite under the name *TP-4/IP*.

Karn's algorithm

An algorithm that allows transport protocols to distinguish between good and bad round-trip time samples and thus improves round-trip estimations.

kbps

(*Kilo Bits Per Second*) A measure of the rate of data transmission. Also see mbps and baud.

LAN

(*Local Area Network*) Any physical network technology that operates at high speed (usually tens of megabits per second through several gigabits per second) over short distances (up to a few thousand meters). Examples include Ethernet and proNET-10.

LAP/LAPB

A modified form of HDLC that CCITT chose as the link level protocol for X.25 networks. LAPB provides for the reliable transfer of a packet from a host to an X.25 packet switch, which then forwards the packet on to its destination. The protocol has evolved through several versions, with relative stability since LAPB replaced LAPA. Also see X.25 and HDLC.

level 2

A reference to link level communication (e.g., frame formats) or link level connections derived from the ISO 7-layer reference model. For long haul networks, level 2 refers to the communication between a host computer and a network packet switch (e.g., HDLC/LAPB). For local area networks, level 2 refers to physical packet transmission. Thus, a level 2 address is a physical hardware address.

level 3

A reference to transport level communication derived from the ISO 7-layer reference model. For the Internet, level 3 refers to IP and IP datagram format. Thus, a level 3 address is a Internet address.

little-endian

A format for storage or transmission of binary data in which the least-significant byte (bit) comes first. See *big-endian*.

mail bridge

Used loosely to refer to any mail gateway. Technically, a mail bridge screens mail passing between two networks to ensure that it meets administrative constraints. In particular, mail bridges between the ARPANET and MILNET do not permit arbitrary mail flow.

mail exploder

Part of an electronic mail system that accepts a piece of mail and a list of addresses as input and sends a copy of the message to each address on the list. Most electronic mail systems incorporate a mail exploder to allow users to define mailing lists locally.

mail gateway

A machine that connects to two or more electronic mail systems (especially dissimilar mail systems on two different networks) and transfers mail messages among them. Mail gateways usually capture an entire mail message, reformat it according to the rules of the destination mail system, and then forward the message. See mail bridge.

MAN

(*Metropolitan Area Network*) Any of several new physical network technologies that operate at high speeds (usually hundreds of megabits per second through several gigabits per second) over distances sufficient for a metropolitan area.

martians

Humorous term applied to packets that turn up unexpectedly on the wrong network, usually because of incorrect routing tables.

maximum segment size

A term used with TCP, it refers to the largest amount of data from the stream that can be transmitted at one time (e.g., to allow a sender with limited buffer space to restrict the size of incoming packets). Sender and receiver negotiate maximum segment size.

maximum transfer unit

See MTU.

mbps

(*Millions of Bits Per Second*) A measure of the rate of data transmission.

mid-level net

One of several networks funded by the National Science Foundation. Mid-level networks operate autonomously but connect to the NSFnet backbone.

MILNET

(*MILitary NETwork*) Originally part of the ARPANET, MILNET was partitioned in 1984 to make it possible for military installations to have reliable network service while the ARPANET continues to be used for research. MILNET uses exactly the same hardware and protocol technology as ARPANET, and there are several interconnection points between the two. Thus, under normal circumstances, MILNET sites are part of the Internet.

MTU

(Maximum Transfer Unit) The largest amount of data that can be transferred across a given physical network. For local area networks like the Ethernet, the MTU is determined by the network standard. For long haul networks that use serial lines to interconnect packet switches, the MTU is determined by software.

multi-homed host

An Internet host with connections to two or more physical networks. Multi-homed hosts can function as gateways if their routing tables are assigned correct values for routes.

multicast

A technique that allows copies of a single packet to be passed to a selected subset of all possible destinations. Some hardware (e.g., Ethernet) supports multicast by allowing a network interface to belong to one or more multicast groups. Broadcast is a special form of multicast in which the subset of machines to receive a copy of a packet consists of the entire set.

Nagle's algorithm

Used to refer to two separate congestion control algorithms used with TCP. One algorithm reduces the sending window in the face of congestion; the other limits the transmission of datagrams containing small segments.

NAK

(Negative Acknowledgement) A response from the recipient of data to the sender of that data to indicate that the transmission was unsuccessful (e.g., that the data was corrupted by transmission errors). Usually, a NAK triggers retransmission of the lost data. NAKs can be sent at the link level between two machines that communicate directly, or they can be sent at the transport level between the original source and ultimate destination. Also see ACK.

name resolution

The process of mapping a name into a corresponding address. The Internet domain name system provides a mechanism for naming computers in which programs use remote name servers to resolve machine names into Internet addresses for those machines.

NetBIOS

(Network Basic Input Output System) NetBIOS is the standard interface to networks on IBM PC and compatible personal computers. In the Internet, NetBIOS refers to a set of guidelines that describes how to map NetBIOS operations into equivalent Internet operations. For example, one of the NetBIOS naming operations maps into Internet domain name system interactions.

NETBLT

(*NETwork BLock Transfer*) A transport level, flow controlled, bulk data transfer protocol used in the Internet. NETBLT controls the rate at which data is sent to allow a steady, high speed flow.

network byte order

The Internet standard for transmission of integers that specifies most significant byte appears first. Sending machines are required to translate from the local integer representation to network byte order, and receiving machines are required to translate from network byte order to the local machine representation.

NFS

(*Network File System*) A protocol developed by SUN Microsystems that uses IP to allow a set of cooperating computers to access each other's file systems as if they were local. The key advantage of NFS over conventional file transfer protocols is that NFS hides the differences between local and remote files by placing them in the same name space. NFS is used primarily on UNIX systems, but has been implemented for many systems including personal computers like the IBM PC and Apple MacIntosh.

NOC

(*Network Operations Center*) The organization at BBN that monitors and controls several networks that form part of the Internet, including the ARPANET, MILNET, and at least one X.25 based network.

NSF

(*National Science Foundation*) A government agency that has funded the development of a cross country backbone network as well as regional networks designed to connect scientists to the Internet and to use the Internet to connect scientists and the supercomputers they need to use. NSF has also funded individual researchers working in the network area as well as large projects spanning multiple institutions like CSNET.

NSFnet

(*National Science Foundation NETwork*) Loosely used to describe collectively the cross country backbone, mid-level networks, and supercomputer consortia networks that have all been started with NSF seed funds. In a narrow sense, NSFnet refers only to the backbone network.

OSI

(*Open Systems Interconnect*) A reference to protocols, specifically ISO standards, for the interconnection of cooperative computer systems.

packet

The unit of data sent across a packet switching network. The term is used loosely. While some Internet literature uses it to refer specifically to data sent across a physical network, other literature views the Internet as a packet switching network and describes IP datagrams as packets.

PAD

(*Packet Assembler Disassembler*) A term used with X.25 networks that refers to a terminal multiplexor device that forms a connection between terminals and hosts across an X.25 network. A PAD accepts characters from a conventional terminal and sends them across an X.25 network; it accepts packets from an X.25 network, extracts characters, and displays them on the terminal.

PING

(*Packet InterNet Groper*) The name of a program used in the Internet to test reachability of destinations by sending them an ICMP echo request and waiting for a reply. The term has survived the original program and is now used like a verb as in, ''please ping host *A* to see if it is alive.''

port

See protocol port.

positive acknowledgement

See ACK.

promiscuous ARP

See proxy ARP.

proNET-10

A commercially available local area network product that operates at 10 Mbps using token passing ring technology.

protocol

A formal description of message formats and the rules two or more machines must follow to exchange those messages. Protocols can describe low level details of machine to machine interfaces (e.g., the order in which the bits from a byte are set across a wire), or high level exchanges between application programs (e.g., the way in which two programs transfer a file across the Internet). Most protocols include both intuitive descriptions of the expected interactions as well as more formal specifications using finite state machine models.

protocol port

The abstraction that transport protocols use to distinguish among multiple destinations within a given host computer. Internet protocols identify ports using small positive integers. Usually, the operating system allows an application program to specify which port it wants to use. Some ports are reserved for standard services (e.g., electronic mail).

proxy ARP

The technique in which one machine, usually a gateway, answers ARP requests intended for another by supplying its own physical address. By pretending to be another machine, the gateway accepts responsibility for routing packets to it. The purpose of proxy ARP is to allow a site to use a single Internet address with two physical networks.

PSN

(*Packet Switch Node*) The name of an ARPANET packet switch; PSNs were formerly called IMPs. PSNs are currently implemented with BBN C30 or BBN C300 minicomputers and execute packet switch software under control of the Network Operation Center at BBN. Each PSN connects to at least two other PSNs as well as from 1 to 16 host computers.

PUP

(*Parc Universal Packet*) In the internet system developed by Xerox Corporation, a PUP is the fundamental unit of transfer, like the IP datagram is in the DARPA Internet. The name was derived from the name of the laboratory at which the Xerox internet was developed, the Palo Alto Research Center (PARC).

RARP

(*Reverse Address Resolution Protocol*) The Internet protocol a diskless machine uses at startup to find its Internet address. The machine broadcasts a request that contains its physical hardware address and a server responds by sending the machine its Internet address. RARP takes its name and the message format from another Internet address resolution protocol, ARP.

RDP

(*Reliable Datagram Protocol*) A protocol that provides reliable datagram service on top of the standard unreliable datagram service that Internet Protocol provides. RDP is not among the most widely implemented Internet protocols.

regional net

The original term applied to NSFnet mid-level networks.

repeater

A hardware device that copies electrical signals from one Ethernet to another. Typically, sites that have repeaters use them to connect a physical Ethernet cable on each floor of a building to a backbone cable. The chief disadvantage of a repeater compared to a bridge is that it transfers electrical noise as well as packets. At most, two repeaters can appear between any two machines connected to an Ethernet.

RFC

(*Request For Comments*) The name of a series of notes that contain surveys, measurements, ideas, techniques, and observations, as well as proposed and accepted Internet protocols standards. RFCs are edited but not refereed. They are available across the Internet.

RIP

(*Routing Information Protocol*) The protocol used by Berkeley 4.3 BSD UNIX systems to exchange routing information among a (usually small) set of computers. Usually, the participating machines all attach to a single local area network. Implemented by the UNIX program *routed*, RIP derives from an earlier protocol of the same name developed at Xerox.

RJE

(*Remote Job Entry*) The service offered by many networks that allows one to submit a (batch) job from a remote site. Although the Internet has a protocol for RJE service, it is not very popular because many machines on the Internet support timesharing instead of batch job processing.

rlogin

(Remote LOGIN) The service offered by Berkeley 4.3 BSD UNIX systems that allows users of one machine to connect to other UNIX systems across the Internet and interact as if their terminals connected to the machines directly. Although rlogin offers essentially the same service as TELNET, it is superior because the software passes information about the user's environment (e.g., terminal type) to the remote machine.

round trip time

See RTT.

route

In general, a route is the path that network traffic takes from its source to its destination. In the Internet, each IP datagram is routed separately; the route a datagram follows may include many gateways and many physical networks.

routed

(Route Daemon) A program that runs under 4.3BSD UNIX to propagate routes among machines on a local area network. It uses the RIP protocol. Pronounced "route-d."

router

Any machine responsible for making decisions about which of several paths network (or Internet) traffic will follow. At the lowest level, a physical network bridge is a router because it chooses whether to pass packets from one physical wire to another. Within a long haul network, each individual packet switch is a router because it chooses routes for individual packets. In the Internet, each IP gateway is a router because it uses IP destination addresses to choose routes.

RS232

A standard by EIA that specifies the electrical characteristics of slow speed interconnections between terminals and computers or between two computers. The specification limits speed to 20 Kbps and distance to 500 feet, but many manufacturers support speeds of 38.4 Kbps and/or longer distances. Although the standard commonly used is RS232C, most people refer to it as RS232.

RTT

(Round Trip Time) A measure of delay between two hosts. The round trip time consists of the total time taken for a single packet or datagram to leave one machine, reach the other and return. In most packet switching network delays vary as a result of congestion. Thus, measures of round trip times usually give averages which may have high standard deviation.

SACK

(Selective ACKnowledgement) An acknowledgement mechanism used with sliding window protocols that allows the receiver to acknowledge packets received out of order, but within the current sliding window. The Internet sliding window protocol, TCP, could be improved if it used selective acknowledgement. Also called extended acknowledgement.

SDLC

(Synchronous Data Link Control) A predecessor of HDLC defined by IBM Corporation and used in their SNA network products.

segment

The unit of transfer sent from TCP on one machine to TCP on another. Each segment contains part of a stream of bytes being sent between the machines as well as additional fields that identify the current position in the stream and contain a checksum to ensure validity of received data.

selective acknowledgement
See SACK.

silly-window syndrome
A condition that can arise in TCP in which the receiver keeps advertising a small window and the sender keeps sending small segments to fill it. The resulting transmission of small segments makes inefficient use of network bandwidth.

sliding window
Characteristic of those protocols that, when sending a stream of bytes, allow the sender to transmit up to n packets before an acknowledgement arrives. After the sender receives an acknowledgement for the first outstanding packet, it "slides" the packet window along the stream and sends another. Values for n are usually on the order of 10.

SMTP
(*Simple Mail Transfer Protocol*) The Internet standard protocol for transferring electronic mail messages from one machine to another. SMTP specifies how two mail systems interact and the format of control messages they exchange to transfer mail.

SNA
(*System Network Architecture*) The name applied to an architecture and a class of network products offered by IBM Corporation. SNA does not interoperate with the TCP/IP Internet.

socket
The abstraction provided by Berkeley 4.3 BSD UNIX that allows a process to access the Internet. A process opens a socket, specifies the service desired (e.g., reliable stream delivery), binds the socket to a specific destination, and then sends or receives data.

source quench
A congestion control technique in which a machine experiencing congestion sends a message back to the source of the packets causing the congestion requesting that the source stop transmitting. In the Internet, gateways use ICMP source quench to stop or reduce the transmission of IP datagrams.

source route
A route that is determined by the source. In the Internet, source routing is implemented using the option field of an IP datagram. The source fills in a sequence of machines that the datagram must visit along its trip to the destination. Each gateway along the path honors source routing by following the list of machines to visit instead of following the usual route to the destination.

subnet address

An extension of the Internet addressing scheme that allows a site to use a single Internet address for multiple physical networks. Outside of the site using subnet addressing, routing continues as usual by dividing the destination address into an Internet portion and local portion. Gateways and hosts inside a site using subnet addressing interpret the local portion of the address by dividing it into a physical network portion and host portion.

SYN

(*SYNchronizing segment*) The first segment sent by the TCP protocol, it is used to synchronize the two ends of a connection in preparation for opening a connection.

TAC

(*Terminal Access Controller*) A program and a piece of hardware that connects terminals to the Internet, usually using dialup modem connections. In essence, a TAC is a host computer that accepts terminal connections from dialup lines and allows the user to invoke Internet remote login software (e.g., TELNET). TACs were formerly called TIPs.

TCP

(*Transmission Control Protocol*) The Internet standard transport level protocol that provides the reliable, full duplex, stream service on which many application protocols depend. TCP allows a process on one machine to send a stream of data to a process on another. It is connection-oriented in the sense that before transmitting data, participants must establish a connection. Software implementing TCP usually resides in the operating system and uses the IP protocol to transmit information across the Internet. It is possible to terminate (shut down) one direction of flow across a TCP connection, leaving a one-way (simplex) connection. The Internet protocol suite is often referred to as TCP/IP because TCP is one of the two most fundamental protocols.

TDM

(*Time Division Multiplexing*) A technique used to multiplex multiple signals onto a single hardware transmission channel by allowing each signal to use the channel for a short time before going on to the next one. Also see FDM.

TDMA

(*Time Division Multiple Access*) A method of network access in which time is divided into slots and each node on the network is assigned one of the slots. Because all nodes using TDMA must synchronize exactly (even though the network introduces propagation delays between them), TDMA technologies are difficult to design and the equipment is expensive.

TELENET

A public packet switched network using the CCITT X.25 protocols owned and operated by GTE. CSNET's X25NET uses TELENET.

TELNET

The Internet standard protocol for remote terminal connection service. TELNET allows a user at one site to interact with a remote timesharing systems at another site as if the user's terminal connected directly to the remote machine. That is, the user invokes a TELNET application program that connects to a remote machine, prompts for a login id and password, and then passes keystrokes from the user's terminal to the remote machine and displays output from the remote machine on the user's terminal.

TFTP

(*Trivial File Transfer Protocol*) The Internet standard protocol for file transfer with minimal capability and minimal overhead. TFTP depends only on the unreliable, connectionless datagram delivery service (UDP), so it can be used on machines like diskless workstations that keep such software in ROM and use it to bootstrap themselves.

time to live

See TTL.

TP-4/IP

A term often given to the ISO protocol suite that closely resembles TCP/IP. Both the Internet TCP and ISO TP-4 protocols provide reliable stream delivery service using basically the same techniques of positive acknowledgement and retransmission. The Internet is expected to move to TP-4 when it becomes viable.

trailer protocol

A nonconventional method of encapsulating IP datagrams for transmission across a local area network (e.g., Ethernet). Trailer protocols place the "header" at the end of the packet, so the operating system can arrange to have the network hardware deposit incoming datagrams with the data area starting on a page boundary. The technique saves on the overhead of copying datagrams once they arrive.

transceiver

A device that connects a host interface to local area network (e.g., Ethernet). Ethernet transceivers contain analog electronics that apply signals to the cable and sense collisions.

TTL

(*Time To Live*) A technique used in best-effort delivery systems to avoid endlessly looping packets. For example, in the Internet, each datagram is assigned an integer time to live when it is created. Gateways decrement the time to live field when they process a datagram and discard the datagram if the time to live counter reaches zero.

type of service routing

A routing scheme in which the choice of path depends on the characteristics of the underlying network technology as well as the shortest path to the destination. In principle, the Internet Protocol accommodates type of service routing because datagrams contain a type of service request field. In practice, few gateways honor type of service requests.

UART

(*Universal Asynchronous Receiver and Transmitter*) An electronic device consisting of a single chip that can send or receive characters on asynchronous serial communication lines that use RS232. UARTs are flexible because they have control lines that allow the designer to select parameters like transmission speed, parity, number of stop bits, and modem control. UARTs appear in terminals, modems, and on the I/O boards in computers that connect the computer to terminal(s).

UDP

(*User Datagram Protocol*) The Internet standard protocol that allows an application program on one machine to send a datagram to an application program on another machine. UDP uses the Internet Protocol to deliver datagrams. Conceptually, the important difference between UDP and IP is that UDP messages include a protocol port number, allowing the sender to distinguish among multiple destinations (application programs) on the remote machine. In practice, UDP also includes a checksum over the data being sent.

universal time

The international standard time reference that was formerly called Greenwich Mean Time. It is also called universal coordinated time.

UUCP

(*Unix to Unix Copy Program*) An application program developed in the mid 1970s for version 7 UNIX that allows one UNIX timesharing system to copy files to or from another UNIX timesharing system over a single (usually dialup) link. Because UUCP is the basis for electronic mail transfer in UNIX, the term is often used loosely to refer to UNIX mail transfer.

VAN gateway

(*Value Added Network gateway*) The gateway that interconnects the commercial X.25 network service offered by GTE Telenet and the DARPA Internet. The VAN gateway supports CSNET's X25NET, allowing subscribers to pass IP datagrams across X.25, through the VAN, and onto the Internet.

virtual circuit

See connection.

VMTP

(*Versatile Message Transaction Protocol*) A protocol developed to provide, among other facilities, efficient, reliable datagram communication service at the user level. Unlike most programs that use UDP, programs using VMTP do not have to implement time out, retransmission, or estimation of network delays because the VMTP protocol provides reliable end-to-end datagram delivery.

well-known port

Any of a set of protocol port numbers preassigned for specific uses by transport level protocols (i.e., TCP and UDP). Servers follow the well-known port assignments so clients can locate them. Examples of well-known port numbers include ports assigned to echo servers, time servers, remote login (TELNET) servers, and file transfer (FTP) servers.

window

See sliding window.

X.25

The CCITT standard protocol for transport level network service. Originally designed to connect terminals to computers, X.25 provides a reliable, stream transmission service that can support remote login. The X25NET service offered by CSNET demonstrates that it is possible to run Internet protocols, IP in particular, over an X.25 network. Also, recent ARPANET PSNs support X.25 interfaces that allow host computers to view the ARPANET as an X.25 network. X.25 is most popular in Europe.

X.400

The ISO protocol for electronic mail that is expected to become widely accepted. Work is underway to make Internet mail systems interoperate with X.400.

XDR

(*eXternal Data Representation*) The standard for a machine independent data structure representation developed by SUN Microsystems, Incorporated. To use XDR, a sender translates from the local machine representation to the standard external representation and a receiver translates from the external representation to the local machine representation.

XNS

(*Xerox Network Standard*) The term used collectively to refer to the suite of internet protocols developed by researchers at Xerox Corporation. Although similar in spirit to the DARPA Internet protocols, XNS uses different packet formats and terminology.

zone of authority

Term used in the Internet domain name system to refer to the group of names for which a given name server is an authority. Each zone must be supplied by two name servers that have no common point of failure.

Appendix 5

Official DARPA Internet Protocols

Introduction

Most of the official DARPA Internet protocols can be found in RFCs (see Appendix 3). They were collected into a three volume set entitled *DDN Protocol Handbook*, dated December, 1985. (This is the set with white covers, approximately 5 inches thick). Several early versions of the material appeared between 1978 and 1985, in a small bound set with a yellow cover entitled *Internet Protocol Transition Workbook* dated March 1982. All of the early documents are now obsolete; even minor parts of the DDN protocol handbook have changed. Although the major Internet protocols remain relatively stable, the research and engineering efforts constantly find new ways to interpret or implement them. Thus, the ultimate source of protocol information is RFCs and the Internet research community.

The list of official protocols in this appendix comes from the RFC entitled *Official Internet Protocols*. The official protocol RFC appears periodically; information in this appendix has been taken from the version published in May, 1987 (RFC 1011). This list is not intended to replace the official RFC, but merely to present a summary to help the reader grasp the scope of the Internet protocol suite. Indeed, the RFC listing official protocols gives much more information about each, including hints and interpretations of troublesome points. It is required reading for anyone implementing protocols.

The *Status* listed with each protocol is one of: *required*, *recommended*, *elective*, *experimental*, or *none*. These are interpreted to mean:

Required
> All hosts must implement a required protocol.

Recommended
> All hosts are encouraged to implement a recommended protocol.

Elective
> Hosts may choose to implement or not implement an elective protocol.

Experimental
> Hosts should not implement an experimental protocol unless they are participating in the experiment.

None
> This is not a protocol, but may contain information pertinent to implementing official protocols.

Contact For Information

For further information about Internet protocols in general, you can contact:

> Joyce K. Reynolds
> USC - Information Sciences Institute
> 4676 Admiralty Way
> Marina del Rey, California 90292-6695
> Phone: (213) 822-1511
> Internet mail: JKREYNOLDS@ISI.EDU

List Of Official Protocols

1. Overview And Model

1.1. Catenet Model

General overview of Internet architecture and underlying principles.
Status: Reference: IEN 48 [Other refs: RFC 871]

2. Network Level Protocols

2.1. Internet Protocol (IP)

The universal protocol of the Internet that defines the unit of transfer to be the IP datagram and provides the universal addressing scheme for hosts and gateways. ICMP (see below) is defines to be an integral part of IP.
Status: Required Reference: RFC 791 [Other refs: RFCs 814, 815, 816, 817, 963]

2.2. Internet Control Message Protocol

The protocol that specifies error and control messages used with the Internet Protocols.
Status: Required Reference: RFC 792 [Other refs: RFC 950]

2.3. Internet Group Multicast Protocol (IGMP)

The protocol that specifies extensions of the Internet Protocol required for a host to support Internet multicasting.
Status: Recommended Reference: RFC 988 [Other refs: RFC 966]

3. Host Level Protocols

3.1. User Datagram Protocol (UDP)

The protocol that provides datagram service to application programs. It adds port addresses to the service provided by IP.
Status: Recommended Reference: RFC 768

3.2. Transmission Control Protocol (TCP)

The protocol that provides reliable, end-to-end stream transport.
Status: Recommended Reference: RFC 793 [Other refs: RFCs 813, 814, 816, 817, 879, 889, 896, 964]

3.3. Bulk Data Transfer Protocol (NETBLT)

This is a preliminary version of the Network Block Transfer protocol for rapid transfer of large volumes of data among computers.
Status: Experimental Reference: RFC 969

3.4. Host Monitoring Protocol

This protocol provides a tool for debugging protocol implementations in remote·ly located computers. It is used by Internet gateways and TACs.
Status: Elective Reference: RFC 869

3.5. Exterior Gateway Protocol

The protocol that allows gateways in two different autonomous systems to exchange network reachability information.
Status: Recommended for Gateways Reference: RFCs 888, 904, 975 [Other refs: RFCs 827, 890]

3.6. Gateway Gateway Protocol (GGP)

The protocol core gateways use to exchange routing information.
Status: Experimental Reference: RFC 823

3.7. Host Monitoring Protocol (HMP)

This protocol provides a tool for debugging protocol implementations in remotely located computers.
Status: Elective Reference: RFC 869

3.8. Reliable Data Protocol (RDP)

This protocol supports the efficient transfer of bulk data. It is intended to be simpler to implement than TCP.
Status: Experimental Reference: RFC 908

3.9. Internet Reliable Transaction Protocol (IRTP)

This protocol provides reliable message transport from host to host across the Internet.
Status: Experimental Reference: RFC 938

3.10. Cross Net Debugger

A protocol that allows access to remote systems like debuggers allow access to local programs.
Status: Elective Reference: IEN 158 [Other refs: RFC 643]

3.11. Multiplexing Protocol (MUX)

This protocol defines a mechanism that can accept segments from multiple high level protocols and combine them into one IP datagram.
Status: Experimental Reference: IEN 90

3.12. Stream Protocol (ST)

This is a gateway resource allocation protocol designed for use in real time applications that involve multiple hosts.
Status: Experimental Reference: IEN 119

3.13. Network Voice Protocol (NVP-II)

This protocol defines the procedures used for real time voice conferencing.
Status: Experimental Reference: ISI Internal Memo [Other refs: RFC 741]

4. Application Level Protocols

4.1. Telnet Protocol (TELNET)

This protocol defines remote terminal access in the Internet.
Status: Recommended Reference: RFC 854 [Other refs: RFC 764]

4.2. Telnet Options (TELNET-OPTIONS)

This set of protocols defines options for the remote terminal protocol, TELNET, according to the table shown below. The column labeled *Use* shows whether the option is currently in use.
Status: Elective Reference: RFC 855

Number	Name	RFC	NIC	Use
0	Binary Transmission	856	-	yes
1	Echo	857	-	yes
2	Reconnection	-	15391	no
3	Suppress Go Ahead	858	-	yes
4	Message Size	-	15393	no
5	Status	859	-	yes
6	Timing Mark	860	-	yes
7	Remote Echo	726	39237	no
8	Output Width	-	20196	no
9	Output Page	-	20197	no
10	Output Return	652	31155	no
11	Output Tabstops	653	31156	no
12	Output Tab Disp.	654	31157	no
13	Output Formfeed	655	31158	no
14	Output ver. Tabstops	656	31159	no
15	Output ver. Tabs	657	31160	no
16	Output Linefeed	658	31161	no
17	Extended ASCII	698	32964	no
18	Logout	727	40025	no
19	Byte Macro	735	42083	no
20	Data Entry	732	41762	no
21	SUPDUP	734,6	42213	no
22	SUPDUP Output	749	45449	no
23	Send Location	779	-	no
24	Terminal Type	930	-	no
25	End of Record	885	-	no
26	TACACS User Ident.	927	-	no
27	Output Marking	933	-	no
28	Terminal Loc. Num.	946	-	no
255	Extended Opts.	861	-	yes

4.3. SUPDUP Protocol (SUPDUP)

This is a special Telnet like protocol for display terminals.
Status: Elective Reference: RFC 734

4.4. File Transfer Protocol (FTP)

This protocol specifies a standard for moving files among Internet hosts. It includes access controls (authentication) as well as negotiation of file parameters.
Status: Recommended Reference: RFC 959 [Other refs: RFC 765]

4.5. Trivial File Transfer Protocol (TFTP)

A simple protocol for moving files. It provides no access control or file parameters.
Status: Elective Reference: RFC 783 [Other refs: IEN 133]

4.6. Simple File Transfer Protocol (SFTP)

This protocol defines a simple file transfer mechanism, more powerful than TFTP but not as complex as FTP.
Status: Experimental Reference: RFC 913

4.7. Simple Mail Transfer Protocol (SMTP)

This protocol defines the procedure for transmitting computer mail between hosts.
Status: Recommended Reference: RFC 821 [Other refs: RFCs 822, 733]

4.8. Network News Transfer Protocol (NNTP)

This protocol defines how news articles are posted, distributed, and accessed among Internet sites.
Status: Experimental Reference: RFC 977

4.9. Post Office Protocol - Version 2 (POP2)

The Post Office Protocol - Version 2 (POP2) allows a user's workstation to access mail from a mailbox server.
Status: Experimental Reference: RFC 937

4.10. NetBIOS Services Protocol (NETBIOS)

This protocol describes how to map personal computer NetBIOS services into a TCP/IP environment.
Status: Recommended Reference: RFCs 1001, 1002

4.11. Bootstrap Protocol (BOOTP)

This proposed protocol provides an IP/UDP bootstrap protocol which allows a diskless client machine to discover its own IP address, the address of a server host, and the name of a file to be loaded into memory and executed.
Status: Experimental Reference: RFC 951

4.12. Loader Debugger Protocol (LDP)

This protocol specifies a method for loading, dumping, and debugging target machines from across the Internet.
Status: Experimental Reference: RFC 909

4.13. Resource Location Protocol (RLP)

This protocol defines a method of automatically locating a resource in the Internet.
Status: Elective Reference: RFC 887

4.14. Remote Job Entry (RJE)

This protocol specifies procedures for submission and retrieval of batch jobs.
Status: Elective Reference: RFC 407

4.15. Remote Job Service (NETRJS)

This protocol specifies batch job submission and retrieval for the UCLA IBM
OS system.
Status: Elective Reference: RFC 740

4.16. Remote Telnet Service (RTELNET)

This protocol provides special access to user Telnet on a remote system.
Status: Elective Reference: RFC 818

4.17. Graphics Protocol (GRAPHICS)

This protocol specifies a standard for communicating vector graphics.
Status: Elective Reference: NIC 24308 [Other refs: RFC 493]

4.18. Echo Protocol (ECHO)

This protocol, used for debugging, returns whatever it is sent.
Status: Recommended Reference: RFC 862

4.19. Discard Protocol (DISCARD)

This protocol, used for debugging, throws away whatever it is sent.
Status: Elective Reference: RFC 863

4.20. Character Generator Protocol (CHARGEN)

This protocol, used for debugging, sends you ASCII data.
Status: Elective Reference: RFC 864

4.21. Quote of the Day Protocol (QUOTE)

This protocol, used for debugging, sends you a short ASCII message.
Status: Elective Reference: RFC 865

4.22. Statistics Server (STATSRV)

This protocol defines how hosts and gateways send statistics data on request to a
monitoring center or debugging host.
Status: Recommended Reference: RFC 996

4.23. Active Users Protocol (USERS)

This protocol sends a list of currently active users.
Status: Elective Reference: RFC 866

4.24. Finger Protocol (FINGER)

This protocol provides information on the current activity of a user.
Status: Elective Reference: RFC 742

4.25. WhoIs Protocol (NICNAME)

This protocol provides user address, telephone number, and mailbox information using a central database.
Status: Elective Reference: RFC 954 (in DPH)

4.26. CSNET Mailbox Name Server Protocol (CSNET-NS)

This protocol provides access to the CSNET data base of users to obtain information about users' names, affiliations, and mailboxes.
Status: Experimental Reference: CS-DN-2

4.27. Domain Name Protocol (DOMAIN)

This protocol defines the domain name system and the messages it uses.
Status: Recommended Reference: RFCs 881, 882, 883 [Other refs: RFCs
920.921 973, 974]

4.28. HOSTNAME Protocol (HOSTNAME)

This (obsolete) protocol provides information about hosts based on a local database.
Status: Elective Reference: RFC 953

4.29. Host Name Server Protocol (NAMESERVER)

This protocol provides a machine-oriented procedure for translating a host name
to an Internet Address.
Status: Experimental Reference: IEN 116

4.30. Daytime Protocol (DAYTIME)

This protocol provides the day and time in an ASCII character string.
Status: Elective Reference: RFC 867

4.31. Network Time Protocol (NTP)

This is a proposed protocol for synchronizing a set of network clocks using a set
of distributed clients and servers.
Status: Experimental Reference: RFC 958 [Other refs: RFCs 778, 891, 956,
957]

4.32. Time Server Protocol (TIME)

This protocol provides the time as the number of seconds from a specified reference time.
Status: Elective Reference: RFC 868

4.33. DCNET Time Server Protocol (CLOCK)

This protocol provides a mechanism for keeping clocks synchronized.
Status: Experimental Reference: RFC 778

4.34. Authentication Service (AUTH)

This server provides a means to determine the identity of a user of a particular TCP connection.
Status: Experimental Reference: RFC 931

4.35. Authentication Scheme (COOKIE-JAR)

This RFC discuss an authentication scheme for the Internet, some problems, and their solution.
Status: Experimental Reference: RFC 1004

4.36. Internet Message Protocol (MPM)

This is an experimental multimedia mail transfer protocol.
Status: Experimental Reference: RFC 759 [Other refs: RFC 767]

4.37. Network Standard Text Editor (NETED)

This protocol describes a simple line editor which could be provided by every Internet host.
Status: Elective Reference: RFC 569

5. Appendices To Internet Official Protocols

5.1. Internet Numbers

This document describes the fields of network numbers and autonomous system numbers that are assigned values and lists the currently assigned values.
Status: None Reference: RFC 997

5.2. Assigned Numbers

Describes the fields of various protocols that are assigned specific values for actual use and lists the currently assigned values.
Status: None Reference: RFC 1010

5.3. Preemption

This document describes how to do preemption of TCP connections.
Status: Elective Reference: RFC 794

5.4. Service Mappings

Describes the mapping of the IP type of service field onto the parameters of some specific networks.
Status: None Reference: RFC 795

5.5. Address Mappings

Describes the mapping between Internet Addresses and the addresses of some specific networks.
Status: None Reference: RFC 796

5.6. Document Formats

Describes standard format rules for several types of documents.
Status: None Reference: RFC 678

5.7. Equations Representation

Describes issues in defining a standard for the exchange of mathematical equations.
Status: None Reference: RFC 1003

5.8. Bitmap Formats

Describes a standard format for bitmap data.
Status: None Reference: RFC 797

5.9. Facsimile Formats

Describes a standard format for facsimile data.
Status: None Reference: RFC 804 [Other refs: RFC 769]

5.10. Host-Front End Protocol (HFEP)

For private use only.
Status: Experimental Reference: RFC 929

5.11. Internet Protocol on ARPANET (IP-ARPA)

Describes a standard for the transmission of IP Datagrams over the ARPANET.
Status: Recommended Reference: BBN Report 1822 [Other refs: RFCs 851, 852, 878, 979]

5.12. Internet Protocol on WBNET (IP-WB)

Describes a standard for the transmission of IP Datagrams over the Wideband Net.
Status: Recommended Reference: RFC 907

5.13. Host Access Protocol (IP-SAT)

Describes a standard for the transmission of IP Datagrams over the SATNET.
Status: Recommended Reference: RFC 907

5.14. Internet Protocol on X.25 Networks (IP-X25)

Describes a standard for the transmission of IP Datagrams over Public Data Networks.
Status: Recommended Reference: RFC 877

5.15. Internet Protocol on DC Networks (IP-DC)

Describes a standard for the transmission of IP Datagrams over DC network.
Status: Elective Reference: RFC 891 [Other refs: RFC 778]

5.16. Internet Protocol on Ethernet Networks (IP-E)

Describes a standard for the transmission of IP datagrams over Ethernet.
Status: Recommended Reference: RFC 894

5.17. Internet Protocol on Experimental Ethernet (IP-EE)

Describes a standard for the transmission of IP datagrams over experimental
Ethernet networks.
Status: Recommended Reference: RFC 895

5.18. Internet Protocol on IEEE 802 (IP-IEEE)

Describes two methods of encapsulating IP datagrams for transmission over
IEEE 802.3 networks.
Status: Recommended Reference: RFC 948

5.19. Internet Subnet Protocol (IP-SUB)

This document specifies procedures for the use of subnets, which are logical
subsections of a single Internet network.
Status: Recommended Reference: RFC 950 [Other refs: RFCs 940, 917, 925,
932, 936, 922]

5.20. Address Resolution Protocol (ARP)

This is a procedure for finding the network hardware address corresponding to
an Internet Address.
Status: Recommended Reference: RFC 826

5.21. A Reverse Address Resolution Protocol (RARP)

This is a procedure for workstations to dynamically find their protocol address
(e.g., their Internet Address), when they only know their hardware address (e.g.,
their attached physical network address).
Status: Elective Reference: RFC 903

5.22. Multi-LAN Address Resolution Protocol (MARP)

Discussion of the various problems and potential solutions of "transparent subnets" in a multi-LAN environment.
Status: Experimental Reference: RFC 925 [Other refs: RFC 917, 826]

5.23. Broadcasting Internet Datagrams (IP-BROAD)

A proposed protocol of simple rules for broadcasting Internet datagrams on local networks that support broadcast, for addressing broadcasts, and for how
gateways should handle them. Recommended in the sense of "if you do broadcasting at all, then do it this way".
Status: Recommended Reference: RFC 919 [Other refs: RFC 922]

5.24. Broadcasting Datagrams with Subnets (IP-SUB-BROAD)

A proposed protocol of simple rules for broadcasting Internet datagrams on local networks that support broadcast, for addressing broadcasts, and for how gateways should handle them. Recommended in the sense of "if you do broadcasting with subnets at all, then do it this way".
Status: Recommended   Reference: RFC 922 [Other refs: RFC 919]

5.25. Reliable Asynchronous Transfer Protocol (RATP)

This paper specifies a proposed protocol which allows two programs to reliably communicate over a communication link.
Status: Experimental   Reference: RFC 916

5.26. Thinwire Protocol (THINWIRE)

This paper discusses a Thinwire Protocol for connecting personal computers to the Internet. It focuses primarily on the particular problems of low speed network interconnection with personal computers and possible methods of solution.
Status: Experimental   Reference: RFC 914

Bibliography

ABRAMSON, N. [1970], The ALOHA System – Another Alternative for Computer Communications, *Proceedings of the Fall Joint Computer Conference.*

ABRAMSON, N. and F. KUO (EDS.) [1973], *Computer Communication Networks,* Prentice Hall, Englewood Cliffs, New Jersey.

ANDREWS, D. W., and G. D. SHULTZ [1982], A Token-Ring Architecture for Local Area Networks: An Update, *Proceedings of Fall 82 COMPCON,* IEEE.

BALL, J. E., E. J. BURKE, I. GERTNER, K. A. LANTZ, and R. F. RASHID [1979], Perspectives on Message-Based Distributed Computing, *IEEE Computing Networking Symposium,* 46-51.

BBN [1981], A History of the ARPANET: The First Decade, *Technical Report* Bolt, Beranek, and Newman, Inc.

BBN [December 1981], Specification for the Interconnection of a Host and an IMP (revised), *Technical Report 1822,* Bolt, Beranek, and Newman, Inc.

BERTSEKAS D. and R. GALLAGER [1987], *Data Networks,* Prentice-Hall, Englewood Cliffs, New Jersey.

BIRRELL, A., and B. NELSON [February 1984], Implementing Remote Procedure Calls, *ACM Transactions on Computer Systems,* 2(1), 39-59.

BOGGS, D., J. SHOCH, E. TAFT, and R. METCALFE [April 1980], Pup: An Internetwork Architecture, *IEEE Transactions on Communications.*

BROWN, M., N. KOLLING, and E. TAFT [November 1985], The Alpine File System, *Transactions on Computer Systems,* 3(4), 261-293.

BROWNBRIDGE, D., L. MARSHALL, and B. RANDELL [December 1982], The Newcastle Connections or UNIXes of the World Unite!, *Software – Practice and Experience,* 12(12), 1147-1162.

CERF, V., and E. CAIN [October 1983], The DOD Internet Architecture Model, *Computer Networks.*

CERF, V., and R. KAHN [May 1974], A Protocol for Packet Network Interconnection, *IEEE Transactions of Communications,* Com-22(5).

CHERITON, D. R. [1983], Local Networking and Internetworking in the V-System, *Proceedings of the Eighth Data Communications Symposium.*

CHERITON, D. R. [April 1984], The V Kernel: A Software Base for Distributed Systems, *IEEE Software*, 1(2), 19-42.

CHERITON, D. [August 1986], VMTP: A Transport Protocol for the Next Generation of Communication Systems, *Proceedings of ACM SIGCOMM '86*, 406-415.

CHERITON, D., and T. MANN [May 1984], Uniform Access to Distributed Name Interpretation in the V-System, *Proceedings IEEE Fourth International Conference on Distributed Computing Systems*, 290-297.

CHESSON, G. [June 1987] Protocol Engine Design, *Proceedings of the 1987 Summer USENIX Conference*, Phoenix, AZ.

CLARK, D., M. LAMBERT, and L. ZHANG [August 1987], NETBLT: A High Throughput Transport Protocol, *Proceedings of ACM SIGCOMM '87.*

COMER, D. E. and J. T. KORB [1983], CSNET Protocol Software: The IP-to-X25 Interface, *Computer Communications Review*, 13(2).

COMER, D. E. [1984], *Operating System Design – The XINU Approach*, Prentice-Hall, Englewood Cliffs, New Jersey.

COMER, D. E. [1987], *Operating System Design Vol II. – Internetworking With XINU*, Prentice-Hall, Englewood Cliffs, New Jersey.

COMER, D. E., T. NARTEN, and R. YAVATKAR [1987], The Cypress Network: A Low-Cost Internet Connection Technology, *Technical Report TR-653*, Purdue University, West Lafayette, IN.

COTTON, I. [1979], Technologies for Local Area Computer Networks, *Proceedings of the Local Area Communications Network Symposium.*

CROWLEY, T., H, FORSDICK, M. LANDAU, and V. TRAVERS [June 1987], The Diamond Multimedia Editor, *Proceedings of the 1987 Summer USENIX Conference, Phoenix, AZ.*

DALAL Y. K., and R. S. PRINTIS [1981], 48-Bit Absolute Internet and Ethernet Host Numbers, Proceedings of the Seventh Data Communications Symposium.

DIGITAL EQUIPMENT CORPORATION., INTEL CORPORATION, and XEROX CORPORATION [September 1980], The Ethernet: A Local Area Network Data Link Layer and Physical Layer Specification..

DION, J. [Oct. 1980], The Cambridge File Server, Operating Systems Review, 14(4), 26-35.

DRIVER, H., H. HOPEWELL, and J. IAQUINTO [September 1979], How the Gateway Regulates Information Control, Data Communications.

EDGE, S. W. [1979], Comparison of the Hop-by-Hop and Endpoint Approaches to Network Interconnection, in Flow Control in Computer Networks, J-L. GRANGE and M. GIEN (EDS.), North-Holland, Amsterdam, 359-373.

EDGE, S. [1983], An Adaptive Timeout Algorithm for Retransmission Across a Packet Switching Network, Proceedings of ACM SIGCOMM '83.

ENSLOW, P. [January 1978], What is a 'Distributed' Data Processing System? Computer, 13-21.

FALK, G. [1983], The Structure and Function of Network Protocols, in Computer Communications, Volume I: Principles, CHOU, W. (ED.), Prentice-Hall, Englewood Cliffs, New Jersey.

FARMER, W. D., and E. E. NEWHALL [1969], An Experimental Distributed Switching System to Handle Bursty Computer Traffic, Proceedings of the ACM Symposium on Probabilistic Optimization of Data Communication Systems, 1-33.

FEINLER, J., O. J. JACOBSEN, and M. STAHL [December 1985], DDN Protocol Handbook Volume Two, DARPA Internet Protocols, DDN Network Information Center, SRI International, 333 Ravenswood Avenue, Room EJ291, Menlo Park, California.

FRANK, H., and W. CHOU [1971], Routing in Computer Networks, Networks, 1(1), 99-112.

FRANK, H., and J. FRISCH [1971]. Communication, Transmission, and Transportation Networks, Addison-Wesley, Reading, Massachusetts.

FRANTA, W. R., and I. CHLAMTAC [1981], Local Networks, Lexington Books, Lexington, Massachusetts.

FRIDRICH, M., and W. OLDER [December 1981], The Felix File Server, Proceedings of the Eighth Symposium on Operating Systems Principles, 37-46.

FULTZ, G. L., and L. KLEINROCK, [June 14-16, 1971], Adaptive Routing Techniques for Store-and-Forward Computer Communication Networks, presented at IEEE International Conference on Communications, Montreal, Canada.

GERLA, M., and L. KLEINROCK [April 1980], Flow Control: A Comparative Survey, IEEE Transactions on Communications.

GRANGE, J-L., and M. GIEN (EDS.) [1979], Flow Control in Computer Networks, North-Holland, Amsterdam.

GREEN, P. E. (ED.) [1982], Computer Network Architectures and Protocols, Plenum Press, New York.

HINDEN, R., J. HAVERTY, and A. SHELTZER [September 1983], The DARPA Internet: Interconnecting Heterogeneous Computer Networks with Gateways, Computer.

INTERNATIONAL STANDARDS ORGANIZATION [June 1986a] Information processing systems — Open Systems Interconnection — Transport Service Definition, International Standard number 8072, ISO, Switzerland.

INTERNATIONAL STANDARDS ORGANIZATION [July 1986b], Information processing systems — Open Systems Interconnection — Connection Oriented Transport Protocol Specification, International Standard number 8073, ISO, Switzerland.

INTERNATIONAL STANDARDS ORGANIZATION [May 1987a], Information processing systems — Open Systems Interconnection — Specification of Basic Specification of Abstract Syntax Notation One (ASN.1), International Standard number 8824, ISO, Switzerland.

INTERNATIONAL STANDARDS ORGANIZATION [May 1987b], Information processing systems — Open Systems Interconnection — Specification of Basic Encoding Rules for Abstract Syntax Notation One (ASN.1), International Standard number 8825, ISO, Switzerland.

JAIN, R. [January 1985] On Caching Out-of-Order Packets in Window Flow Controlled Networks, Technical Report, DEC-TR-342, Digital Equipment Corporation.

JAIN, R. [March 1986] Divergence of Timeout Algorithms for Packet Retransmissions, *Proceedings Fifth Annual International Phoenix Conference on Computers and Communications*, Scottsdale, AZ.

JAIN, R. [October 1986] A Timeout-Based Congestion Control Scheme for Window Flow-Controlled Networks, *IEEE Journal on Selected Areas in Communications*, Vol. SAC-4, no. 7.

JAIN, R., K. RAMAKRISHNAN, and D-M. CHIU [August 1987], Congestion Avoidance in Computer Networks With a Connectionless Network Layer. *Technical Report*, DEC-TR-506, Digital Equipment Corporation.

JUBIN, J. and J. TORNOW [January 1987], The DARPA Packet Radio Network Protocols, *IEEE Proceedings*.

KAHN, R. [November 1972], Resource-Sharing Computer Communications Networks, *Proceedings of the IEEE*, 60(11), 1397-1407.

KARN, P., H. PRICE, and R. DIERSING [May 1985], Packet Radio in the Amateur Service, *IEEE Journal on Selected Areas in Communications*,

KARN, P., and C. PARTRIDGE [August 1987], Improving Round-Trip Time Estimates in Reliable Transport Protocols, *Proceedings of ACM SIGCOMM '87*.

KENT, C., and J. MOGUL [August 1987], Fragmentation Considered Harmful, *Proceedings of ACM SIGCOMM '87*.

KLINE, C. [August 1987], Supercomputers on the Internet: A Case Study, *Proceedings of ACM SIGCOMM '87*.

LAMPSON, B. W., M. PAUL, and H. J. SIEGERT (EDS.) [1981], *Distributed Systems - Architecture and Implementation (An Advanced Course)*, Springer-Verlag, Berlin.

LAZAR, A. [November 1983], Optimal Flow Control of a Class of Queuing Networks in Equilibrium. *IEEE Transactions on Automatic Control*, Vol. AC-28:11.

LYNCH, D. C., and O. J. JACOBSEN (PUBLISHER and EDITOR) [1987-], ConneXions, the Interoperability Report, *Advanced Computing Environments*, 21370 Vai Avenue, Cupertino, California.

MCNAMARA, J. [1982], *Technical Aspects of Data Communications*, Digital Press, Digital Equipment Corporation, Bedford, Massachusetts.

MCQUILLAN, J. M., I. RICHER, and E. ROSEN [May 1980], The New Routing Algorithm for the ARPANET, *IEEE Transactions on Communications*, (COM-28), 711-719.

METCALFE, R. M., and D. R. BOGGS [July 1976], Ethernet: Distributed Packet Switching for Local Computer Networks, *Communications of the ACM*, 19(7), 395-404.

MILLER, C. K., and D. M. THOMPSON [March 1982], Making a Case for Token Passing in Local Networks, *Data Communications*.

MILLS, D., and H-W. BRAUN [August 1987], The NSFNET Backbone Network, *Proceedings of ACM SIGCOMM '87*.

MITCHELL, J., and J. DION [April 1982], A Comparison of Two Network-Based File Servers, *Communications of the ACM*, 25(4), 233-245.

MORRIS, R. [1979], Fixing Timeout Intervals for Lost Packet Detection in Computer Communication Networks, *Proceedings AFIPS National Computer Conference*, AFIPS Press, Montvale, New Jersey.

NAGLE, J. [April 1987], On Packet Switches With Infinite Storage, *IEEE Transactions on Communications*, Vol. COM-35:4.

NEEDHAM, R. M. [1979], System Aspects of the Cambridge Ring, *Proceedings of the ACM Seventh Symposium on Operating System Principles*, 82-85.

NELSON, J. [September 1983], 802: A Progress Report, *Datamation*.

OPPEN, D., and Y. DALAL [October 1981], The Clearinghouse: A Decentralized Agent for Locating Named Objects, Office Products Division, XEROX Corporation.

PARTRIDGE, C. [June 1986], Mail Routing Using Domain Names: An Informal Tour, *Proceedings of the 1986 Summer USENIX Conference*, Atlanta, GA.

PARTRIDGE, C. [June 1987], Implementing the Reliable Data Protocol (RDP), *Proceedings of the 1987 Summer USENIX Conference*, Phoenix, Arizona.

PETERSON, L. [1985], *Defining and Naming the Fundamental Objects in a Distributed Message System*, Ph.D. Dissertation, Purdue University, West Lafayette, Indiana.

PIERCE, J. R. [1972], Networks for Block Switching of Data, *Bell System Technical Journal*, 51.

POSTEL, J. B. [April 1980], Internetwork Protocol Approaches, *IEEE Transactions on Communications*, COM-28, 604-611.

POSTEL, J. B., C. A. SUNSHINE, and D. CHEN [1981], The ARPA Internet Protocol, *Computer Networks*.

QUARTERMAN, J. S., and J. C. HOSKINS [October 1986], Notable Computer Networks, *Communications of the ACM*, 29(10).

REYNOLDS, J., J. POSTEL, A. R. KATZ, G. G. FINN, and A. L. DESCHON [October 1985], The DARPA Experimental Multimedia Mail System, *IEEE Computer*.

RITCHIE, D. M., and K. THOMPSON [July 1974], The UNIX Time-Sharing System, *Communications of the ACM*, 17(7), 365-375; revised and reprinted in *Bell System Technical Journal*, 57(6), [July-August 1978], 1905-1929.

ROSENTHAL, R. (ED.) [November 1982], *The Selection of Local Area Computer Networks*, National Bureau of Standards Special Publication 500-96.

SALTZER, J. [1978] Naming and Binding of Objects, *Operating Systems, An Advanced Course*, Springer-Verlag, 99-208.

SALTZER, J. [April 1982] Naming and Binding of Network Destinations, *International Symposium on Local Computer Networks*, IFIP/T.C.6, 311-317.

SALTZER, J., D. REED, and D. CLARK [November 1984], End-to-End Arguments in System Design, *ACM Transactions on Computer Systems*, 2(4), 277-288.

SCHWARTZ, M., and T. STERN [April 1980] *IEEE Transactions on Communications*, COM-28(4), 539-552.

SHOCH, J. F. [1978], Internetwork Naming, Addressing, and Routing, *Proceedings of COMPCON*.

SHOCH, J. F., Y. DALAL, and D. REDELL [August 1982], Evolution of the Ethernet Local Computer Network, *Computer*.

SNA [1975], *IBM System Network Architecture – General Information*, IBM System Development Division, Publications Center, Department E01, P.O. Box 12195, Research Triangle Park, North Carolina, 27709.

SOLOMON, M., L. LANDWEBER, and D. NEUHEGEN [1982], The CSNET Name Server, *Computer Networks* (6), 161-172.

STALLINGS, W. [1984], *Local Networks: An Introduction*, Macmillan Publishing Company, New York.

STALLINGS, W. [1985], *Data and Computer Communications*, Macmillan Publishing Company, New York.

SWINEHART, D., G. MCDANIEL, and D. R. BOGGS [December 1979], WFS: A Simple Shared File System for a Distributed Environment, *Proceedings of the Seventh Symposium on Operating System Principles*, 9-17.

TANENBAUM, A. [1981], *Computer Networks: Toward Distributed Processing Systems*, Prentice-Hall, Englewood Cliffs, New Jersey.

TICHY, W., and Z. RUAN [June 1984], Towards a Distributed File System, *Proceedings of Summer 84 USENIX Conference*, Salt Lake City, Utah, 87-97.

TOMLINSON. R. S. [1975], Selecting Sequence Numbers, *Proceedings ACM SIGOPS/SIGCOMM Interprocess Communication Workshop*, 11-23, 1975.

WARD, A. A. [1980], TRIX: A Network-Oriented Operating System, *Proceedings of COMPCON*, 344-349.

WATSON, R. [1981], Timer-Based Mechanisms in Reliable Transport Protocol Connection Management, *Computer Networks*, North-Holland Publishing Company.

WEINBERGER, P. J. [1985], The UNIX Eighth Edition Network File System, *Proceedings 1985 ACM Computer Science Conference*, 299-301.

WELCH, B., and J. OSTERHAUT [May 1986], Prefix Tables: A Simple Mechanism for Locating Files in a Distributed System, *Proceedings IEEE Sixth International Conference on Distributed Computing Systems*, 1845-189.

WILKES, M. V., and D. J. WHEELER [May 1979], The Cambridge Digital Communication Ring, *Proceedings Local Area Computer Network Symposium*.

XEROX [1981], Internet Transport Protocols, *Report XSIS 028112*, Xerox Corporation, Office Products Division, Network Systems Administration Office, 3333 Coyote Hill Road, Palo Alto, California.

ZHANG, L. [August 1986] Why TCP Timers Don't Work Well, *Proceedings of ACM SIGCOMM '86*.

Index